WEBSTER'S
NEW WORLD
GUIDE TO
PRONUNCIATION

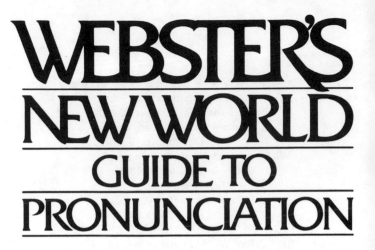

WEBSTER'S NEW WORLD GUIDE TO PRONUNCIATION

Easy pronunciations for
over 13,000 words

*

William S. Chisholm, Jr.

SIMON AND SCHUSTER

Copyright © 1984 by Simon & Schuster, Inc.
Published by New World Dictionaries/Simon and Schuster
A Division of Simon & Schuster, Inc.
Simon & Schuster Building
Rockefeller Center
1230 Avenue of the Americas
New York, New York 10020
SIMON AND SCHUSTER/TREE OF KNOWLEDGE,
WEBSTER'S NEW WORLD and colophon are registered
trademarks of Simon & Schuster, Inc.

*Dictionary Editorial Offices: New World Dictionaries,
850 Euclid Avenue, Cleveland, Ohio 44120.*

Manufactured in the United States of America

1 3 5 7 9 10 8 6 4 2

Library of Congress Cataloging in Publication Data
Chisholm, William.
Webster's new world guide to pronunciation.
1. English language—Pronunciation—Dictionaries.
I. Title. II. Title: New world guide to pronunciation.
III. Title: Guide to pronunciation.
PE1137.C428   1984   421'.52   84-13967
ISBN 0-671-50035-X

BRIEF USER'S GUIDE

This book records standard pronunciations for more than 13,000 words listed alphabetically. Each page has two columns with the words spelled on the left side of each column and pronounced on the right side. The pronunciations are indicated by means of the ordinary letters of the English alphabet; there are no special phonetic characters of any kind. Both capital letters and lower-case letters are used depending on whether the syllables indicated are "accented," that is, stressed (like the first syllable of *sister*), or are not loudly stressed (like the second syllable of *sister*).

sister . . . . **SIS** tur

All told, three degrees of stress are recognized:

generation . . . . JEN uh **RAY** shun

The dark capitals (**RAY**) mark the prominently stressed syllable, the plain capitals (JEN) mark the second loudest syllable, and the lower-case letters mark the weakly stressed or unstressed syllables.

Representation of consonant sounds

The letters b, d, f, h, j, k, l, m, n, p, r, v, w, y, z are used to represent their usual sounds: b as in *bib*, d as in *dud*, f as in *fit*, h as in *hit*, j as in *jet*, k as in *kit*, l as in *let*, m as in *mat*, n as in *nut*, p as in *pit*, r as in *rat*, v as in *vat*, w as in *wet*, y as in *yet*, z as in *zoo*. The following additional consonant letters are used:

Letters	Represent the Sound of	Shown as
G, g	g *in* gap	**GAP**
S, s	s *in* sit	**SIT**
T, t	t *in* late	**LAYT**

v

Brief User's Guide

Letters	Represent the Sound of	Shown as
CH, ch	*ch* in church	**CHURCH**
SH, sh	*sh* in shut	**SHUT**
TH, th	*th* in thin	**THIN**
DH, dh	*th* in then	**DHEN**
ZH, zh	*s* in leisure *and the*	**LEE** zhur
	z in azure	**AZH** ur
NG, ng	*ng* in sing	**SING**

In a few foreign words, the sound of *ch*, as in the name *Bach*, is represented by KH or kh, produced like the sound of clearing the throat. Many Americans, however, use the simple sound K or k in such borrowed words.

Representation of vowel sounds

Letters	Represent the Sound of	Shown as
A, a	*a* in mat	**MAT**
AH, ah	*o* in lot	**LAHT**
AHR, ahr	*ar* in jar	**JAHR**
AR, ar	*ar* in daring	**DARING**
AW, aw	*aw* in law	**LAW**
AWR, awr	*or* in store	**STAWR**
AY, ay	*ay* in hay	**HAY**
E, e	*e* in let	**LET**
EE, ee	*ee* in feed	**FEED**
ER, er	*ear* in bear	**BER**
EYE, eye* (*see note on next page*)	*i* in ivy	**EYE** vee
I, i	*i* in lip	**LIP**
IR, ir	*ear* in dear	**DIR**
OH, oh	*o* in bone	**BOHN**

Letters	*Represent the Sound of*	*Shown as*
OO, oo	oo *in* look	**LOOK**
OOH, ooh	oo *in* soon	**SOOHN**
OOR, oor	our *in* tour	**TOOR**
OW, ow	ow *in* cow	**KOW**
OWR, owr	our *in* sour	**SOWR**
OY, oy	oy *in* boy	**BOY**
U, u	u *in* rut	**RUT**
uh	a *in* ago	uh **GOH**
UR, ur	ur *in* fur	**FUR**

In French words, vowels followed by the letter n are nasalized, that is, produced by breathing out slightly through the nose while pronouncing the vowel. That nasalization is shown by the use of **N** or n after the vowel sound, as for *bonbon* (bohn **BOHN**).

The reader will find here and there among the words entered some notes on pronunciation, where brief comments, we felt, would be helpful. Also, reference numbers appear after a paragraph sign (¶) at many entries. These numbers direct the reader's attention to numbered paragraphs (on pages xxix-xxxviii) where certain regular variations in pronunciation are discussed.

---

*But this sound in *rise, file*, etc. is represented somewhat differently so that the pronunciations are shown as **RYZE** and **FYLE**; in such words as *lye* and *cry*, the pronunciations are represented as **LYE** and **KRYE**.

INTRODUCTION

What's the correct pronunciation of *coupon*? How are you supposed to pronounce *nuclear*? Doesn't *athlete* have only two syllables, not three? Is it wrong to say **AY** purn for *apron*? How do you pronounce *diastole*? Why doesn't English spelling represent its sounds better? Is British pronunciation more refined than American? These and similar questions are often asked. Although it is not easy to answer such questions simply, it is possible to propose answers based on facts about the rise and development of English, about the nature of regional and social dialects, and about the sounds of English speech. As in any inquiry, a good understanding of the subject matter encourages the posing of answerable questions. With this in mind, we present in the following paragraphs brief discussions of some of the pertinent facts about the English language. First, a short account of where Standard American English has come from.

English in the earliest period

English began about 1,300 years ago after some members of West Germanic tribes living in Northern Europe had journeyed from their homeland to what we now call England. The name of the country and that of the language derive from the name of one of these tribes, the Angles. *England* is the modern form of the Anglo-Saxon word *Angalond*, the land of the Angles; *English* comes from *Englisc*, the language of these people. The Angles settled in the east central part of England and were joined in a collective invasion of the island by Jutes, Frisians, and Saxons, the latter occupying the southwestern part of England. By 700 A.D. these people had successfully won the land from the Britons and had established their culture and language, subjugating the natives in the process or driving them westward or northward.

The tribesmen spoke different dialects, and so they could understand each other with some cooperative effort. Nevertheless, within a century or two, their related dialects developed into a new language in the world—English. The speakers of the new language had fashioned English out of the accumulation of changes that time inevitably produces in any language. Such changes—in pronunciation, in vocabulary, in grammar—are adopted subconsciously by the speakers of a language as they occur. When it happens that some of the speakers are cut off from others, then it may happen that a new language is born. These were the circumstances and this was the result for English in the period 450–650 A.D.

Old English

The words of early English were mostly Germanic, of course, with a sprinkling of Latin terms (*street, pound, wine, kettle, cheese, chalk, Saturday*) which had come into Germanic even before the speakers had left Europe. The most common words in English 1,300 years ago are today still the most common (*hand, house, mother, the, of, and, who, I, you, go, come, have, do*, etc.), but in most cases both the spelling and the pronunciation have since changed. The *basic* vocabulary of English, nevertheless, is virtually the same today as it was in the beginning.

The structure of Old English was different in some respects from that of Modern English. The rules that governed how words could be arranged to form sentences were less strict, partly because the endings on words in Old English communicated what we today express by arranging words in certain orders. In Modern English one is obliged to construct a sentence like "He said that the men should harvest the crops now" with the words ordered one after the other the way they appear here. But in Old English (here restated in Modern English), other arrangements were possible, even commonplace:

Now said he the men harvest should the crops.
He said the men the crops harvest should now.
He said now the crops harvest should the men.

In Old English, in other words, the information about who was doing what to whom was expressed more by inflections (word endings) than by syntax (word ordering).

The individual sounds of Old English are not much different from those of Modern English. To be sure, a few Old English sounds have disappeared, and some sounds are new, although the newest sound in English, the consonant sound at the end of *beige*, is now 500 years old. Among the "new" vowel sounds of English is the one which is today the most frequent of all—the one at the beginning of *ago*. This weak vowel began to be used toward the end of the Old English period.

Middle English

The Battle of Hastings in 1066 is important in English history. On October 14, 1066, William II, the Duke of Normandy, defeated the English under King Harold and was king of England for twenty years following. Centuries afterward, the Norman-French influence was still being felt in England. In culture, in the arts, in science, education, government, medicine, and even in lowly arts like cooking and fashion, the French influence was extensive. During the period 1066–1550, more than 1,500 French words were borrowed into English and most of these are common coin today: *people, tax, poet, war, government, religion, dance, dress, apparel, letter, chair, city, lamp, cream, roast, supper*. Considering that the country was run by "for-

eigners" (Normans), it is not surprising that the language these rulers
used should have been adopted by many of the English-speaking
people, especially those who dealt with the new rulers on a day-to-
day basis. Actually, many Normans learned English and spoke it,
dropping French words into their English sentences. But the citizens,
in fact, had little contact with their lords and masters. For this reason,
English persisted and the outcome of the Norman invasion was different from what had happened nearly 600 years earlier when the
Anglo-Saxons had invaded England (actually, they had been invited
to come to the Britons' aid in their continuing struggle with the Picts)
and had thoroughly conquered the territories they wished to occupy.
In Medieval England, English rule was eventually restored, but not
before the vocabulary of English had been enriched by French. All
languages change all the time, because they are "living" organisms.
Old English had set itself on an inexorable course for *change* even
before 1066. The elaborate word-ending system was simplifying itself,
and, consequently, the word-order system was becoming more and
more fixed. The effect of the changes was that English was taking
on a modern look.

The Great Vowel Shift

From about 1250 to 1750, a vast change occurred in the English
vowel system, with most of the changes being effected in the relatively
short period 1400–1550. Few if any of the vowel sounds were dropped
and very few vowel sounds were added, however. What happened
was that many of the stressed vowels of English syllables exchanged
places. For instance, the vowel sound in Modern English *street* 700
years ago was more like that of modern *straight*, so that Middle
English *street* was pronounced as Modern English *straight* is. But in
Middle English, *straight* was pronounced something like **STRAT**.
Meanwhile, where we today have the long vowel of *ride*, Middle English

had the vowel sound of modern *street* in the same word: *ride* sounded like modern *reed*. Today, we might *ride* down a *straight street*, but our Middle English linguistic forebears would **REED** down a **STRAT STRAYT**. In fact, *down* was pronounced as **DOOHN**. All of the long vowels, not just these four, displaced each other similarly, moving out of one set of word-rhymes and into another: thus, the vowel of Middle English *stone*, pronounced **STAWN**, became the modern **OH** (in Old English, the vowel in this word was a long **AH**-sound); the vowel of *boot* pronounced in Middle English as in modern *boat*, became **OOH**, and Middle English **OOH** in *mouse* became the familiar diphthong sounded today in this word (**OW**, that is, **AH** + **OOH**).

Sound change and fixed spelling

Among the curiosities resulting from these shiftings, we can cite the spelling pronunciation of *brooch*, rhyming with *hooch*. This word had the **AW**-vowel in Middle English (**BRAWCH**) and so in Modern English has the **OH**-sound (as in *stone*), but the exceptional *oo*-spelling has encouraged a pronunciation with the **OOH**-sound. In addition, other double-*o* spellings (*food, root, flood*), which were conventionalized before the sounds had changed, camouflage the distinct sounds they represent today. Middle English **OH** generally appears in Modern English as **OOH**; and so Middle English *root* pronounced as we pronounce *wrote* ends up with the **OOH**-sound. But in *good*, this same tense vowel was later relaxed to short **OO**; and in *flood*, the vowel was further altered to the **UH**-sound. The fact that some speakers even today pronounce *root* and *room* with the vowel of *look* attests to the ongoing vowel alternations begun more than 700 years ago and also to the uncertain guide called spelling.

"Silent" letters are common in English spelling these days. However, most silent letters are a reflection of what once were sounds. The *e*'s of *wives, come*, and *home* are remnants of earlier grammatical inflections. The first of these words (*wives*), for instance, emerged during the Old English period as the plural form of *wife* and was pronounced **WEE** vez. The word *wife* was originally a neuter noun and had no ending in the plural, but the plural of the masculine nouns (-*as*) eventually spread through the whole noun system. English speakers long ago would speak of "one wife" and "two wife"; today, of course, it is "one wife" and "two wives." And the older vowel sound in what used to be a second syllable is now silent.

Silent consonant letters are somewhat more difficult to account for partly because some of them owe their existence to spelling reformers, not to linguistic change. The words *doubt* and *limb* will serve as illustrations of "unhistorical" silent letters. The *b* in *doubt* was put there (restored) by enthusiasts who recognized the word's relation to Latin *dubitare*. And the *b* in *limb* (Old English and Middle English *lim*) got into the spelling after the Old English sound sequence *m* followed by *b* in words like *lamb* and *dumb* had lost the *b*-sound. Scribes introduced the *b* in *limb* on a false analogy with those words.

The *gh* in *light* and *though*, now "silent," is the reflection of a consonant sound of Old and Middle English which ceased to exist in such words about 1500. The *gh* of *laugh* and *enough* represents the change of the old sound to an *f*-sound. The spelling in this case preserves the older state of affairs. It is the same story with *two*. Here, of course, the *w* is silent now. But it was pronounced in Old English. Because it was sounded between *t* and a back vowel, it was lost here as in some similar words. A back vowel is one uttered with the tongue drawn toward the back of the mouth, as in the OH-sound in *cold* and the AW-sound in *jaw*. (A similar explanation may be given for the loss of the *w*-sound in *sword, answer*, and some other words.) The related form *twain* (now archaic) retains the *w*-sound because of the front vowel following the *w*. A front vowel is one uttered with the tongue extended toward the front of the mouth, like the AY-sound in *say* and the I-sound in *bid*.

In many ways, English spelling today is "regular." The sounds articulated at the beginning and the end of *bed* are regularly represented in writing by *b* and *d* (sometimes *bb* and *dd* as in *webbing* and *bedding*). Similarly, the sounds at the beginnings of *fan, get, hem, lot, map, nut, pod, run, tap, vim, wall, yet, zone* are commonly spelled with the letters standing at the beginning of these words. The vowel sounds of *pit, set, lap, luck, lock* are commonly spelled with *i, e, a, u, o* followed by a consonant letter or two. The vowel sounds of *lame, wine, tune, bone* are commonly spelled with *a, i, u, o* + a single consonant letter + *e* and sometimes some other consonant letter. These last two sets of facts explain why *dinner* and *diner* are spelled as they are.

Among the consonant letters, very often the English spelling of the *k*-sound will show a *c* (*call, coat*) rather than a *k*, and then to make matters somewhat worse, this same letter *c* is often used to represent an *s*-sound (*city, cell*). Here, however, there is regularity, because the *c* letter systematically has the *s*-sound value when it precedes the letters *i, e,* or *y,* and has the *k*-sound value when any other vowel letter or a consonant follows it (*cold, fact*). To be sure, there are many "irregularities" (in addition to those already mentioned) as when the *f*-sound is spelled with the letters *ph* (*philosophy*), when the *j*-sound appears with a *g* (*gem, ginger*); or when three different sounds, the *k*-sound, the *ch*-sound, and the *sh*-sound, are all spelled *ch* (*chemistry, chamber, chamois*). *Chamois* is irregular in another way: no other word in English uses the letters *ois* to represent the EE-sound. Also, all of the vowel letters are used variously to represent the weakly stressed UH-sound in words, for instance, an *a* in the third syllable of *predictable* but an *i* in the third syllable of *contemptible*.

The irregularities mentioned here arise generally from two sources, each very different from the other. The first has to do with words borrowed from Greek and Latin and its derivatives. It would be hard to guess how to spell *psyche* (Greek) or *leukemia* (Modern Latin) without knowing something about the spelling traditions involved in making these words English. The second cause of unpredictable spelling relates to the oldest, simplest words native to English—words like *come, of, have, been, do, two.* Spelled regularly, these words would be *cum, uv, hav, bin, doo, too.* The difficulty in these cases comes from the fact that the spellings had become fixed *before* the sound changes occurred, as was mentioned earlier.

1620 and all that

The first English-speaking people to set foot on the North American continent were not the Pilgrims, but those who landed at Plymouth were the most important settlers linguistically speaking. Typically, they came from eastern or southern England, or from an area just northwest of London, bringing with them different regional dialects. All together, they brought Early Modern English, the language of Shakespeare's time, to America. For a generation or two, the English language in America was the same as the English of Britain, there being no reason for the first settlers to start right in talking differently. Because the settlers could have no conversation with the people they had left behind in England, the natural forces of linguistic change eventually made two dialects, British English and American English, out of one. The same thing happened when Australia was settled later, although it might have turned out otherwise, as in fact it did in another part of the world after some Dutchmen left Holland and settled in South Africa. There, Afrikaans came into being, a language separate from Dutch and more than a little difficult for Dutch speakers to understand. In these particulars, the establishment of Afrikaans in the 19th century parallels the success of English back in the 5th through the 7th centuries. Though German, Dutch, French, and Spanish competed with English early on, English has prevailed in America as the national language.

Modern English

Correctness

The differences between American English and British English are not great, though they are notorious: American English has *elevator* where British English has *lift*; similarly, in America somebody is "in the hospital" but in England is "in hospital"; and the pronunciation of *laboratory*, which in America is stressed on the first syllable, is stressed on the second syllable in Britain. Such American ways are neither better nor worse than the British ways, neither "correct" nor "incorrect." They are merely different. It would be unnatural, however, for an American to stress the second syllable of *laboratory*, because such a pronunciation is *nonstandard* in America. *Correctness* is nothing more than common practice: correct Standard American English is that which Standard American English speakers use. (See the discussion of *social dialects* in a later section.)

Foreign influence

The American English vocabulary has been enriched by American Indian languages, by French, by Spanish, in fact, by many of the world's languages. The continuous and extensive contact that English speakers had with American Indians during the early settlement years and then during the westward expansion resulted in the infusion of many words from Algonquian and other Amerindian families of languages. As examples, *hickory, moose, skunk, toboggan, totem,* and *wigwam* may be cited; similarly, from French, American English took such words as *portage, chowder, bureau,* and *levee*; from Spanish, we incorporated *adobe, bonanza, bronco, canyon, patio, ranch,* and *siesta*; from Dutch, we benefited from *cruller, coleslaw, cookie, boss,* and *scow*; from German, *noodle* and *sauerkraut* were borrowed in the early period.

Introduction

The speech of an American

Everyone who speaks American English has his own *idiolect*, his own speechways. The differences among the idiolects in one family are not great, especially among brothers and sisters. The differences are perceptibly greater among individuals of different generations, in different households and different neighborhoods, greater still among people in different cities and towns, and sometimes very wide among people who live in different parts of the country. In addition, people in different social stations talk differently. So, there are both regional dialects and social ones.

Regional American dialects

There are convenient geographical terms for four of the major regional dialect areas in the United States: Eastern New England, Northern, Midland, and Southern. The first of these includes all of Maine, New Hampshire, and Rhode Island and the eastern halves of Vermont, Massachusetts, and Connecticut. The Northern dialect area includes the western halves of the last three named states and all of New York (except New York City itself), Michigan, and Wisconsin, as well as the northernmost parts of Ohio, Indiana, and Illinois. The Southern dialect area consists of the Atlantic States beginning with Virginia, then eastern North Carolina, most of South Carolina, all of Georgia, Florida, Alabama, Mississippi, and Louisiana, and most of eastern Texas. The North Midland and the South Midland are divided by a line that runs east to west through West Virginia (but Appalachian speech sprawls across this line), Kentucky, Missouri, and Kansas and then sweeps south through the eastern third of New Mexico. The northern and southern boundaries of the Midland are, respectively, the same as the southern boundary of Northern and the northern boundary of Southern. Generally, North Midland stretches all the way to the Pacific, but the whole of the West is somewhat mixed dialectally, having been settled relatively recently. Northern probably predominates in metropolitan centers like Los Angeles and San Francisco.

The lines that dialecticians draw on a map are called *isoglosses*, and each reflects a number of dialect differences. A dialectician can draw a line, for instance, that marks the western limit of the pronunciation of *car* that has no *r*-sound. Then he can draw lines that similarly mark the western limits of *dear, care, store*, and *tour*, all with no *r*-sound. Next, he marks the western limit of the pronunciation of *aunt* with an AH-sound, and then the western limit of *news* rhyming with *cues*. Continuing, he discovers that he is drawing lines on top of lines. The isogloss designates a *major dialect boundary*, in the case of the differences just cited, the line that separates Eastern New England from Northern. Field studies of such pronunciations, together with other kinds of dialect differences (as, for instance, the word *rotary* in the East versus *traffic circle* in the North), lead to dialect-geography maps and to brief descriptions of them like the one presented here.

Settlement history

Regional dialects are founded on settlement history. Most of East Texas was settled from the South while the rest of Texas was settled from the Midland, and we witness even today the effects of those diverse beginnings. The speechways in the two parts of Texas are as different as those in the two halves of Connecticut. Though some outsiders lump all Texas speech under the general heading of the "Texas Drawl," Texans themselves know better.

Now the Midwest was generally settled first from the East, as the South was settled from the Mid-Atlantic seaports and neighboring inland areas. But no one can say why the early Northern speakers who had responded to the call of Westward Ho should have retained the *r*-sound after vowel sounds (*dear, care*, etc.) while their kinsmen and neighbors whom they had left behind decided to put an UH-sound in the place where the *r*-sound had been—to drop their r's. And no one can say why Southern speech has come through to the last moments of the 20th century in the specific form that it has, but the fact that the landed gentry of the Old South continued to send their children (mostly the boys) to England for their education well into the 19th century probably has much to do with it.

It can be stressed, however, that if a person left home toward the end of the 18th century (the Revolutionary War period) or at the beginning of the 19th century (President Jackson's time—he was a Midlander as was Lincoln a generation later), it was likely that the person would not return. So the person's speech would mingle with the speech of those who had come to the new surroundings earlier and then with the speech of those who followed. In this way, dialects arise and spread.

Dialect leveling

The Age of Technology, our own age, has considerably lessened the chances for dialect development and has increased the chances for reducing the number of dialects. Transportation of persons and voices—by cars, trains, and airplanes in the case of people, and by telephones, radios, and TVs in the case of people's voices—has tended to smooth the sharp edges of regional differences. Voices are in our ears now from *everywhere*, not just from people down the lane. And so, regional dialects are no longer insulated from "outside" influence. It happens, though, that national newscasters (and even local ones), talk-show hosts, most voices for commercials, etc., all speak the "prestige social dialect," and this is the one with a Northern regional base. This is so because the North "won" the Civil War and educational and cultural prestige still attaches to the area and, to a lesser degree, because the major media emanate from New York City, Chicago, and Los Angeles, places where the Northern dialect has status.

Social dialects

Generally, social dialects exist side by side with regional ones. In every region, there is language variation brought about by the social stratification of the people. Both regional and social dialects are inevitable in any linguistic nation whose people occupy a good stretch of land as well as different social niches. In most nations (not all), there are wealthy people, poor people, and people with *some* money (the majority); there are people with power and authority and others with little of either; there are educated people and uneducated people. The *prestige* dialect in any nation is always the one which the people with prestige speak. This dialect is neither better nor worse than any other dialect, because all dialects enable their speakers to carry on their affairs.

The people who collectively speak the prestige dialect in America are managers, executives, professionals, government officials, teachers, religious leaders, and the like. (By no means are they universally admired, either as persons or as speakers. But because their speech has prestige, it enjoys esteem.) They are educated, whether by schools or by themselves. And to be educated is to be literate. So Standard Spoken English is the corollary of Standard Written English. These are not the same, however. One does not speak the way one writes (as this sentence and others in this introduction will testify). But speakers of Standard Spoken English are the same individuals who write Standard Written English. Put another way, they are masters of three dialects; a regional dialect (this comes naturally), a social dialect (this does, too, commonly), and Standard Written English (this has to be learned).

Introduction

If not all "educated" people speak the Standard, it is true that most people who wish to attach themselves to the educated class *aspire* to the educated dialect. And it is the pronunciation practices of the speakers of this dialect that are reflected in this volume.

Variation

For a large number of words, there is more than one pronunciation. This is true not only across dialects or within a particular dialect, but also of an individual's speech. Anyone using this book will discover quickly that more than one pronunciation is recorded as standard for many words. This may raise the legitimate question in the reader's mind about whether there aren't "correct" pronunciations for words, other pronunciations being "incorrect." Why doesn't someone decide what's right and what's wrong? Shouldn't *roof* be pronounced with the vowel sound of *wool*, not that of *tool*? Or shouldn't *patio* be pronounced so that the first syllable sounds like *pat*, not *pot*? In fact, might it not be the other way around in both of these cases? Can't we resort to *reason* to decide, or to what our elders said, or to the history of the word? Isn't it true that spelling dictates pronunciation? Actually, there are standard "spelling pronunciations," like *often* pronounced with the *t*-sound, and nonstandard ones, like *sword* pronounced with a *w*-sound near the beginning (**SWAWRD**). The universal pronunciation of *author* was originally a spelling pronunciation that got started after the spelling of the word—*autor*—was changed to *author*. And there are pronunciation spellings, too, like spelling the auxiliary verb *have* as *of*. This happens because *have* sounds like *of* in sentences like "You should have started earlier."

Authority

Implicit in the posing of questions about what's right and what's wrong is an appeal to *authority*. One attempts to verify or prove the correctness of a pronunciation by citing the authority for it. But the arbiter can only be the people; the usual practices of the educated population are the authority for correct standard pronunciation. If among the speakers of Standard Spoken English, some say *roof* one way and others say it another way, then both pronunciations are correct. Variety in this case is the standard. If no one who speaks the dialect pronounces *roof* to rhyme with *rough*, then such a pronunciation is nonstandard, that is, incorrect. One who aspires to speak Standard English can feel comfortable pronouncing *roof* in either of two standard ways. It should be added that it is not the opinion of standard speakers as to how words ought to be pronounced that has informed the compiling of this book. It is their pronunciations as we have heard them, monitored them, recorded them.

American English phonology

The syllable

The spoken syllable has a minimum requirement. There must be a "vowel" sound, and there can be only one. The vowel can be a monophthong (a sound produced without moving the tongue or the jaw) like the one in *cup*, or it can be a diphthong (a sound produced with movement of both tongue and jaw) like the one in *cope*. A consonant sound, designated in the following discussion as C, may precede a vowel sound, designated as V, to form a syllable as in *day* or *key*. Or a C may follow a V: *up, ache, ouch*. We can represent these possibilities in the following way: (C) V (C). In other words, a syllable can consist merely of a V as the first syllable of *ago* does, or it can consist of a C followed by a V as *day* does, or of a V followed by a C as *up* does. In fact, the formula specifies that a syllable can consist of a C then a V then another C, as *top* does.

Introduction

Continuing, we find that all English syllables can be successfully represented by this formula: (C) (C) (C) V (C) (C) (C). There can be as many as three consonant sounds before the required vowel sound (*strike, splash*), and there can be as many as three consonant sounds after the vowel (*lamps*). But English phonology is such that not all possible combinations of consonants and vowels can be used to form syllables and words. Consonant clusters like *dl* or *mk* or *pch* do not exist. And though *fl* and *gr* can be combined to form a cluster at the beginning of an English syllable (*flub, grub*), they may not combine at the end of one. There are many such constraints on cluster formation.

Tone and rhythm

When single-syllable words are recited as if they were on a shopping list, they normally have a falling pitch pattern; that is, the tone of the voice starts high and then goes lower, as the reader can appreciate if he reads successively and separately *beans, meat,* and then *milk.* If a word has more than one syllable, the same principle applies though there may be a low tone for the first syllable or two, then a higher tone, and once again a low tone: *asparagus.* Also, phrases and whole sentences usually follow the rule of falling pitch, or of first rising and then falling pitch: *paper towels, a small package of cheddar cheese*, and *You'll find it in the dairy section.*

English rhythm is based in part on its *stress* patterns. Some syllables are "accented" more than others; that is, they are stressed more than others. In fact, there are four degrees of stress in English and all four can be heard in a phrase like *paper airplane*. The loudest, most stressed syllable in this expression is the first syllable of the second word, namely, *air*; the second loudest syllable is the first syllable of *paper*; the third loudest is the second syllable of *airplane*; and the softest syllable is the second syllable of *paper*. It can be seen that the loudest syllable (*air*) is also the one spoken with the highest pitch, both syllables of *paper* are pronounced with a relatively low pitch, and the lowest pitch is used for the pronunciation of the last syllable of *airplane*.

In any stretch of speech there is an alternation between soft syllables and loud ones. Sometimes this alternation is strict as when the syllables come in pairs, each having a soft syllable then a loud one. Much English poetry is written with this rhythm.

> The harp that once through Tara's halls
> The soul of music shed,
> Now hangs as mute on Tara's walls
> As if that soul were fled.
> —*Thomas Moore*

But speech can be like this too: "a MAN from ALbuQUERque CALLED you YESterDAY." When the pattern is not strict, we can still detect it working generally: "He SAID he'd MAIL the PApers by FRIday."

These aspects of English pronunciation are recorded in this book in the following ways: first, the loudest syllable and the one with the highest pitch is spelled in bold-faced capitals, that is, in dark capital letters; for instance:

calendar . . . . **KAL** un dur

Next, the second loudest syllable is recorded in plain capitals, for instance, the last syllable of *reactivate*:

reactivate . . . . ree **AK** tuh VAYT

Finally, soft syllables are spelled in lower-case letters, as the first and third syllables of *reactivate*.

Introduction

Systematic patterns of variation

Some variations in pronunciation are not systematically represented in this book, but we mention them here and they may be inferred. First, when a *t*-sound comes between voiced sounds, usually vowels, it is often voiced to a *d*-sound. (A *voiced sound* is a sound produced with vibration in the vocal cords, for instance, a *v*-sound, a *z*-sound, or any vowel sound; a *voiceless sound* is one produced with no vibration in the vocal cords, for instance, an *f*-sound or an *s*-sound.) Both *latter* and *ladder* are pronounced identically by most Americans. And the *t*'s in such words as *arbiter, brevity, greater, satisfy, artery, seventy*, which are shown as a t in the pronunciations, may be taken as representing either a *t*-sound or a *d*-sound. Second, *n* and *l* serve English syllables not only as consonants, but as vowels. The second syllable of *brighten* consists merely of an *n*-sound, and the second syllable of *bridal* consists of just an *l*-sound. Because each syllable in English must have a "vowel" sound, the sounds in question here are called *vocalic consonants*. In this book, *brighten* and *bridal* are respelled for pronunciation as **BRYTE** un and **BRYDE** ul, respectively, but the vocalic consonants are meant. Third, the vowel before *r* in *charity* varies between that of *set* and *sat*, and so, **CHAR** uh tee and **CHER** uh tee are both heard. And i + r varies with ee + r in *fear*; oo + r varies with ooh + r in *tour*; aw + r varies with oh + r in *store*. These alternatives are not generally indicated in this book, but the user can rightly assume them.

Conclusion

The pronunciation of Standard English varies in some ways from person to person and group to group. Despite arbitrary standards which some guardians of English have sought to impose on the population, the people have gone their own way as they have always done, making, then remaking the standards as they go. The author has tried to record the variety of current pronunciation practices of the speakers of Standard Spoken English.

Things change rapidly though. No pronunciation recorded in this book is immutable. In fact, some of the pronunciations given are different from those which appear in dictionaries and other guides. This is as it must be. (This book will have little value, except as a historical document, one hundred years from now.) It is seldom possible to say *why* pronunciations change, but it is possible to predict that they will. Growth, after all, depends upon change.

The author's responsibility has been to listen to standard speakers talk, to monitor their pronunciations, to consult individuals who regularly use specialized vocabularies (art, music, the sciences, and so on), and then to report his findings. Any errors in fact or judgment are his alone.

William S. Chisholm, Jr.
Cleveland, Ohio
February, 1984

¶

Some alternative pronunciations are indicated by means of paragraph references as set forth below. If you look up a word and see a paragraph sign, ¶, followed by a number, refer to that numbered paragraph in this section, where you will find a brief description of the variation and some examples of it. At *solve*, for example, you will see:

solve . . . . **SAHLV** ¶19

At ¶19 below, it is explained that in words of this sort the AH-sound is replaced by the AW-sound in some parts of the country. Thus, both **SAHLV** and **SAWLV** are indicated as standard pronunciations.

¶1 Weakly stressed syllables

English words with weakly stressed syllables commonly have the vowel sound uh in them (or sometimes i) as in the first syllable of *machinery* (muh **SHEEN** ur ee), the second syllable of pendant (**PEN** dunt), or the middle syllable of *obligate* (**AHB** luh gayt). But in many weakly stressed syllables, uh or i will vary with unstressed ee, ay, e, a, ooh, oo, oh, ah, aw, or eye.

Here are some examples of these:
—ee varies with i: elope (i **LOHP** or ee **LOHP**); ecology (ee **KAHL** uh jee or i **KAHL** uh jee)
—ay varies with uh and i: satanic (say **TAN** ik or suh **TAN** ik); creativity (KREE ay **TIV** uh tee or KREE uh **TIV** uh tee)
—e varies with uh and i: embrace (im **BRAYS** or em **BRAYS**); September (sep **TEM** bur or sup **TEM** bur or sip **TEM** bur)
—a varies with uh: trapeze (tra **PEEZ** or truh **PEEZ**); allude (uh **LOOHD** or a **LOOHD**)

¶

—ooh and oo vary with uh: superb (soo **PURB** *or* suh **PURB** *or* sooh **PURB**); conspicuous (kun **SPIK** yoo wus *or* kun **SPIK** yuh wus *or* kun **SPIK** yooh us)

—oh varies with uh: esoteric (ES uh **TER** ik *or* ES oh **TER** ik); proceed (pruh **SEED** *or* proh **SEED**)

—ah varies with uh: concoct (kun **KAHKT** *or* kahn **KAHKT**); ah before *r* varies with ur: partition (pahr **TISH** un *or* pur **TISH** un)

—aw varies with uh: Caucasian (kaw **KAY** zhun *or* kuh **KAY** zhun); morale (muh **RAL** *or* maw **RAL**)

—eye varies with uh: binocular (bye **NAHK** yuh lur *or* buh **NAHK** yuh lur); tribunal (trye **BYOOH** nul *or* truh **BYOOH** nul)

¶2 Stress and pitch reversal

The syllable with the main stress is either one or another of two syllables in a word; that is, the stress may be rising (going from weak to strong) or falling (going from strong to weak).

capsize	**KAP** syze *or* kap **SYZE**
décor	day **KAWR** *or* **DAY** kawr
dictator	**DIK** tayt ur *or* dik **TAYT** ur
rutabaga	ROOHT uh **BAY** guh *or* **ROOHT** uh BAY guh

¶3 Dissimilation

The first of two r-sounds, l-sounds, or n-sounds in a word may not be pronounced.

caterpillar	**KAT** ur PIL ur *or* **KAT** uh PIL ur
surprise	sur **PRYZE** *or* suh **PRYZE**
government	**GUV** ur munt *or* **GUV** urn munt
ophthalmology	AHF thul **MAHL** uh jee *or* AHP thuh **MAHL** uh jee
badminton	**BAD** min tun *or* **BAD** mit un

¶4 Metathesis
The order of two sounds, usually an uh-sound and an r-sound, can be reversed.

irony .... **EYE** ruh nee *or* **EYE** ur nee
hundred .... **HUN** drud *or* **HUN** durd
jewelry .... **JOOH** ul ree *or* **JOOH** lur ee

¶5 Syncopation
Some words, especially those with n-, r-, or l-sounds in weakly stressed syllables, can have the number of syllables reduced by one; that is, the word can be syncopated.

arsenic .... **AHR** suh nik *or* **AHRS** nik
conference .... **KAHN** fur uns *or* **KAHN** fruns
family .... **FAM** uh lee *or* **FAM** lee

¶6 Assimilation
Assimilation is a process which changes sounds because of the position they occupy in words.

A. Two identical sounds coming one after the other tend to reduce to one:

eighteen (eigh*t* + *t*een) .... ay **TEEN**

B. (1) Voiceless consonants (those with no vibration in the vocal cords) coming next to voiced sounds (those with vibration in the vocal cords) tend to become voiced, as, for instance, the *t*-sound of *late*, which becomes a *d*-sound in *later*.

(2) Voiced consonants coming next to voiceless ones may become voiceless. This accounts for the pronunciation of *disgust* as dis **KUST** (making it rhyme perfectly with "discussed"). The

d-sound in *width* is often made voiceless because of the voiceless *th*-sound following it; that is, **WIDTH** varies with **WITTH**.

C. (1) For "ease of articulation," a consonant sound standing next to a similar consonant sound may disappear entirely or may be modified so that it has exactly the same sound. For *horseshoe*, **HAWR** shooh and **HAWRSH** shooh, illustrate the two processes.

(2) A sound can be moved from one place in the mouth to another to make it easier to pronounce the next sound. The *f*-sound at the beginning of the second syllable of *symphony* is easier to pronounce if the first syllable ends in an *n*-sound (**SIN** fuh nee) than if it ends in an *m*-sound (**SIM** fuh nee).

¶7 Syllable splitting

Single syllables can be split, or divided; for instance, words like toil *and* fire *can be pronounced as one syllable or two.*

toil . . . . **TOYL** *or* **TOY** ul
fire . . . . **FYRE** *or* **FYE** ur

¶8 Restressing

In some words a single syllable, other than the one receiving primary stress, will be spoken with either a weak stress or a relatively strong stress. In recent years, restressing of weakly stressed syllables has increased, as, for instance, for the days of the week, which formerly were pronounced by nearly everyone with the -day syllable weakly stressed. The consequence of restressing is that the quality of the vowel changes from an uh-sound or an i-sound (see ¶1) to some other vowel.

accent . . . . **AK** sent *or* **AK** sunt
consequence . . . . **KAHN** suh kwens *or* **KAHN** suh kwuns
Wednesday . . . . **WENZ** dee *or* **WENZ** day

¶9 Syllable stopping

Some syllables are "stopped" by sounding a p, t, or k between certain consonants in clusters. (The sounding of these consonants causes a momentary stoppage of the outgoing breath.) This process accounts for the identical pronunciations of cents *and* sense.

nymph.................................... **NIMF** *or* **NIMPF**
sense..................................... **SENS** *or* **SENTS**
length .... **LENGTH** *or* **LENGKTH**

¶10 Consonant cluster reduction

Clusters of two or more consonant sounds may be reduced by one.

architects .... **AHR** kuh tekts *or* **AHR** kuh teks
bondsman.......................... **BAHNDZ** mun *or* **BAHNZ** mun
fifth .... **FIFTH** *or* **FITH**
postpone........................... pohst **POHN** *or* pohs **POHN**

In paragraphs 11–17, we have listed pairs of sounds that are heard interchangeably in some words.

¶11 s *or* sh

commensurate.................... kuh **MEN** shur it *or* kuh **MEN** sur it
sociology .... SOH see **AHL** uh jee *or* SOH shee **AHL** uh jee
species .... **SPEE** sheez *or* **SPEE** seez
sumac .... **SHOOH** mak *or* **SOOH** mak

¶12 sh *or* ch

chassis .... **CHAS** ee *or* **SHAS** ee
welsh....................................... **WELSH** *or* **WELCH**
century .... **SEN** chur ee *or* **SEN** shur ee

¶

¶13 t *or* ch

mature	muh **TOOR** *or* muh **CHOOR**
pasteurize	**PAS** chuh ryze *or* **PAS** tuh ryze
Neptune	**NEP** toohn *or* **NEP** choohn

¶14 s *or* z

citizen	**SIT** uh zun *or* **SIT** uh sun
cortisone	**KAWR** tuh sohn *or* **KAWR** tuh zohn
newspaper	**NOOHZ** pay pur *or* **NOOHS** pay pur

¶15 j *or* zh

Words borrowed from French with the zh-sound are usually made American by substituting the j-sound.

massage	muh **SAHZH** *or* muh **SAHJ**
prestige	pres **TEEZH** *or* pres **TEEJ**
garage	guh **RAHJ** *or* guh **RAHZH**

¶16 n *or* ng

The principle stated in ¶6, C.2 is often responsible for this variation.

conquest	**KAHNG** kwest *or* **KAHN** kwest
dungarees	dung guh **REEZ** *or* dun guh **REEZ**
bronchitis	brahng **KYTE** is *or* brahn **KYTE** is

¶17 ch *or* ty; j *or* dy

In some words a process called palatalization *takes place. In this process the sound ty becomes ch or the dy-sound evolves into a j-sound. This does not happen universally in all words where it might, but if it does happen, the t-sound (or the comparable d-sound) may remain nearly as common as the palatalized sound (the ch or j), but it will have a y-sound following immediately. A historical illustration of this process can be seen in the word* nature, *which, until about 1650, was pronounced* **NAY** tur, *but since that time the t-sound has been a ch-sound (***NAY** chur*) or, rarely, a ty-sound (***NAY** tyoor*).*

petulant.............................	**PECH** oo lunt *or* **PET** yoo lunt
fraudulent......................	**FRAW** juh lunt *or* **FRAWD** yuh lunt
celestial	suh **LES** chul *or* suh **LEST** yul

In paragraphs 18–25, we have listed pairs of vowel sounds that are heard interchangeably in some words.

¶18 a *or* ah

Words like bath *and* path *are pronounced as* **BAHTH** *and* **PAHTH** *in Eastern New England and as* **BATH** *and* **PATH** *elsewhere. Also, some words borrowed from Italian and Spanish show the same variation, the ah-sound reflecting the original vowel and the a-sound being the native, Anglicized vowel.*

bath	**BATH** *or* **BAHTH**
madras	**MAD** rus *or* **MAHD** rus
patio	**PAT** ee oh *or* **PAHT** ee oh

¶19 ah *or* aw

In the North, the word on *is pronounced* **AHN**, *but elsewhere it is pronounced* **AWN**, *except in some few places, Pittsburgh and neighboring areas for instance, where an intermediate vowel (a sound midway between* **AH** *and* **AW***) is heard. In the North,* cot *and* caught *contrast, that is,* **KAHT** *for* cot, *and* **KAWT** *for* caught; *again, in Pittsburgh, the intermediate vowel is heard in both words. In addition, one hears either the ah-sound or the aw-sound before an r-sound in a word like* minority.

¶

resolve .... ri **ZAHLV** *or* ruh **ZAWLV**
minority .... muh **NAWR** uh tee *or* muh **NAHR** uh tee
water...**WAWT** ur *or* **WAHT** ur

¶20 ah *or* oh

These two sounds are heard interchangeably in many words, especially certain specialized words borrowed from Latin.

solstice .... **SAHL** stis *or* **SOHL** stis
solenoid .... **SOH** luh noyd *or* **SAH** luh noyd
obelisk ....**AHB** uh lisk *or* **OH** buh lisk

¶21 ooh *or* yooh; oo *or* yoo

In certain words, like cute *and* beauty, *yooh is universal, whereas ooh is universal in* lute, rule, *and the like. In some other words, however, generally of the* new, tune *type, there are regional and social variations between yooh and ooh. But in situations where neither predominates, the ooh-sound is generally replacing the* yooh.

nuisance .... **NOOH** suns *or* **NYOOH** suns
bubonic............................ byoo **BAHN** ik *or* boo **BAHN** ik
tube .... **TOOHB** *or* **TYOOHB**

¶22 eye *or* ee *or* i

mercantile .... **MUR** kun tyle *or* **MUR** kun teel *or* **MUR** kun tul
serpentine......................... **SUR** pun teen *or* **SUR** pun tyne
strychnine .... **STRIK** nyne *or* **STRIK** neen *or* **STRIK** nun
turbine .... **TUR** bun *or* **TUR** byne
destine ....**DES** tin
Note: *The* -ine *and* -ile *endings have varying and unpredictable pronunciations; in some words (such as* mercantile) *there are three*

choices, others (like turbine) *have two variations, and still others (like* turpentine... **TUR** pun tyne *and* intestine... in **TES** tin) *have only a single standard pronunciation. Readers may wish to consult* Webster's New World Dictionary *if they have doubts as to which variations for any such words are current in Standard American English.*

¶23 ar or er

Most Southerners pronounce Mary *as* **MAY** ree, merry *as* **MER** ee, *and* marry *as* **MAR** ee. *Elsewhere, generally, these three words are pronounced alike, that is, as* **MER** ee. *More and more frequently, one hears* charity *pronounced with the same first syllable of* cherish, *that is,* **CHER** uh tee *and* **CHER** ish.

```
carriage.........................................KAR ij or KER ij
charity............................. CHAR i tee or CHER i tee
capillary ....................... KAP uh LER ee or KAP uh LAR ee
```

¶24 oor or ur; yoor or yur

Usage is very much unsettled in words where these sounds compete with each other. One almost always hears tour *pronounced* **TOOR**, *but for* tourist, **TUR** ist *competes well with* **TOOR** ist. *Most insurance salesmen these days are selling in* **SHUR** uns, *not in* **SHOOR** uns, *but the second of these remains the standard.*

```
Europe .................................. YOOR up or YUR up
furious ............................ FYOOR ee us or FYUR ee us
tournament..................... TOOR nuh munt or TUR nuh munt
```

¶25 yuh or ee uh

The last two syllables of California *pronounced as* KAL uh **FAWR** nee uh *can be syncopated, producing* KAL uh **FAWR** nyuh, *which is the more frequent pronunciation. Syncopation of* ee uh *to* yuh *prevails in state and*

¶

nation names, but the unsyncopated pronunciation probably predominates in the examples listed below.

trivial .... **TRIV** ee ul *or* **TRIV** yul
opium .... **OH** pee um *or* **OH** pyum
malleable .... **MAL** ee uh bul *or* **MAL** yuh bul

A

a *(article)* .... uh
*AY is properly used only when the
article is emphasized.*

aardvark .... **AHRD** vahrk

abacus .... **AB** uh kus
uh **BAK** us *is now sometimes heard.*

abalone .... AB uh **LOH** nee

abandon .... uh **BAN** dun

abatement .... uh **BAYT** munt

abattoir .... **AB** uh twahr ¶2

abbess .... **AB** is

abbey .... **AB** ee

abbot .... **AB** ut

abbreviate .... uh **BREE** vee ayt

abbreviation ..... uh **BREE** vee **AY** shun

abdicate .... **AB** duh kayt

abdomen .... **AB** duh mun *or*
ab **DOH** mun ¶1

abdominal .... ab **DAHM** uh nul ¶1

abduction .... ab **DUK** shun ¶1

aberrant .... a **BER** unt ¶1
now also **AB** ur unt

aberration .... AB ur **RAY** shun

abeyance .... uh **BAY** uns ¶9

abhor .... ub **HAWR**

abject .... **AB** jekt *or* ab **JEKT**

abjure .... ub **JOOR** ¶1, 24

ablative .... **AB** luh tiv

–able .... uh bul
*There are many derived
adjectives ending with this suffix
that could not be entered here.*

ablution .... ab **LOOH** shun ¶1

abnegate .... **AB** nuh gayt

abnormal .... ab **NAWR** mul ¶1

abnormality ....
.... AB nawr **MAL** uh tee ¶1

abode .... uh **BOHD**

abolish .... uh **BAHL** ish

abolition .... AB uh **LISH** un

abominable .... uh **BAHM** uh nuh bul

abominate .... uh **BAHM** uh nayt

abomination ... uh **BAHM** uh **NAY** shun

aborigine .... AB uh **RIJ** uh nee

abortion .... uh **BAWR** shun

abracadabra .... AB ruh kuh **DAB** ruh

abrasion .... uh **BRAY** zhun

abrasive .... uh **BRAY** siv

abridgment .... uh **BRIJ** munt

abrogate .... **AB** ruh gayt ¶1

abscess .... **AB** ses

abscond .... ub **SKAHND** ¶1

absent *(verb)* .... ab **SENT** ¶2

absent *(adjective)* .... **AB** sunt

absentee .... ab sun **TEE**

absinthe .... **AB** sinth ¶9

absolute .... **AB** suh looht ¶2

absolve .... ub **ZAHLV** ¶1, 14, 19

absorbent ..... ub **ZAWR** bunt ¶1, 14

absorption ... ub **ZAWRP** shun ¶1, 14

abstemious ...... ub **STEE** mee us ¶1

abstention .... ub **STEN** shun ¶1

abstinence .... **AB** stuh nuns ¶9

SPELLED	PRONOUNCED
abstract (verb and adjective)	
.... ab **STRAKT** or **AB** strakt	
abstract (noun) .... **AB** strakt	
abstraction .... ab **STRAK** shun ¶1	
abstruse .... ab **STROOHS** ¶1	
absurd .... ub **SURD** ¶1, 14	
Abu Dhabi .... AH booh **DAH** bee	
abundant .... uh **BUN** dunt	
abuse (verb) .... uh **BYOOZ**	
abuse (noun) .... uh **BYOOHS**	
abusive .... uh **BYOOH** siv	
abutment .... uh **BUT** munt	
abysmal .... uh **BIZ** mul	
abyss .... uh **BIS**	
acacia .... uh **KAY** shuh	
academe .... **AK** uh deem ¶2	
academia ..... AK uh **DEE** mee uh ¶25	
academic .... AK uh **DEM** ik	
academician .... uh KAD uh **MISH** un or	
AK uh duh **MISH** un	
academy .... uh **KAD** uh mee	
a cappella .... AH kuh **PEL** uh	
Acapulco .... AK uh **POOL** koh or	
AHK uh **POOL** koh	
accede .... ak **SEED** ¶1	
accelerate .... uk **SEL** uh rayt ¶1	
acceleration	
.... uk SEL uh **RAY** shun ¶1	
accent (verb) .... **AK** sent ¶2	
accent (noun) .... **AK** sent	
AK sunt is becoming rare ¶8.	
accentuate	
.... ak **SEN** choo wayt ¶1, 12	
accept .... ak **SEPT** ¶1	
access .... **AK** ses	

SPELLED	PRONOUNCED
accession .... ak **SESH** un ¶1	
accessory .... uk **SES** ur ee ¶1	
accident .... **AK** suh dunt	
accidental .... AK suh **DEN** tul	
accipiter .... ak **SIP** uh tur ¶1	
acclimate .... **AK** luh mayt or	
uh **KLYE** mut	
acclimatize .... uh **KLYE** muh TYZE	
accolade .... **AK** uh layd	
accommodate .... uh **KAHM** uh dayt	
accommodation	
.... uh KAHM uh **DAY** shun	
accompaniment	
.... uh **KUMP** ni munt ¶5	
accompany ...... uh **KUM** puh nee ¶5	
accomplice .... uh **KAHM** plis or	
uh **KUM** plis	
accomplish .... uh **KAHM** plish or	
uh **KUM** plish	
accord .... uh **KAWRD**	
accordion .... uh **KAWR** dee un	
accost .... uh **KAWST** ¶19	
accounting .... uh **KOWN** ting	
accouterment .. uh **KOOHT** ur munt or	
uh **KOOH** truh munt	
The second is heard especially as	
a reading pronunciation of the	
alternate spelling accoutrement.	
accretion .... uh **KREE** shun	
accrue .... uh **KROOH**	
acculturate .... uh **KUL** chuh rayt	
accumulate .... uh **KYOOH** myuh layt	
uh **KYOOH** muh layt is also heard.	
accuracy .... **AK** yur uh see ¶5	
accurate .... **AK** yur it ¶5	

SPELLED	PRONOUNCED
accursed	uh KUR sid *or* uh KURST
accusative	uh KYOOH zuh tiv
accuse	uh KYOOHZ
accustom	uh KUS tum
acerbic	uh SUR bik
acetate	AS uh tayt
acetone	AS uh tohn
acetyl	uh SEET ul *or* AS uh tul
acetylene	uh SET uh LEEN
ache	AYK
achene	ay KEEN *or* uh KEEN
achieve	uh CHEEV
Achilles	uh KIL eez
acid	AS id
acidic	uh SID ik
acidity	uh SID uh tee
acidulous	uh SIJ oo lus ¶17
acknowledge	uk NAHL ij ¶1
acme	AK mee
acne	AK nee
acolyte	AK uh lyte
acorn	AY kawrn
AY kurn *is also heard.*	
acoustics	uh KOOHS tiks
acquaint	uh KWAYNT
acquiesce	ak wee ES
acquire	uh KWYRE
acquisition	AK wuh ZISH un
acquisitive	uh KWIZ uh tiv
acquit	uh KWIT
acre	AY kur
acreage	AY kur ij ¶5
acrid	AK rid
acrimonious	
	AK ruh MOH nee us ¶25

SPELLED	PRONOUNCED
acrimony	AK ruh MOH nee
acrobat	AK ruh bat
acronym	AK ruh nim
acrophobia	AK ruh FOH bee uh ¶25
acropolis	uh KRAHP ul is
across	uh KRAWS ¶19
acrostic	uh KRAWS tik ¶19
acrylic	uh KRIL ik
actinic	ak TIN ik
action	AK shun
activate	AK tuh vayt
active	AK tiv
activity	ak TIV uh tee ¶1
actor	AK tur
actress	AK tris
actual	AK choo wul ¶5, 12
actually	AK choo wul ee *or* AK choo lee ¶5, 12
actuary	AK choo WER ee
actuate	AK choo wayt
acuity	uh KYOOH uh tee
acumen	uh KYOOH mun *or* AK yuh mun
acupuncture	AK yuh PUNGK chur ¶12
acute	uh KYOOHT
adage	AD ij
adagio	uh DAH joh ¶15, 25
adamant	AD uh munt
adamantine	AD uh MAN teen ¶22
adapt	uh DAPT
adaptation	AD up TAY shun ¶1
addend	AD end *or* uh DEND
addendum	uh DEN dum
addict *(verb)*	uh DIKT

SPELLED	PRONOUNCED
addict *(noun)*	**AD** ikt
addiction	uh **DIK** shun
addictive	uh **DIK** tiv
addition	uh **DISH** un ¶1
additive	**AD** uh tiv
addlepated	**AD** ul payt id
address *(verb)*	uh **DRES**
address *(noun)*	uh **DRES** or **AD** res
adduce	uh **DOOHS** ¶1, 21
adenoids	**AD** uh noydz
adept *(noun)*	**AD** ept
adept *(adjective)*	uh **DEPT**
adequacy	**AD** i kwuh see
adequate	**AD** uh kwuht
adhere	ud **HIR** ¶1
adhesion	ud **HEE** zhun ¶1
adhesive	ud **HEE** siv ¶1, 14
ad hoc	ad **HAHK** or ahd **HOHK** or ad **HOHK**
ad hominem	ad **HAHM** uh **NEM**
adieu	uh **DYOOH** ¶21
ad infinitum	ad **IN** fuh **NYTE** um ¶18
adios	ah dee **OHS** or ad ee **OHS**
adipose	**AD** uh pohs
adjacent	uh **JAY** sunt
adjectival	**AJ** ik **TYE** vul
adjective	**AJ** ik tiv
adjourn	uh **JURN**
adjudicate	uh **JOOH** duh kayt
adjunct	**AJ** ungkt
adjust	uh **JUST**
adjustment	uh **JUST** munt ¶10
adjutant	**AJ** uh tunt
ad–lib	ad **LIB**

SPELLED	PRONOUNCED
adman	**AD** man

This is one of the words formed with –man where it is never pronounced muhn.

administer	ud **MIN** uh stur ¶1
administrate	ud **MIN** uh strayt ¶1
admirable	**AD** mur uh bul ¶5
admiral	**AD** mur ul ¶5
admiration	AD muh **RAY** shun
admire	ud **MYRE** ¶1
admissible	ud **MIS** uh bul ¶1
admission	ud **MISH** un ¶1
admit	ud **MIT** ¶1
admixture	ad **MIKS** chur ¶1
admonish	ud **MAHN** ish ¶1
admonition	AD muh **NISH** un
ad nauseam	ad **NAW** zee um or ahd **NAW** shee um ¶11
ado	uh **DOOH**
adobe	uh **DOH** bee
adolescent	AD uh **LES** unt
Adonis	uh **DAHN** is
adoration	AD uh **RAY** shun
adrenal	uh **DREE** nul
adrenaline	uh **DREN** uh lun
Adriatic	AY dree **AT** ik
adroit	uh **DROYT**
adulate	**AJ** uh layt
adult	uh **DULT** or **AD** ult
adulterate	uh **DUL** tuh rayt
adulterer	uh **DUL** tur ur
adulteress	uh **DUL** tur is ¶5
adultery	uh **DUL** tur ee ¶5
adumbrate	**AD** um brayt or uh **DUM** brayt

SPELLED	PRONOUNCED	SPELLED	PRONOUNCED
ad valorem	AD vuh LAWR um	aerobe	ER ohb
advance	ud VANS ¶1, 9, 18	aerobic	e ROH bik
advantage	ud VAN tij ¶1, 18	aerodynamics	
advantageous	AD van TAY jus ¶1		ER oh dye NAM iks ¶1
Advent	AD vent	aeronautics	ER uh NAWT iks ¶1
adventitious	AD ven TISH us ¶1	aerosol	ER uh sawl ¶1, 19
adventure	ud VEN chur ¶1	Aeschylus	ES kuh lus
adverb	AD vurb	Aesop	EE sahp
adverbial	ud VUR bee ul ¶1, 25	EE sup *is occasionally heard* ¶8.	
adversary	AD vur SER ee ¶3	aesthete	ES theet ¶2
adversative	ud VUR suh tiv	aesthetics	es THET iks
adverse	ad VURS *or* AD vurs ¶1	afebrile	ay FEE brul *or*
adversity	ad VURS uh tee ¶1		ay FEB rul ¶22
advertise	AD vur tyze	affable	AF uh bul
advertisement	AD vur TYZE munt *or*	affair	uh FER
	ud VUR tiz munt ¶1, 14	affect	uh FEKT
advice	ud VYSE ¶1	affectation	AF ek TAY shun ¶1
advise	ud VYZE ¶1	affection	uh FEK shun
advisedly	ud VYE zid lee ¶1	affenpinscher	AHF un PIN chur *or*
advocacy	AD vuh kuh see		AF un PIN chur
advocate *(verb)*	AD vuh kayt	affiance	uh FYE uns ¶9
advocate *(noun)*	AD vuh kit *or*	affidavit	AF uh DAY vit
	AD vuh kayt	AF uh DAY vid *is sometimes heard.*	
Aegean	i JEE un	affiliate *(verb)*	uh FIL ee ayt
aegis	EE jis	affiliate *(noun)*	uh FIL ee it
Aeneid	i NEE id	affinity	uh FIN uh tee
Aeolian	ee OH lee un	affirm	uh FURM
aerate	ER ayt	affirmation	AF ur MAY shun
AY ur ayt *has become rare.*		affirmative	uh FUR muh tiv
aerial	ER ee ul	affix *(verb)*	uh FIKS *or* AF iks
ay IR ee ul *is no longer heard for*		affix *(noun)*	AF iks
the noun and is rare for the		affixation	AF ik SAY shun
adjective.		afflatus	uh FLAYT us
aerie	ER ee *or* IR ee	afflict	uh FLIKT
aerobatics	ER uh BAT iks	affliction	uh FLIK shun

5

affluence .... **AF** loo wuns *or*
         uh **FLOOH** uns ¶9

affront .... uh **FRUNT**

Afghan .... **AF** gan

Afghanistan .... af **GAN** uh **STAN**

aficionado ..... uh **FISH** uh **NAH** doh *or*
        uh **FEESH** uh **NAH** doh
also uh **FIS** ee uh **NAH** doh ¶25

Africa .... **AF** ri kuh

Afrikaans .... af ri **KAHNZ** *or*
   af ri **KAHNS** *or* af ri **KANZ**

Afrikaner .... **AF** ri **KAHN** ur

Afro .... **AF** roh

after .... **AF** tur ¶18

afterward .... **AF** tur wurd ¶18

afterword .... **AF** tur **WURD** ¶18

against .... uh **GENST**
  uh **GAYNST** *is also heard, but
  mainly in British and Canadian
  usage.*

agape ("wide open") .... uh **GAYP**

agape ("divine love") ....
         AH gah pay ¶1

agate .... **AG** ut

agave .... uh **GAH** vee

aged ("old" *or* "old people") ... **AY** jid
  *When the meaning is made old,
  as in* "aged wine," *or of the age
  of, as in* "a girl aged nine," *it is*
  AYJD.

agency .... **AY** jun see

agenda .... uh **JEN** duh

ageratum .... AJ uh **RAYT** um

agglomerate *(verb)* ....
         uh **GLAHM** uh rayt

agglomerate *(noun and adjective)* ..
        uh **GLAHM** ur it

aggrandize .... uh **GRAN** dyze *or*
        AG run dyze

aggravate .... **AG** ruh vayt

aggregate *(verb)* .... **AG** ruh gayt

aggregate *(noun and adjective)* .....
        AG ruh gut

aggression .... uh **GRESH** un

aggressive .... uh **GRES** iv

aggressor .... uh **GRES** ur

aggrieve .... uh **GREEV**

aghast .... uh **GAST** ¶18

agile .... **AJ** ul ¶22

agitate .... **AJ** uh tayt

agnate .... **AG** nayt

agnostic .... ag **NAHS** tik ¶1, 19

agnosticism ....
        ag **NAHS** tuh siz um ¶1, 19

agog .... uh **GAHG** ¶19

agonize .... **AG** uh nyze

agony .... **AG** uh nee

agora .... **AG** ur uh
  uh **GAWR** uh *is now sometimes
  heard.*

agouti .... uh **GOOH** tee

agrarian ..... uh **GRAR** ee un ¶23, 25

agriculture .... **AG** ri **KUL** chur

agronomy .... uh **GRAHN** uh mee

ague .... **AY** gyooh

Ahab .... **AY** hab

aigrette .... **AY** gret *or* ay **GRET**

aikido .... eye **KEE** doh *or* eye kee **DOH**

ailanthus .... ay **LAN** thus ¶9

aileron .... **AY** luh rahn

SPELLED	PRONOUNCED	SPELLED	PRONOUNCED
Ainu	**EYE** nooh	al dente	ahl **DEN** tay
airily	**ER** uh lee	*an Italian phrase that is now*	
airiness	**ER** ee nis	*occasionally Anglicized to*	
airman	**ER** mun	al **DEN** tee	
aisle	**EYLE**	alder	**AWL** dur
akimbo	uh **KIM** boh	alderman	**AWL** dur mun
akin	uh **KIN**	aleatory	**AY** lee uh **TAWR** ee
alabaster	**AL** uh **BAS** tur	alert	uh **LURT**
a la carte	AH luh **KAHRT** *or*	Aleut	**AL** ee ooht *or* **AL** yooht *or*
	AL uh **KAHRT**		uh **LOOHT**
alacrity	uh **LAK** ruh tee	Aleutian	uh **LOOH** shun
Aladdin	uh **LAD** un	alexandrine	**AL** ig **ZAN** drin ¶22
à la king	AH luh **KING** *or* **AL** uh **KING**	alexia	uh **LEK** see uh
Alamo	**AL** uh moh	alfalfa	al **FAL** fuh
a la mode	AH luh **MOHD** *or*	alfresco	al **FRES** koh
	AL uh **MOHD**	algae	**AL** jee
alas	uh **LAS** ¶18	*The singular* alga *is* **AL** guh.	
Alaska	uh **LAS** kuh	algebra	**AL** juh bruh
albacore	**AL** buh kawr	algebraic	**AL** juh **BRAY** ik
Albania	al **BAY** nee uh ¶25	Algeria	al **JIR** ee uh
albatross	**AL** buh traws ¶19	Algiers	al **JIRZ**
albeit	awl **BEE** it *or* al **BEE** it	Algonquian	al **GAHNG** kee un *or*
albino	al **BYE** noh		al **GAHNG** kwee un
Albion	**AL** bee un	Algonquin	al **GAHNG** kin *or*
album	**AL** bum		al **GAHNG** kwin
albumen	al **BYOOH** mun	algorithm	**AL** guh **RIDH** um
AL byuh mun *is occasionally heard.*		alias	**AY** lee us ¶25
albumin	al **BYOOH** mun	Ali Baba	AH lee **BAH** buh *or*
Albuquerque	**AL** buh **KUR** kee		AL ee **BAB** uh
alburnum	al **BUR** num	alibi	**AL** uh bye
alchemy	**AL** kuh mee	alien	**AY** lee un ¶25
alcohol	**AL** kuh hawl ¶19	alienation	AY lee uh **NAY** shun ¶25
alcoholic	AL kuh **HAWL** ik ¶19	alight	uh **LYTE**
alcove	**AL** kohv	align	uh **LYNE**
aldehyde	**AL** duh hyde	aliment	**AL** uh munt

alimentary	AL uh **MEN** tur ee ¶5	alloy *(noun)*	AL oy
alimentation		allspice	AWL spyse
	AL uh men **TAY** shun ¶1	allude	uh LOOHD ¶1
alimony	AL uh MOH nee	allure	uh LOOR
alive	uh LYVE	allusion	uh LOOH zhun
alkali	AL kuh lye	allusive	uh LOOH siv
alkaline	AL kuh lin *or* AL kuh lyne	alluvial	uh LOOH vee ul ¶25
allay	uh LAY	ally *(verb)*	uh LYE *or* AL eye
allegation	AL uh **GAY** shun	ally *(noun)*	AL eye *or* uh LYE
allege	uh LEJ	alma mater	AL muh **MAHT** ur *or*
alleged	uh LEJD		AHL muh **MAHT** ur *(or* **MAYT** ur*)*
uh **LEJ** id *is heard occasionally.*		almanac	AWL muh nak *or*
allegedly	uh LEJ id lee		AL muh nak
allegiance	uh **LEE** juns ¶9	almighty	awl MYTE ee
allegorical	AL uh **GAWR** i kul ¶19	almond	AH mund *or* AHL mund *or*
allegory	AL uh GAWR ee		AL mund *or* AM und ¶10
allegretto	AL uh **GRET** oh	alms	AHMZ
allegro	uh **LEG** roh *or* uh LAY groh	*The spelling pronunciation* **AHLMZ**	
allergen	AL ur jun	*is sometimes heard.*	
allergic	uh LUR jik	aloe	AL oh
allergy	AL ur jee	aloha	uh LOH uh *or* ah LOH hah
alleviate	uh **LEE** vee ayt	aloof	uh LOOHF
alley	AL ee	alpaca	al PAK uh
alliance	uh **LYE** uns ¶9	alpha	AL fuh
allied	uh LYDE *or* AL yde	alphabet	AL fuh bet
alligator	AL uh gayt ur	alphabetical	AL fuh **BET** i kul
alliteration	uh LIT uh **RAY** shun	alphabetize	AL fuh buh TYZE
alliterative	uh **LIT** uh rayt iv *or*	alpine	AL pyne
	uh **LIT** ur uh tiv	already	awl RED ee
allocate	AL uh kayt ¶1	Alsatian	al **SAY** shun
allot	uh LAHT	altar	AWL tur
allow	uh LOW	alter	AWL tur
allowance	uh LOW uns ¶9	alteration	AWL tur **RAY** shun
allowedly	uh LOW id lee	altercation	AWL tur **KAY** shun
alloy *(verb)*	uh LOY *or* AL oy	alter ego	AWL tur **EE** goh

alternate *(verb)*	AWL tur nayt	Amazon	AM uh zahn
alternate *(adjective)*	AWL tur nit	ambassador	am BAS uh dur *or*
alternative	awl TUR nuh tiv		am BAS uh DAWR
alternator	AWL tur nayt ur	ambassadorial	
although	awl DHOH		am BAS uh DAWR ee ul
altimeter	al TIM uh tur	ambergris	AM bur gris *or*
altitude	AL tuh toohd ¶21		AM bur grees
altogether	AWL tuh GEDH ur ¶2	ambidextrous	AM bi DEK strus
altruism	AL troo wiz um	ambience *or* ambiance	AM bee uns
altruistic	AL troo WIS tik	ahm BYAHNS *approximates the*	
alum	AL um	*French pronunciation.*	
aluminum	uh LOOH muh num	ambient	AM bee unt
alumna	uh LUM nuh	ambiguity	AM buh GYOOH uh tee

The plural alumnae *is*
uh LUM nee, *but* uh LUM nye, *which*
is also heard, causes confusion
with the plural of alumnus.

alumnus	uh LUM nus	ambiguous	am BIG yoo wus
		ambition	am BISH un
The plural alumni *is* uh LUM nye.		ambivalence	am BIV uh luns ¶9
alveoli	al VEE uh LYE	amble	AM bul
always	AWL wiz *or* AWL wayz ¶1	ambrosia	am BROH zhuh ¶25
alyssum	uh LIS um	ambulance	AM byuh luns ¶9
amalgam	uh MAL gum	ambulatory	AM byuh luh TAWR ee
amalgamation		ambush	AM boosh
	uh MAL guh MAY shun	ameliorate	uh MEEL yuh rayt ¶25
amandine	AH mun deen *or*	amen	ay MEN *or* ah MEN ¶2
	AM un deen	amenable	uh MEE nuh bul *or*
amanuensis	uh MAN yoo WEN sis		uh MEN uh bul
amaranth	AM uh ranth ¶9	amend	uh MEND
amaryllis	AM uh RIL us	amendment	uh MEND munt ¶10
amateur	AM uh chur *or*	amenity	uh MEN uh tee *or*
	AM uh toor ¶13, 21, 24		uh MEE nuh tee
amateurish		amerce	uh MURS
	AM uh CHOOR ish ¶13, 17, 21	Americana	uh MER uh KAN uh *or*
amaze	uh MAYZ		uh MER uh KAH nuh
		Ameslan	AM us lan
		amethyst	AM uh thist
		amiable	AY mee uh bul ¶25

9

amicable .... **AM** i kuh bul

amice .... **AM** is

amidst .... uh **MIDST** ¶6

amigo .... uh **MEE** goh

amino (acids) .... uh **MEE** noh
AM uh noh *is no longer much
heard.*

amir .... uh **MIR**

Amish .. **AH** mish *or* **AM** ish *or* **AY** mish

amiss .... uh **MIS**

amity .... **AM** uh tee

ammeter .... **AM** meet ur

ammonia .... uh **MOHN** yuh ¶25

ammunition .... **AM** yuh **NISH** un

amnesia .... am **NEE** zhuh ¶25

amnesiac .... am **NEE** zee **AK**

amnion ...... **AM** nee un *or* **AM** nee ahn

amniotic .... **AM** nee **AHT** ik

amoeba .... uh **MEE** buh

amok .... uh **MUK**

amoral .... ay **MAWR** ul ¶20

amoretto .... **AM** uh **RET** oh

amorist .... **AM** ur ist

amorous .... **AM** ur us

amorphous .... uh **MAWR** fus

amortization ...... **AM** ur tuh **ZAY** shun
uh **MAWR** tuh **ZAY** shun *is
occasionally heard.*

amortize .... **AM** ur tyze
uh **MAWR** tyze *is occasionally
heard.*

amount .... uh **MOWNT**

amour .... uh **MOOR**

amperage .... **AM** pur ij ¶5

ampere .... **AM** pir

ampersand .... **AM** pur sand

amphetamine ....
.... am **FET** uh meen ¶6, 22

amphibian ...... am **FIB** ee un ¶6, 25

amphitheater ....
.... **AM** fuh **THEE** uh tur ¶6

amphora .... **AM** fur uh
now sometimes am **FAWR** uh

amplification ..... **AM** pluh fi **KAY** shun

amplify .... **AM** pluh fye

amplitude .... **AM** pluh toohd ¶21

ampule .... **AM** pyool *or* **AM** pool

amputate .... **AM** pyuh tayt

amulet .... **AM** yuh lit

amuse .... uh **MYOOHZ**

Anabaptist .... **AN** uh **BAP** tist ¶2

anachronism .... uh **NAK** ruh niz um

anaconda .... **AN** uh **KAHN** duh

anaerobe ..... **AN** uh rohb *or* an **ER** ohb

anagram .... **AN** uh gram

anal .... **AY** nul

analgesia .... **AN** ul **JEE** zee uh *or*
AN ul **JEE** zhee uh ¶14, 25

analgesic .... **AN** ul **JEE** zik ¶14

analog .... **AN** uh lawg ¶19

analogical .... **AN** uh **LAHJ** i kul

analogous .... uh **NAL** uh gus

analogy .... uh **NAL** uh jee

analysis .... uh **NAL** uh sis

analyst .... **AN** uh list

analytic .... **AN** uh **LIT** ik

analyze .... **AN** uh lyze

anapest .... **AN** uh pest

anaphora .... uh **NAF** ur uh ¶5

anarchic .... an **AR** kik

SPELLED	PRONOUNCED	SPELLED	PRONOUNCED
anarchism	**AN** ur kiz um	anesthetist	uh **NES** thuh tist
anarchist	**AN** ur kist	anesthetize	uh **NES** thuh tyze
anarchy	**AN** ur kee	aneurysm	**AN** yuh riz um
anathema	uh **NATH** uh muh	anew	uh **NOOH** ¶21
Anatolian	AN uh **TOH** lee un	angel	**AYN** jul
anatomical	AN uh **TAHM** i kul	angelic	an **JEL** ik
anatomy	uh **NAT** uh mee	angelica	an **JEL** i kuh
–ance	uns ¶9	Angelus	**AN** juh lus
ancestor	**AN** ses tur	anger	**ANG** gur
also, but becoming less common,		angina	an **JYE** nuh
AN sus tur ¶8		*also, especially among doctors,*	
ancestral	an **SES** trul	**AN** juh nuh	
anchor	**ANG** kur	angioma	AN jee **OH** muh
anchorage	**ANG** kur ij ¶5	angle	**ANG** gul
anchorman	**ANG** kur man	angled	**ANG** guld
anchovy	AN **choh** vee *or* AN **chuh** vee	Anglican	**ANG** gli kun
	or an **CHOH** vee	Anglicism	**ANG** gluh siz um
ancient	**AYN** shunt ¶12	Anglicize	**ANG** gluh syze
ancillary	**AN** suh **LER** ee ¶23	Anglophile	**ANG** gluh fyle
andante	ahn **DAHN** tay *or*	Anglophobe	**ANG** gluh fohb
	an **DAN** tee	Angora	ang **GAWR** uh ¶16
andiron	**AN** dye urn	angostura	AN gus **TOOR** uh ¶21
Androcles	**AN** druh kleez	angry	**ANG** gree
androgynous	an **DRAHJ** uh nus	angstrom	**ANG** strum
Andromeda	an **DRAHM** uh duh	anguish	**ANG** gwish
anecdotal	AN ik **DOHT** ul ¶1	angular	**ANG** gyuh lur
anecdote	**AN** ik doht	angularity	
anemia	uh **NEE** mee uh ¶25		**ANG** gyuh **LAR** uh tee ¶23
anemometer	AN uh **MAHM** uh tur	anhydrous	an **HYE** drus
anemone	uh **NEM** uh nee	aniline	**AN** ul in ¶22
anesthesia	AN us **THEE** zhuh *or*	animadversion	AN uh mad **VUR** zhun
	AN us **THEE** zyuh ¶25	animal	**AN** uh mul
anesthesiologist		animate *(verb)*	**AN** uh mayt
	AN us THEE zee **AHL** uh jist	animate *(adjective)*	**AN** uh mit
anesthetic	AN us **THET** ik	animation	AN uh **MAY** shun

11

SPELLED	PRONOUNCED
animator	**AN** uh mayt ur
animism	**AN** uh miz um
animosity	AN uh **MAHS** uh tee
animus	**AN** uh mus
anion	**AN** eye un
anise	**AN** is
anisette	AN uh set ¶2, 14
ankh	**AHNGK** or **ANGK**
ankle	**ANG** kul
anklet	**ANG** klit
annals	**AN** ulz
anneal	uh **NEEL**
annex (verb)	uh **NEKS** or AN eks
annex (noun)	**AN** eks
annihilate	uh **NYE** uh layt
anniversary	AN uh **VUR** sur ee ¶5
annotate	**AN** uh tayt ¶1
annotation	AN uh **TAY** shun ¶1
announce	uh **NOWNS** ¶9
annoy	uh **NOY**
annual	**AN** yoo wul ¶5
annuity	uh **NOOH** uh tee ¶21
annul	uh **NUL**
annunciation	
	uh NUN see **AY** shun ¶9
anode	**AN** ohd
anodize	**AN** uh dyze
anodyne	**AN** uh dyne
anoint	uh **NOYNT**
anomalous	uh **NAHM** uh lus
anomaly	uh **NAHM** uh lee
anomie	**AN** uh mee
anon	uh **NAHN**
anonymity	AN uh **NIM** uh tee
anonymous	uh **NAHN** uh mus

SPELLED	PRONOUNCED
anopheles	uh **NAHF** uh LEEZ
anorexia	AN uh **REK** see uh ¶25
anorexic	AN uh **REK** sik
anserine	**AN** sur eyne ¶22
answer	**AN** sur ¶9, 18
antacid	ant **AS** id ¶2
antagonism	an **TAG** uh niz um
antagonistic	an TAG uh **NIS** tik
antagonize	an **TAG** uh NYZE
antarctic	ant **ARK** tik or
	ant **AR** tik ¶10
ante	**AN** tee
ante–	**AN** ti or **AN** tuh or **AN** tee
antebellum	AN ti **BEL** um ¶1
antecedent	AN tuh **SEED** unt
antechamber	**AN** ti CHAYM bur
antedate	**AN** ti dayt
antediluvian	AN ti duh **LOOH** vee un
antelope	**AN** tuh lohp
ante meridiem	
	AN tee muh **RID** ee um
antenna	an **TEN** uh

The biological plurals, antennae *or* antennas, *are* an **TEN** ee *and* an **TEN** uz; *only the second is used for the radio and television apparatus.*

antepenult	**AN** ti **PEE** nult
anterior	an **TIR** ee ur
anthem	**AN** thum ¶9
anthology	an **THAHL** uh jee
anthracite	**AN** thruh syte
anthrax	**AN** thraks
anthropoid	**AN** thruh poyd
anthropology	AN thruh **PAHL** uh jee

SPELLED	PRONOUNCED	SPELLED	PRONOUNCED

anti– ..... **AN** ti *or* **AN** tee *or* **AN** tye *or* **AN** tuh

These pronunciations are heard variously for the following words that begin with this prefix.

antibiotic .... AN ti bye **AHT** ik ¶1
antibody .... **AN** ti BAHD ee
anticipate .... an **TIS** uh payt
anticipation .... an TIS uh **PAY** shun
anticipatory ... an TIS uh puh **TAWR** ee
anticlimactic .... AN ti klye **MAK** tik
anticlimax .... AN ti **KLYE** maks
antidote .... **AN** ti doht
Antietam .... an **TEET** um
antifreeze .... **AN** ti freez
antigen .... **AN** tuh jun
Antigone .... an **TIG** uh nee
antihistamine ....
.... AN ti **HIS** tuh MEEN ¶22
Antilles .... an **TIL** eez
antimacassar .... AN ti muh **KAS** ur
antimatter .... **AN** ti MAT ur
antimony .... **AN** tuh MOH nee
antinomy .... an **TIN** uh mee
antipasto .... AN ti **PAS** toh *or* AHN tee **PAHS** toh
antipathy .... an **TIP** uh thee
antiperspirant ....
.... AN ti **PUR** spur unt ¶5
antiphonal .... an **TIF** un ul
antiphony .... an **TIF** uh nee
antipodes .... an **TIP** uh DEEZ
antiquary .... **AN** tuh KWER ee
antiquated .... **AN** tuh kwayt id
antique .... an **TEEK**

antiquity .... an **TIK** wuh tee
anti–Semite .... AN ti **SEM** yte
anti–Semitic .... AN ti suh **MIT** ik
anti–Semitism .... AN ti **SEM** uh tiz um
antiseptic .... AN ti **SEP** tik
antistrophe .... an **TIS** truh fee
antithesis .... an **TITH** uh sis
antithetical .... AN tuh **THET** i kul
antitoxin .... AN ti **TAHK** sin ¶2
antonym .... **AN** tuh nim
antonymous .... an **TAHN** uh mus
anus .... **AY** nus
anvil .... **AN** vul
anxiety .... ang **ZYE** uh tee
anxious .... **ANGK** shus *or* **ANG** shus
aorta .... ay **AWR** tuh
Apache .... uh **PACH** ee
apache .... uh **PASH** *or* uh **PAHSH**
apartheid .... uh **PAHRT** hayt *or* uh **PAHRT** hyte *or* uh **PAHRT** ayt *popularly* uh **PAHRT** yte
apathetic .... AP uh **THET** ik
apathy .... **AP** uh thee
apatite .... **AP** uh tyte
Apennines .... **AP** uh nynze
aperitif .... AH per uh **TEEF**
aperture .... **AP** ur chur ¶3
apex .... **AY** peks
aphasia .... uh **FAY** zhuh ¶25
aphid .... **AY** fid *or* **AF** id
aphorism .... **AF** ur iz um
aphrodisiac .... AF ruh **DIZ** ee AK *or* AF ruh **DEE** zee AK
Aphrodite .... AF ruh **DYTE** ee
apiary .... **AY** pee ER ee

aplomb .. uh **PLAHM** or uh **PLUM** ¶19
apocalypse .... uh **PAHK** uh lips
apocalyptic .... uh PAHK uh **LIP** tik
apocrypha .... uh **PAHK** ruh fuh
apogee .... **AP** uh jee
Apollo .... uh **PAHL** oh
apologetic .... uh PAHL uh **JET** ik
apologia .... AP uh **LOH** jee uh
apology .... uh **PAHL** uh jee
apoplectic .... AP uh **PLEK** tik
apoplexy .... **AP** uh PLEK see
apostasy .... uh **PAHS** tuh see
apostate .. uh **PAHS** tayt or uh **PAHS** tit
apostle .... uh **PAHS** ul
apostolic .... AP uh **STAHL** ik
apostrophe .... uh **PAHS** truh fee
apothecary .... uh **PAHTH** uh ker ee
apothegm .... **AP** uh them
apotheosis ..... uh **PAHTH** ee **OH** sis or
                     AP uh **THEE** uh sis
appall .... uh **PAWL**
appaloosa .... AP uh **LOOH** suh
apparatus .... AP uh **RAT** us or
                     AP uh **RAYT** us
apparel .... uh **PAR** ul ¶23
apparent .... uh **PAR** unt ¶23
apparition .... AP uh **RISH** un
appearance .... uh **PIR** uns
appeasement .... uh **PEEZ** munt
appellate .... uh **PEL** it
appellation .... AP uh **LAY** shun
appellative .... uh **PEL** uh tiv
appendage .... uh **PEN** dij
appendectomy .... AP un **DEK** tuh mee
appendicitis ...... uh PEN duh **SYTE** us

appendix .... uh **PEN** diks
The plural is appendixes
uh **PEN** dik siz *or* appendices
uh **PEN** duh SEEZ.
appertain .... ap ur **TAYN**
appetite .... **AP** uh tyte
applause .... uh **PLAWZ**
appliance .... uh **PLYE** uns ¶9
applicable .... **AP** luh kuh bul
application .... AP luh **KAY** shun
applicator .... **AP** luh kayt ur
appliqué .... ap luh **KAY**
apply .... uh **PLYE**
Appomattox .... AP uh **MAT** uks
apposition .... AP uh **ZISH** un
appreciable .... uh **PREE** shuh bul or
                  uh **PREE** shee uh bul
appreciate .... uh **PREE** shee ayt ¶1
appreciative ...... uh **PREE** shuh tiv or
                  uh **PREE** shee uh tiv
apprehend .... ap ruh **HEND**
apprehensive ...... AP ruh **HEN** siv ¶9
apprentice .... uh **PREN** tis
approachable .... uh **PROHCH** uh bul
approbation .... AP ruh **BAY** shun
appropriate *(verb)* ....
          .... uh **PROH** pree ayt
appropriate *(adjective)* ....
           .... uh **PROH** pree it
approximate *(verb)* ....
          .... uh **PRAHK** suh mayt
approximate *(adjective)* ....
          .... uh **PRAHK** suh mit
appurtenance .... uh **PURT** un uns ¶9
apricot .... **AP** ruh kaht or **AY** pruh kaht

a priori .... AH pree **AWR** ee *or*
            AY prye **AWR** eye

apron .... AY prun ¶4

apropos .... ap ruh **POH**

aptitude .... **AP** tuh toohd ¶21

.... AHK wuh muh **REEN** ¶18

aquarium .... uh **KWER** ee um ¶23

Aquarius .... uh **KWER** ee us

aquatic ... uh **KWAHT** ik *or* uh **KWAT** ik

aquatint .... **AK** wuh tint ¶18

aquavit .... **AK** wuh veet ¶18

aqueduct .... **AK** wuh dukt

aqueous ..... AY kwee us *or* AK wee us

aquiline .... **AK** wuh lyne ¶22

Aquinas .... uh **KWYE** nus

Arab .... AR ub ¶23

  AY rab *is not a standard*
  pronunciation.

arabesque .... ar uh **BESK** ¶23

Arabic .... **AR** uh bik ¶23

arable .... **AR** uh bul ¶23

arachnid .... uh **RAK** nid

Aramaic .... AR uh **MAY** ik ¶23

Ararat .... **AR** uh rat ¶23

arbiter .... **AHR** buh tur

arbitrage .... **AHR** buh trazh

arbitrament .... ahr **BIT** ruh munt

arbitrary ...... **AHR** buh **TRER** ee ¶23

arbitrate .... **AHR** buh trayt

arboreal .... ahr **BAWR** ee ul ¶25

arboretum .... AHR buh **REET** um

arbutus .... ahr **BYOOHT** us

arcade .... ahr **KAYD**

arcane .... ahr **KAYN**

archaeology ...... AHR kee **AHL** uh jee

archaic .... ahr **KAY** ik

archaism .... **AHR** kee iz um *or*
            AHR kay iz um

archangel .... **AHRK** ayn jul

archbishop .... **AHRCH** bish up

archery .... **AHR** chur ee ¶5

archetypal .... AHR kuh **TYPE** ul

archetype .... **AHR** kuh type

Archimedes .... AHR kuh **MEE** deez

archipelago .... AHR kuh **PEL** uh goh

architect .... **AHR** kuh tekt

architecture ....
           AHR kuh **TEK** chur ¶12

archive .... **AHR** kyve

archivist .... **AHR** kye vist *or*
            AHR kuh vist

arctic .... **AHRK** tik *or* **AHR** tik ¶10

ardent .... **AHR** dunt

ardor .... **AHR** dur

arduous .... **AHR** joo wus ¶5

area .... **ER** ee uh ¶23

arena .... uh **REE** nuh

Argentina .... AHR jun **TEE** nuh

Argentine .... **AHR** jun teen ¶22

argon .... **AHR** gahn

argosy .... **AHR** guh see

argot .... **AHR** goh *or* **AHR** gut

arguable .... **AHR** gyoo wuh bul

argument .... **AHR** gyuh munt

argumentative .. AHR gyuh **MEN** tuh tiv

argyle .... **AHR** gyle

aria .... **AHR** ee uh
  AR ee uh *is occasionally heard.*

arid .... **AR** id ¶23

Aries .... **AR** eez *or* **AR** ee eez ¶23
aristocracy ....
.... **AR** uh **STAH** kruh see ¶23
aristocrat .... uh **RIS** tuh **KRAT** *or*
     AR is tuh **KRAT** ¶23
aristocratic ..... uh **RIS** tuh **KRAT** ik *or*
     AR is tuh **KRAT** ik ¶23
Aristotelian ....
.... **AR** is tuh **TEEL** yun ¶23, 25
Aristotle .... **AR** is **TAHT** ul ¶23
arithmetic *(noun)* .... uh **RITH** muh tik
arithmetic *(adjective)* ....
.... **AR** ith **MET** ik ¶23
Arkansas .... **AHR** kun saw
The river is also pronounced
  ahr **KAN** zus.
armada .. ahr **MAH** duh *or* ahr **MAY** duh
armadillo .... **AHR** muh **DIL** oh
Armageddon .... **AHR** muh **GED** un
armament .... **AHR** muh munt
armature .... **AHR** muh chur
Armenia ...... ahr **MEE** nee uh ¶25
armistice .... **AHR** muh stis
armor .... **AHR** mur
armory .... **AHR** mur ee ¶5
aroma .... uh **ROH** muh
aromatic .... **AR** uh **MAT** ik ¶23
arpeggio .. ahr **PEJ** oh *or* ahr **PEJ** ee oh
arraignment .... uh **RAYN** munt
arrant .... **AR** unt ¶23
array .... uh **RAY**
arrears .... uh **RIRZ**
arrogance .... **AR** uh guns ¶9, 23
arroyo .... uh **ROY** oh
arsenal .... **AHR** suh nul

arsenic *(noun)* ...... **AHR** suh nik ¶5
arsenic *(adjective)* .... ahr **SEN** ik
arson .... **AHR** sun
Artemis .... **AHR** tuh mis
arterial .... ahr **TIR** ee ul ¶25
arteriosclerosis ....
.... ahr **TIR** ee oh skluh **ROH** sis
artery .... **AHR** tur ee
artesian (well) .... ahr **TEE** zhun
arthritis .... ahr **THRYTE** is
artichoke .... **AHR** tuh chohk
article .... **AHR** ti kul
articulate *(verb)* ...... ahr **TIK** yuh layt
articulate *(adjective)* .. ahr **TIK** yuh lit
artifact .... **AHR** tuh fakt
artifice .... **AHR** tuh fis
artificer .... ahr **TIF** uh sur
artificial .... **AHR** tuh **FISH** ul
artillery .... ahr **TIL** ur ee ¶5
artisan .... **AHR** tuh sun ¶14
artiste .... ahr **TEEST**
Aryan .... **AR** ee un ¶23, 25
asafetida .... **AS** uh **FET** uh duh
asbestos ...... as **BES** tus *or* az **BES** tus
ascend .... uh **SEND**
ascension .... uh **SEN** shun ¶12
ascent .... uh **SENT**
ascertain .... as ur **TAYN**
ascetic .... uh **SET** ik
asceticism .... uh **SET** uh siz um
ascorbic (acid) .... uh **SKAWR** bik ¶1
ascot .... **AS** kaht
  AS kut *is more British than*
  American. ¶8
ascribe .... uh **SKRYBE**

SPELLED	PRONOUNCED	SPELLED	PRONOUNCED
ascription	uh **SKRIP** shun ¶1	asset	**AS** et
aseptic	ay **SEP** tik	assiduity	**AS** uh **DYOOH** uh tee ¶21
asexual	ay **SEK** shoo wul	assiduous	uh **SIJ** oo wus
ashamed	uh **SHAYMD**	assignation	**AS** ig **NAY** shun
Asia	**AY** zhuh	assignee	uh sye **NEE**
AY shuh *is mainly British.*		assignment	uh **SYNE** munt
asinine	**AS** uh nyne	assimilate	uh **SIM** uh layt
asininity	**AS** uh **NIN** uh tee	assistance	uh **SIS** tuns ¶9
ask	**ASK** ¶18	assize	uh **SYZE**
askance	uh **SKANS** ¶9, 18	associate *(verb)*	uh **SOH** shee ayt *or*
askew	uh **SKYOOH**		uh **SOH** see ayt
asocial	ay **SOH** shul	associate *(noun and adjective)*	
asparagus	uh **SPAR** uh gus ¶23		uh **SOH** shee it *or* uh **SOH** see it
asperity	a **SPER** uh tee	assonance	**AS** uh nuns ¶9
aspersion	a **SPUR** zhun ¶1	assortment	uh **SAWRT** munt
asphalt	**AS** fawlt	assuage	uh **SWAYJ**
asphodel	**AS** fuh del	assume	uh **SOOHM** ¶21
asphyxiate	as **FIK** see ayt ¶1	assumption	uh **SUMP** shun ¶10
aspidistra	**AS** puh **DIS** truh	assurance	uh **SHOOR** uns ¶9, 24
aspirant	**AS** pur unt *or* uh **SPYRE** unt	asterisk	**AS** tur isk
aspiration	**AS** puh **RAY** shun	asteroid	**AS** tuh royd
aspirator	**AS** puh rayt ur	*Although* **AS** tur ik *and* **AS** tur iks	
aspirin	**AS** pur in *or* **AS** prin ¶5	*are now sometimes heard, they*	
assailant	uh **SAYL** unt	*are not considered standard* ¶4.	
assassin	uh **SAS** un	asteroid	**AS** tuh royd
assassinate	uh **SAS** uh nayt	asthma	**AZ** muh
assault	uh **SAWLT**	asthmatic	az **MAT** ik
assay *(verb)*	a **SAY** ¶1	astigmatic	**AS** tig **MAT** ik
assay *(noun)*	**AS** ay *or* a **SAY**	astigmatism	uh **STIG** muh tiz um
assemblage	uh **SEM** blij	astonish	uh **STAHN** ish
assemble	uh **SEM** bul	astound	uh **STOWND**
assent	uh **SENT**	astringent	uh **STRIN** junt
assert	uh **SURT**	astrodome	**AS** truh dohm
assertion	uh **SUR** shun	astrolabe	**AS** truh layb
assess	uh **SES**	astrology	uh **STRAHL** uh jee
		astronaut	**AS** truh nawt ¶19

astronomical	AS truh **NAHM** i kul	atrium	**AY** tree um
astronomy	uh **STRAHN** uh mee	atrocious	uh **TROH** shus
astute	uh **STOOHT** ¶21	atrocity	uh **TRAHS** uh tee
asunder	uh **SUN** dur	atrophy	**A** truh fee
asylum	uh **SYE** lum	atropine	**A** truh peen ¶22
asymmetric	AY suh **MET** rik	attaché	at uh **SHAY** *or* a ta **SHAY**
asymmetry	ay **SIM** uh tree		uh **TASH** ay *is chiefly British.*
asymptote	**AS** im toht ¶10	attainder	uh **TAYN** dur
atavism	**AT** uh viz um	attar	**AT** ur
ataxia	uh **TAK** see uh	attempt	uh **TEMPT** ¶10
–ate *(verb suffix)*	ayt	attenuate *(verb)*	uh **TEN** yoo wayt
–ate *(noun suffix)*	it *or* ayt	attenuate *(adjective)*	uh **TEN** yoo wit
	variously	attestation	A tes **TAY** shun
–ate *(adjective suffix)*	it *or* ayt	Attila	uh **TIL** uh
	variously	**AT** uh luh, *the older pronunciation,*	
atelier	**AT** ul yay *or* at ul **YAY**	*is still sometimes heard.*	
Athapascan	ATH uh **PAS** kun	attitude	**AT** uh toohd ¶21
atheism	**AY** thee iz um	attorney	uh **TUR** nee
atherosclerosis		attribute *(verb)*	uh **TRIB** yoot ¶1
	ATH ur oh skluh **ROH** sis	attribute *(noun)*	**A** truh byooht
athlete	**ATH** leet	attrition	uh **TRISH** un
ATH uh leet *is not considered*		attune	uh **TOOHN** ¶21
standard.		atypical	ay **TIP** i kul
athletics	ath **LET** iks	auburn	**AW** burn
athwart	uh **THWAWRT**	auction	**AWK** shun
–ative	uh tiv *or* ayt iv *variously*	audacious	aw **DAY** shus
atmosphere	**AT** mus fir	audacity	aw **DAS** uh tee
atmospheric	**AT** mus **FIR** ik *or*	audience	**AW** dee uns ¶9, 25
	AT mus **FER** ik	audiology	AW dee **AHL** uh jee
atoll	**A** tawl *or* **AY** tawl ¶19, 20	audiometer	AW dee **AHM** uh tur
atom	**AT** um	audio–visual	AW dee oh **VIZH** oo wul
atomic	uh **TAHM** ik	audit	**AW** dit
atomize	**AT** uh myze	audition	aw **DISH** un
atonal	ay **TOHN** ul	auditorium	
atonement	uh **TOHN** munt		AW duh **TAWR** ee um ¶25

SPELLED	PRONOUNCED
auditory	**AW** duh **TAWR** ee
Audubon	**AW** duh bahn *or* **AW** duh bun
au fait	oh **FAY**
Augean	aw **JEE** un
auger	**AW** gur
augment *(verb)*	awg **MENT** ¶2
augment *(noun)*	**AWG** ment
augmentation	AWG men **TAY** shun
au gratin	oh **GRAHT** un *or* aw **GRAT** un
augur	**AW** gur
augury	**AW** gyur ee
Augustan	aw **GUS** tun ¶1
Augustine	**AW** gus teen *or* aw **GUS** tun
au jus	oh **ZHOOH**
An Englished pronunciation, oh **JOOHS**, *is commonly heard.*
auk	**AWK**
auld lang syne	**OHLD LANG ZYNE** *or* **AWLD LANG SYNE** ¶10, 19
aunt	**ANT** ¶18
aura	**AWR** uh
aureola	aw **REE** uh luh
aureole	**AWR** ee ohl
au revoir	oh ruh **VWAHR** *or* awr uh **VWAHR**
auricle	**AWR** i kul
auricular	aw **RIK** yoo lur
aurochs	**AWR** ahks
aurora borealis	aw **RAWR** uh **BAWR** ee **AL** is ¶1
auspices	**AWS** puh siz *or* **AWS** puh seez
auspicious	aw **SPISH** us
austere	aw **STIR**
austerity	aw **STER** uh tee
Australia	aw **STRAYL** yuh
autarchy	**AW** tahr kee
autarky	**AW** tahr kee
authentic	aw **THEN** tik
authenticate	aw **THEN** tuh kayt
authenticity	AW thun **TIS** uh tee
author	**AW** thur
authoritarian	uh THAWR ee **TAR** ee un ¶25
authoritative	uh **THAWR** uh tayt iv
authority	uh **THAWR** uh tee
authorization	AW thur i **ZAY** shun
authorize	**AW** thuh ryze
autism	**AW** tiz um
autistic	aw **TIS** tik
Autobahn	**AWT** oh bahn
autochthon	aw **TAHK** thun
autoclave	**AWT** uh klayv
autocracy	aw **TAHK** ruh see
autocrat	**AWT** uh krat
auto–da–fé	AWT oh duh **FAY** *or* OWT oh duh **FAY**
autoerotism	AWT oh **ER** uh tiz um
autogenous	aw **TAHJ** uh nus
autogiro	AWT uh **JYE** roh ¶1
autograph	**AWT** uh graf ¶18
automat	**AWT** uh mat
automata	aw **TAHM** uh tuh
automate	**AWT** uh mayt
automatic	AWT uh **MAT** ik
automation	AWT uh **MAY** shun
automatism	aw **TAHM** uh tiz um

automaton	aw TAHM uh tun *or* aw TAHM uh TAHN	avidity	uh VID uh tee
automobile	AWT uh muh **BEEL** *or* AWT uh moh BEEL *also* AWT uh **MOH** beel	avionics	AY vee **AHN** iks *occasionally* AV ee **AHN** iks
		avocado	AV uh **KAH** doh *or* AHV uh **KAH** doh
autonomous	aw TAHN uh mus	avocation	AV uh KAY shun ¶1
autopsy	AW tahp see **AWT** up see *is also heard but is chiefly British.*	Avogadro	AHV uh GAH droh
		avoidance	uh VOID uns ¶19
		avoirdupois	AV ur duh POYZ ¶2
autumn	AWT um	Avon	AY vun *or* AY vahn
autumnal	aw TUM nul	avouch	uh VOWCH
auxiliary	awg ZIL yur ee *or* awg ZIL ur ee	avowal	uh VOW ul
		avuncular	uh VUNG kyuh lur
available	uh VAY luh bul	AWACS	AY waks
avalanche	AV uh lanch	awash	uh WAWSH ¶19
avant–garde	ah vahnt **GAHRD** *or* ah vahn GAHRD *or* av awnt GAHRD	awesome	AW sum
		awful	AW ful
avarice	AV ur is ¶5	awfully	AW flee ¶5
avaricious	AV uh **RISH** us	*In its literal sense,* in a way to inspire awe, *it is* AW fuh lee.	
avatar	AV uh tahr		
ave	AH vay *or* AH vee	awkward	AWK wurd ¶19
avenge	uh VENJ	awl	AWL
avenue	AV uh nooh ¶21	AWOL	AY WAWL
aver	uh VUR	awry	uh RYE
average	AV rij ¶5	axial	AK see ul ¶25
averse	uh VURS	axiom	AK see um ¶25
aversion	uh VUR zhun uh VUR shun, *which is also heard, is chiefly British.*	axis	AK sis
		The plural axes *is* AK seez.	
		axle	AK sul
avert	uh VURT	ayatollah	EYE uh TOH luh
Avestan	uh VES tun	aye	EYE
aviary	AY vee ER ee ¶23	azalea	uh ZAYL yuh
aviation	AY vee AY shun AV ee AY shun *has become rare.*	azimuth	AZ uh muth
		Azores	AY zawrz *or* uh ZAWRZ
avid	AV id	azure	AZH ur

20

B

Babel .... **BAY** bul *or* **BAB** ul
baboon .... ba **BOOHN** ¶1
babushka .... buh **BOOSH** kuh ¶1
Babylon .... **BAB** uh lahn *or* **BAB** uh lun
Babylonian ....
.... **BAB** uh **LOH** nee un ¶25
baccalaureate ..... **BAK** uh **LAWR** ee it
baccarat .... bak uh **RAH** ¶2, 18
bacchanal .... bak uh **NAL** *or*
.... **BAK** uh nul ¶2
Bacchus .... **BAK** us ¶18
Bach .... **BAHKH**
*Most Americans try to reproduce
the German* ach *sound,
represented here by* **AHKH**;
otherwise, **BAHK**.
bachelor .... **BACH** uh lur ¶5
bacillus .... buh **SIL** us
The plural is bacilli buh **SIL** eye
or, occasionally, buh **SIL** ee.
bacitracin .... **BAS** uh **TRAY** sun
backgammon .... **BAK** gam un
backward .... **BAK** wurd
bacteria .... bak **TIR** ee uh
bacteriology .... bak TIR ee **AHL** uh jee
bade .... **BAD**
BAYD *is a spelling pronunciation.*
badinage .. bad uh **NAHZH** *or* **BAD** un ij

badminton .... **BAD** mint un ¶3
BAD mit un *is now common.*
bagatelle .... bag uh **TEL**
bagel .... **BAY** gul
Baghdad ...... **BAG** dad *or* bahg **DAHD**
baguette .... ba **GET**
Bahai .... buh **HYE** *or* buh **HAH** ee
Bahamas .... buh **HAH** muz *or*
.... buh **HAY** muz
bailiff .... **BAY** lif
bailiwick .... **BAY** luh wik ¶1
Baja .... **BAH** hah
baklava .... bahk luh **VAH** ¶2
balaclava .... **BAHL** uh **KLAH** vuh
balalaika .... **BAL** uh **LYKE** uh
balance .... **BAL** uns ¶9
balcony .... **BAL** kuh nee
baldachin .... **BAL** duh kin *or*
.... **BAWL** duh kin
baleen .... buh **LEEN** ¶1
Bali .... **BAH** lee *or* **BAL** ee
Balinese .... bah luh **NEEZ** *or*
.... bal uh **NEEZ**
balk .... **BAWK**
Balkans .... **BAWL** kunz
ballad .... **BAL** ud
ballade .... buh **LAHD** ¶1
ballast .... **BAL** ust
ballerina .... BAL uh **REE** nuh
ballet .... ba **LAY** *or* **BAL** ay
ballistics .... buh **LIS** tiks
balloon .... buh **LOOHN**
ballot .... **BAL** ut
ballyhoo *(noun)* .... **BAL** ee hooh
The verb is also bal ee **HOOH**.

balm .... **BAHM**
Some people have adopted the spelling pronunciation **BAHLM.**

baloney .... buh **LOH** nee

balsa .... **BAWL** suh

balsam .... **BAWL** sum

Baltic .... **BAWL** tik

baluster .... **BAL** us tur

balustrade .... **BAL** uh strayd ¶2

Balzac .... **BAWL** zak *or* bahl **ZAHK**

bambino .... bam **BEE** noh ¶18

bamboo .... bam **BOOH**

bamboozle .... bam **BOOH** zul

banal ...... **BAY** nul *or* buh **NAL** *or* buh **NAHL**

banana .... buh **NAN** uh ¶18

bandicoot .... **BAN** di kooht

bandolier .... ban duh **LIR**

Bangkok .... **BANG** kahk

Bangladesh .... bahng gluh **DESH**

bangle .... **BANG** gul

banister .... **BAN** us tur

banjo .... **BAN** joh

bankrupt .... **BANGK** rupt

banquet .... **BANG** kwit

bantam .... **BAN** tum

Bantu .... **BAN** tooh

banyan .... **BAN** yun

baptistery .... **BAP** tis tree *or* **BAP** tis tur ee ¶5

baptize .... **BAP** tyze ¶2

Barbados .... bahr **BAY** dohz ¶14
Occasionally **BAHR** buh dohz *is heard.*

barbarian .. bahr **BAR** ee un ¶23, 25

barbaric .... bahr **BAR** ik ¶23

barbarism .... **BAHR** bur iz um

barbecue .... **BAHR** buh kyooh

barberry .... **BAHR** ber ee

barbiturate .... bahr **BICH** ur it *or* bahr **BICH** uh rayt
also BAHR buh **TYOOR** it

barcarole .... **BAHR** kuh rohl

Barcelona .... BAHR suh **LOH** nuh

bargain .... **BAHR** gun

baritone .... **BAR** uh tohn ¶23

barium .... **BAR** ee um ¶23, 25

bar mitzvah .... bahr **MITS** vuh

barometer .... buh **RAHM** uh tur

barometric ...... BAR uh **MET** rik ¶23

baron .... **BAR** un ¶23

baronet .... **BAR** uh nit *or* **BAR** uh net ¶23

baronial .... buh **ROH** nee ul

baroque .... buh **ROHK**

barracks .... **BAR** uks ¶23

barracuda .... BAR uh **KOOH** duh ¶23

barrage ("an attack") ....
.... buh **RAHZH** ¶15

barrage ("a barrier") .... **BAHR** ij

barrel .... **BAR** ul ¶23

barren .... **BAR** un ¶23

barricade .... **BAR** uh kayd ¶23

barrier .... **BAR** ee ur ¶23, 25

barrister .... **BAR** is tur ¶23

barrow .... **BAR** oh ¶23

Bartók .... **BAHR** tawk

basal .... **BAY** sul

basalt .... buh **SAWLT** *or* **BAY** sawlt

basil .... **BAY** zul *or* **BAZ** ul

SPELLED	PRONOUNCED
basilica	buh SIL i kuh
basilisk	BAS uh lisk
basis	BAY sis

The plural bases *is* BAY seez, *but the plural of* base *is* BAY suz.

basket	BAS kit ¶18
Basque	BASK or BAHSK
bas–relief	BAH ruh LEEF
bass ("voice")	BAYS

This word invites a spelling pronunciation BAS.

bass ("fish")	BAS
bassinet	bas uh NET
bassoon	buh SOOHN
bastille	bas TEEL
bastion	BAS chun ¶17
bateau	ba TOH
bath	BATH

The plural is BATHS *or* BADHZ. ¶18

bathe	BAYDH
bathos	BAY thahs ¶19
Bathsheba	bath SHEE buh or BATH shi buh
bathyscaph	BATH uh skaf
batik	buh TEEK or BAT ik
batiste	ba TEEST
bat mitzvah	baht MITS vuh
baton	buh TAHN
Baton Rouge	BAT un ROOHZH
battalion	buh TAL yun
battery	BAT ur ee ¶5
Bauhaus	BOW hows
bauxite	BAWK syte or BOH zyte
bayberry	BAY ber ee or BAY bur ee

SPELLED	PRONOUNCED
bayonet	BAY uh net ¶2

BAY uh nit *is now old–fashioned.*

bazaar	buh ZAHR
beagle	BEE gul
beard	BIRD
beatific	BEE uh TIF ik
beatification	bee AT uh fi KAY shun
beatify	bee AT uh FYE
beatitude	bee AT uh TOOHD ¶21
beaucoup	boh KOOH
beau geste	boh ZHEST
Beaujolais	boh zhuh LAY ¶2
beautician	byooh TISH un
beautiful	BYOOHT uh ful
beautify	BYOOHT uh fye
beaux–arts	boh ZAHR or boh ZAHRT
because	bi KAWZ
bedizen	bi DYE zun or bi DIZ un
bedlam	BED lum
Bedouin	BED oo win
bedraggled	bi DRAG uld
beefalo	BEEF uh loh
Beelzebub	bee EL zuh bub
beestings	BEES tingz
Beethoven	BAY toh vun
begonia	buh GOHN yuh
beguile	bi GYLE
beguine	bi GEEN
behave	bi HAYV
behemoth	bi HEE muth

BEE uh muth *has become rare.*

behest	bi HEST
beholden	bi HOHL dun
behoove	bi HOOHV
beige	BAYZH

23

SPELLED	PRONOUNCED	SPELLED	PRONOUNCED

bel canto .... bel **KAHN** toh
also, especially more recently,
bel **KAN** toh

beleaguer .... bi **LEE** gur

belfry .... **BEL** free

Belgium .... **BEL** jum

belladonna .... BEL uh **DAHN** uh

belles–lettres .. bel **LET** ruh *or* bel **LET**

belletristic .... BEL uh **TRIS** tik

bellicose .... **BEL** uh kohs

belligerent .... buh **LIJ** ur unt

bellows .... **BEL** ohz
also, especially formerly,
BEL uz ¶8

benedictine .... BEN uh **DIK** teen ¶22

Benedictine ...... BEN uh **DIK** tin ¶22

benediction .... BEN uh **DIK** shun

benefactor .... BEN uh **FAK** tur

beneficence .... buh **NEF** uh suns ¶9

beneficial .... BEN uh **FISH** ul

beneficiary
.... BEN uh **FISH** ee ER ee ¶23

benefit .... **BEN** uh fit

benevolence ..... buh **NEV** uh luns ¶9

Bengali .... ben **GAHL** ee ¶16

benign .... bi **NYNE**

benignant .... bi **NIG** nunt

benison .... BEN uh zun *or* BEN uh sun

benzene .... **BEN** zeen

bequeath ... bi **KWEEDH** *or* bi **KWEETH**

beret .... buh **RAY**

bergère .... ber **ZHER**

beriberi .... BER ee **BER** ee

Bering (Sea) .... **BER** ing *or* **BIR** ing

Berlioz .... **BER** lee ohz

berm .... **BURM**

Bermuda .... bur **MYOOH** duh

berserk .... bur **SURK** ¶2, 14

berth .... **BURTH**

beryl .... **BER** ul

besiege .... bi **SEEJ** ¶15

besom .... **BEE** zum

Bessemer (process) .... **BES** uh mur

bestial .... BES chul *or* BES tyul
also BEES chul *or* BEES tyul
by association with the related
word beast ¶17, 25

bestiary .... BES chee ER ee *or*
BES tee ER ee ¶23: *see* bestial

beta .... **BAYT** uh

betatron .... **BAYT** uh trahn

Betelgeuse .... BET ul jooz
The first syllable is also BAYT *or*
BEET, *and the last may be* joohz *or*
goohz.

bête noire .... bet **NWAHR** *or*
bayt **NWAHR**

Bethlehem .... BETH luh hem *or*
BETH lee um

betroth .... bi **TROHDH** *or*
bi **TRAWTH** ¶19

bevel .... **BEV** ul

beverage .... BEV rij ¶5

bevy .... **BEV** ee

bewilder .... bi **WIL** dur

beyond .... bi **YAHND**

bezel .... **BEZ** ul

bias .... **BYE** us

Biblical .... **BIB** li kul

bibliography ..... BIB lee **AHG** ruh fee

SPELLED	*PRONOUNCED*
bibliophile	**BIB** lee uh **FYLE**
bibliotheca	**BIB** lee uh **THEE** kuh
bibulous	**BIB** yoo lus
bicameral	bye **KAM** ur ul ¶5
biceps	**BYE** seps
bicuspid	bye **KUS** pid
bicycle	**BYE** si kul
bidet	bi **DAY** ¶1
biennial	bye **EN** ee ul ¶25
bier	**BIR**
bifocal	bye **FOH** kul ¶2
bifocals	**BYE** foh kulz
bigamy	**BIG** uh mee
bigot	**BIG** ut
bigotry	**BIG** uh tree
bikini	bi **KEE** nee
bilingual	bye **LING** gwul
bilious	**BIL** yus
billet	**BIL** it
billet–doux	bil ee **DOOH** or
	BEE yay **DOOH**
billiards	**BIL** yurdz
binary	**BYE** nur ee or **BYE** ner ee
binaural	bye **NAWR** ul
binocular	bye **NAHK** yuh lur ¶1
binoculars	bi **NAHK** yuh lurz
binomial	bye **NOH** mee ul
biodegradable	
	BYE oh di **GRAY** duh bul
biographer	bye **AHG** ruh fur or
	bee **AHG** ruh fur
biographical	
	BYE uh **GRAF** uh kul ¶18
biography	bye **AHG** ruh fee or
	bee **AHG** ruh fee

SPELLED	*PRONOUNCED*
biological	**BYE** uh **LAHJ** i kul
biology	bye **AH** luh jee
bionics	bye **AHN** iks
biopsy	**BYE** ahp see
biorhythm	**BYE** oh **RIDH** um
biosphere	**BYE** uh sfir
biped	**BYE** ped
biscuit	**BIS** kit
bisect	bye **SEKT** ¶2
bishop	**BISH** up
bismuth	**BIZ** muth
bison	**BYSE** un or **BYE** zun
bisque	**BISK**
bittern	**BIT** urn
bitumen	bi **TOOH** mun ¶1
bivouac	**BIV** wak ¶5
bizarre	bi **ZAHR**
Bizet	bee **ZAY**
blackguard	**BLAG** urd

*A spelling pronunciation is
rarely heard, but the Canadians
say* **BLA** gahrd, *and the British say*
BLA gahd.

blamable	**BLAYM** uh bul
blancmange	bluh **MAHNZH** ¶15
blasé	blah **ZAY**
blaspheme	blas **FEEM** ¶2
blasphemy	**BLAS** fuh mee
blastula	**BLAS** choo luh ¶17
blatant	**BLAYT** unt
blather	**BLADH** ur
blazon	**BLAY** zun
blemish	**BLEM** ish
Blenheim (spaniel)	**BLEN** um
blesbok	**BLES** bahk

25

blessed *(adjective)* .... **BLES** id
*When the word is used in
nonreligious contexts,* **BLEST** *is
also occasionally heard.*

bleu (cheese) .... **BLOOH**

blight .... **BLYTE**

blintz .... **BLINTS**

blithe .... **BLYDHE** *or* **BLYTHE**

blithering .... **BLIDH** ur ing ¶5

blizzard .... **BLIZ** urd

blockade .... blah **KAYD**

blossom .... **BLAHS** um

blotto .... **BLAHT** oh

blouse .... **BLOWS**
  BLOWZ *has become rare.*

blucher .... **BLOOH** chur *or* **BLOOH** kur

bludgeon .... **BLUJ** un

blunderbuss .... **BLUN** dur BUS

B'nai B'rith .... buh **NAY BRITH** *or*
                      buh **NAY BRIT**

boa .... **BOH** uh

boatswain .... **BOHS** un

bobolink .... **BAHB** uh lingk

Boccaccio ..... boh **KAHCH** ee oh ¶25

boccie .... **BAHCH** ee

bodega ... boh **DAY** guh *or* boh **DEE** guh

bodice .... **BAHD** is

bodied .... **BAHD** eed

Boer .... **BOHR** *or* **BOOR** *or* **BOH** ur

boffo .... **BAHF** oh ¶19

bogey .... **BOH** gee

Bogotá .... boh guh **TAH**

bogyman .... **BOH** gee man *or*
                      BOOG ee man

Bohemian ...... boh **HEE** mee un ¶25

boisterous .... **BOYS** tur us ¶5

bolero .... buh **LER** oh ¶1

Bolívar .. **BAHL** uh vur *or* boh **LEE** vahr

bollix .... **BAHL** iks

Bologna ("city") .... buh **LOHN** yuh *or*
                    buh **LOH** nuh

bologna (sausage) .... buh **LOH** nee
buh **LOH** nyuh *and* buh **LOH** nuh *are
occasional pronunciations
influenced by that of the city.*

Bolshevik .... **BOHL** shuh vik ¶20

bolus .... **BOH** lus

bomb .... **BAHM**

bombard .... bahm **BAHRD** ¶1

bombardier .... bahm buh **DIR** ¶3

bona fide .... **BOH** nuh fyde *or*
    BAH nuh fyde *or* **BOH** nuh **FYE** dee
*Many people still cling to this
last, "correct" pronunciation.*

bonanza .... buh **NAN** zuh ¶1

Bonaparte .... **BOH** nuh pahrt

bonbon .... **BAHN** bahn
The "French" bohn **BOHN** *is
sometimes heard, the* n's *marking
nasalized vowels.*

bondage .... **BAHN** dij

bondsman .... **BAHNDZ** mun ¶10

bongo .... **BAHNG** goh

bonhomie .... **BAHN** uh mee *or*
              boh noh **MEE** ¶2

bonito .... buh **NEET** oh

bon mot .... bohn **MOH**

bonnet .... **BAHN** it

bon vivant .... BAHN vee **VAHNT** *or*
               BOHN vee **VAHNT**

SPELLED	PRONOUNCED
bon voyage	BAHN voy AHZH
boogie	BOOG ee
Boolean	BOOH lee un
boomerang	BOOHM uh rang
boondocks	BOOHN dahks
boondoggle	BOOHN dawg ul ¶19
Boötes	boh OH teez
borax	BAWR aks
Bordeaux	bawr DOH ¶2
bordello	bawr DEL oh
Borgia	BAWR jah ¶1
Borodin	BAWR uh din
boron	BAWR ahn
borough	BUR oh
borsch, borsht	BAWRSH or BAWRSHT
borzoi	BAWR zoy
boscage	BAHS kij
bo's'n	BOHS un
bosom	BOOZ um or BOOH zum
Bosporus	BAHS pur us ¶5
bosque	BAHS kay
bossa nova	BAHS uh NOH vuh
bossism	BAWS iz um ¶19
Boston	BAWS tun ¶19
botanical	buh TAN i kul
botany	BAHT un ee
bothersome	BAHDH ur sum
Botswana	baht SWAH nuh
Botticelli	BAHT uh CHEL ee ¶20
botulism	BAHCH uh liz um
bouclé	booh KLAY
boudoir	BOOHD wahr or BOOD wahr ¶2
bouffant	booh FAHNT

SPELLED	PRONOUNCED
bougainvillea	BOOH gun VIL ee uh ¶25
bough	BOW
bouillabaisse	boohl yuh BAYS or booh yuh BES or booh luh BAYS ¶2
bouillon	BOOL yahn or BOOL yun
boulder	BOHL dur
boules	BOOHLZ
boulevard	BOOL uh vahrd
boundary	BOWN dree ¶5
bountiful	BOWN tuh ful
bounty	BOWN tee
bouquet	boh KAY or booh KAY

Either of these is common when speaking of cut flowers, but when speaking of aroma, booh KAY *prevails.*

SPELLED	PRONOUNCED
bourbon	BUR bun
bourgeois	boor ZHWAH ¶2
bourgeoisie	boor zhwah ZEE
bourse	BOORS
bout	BOWT
boutique	booh TEEK

boh TEEK *is now widespread.*

SPELLED	PRONOUNCED
boutonniere	booht un IR or booht un ER or booh tuh NYER
bouzouki	booh ZOOH kee
bovine	BOH vyne ¶22
bowdlerize	BOWD luh ryze or BOHD luh ryze
bowel	BOW ul ¶7
bower	BOW ur ¶7
bowery	BOW ur ee ¶5
bowie (knife)	BOOH ee or BOH ee
bowler	BOHL ur

bowline	**BOH** lin *or* **BOH** lyne
bowls	**BOHLZ**
bowsprit	**BOW** sprit *or* **BOH** sprit
boycott	**BOY** kaht
boysenberry	**BOY** zun **BER** ee
less frequently **BOYS** un **BER** ee	
brachiopod	**BRAK** ee uh **PAHD**
braciola	brah **CHYOH** luh *or*
	BRAH chee **OH** luh
braggadocio	
	BRAG uh **DOH** shee oh ¶25
braggart	**BRAG** urt
Brahma	**BRAH** muh
Brahman ("a class of Hindu")	
	BRAH mun
Brahman ("breed of cattle")	
	BRAY mun
Brahmin	**BRAH** mun
Brahms	**BRAHMZ**
Braille	**BRAYL**
braise	**BRAYZ**
Brandeis	**BRAN** dyse ¶14
brassiere	bruh **ZIR**
bratwurst	**BRAT** wurst *or*
	BRAHT voorsht
bravado	bruh **VAH** doh
bravery	**BRAY** vur ee ¶15
bravura	bruh **VYOOR** uh ¶21
brawl	**BRAWL**
brawn	**BRAWN**
brazier	**BRAY** zhur
bread	**BRED**
breadth	**BREDTH** ¶16
breakfast	**BREK** fust
breath	**BRETH**

breeches ("trousers")	**BRICH** iz
breeches (buoy)	**BREECH** iz *or*
	BRICH iz
br'er	**BRUR**
BRER *is a spelling pronunciation.*	
brethren	**BREDH** run ¶14
breve	**BREV**
occasionally **BREEV**, *but not in*	
linguistics	
breviary	**BREE** vee **ER** ee ¶15, 24
brevity	**BREV** uh tee
bribery	**BRYE** bur ee ¶15
bric–a–brac	**BRIK** uh **BRAK**
bridal	**BRYDE** ul
bridegroom	**BRYDE** groohm *or*
	BRYDE groom
bridle	**BRYDE** ul
Brie (cheese)	**BREE**
brier	**BRYE** ur ¶7
brigade	bri **GAYD**
brigadier	brig uh **DIR**
brigand	**BRIG** und
brigantine	**BRIG** un teen
brilliant	**BRIL** yunt
brilliantine	**BRIL** yun teen
brindled	**BRIN** duld
Brinell	bri **NEL**
brioche	bree **OHSH** *or*
	bree **AWSH** ¶2
briquette	bri **KET**
Brisbane	**BRIZ** bayn *or* **BRIZ** bun
brisket	**BRIS** kit
brisling	**BRIZ** ling *or* **BRIS** ling
bristle	**BRIS** ul
Briticism	**BRIT** uh siz um

broadcast	**BRAWD** kast ¶18
brocade	broh **KAYD**
broccoli	**BRAHK** uh lee ¶5
brochette	broh **SHET**
brochure	broh **SHOOR** ¶24
brogan	**BROH** gun
brogue	**BROHG**
brokerage	**BROH** kur ij ¶5
bromine	**BROH** meen
bronchial	**BRAHNG** kee ul ¶25
bronchitis	brahng **KYTE** is ¶16
Brontë	**BRAHN** tee
brontosaurus	BRAHN tuh **SAWR** us
Bronx	**BRAHNGKS**
bronze	**BRAHNZ**
brooch	**BROHCH**
less commonly, **BROOHCH**
brothel	**BRAHTH** ul ¶19
brougham	**BROHM** *or* **BROH** um
also, especially for the carriage,
BROOHM *or* **BROOH** um
brouhaha	**BROOH** hah hah *or*
	brooh **HAH** hah
browse	**BROWZ**
Bruegel	**BROOH** gul *or* **BROY** gul
bruise	**BROOHZ**
brunet, brunette	brooh **NET** ¶1
brusque	**BRUSK**
brutal	**BROOHT** ul
brutality	brooh **TAL** uh tee ¶1
bubonic (plague)	
	byooh **BAHN** ik ¶21
buccaneer	buk uh **NIR**
Bucharest	**BOOH** kuh rest ¶2
buckaroo	buk uh **ROOH** ¶2

| Buckingham | **BUK** ing um |
| *from the spelling, also* |
| **BUK** ing ham |
buckram	**BUK** rum
bucolic	byooh **KAHL** ik ¶1
Buddha	**BOOD** uh *or* **BOOH** duh
Buddhism	**BOOD** iz um *or*
	BOOH diz um
budgerigar	**BUJ** ur i **GAHR**
budget	**BUJ** it
Buenos Aires	**BWAY** nus **ER** eez *or*
	BWAY nus **EYE** reez
buffalo	**BUF** uh loh
buffet ("to hit or slap")	**BUF** it
buffet ("furniture" *or* "a kind of*
meal")	buh **FAY** *or* boo **FAY**
buffo	**BOOH** foh
buffoon	buh **FOOHN**
bugle	**BYOOH** gul
buhl	**BOOHL**
bulbous	**BUL** bus
Bulgaria	bul **GAR** ee uh *or*
	bool **GAR** ee uh ¶23
bulletin	**BOOL** ut un
bullion	**BOOL** yun
bullock	**BOOL** uk
bull's–eye	**BOOLZ** eye
bully	**BOOL** ee
bulrush	**BOOL** rush
bulwark	**BOOL** wurk *or* **BUL** wurk
bumpkin	**BUMP** kin ¶9
bumptious	**BUMP** shus ¶9
bunco	**BUNG** koh
buncombe	**BUNG** kum
bungalow	**BUNG** guh loh

bunion	**BUN** yun
buoy *(verb)*	**BOY** or **BOOH** ee
buoy *(noun)*	**BOOH** ee
buoyancy	**BOY** un see or
	BOOH yun see
bureau	**BYOOR** oh ¶24
bureaucracy	byoo **RAH** kruh see ¶1
bureaucrat	**BYOOR** uh krat ¶24
burette	byoo **RET**
burgeon	**BUR** jun
burglar	**BUR** glur ¶5
Burgundy	**BUR** gun dee
burial	**BER** ee ul ¶25
burlesque	bur **LESK**
Burmese	bur **MEEZ** ¶2
burnish	**BUR** nish
burrito	buh **REE** toh
burro	**BUR** oh or **BOOR** oh
burrow	**BUR** oh
bursa	**BUR** suh
bursar	**BUR** sur
bursitis	bur **SYTE** is
Burundi	boo **ROON** dee or
	boo **RUN** dee
bury	**BER** ee
bushman	**BOOSH** mun
bushwhack	**BOOSH** wak: *see* wh-
business	**BIZ** nis
busing	**BUS** ing
bustle	**BUS** ul
busy	**BIZ** ee
butane	**BYOOH** tayn ¶2
butte	**BYOOHT**
butterfly	**BUT** ur flye
buttock	**BUT** uk

buttress	**BUT** ris
buxom	**BUK** sum
buzzard	**BUZ** urd
bwana	**BWAH** nuh
Byron	**BYE** run
Byronic	bye **RAHN** ik
Byzantine	**BIZ** un teen or
	bi **ZAN** tin ¶22

C

cabal	kuh **BAL** ¶18
cabala	**KAB** uh luh
now also kuh **BAHL** uh	
caballero	KAB uh **LER** oh or
	KAB ul **YER** oh
cabana	kuh **BAHN** uh or
	kuh **BAHN** yuh ¶18
cabaret	kab uh **RAY** ¶2
Cabernet	kab ur **NAY**
cabinet	**KAB** uh nit ¶5
caboose	kuh **BOOHS**
cabriole	**KAB** ree ohl
cabriolet	KAB ree uh **LAY** or
	KAB ree uh **LET**
cacao	kuh **KAY** oh or kuh **KAH** oh
cacciatore	KACH uh **TAWR** ee ¶18
cache	**KASH**
cachepot	**KASH** paht or **KASH** poh

SPELLED	PRONOUNCED
cachet	ka **SHAY** ¶2
cacophony	kuh **KAHF** uh nee ¶1
cadaver	kuh **DAV** ur
cadence	**KAYD** uns ¶9
cadenza	kuh **DEN** zuh
cadet	kuh **DET**
cadge	**KAJ**
cadmium	**KAD** mee um
cadre	**KAD** ree
now also **KAHD** ray	
Caesar	**SEE** zur
Caesarean	si **ZAR** ee un ¶23
café	ka **FAY** *or* kuh **FAY**
café au lait	ka **FAY** oh **LAY**
cafeteria	KAF uh **TIR** ee uh ¶25
caffeine	**KAF** een ¶2
KAF ee in *is now rare.*	
cairn	**KERN**
Cairo	**KYE** roh
The city in Illinois is pronounced **KER** oh, *or, sometimes,* **KAY** roh.	
caisson	**KAY** sahn *or* **KAYS** un
cajole	kuh **JOHL**
Cajun	**KAY** jun
calamine	**KAL** uh myne ¶22
calamity	kuh **LAM** uh tee
calcify	**KAL** suh fye
calcium	**KAL** see um ¶25
calculable	**KAL** kyuh luh bul
calculate	**KAL** kyuh layt
calculus	**KAL** kyuh lus
Calder	**KAWL** dur
caldron	**KAWL** drun
calendar	**KAL** un dur

SPELLED	PRONOUNCED
calends	**KAL** unz ¶10
calf	**KAF** ¶18
caliber	**KAL** uh bur
calibrate	**KAL** uh brayt
calico	**KAL** uh koh
California	KAL uh **FAWR** nyuh ¶25
Caligula	kuh **LIG** yoo luh
caliper	**KAL** uh pur
calisthenics	KAL uhs **THEN** iks
calk	**KAWK**
calligraphy	kuh **LIG** ruh fee
Calliope	kuh **LYE** uh pee
KAL ee ohp *is also used when* calliope, *the musical instrument, is meant.*	
calm	**KAHM**
also **KAHLM**	
caloric	kuh **LAWR** ik
calorie	**KAL** ur ee ¶5
calque	**KALK**
calumet	**KAL** yuh met ¶2
calumny	**KAL** um nee
Calvary	**KAL** vur ee ¶5
calve	**KAV** ¶18
Calvin	**KAL** vin
calypso	kuh **LIP** soh
camaraderie	KAHM uh **RAHD** ur ee *or* KAM uh **RAHD** ur ee
camber	**KAM** bur
Cambrian	**KAM** bree un
Cambridge	**KAYM** brij
camellia	kuh **MEEL** yuh ¶25
Camelot	**KAM** uh laht
Camembert	**KAM** um ber
cameo	**KAM** ee oh

camera	**KAM** ruh ¶5	cantabile	kahn **TAH** bi LAY
Cameroon	kam uh **ROOHN**	cantaloupe	**KAN** tuh lohp
camisole	**KAM** uh sohl	cantankerous	kan **TANG** kur us
camomile	**KAM** uh myle *or*	cantata	kun **TAHT** uh
	KAM uh meel	Canterbury	**KAN** tur BER ee *or*
camouflage	**KAM** uh flahzh ¶15		**KAN** tur bur ee
campaign	kam **PAYN**	cantilever	**KAN** tuh LEE vur *or*
camphor	**KAM** fur ¶9		**KAN** tuh LEV ur
Canaan	**KAY** nun	canto	**KAN** toh
Canadian	kuh **NAY** dee un	canton	**KAN** tun *or* **KAN** tahn *or*
canal	kuh **NAL**		kan **TAHN**
canapé	**KAN** uh pee *or* **KAN** uh pay	cantor	**KAN** tur
canard	kuh **NAHRD**	Canuck	kuh **NUK**
canary	kuh **NAR** ee ¶23	canvass	**KAN** vus
Canberra	**KAN** bur uh	canyon	**KAN** yun
cancellation	KAN suh **LAY** shun	*The Spanish word* cañon, *from*
cancer	**KAN** sur	*which this word derives, is still*
candelabrum	KAN duh **LAH** brum *or*	*sometimes used in English and*
	KAN duh **LAY** brum	*is also pronounced* **KAN** yun.
candidacy	**KAN** duh duh see	capable	**KAY** puh bul
candidate	**KAN** duh dayt *or*	capacious	kuh **PAY** shus
	KAN duh dit	capacity	kuh **PASS** uh tee
candied	**KAN** deed	cap–a–pie	kap uh **PEE**
Candlemas	**KAN** dul mus	caparison	kuh **PAR** uh sun ¶23
candor	**KAN** dur	caper	**KAY** pur
canine	**KAY** nyne	capillary	**KAP** uh **LER** ee ¶23
canister	**KAN** is tur	capital	**KAP** uh tul
canker	**KANG** kur	Capitol	**KAP** uh tul
cannabis	**KAN** uh bis	capitulate	kuh **PICH** uh layt
cannelloni	KAN uh **LOH** nee	capon	**KAY** pahn
Cannes	**KAN** *or* **KANZ**	*also, but less frequently now,*
cannibal	**KAN** uh bul	**KAY** pun ¶8
canon	**KAN** un	cappuccino	KAP uh **CHEE** noh *or*
canonical	kuh **NAHN** i kul		KAHP ooh **CHEE** noh
canopy	**KAN** uh pee	capriccio	kuh **PREE** choh ¶25

SPELLED	PRONOUNCED
caprice	kuh **PREES**
capricious	kuh **PRISH** us
Capricorn	**KAP** ruh kawrn
capsize	**KAP** syze ¶2
capstan	**KAP** stun
capsule	**KAP** sul

occasionally **KAP** syool

captain	**KAP** tun

Also, among some speakers the second syllable is pronounced as if it had no vowel, as **KAP** n *or* **KAP** m.

captious	**KAP** shus
captivate	**KAP** tuh vayt
captive	**KAP** tiv
capture	**KAP** chur ¶12
Capuchin	**KAP** yoo shin *or*
	kuh **PYOOH** shin
carabinieri	KAHR ah bee **NYER** ee
Caracas	kuh **RAHK** us ¶18
carafe	kuh **RAF** ¶18
caramel	**KAR** uh mul ¶23

For the candy, it is very often **KAHR** mul.

carat	**KAR** ut ¶23
caravan	**KAR** uh van ¶23
caravansary	
	KAR uh **VAN** sur ee ¶23
caraway	**KAR** uh way ¶23
carbine	**KAHR** byne *or* **KAHR** been
carbohydrate	KAHR buh **HYE** drayt
carbonate *(verb)*	**KAHR** buh nayt
carbonate *(noun)*	**KAHR** buh nit *or*
	KAHR buh nayt
carbuncle	**KAHR** bung kul

SPELLED	PRONOUNCED
carburetor	**KAHR** buh rayt ur

also, especially formerly, **KAHR** byoo rayt ur

carcass	**KAHR** kus
carcinogen	kahr **SIN** uh jin
carcinoma	KAHR suh **NOH** muh
cardiac	**KAHR** dee ak
cardigan	**KAHR** duh gun
cardinal	**KAHR** duh nul ¶5
cardiology	KAHR dee **AHL** uh jee
careen	kuh **REEN**
career	kuh **RIR**
caress	kuh **RES**
Caribbean	KAR uh **BEE** un *or*
	kuh **RIB** ee un ¶23
caribou	**KAR** uh booh ¶23
caricature	**KAR** uh kuh chur ¶23
caries	**KAR** eez ¶23
carillon	**KAR** uh lahn ¶23
carillonneur	KAR uh luh **NUR** ¶23
Carmel (Mount)	**KAHR** mul
Carmelite	**KAHR** muh lyte
carminative	kahr **MIN** uh tiv *or*
	KAHR muh nayt iv
carmine	**KAHR** min *or* **KAHR** myne
carnage	**KAHR** nij
carnal	**KAHR** nul
carnauba	kahr **NAW** buh *or*
	kahr **NOW** buh
Carnegie	**KAHR** nuh gee *or*
	kahr **NAY** gee
carnival	**KAHR** nuh vul
carnivore	**KAHR** nuh vawr
carnivorous	kahr **NIV** ur us
carob	**KAR** ub ¶23

carom .... **KAR** um ¶23

carotid .... kuh **RAHT** id

carouse .... kuh **ROWZ**

Carpathian .... kahr **PAY** thee un

carrel .... **KAR** ul ¶23

carriage ("vehicle") ..... **KAR** ij ¶23

carriage ("carrying charge") ....
.... **KAR** ee ij *or* **KAR** ij ¶23

carrier .... **KAR** ee ur

carrion .... **KAR** ee un ¶23

carrousel .... kar uh **SEL**
occasionally kar uh **ZEL** ¶23

carte blanche ... kahrt **BLAHNSH** ¶9

cartel .... kahr **TEL**

Cartesian .... kahr **TEE** zhun

Carthage .... **KAHR** thij

Carthusian ... kahr **THOOH** zhun ¶25

cartilage .... **KAHRT** ul ij ¶5

cartilaginous ...... KAHRT ul **AJ** uh nus

cartography .... kahr **TAHG** ruh fee

cartoon .... kahr **TOOHN**

cartridge .... **KAHR** trij

Caruso .... kuh **ROOH** soh ¶14

caryatid .... **KAR** ee **AT** id ¶23

casaba .... kuh **SAH** buh

Casablanca ..... KAS uh **BLANG** kuh *or*
KAH suh **BLAHNG** kuh

Casanova ...... KAS uh **NOH** vuh ¶14

casbah .... **KAHZ** bah *or* **KAS** bah

cascade .... kas **KAYD** ¶2

casein .... **KAY** seen *or* **KAY** see un

cashew .... **KASH** ooh
The older kuh **SHOOH** *is no longer
much heard.*

cashier .... ka **SHIR**

cashmere .... **KAZH** mir
less frequently **KASH** mir

casino .... kuh **SEE** noh

casket .... **KAS** kit ¶18

Caspian ..... **KAS** pee un ¶18, 25

cassava .... kuh **SAH** vuh

casserole .... **KAS** uh rohl

cassette .... kuh **SET** *or* ka **SET**

cassia .... **KASH** uh

Cassiopeia .... KAS ee uh **PEE** uh

cassock .... **KAS** uk

cassowary ..... **KAS** uh **WER** ee ¶23

castanets .... kas tuh **NETS**

caster .... **KAS** tur ¶18

castigate .... **KAS** tuh gayt

Castile (soap) .... kas **TEEL**

Castilian .... kas **TIL** yun

castle .... **KAS** ul ¶18

castor .... **KAS** tur ¶18

castrate .... **KAS** trayt

Castro .... **KAS** troh *or* **KAHS** troh

casual .... **KAZH** oo wul ¶5

casuistry .... **KAZH** oo wis tree

cataclysm .... **KAT** uh **KLIZ** um

catacomb .... **KAT** uh kohm

catafalque .... **KAT** uh falk *or*
KAT uh fawlk

Catalan .... **KAT** uh lan

catalepsy .... **KAT** uh **LEP** see

catalog .... **KAT** uh lawg ¶19

catalpa .... kuh **TAL** puh

catalyst .... **KAT** uh list

catalytic .... KAT uh **LIT** ik

catamaran .... KAT uh muh **RAN**

catapult .. **KAT** uh pult *or* **KAT** uh poolt

cataract .... **KAT** uh rakt
    Careful speakers do not reduce
    the consonant cluster to
    KAT uh rak, *except perhaps for the*
    plural **KAT** uh raks.

catarrh .... kuh **TAHR**

catastrophe .... kuh **TAS** truh fee

catastrophic .... KAT uh **STRAHF** ik

catatonic .... KAT uh **TAHN** ik

Catawba .... kuh **TAW** buh

catcher .... **KACH** ur *or* **KECH** ur

catechism .... **KAT** uh kiz um

catechumen ...... KAT uh **KYOOH** mun

categorical ....
    .... KAT uh **GAWR** uh kul   ¶19

categorize .... **KAT** uh guh RYZE

category .... **KAT** uh GAWR ee

caterpillar .... **KAT** ur PIL ur   ¶3

caterwaul .... **KAT** ur wawl

catharsis .... kuh **THAR** sis

cathedral .... kuh **THEE** drul

catheter .... **KATH** uh tur

cathode .... **KATH** ohd

catholic .... **KATH** uh lik   ¶5

Catholicism ..... kuh **THAHL** uh siz um

catsup .... **KECH** up *or* **KACH** up *or*
                     KAT sup

Caucasian .... kaw **KAY** zhun   ¶1

Caucasus .... **KAW** kuh sus

caucus .... **KAWK** us

caudal .... **KAW** dul

cauliflower .... **KAHL** uh flow ur   ¶19

caulk .... **KAWK**

causal .... **KAWZ** ul

causality .... kaw **ZAL** uh tee

cause célèbre .... KAWZ suh **LEB** ruh *or*
    KOHZ say **LEB** ruh *or* KAWZ suh **LEB**

causerie .... koh zuh **REE**

caustic .... **KAWS** tik

cauterize .... **KAWT** uh ryze

cavalcade .... **KAV** ul kayd

cavalier .... kav uh **LIR**

cavalry .... **KAV** ul ree
    This word is sometimes
    incorrectly pronounced **KAL** vur ee.

caveat .... **KAV** ee at *or* **KAH** vee aht *or*
               KAY vee at

cavern .... **KAV** urn

caviar .... **KAV** ee ahr *or*
             KAH vee ahr   ¶2

cavil .... **KAV** ul

cavity .... **KAV** uh tee

cayenne .... kye **EN** *or* kay **EN**

cecum .... **SEE** kum

cedilla .... si **DIL** uh

Celebes .... **SEL** uh beez

celebrant .... **SEL** uh brunt

celebrate .... **SEL** uh brayt

celebrity .... suh **LEB** ruh tee

celerity .... suh **LER** uh tee

celery .... **SEL** uh ree   ¶5

celestial .... suh **LES** chul   ¶17

celiac .... **SEE** lee ak

celibacy .... **SEL** uh buh see

celibate .... **SEL** uh but

cello .... **CHEL** oh

cellophane .... **SEL** uh fayn

cellular .... **SEL** yoo lur

cellulite .... **SEL** yoo leet   ¶2

cellulose .... **SEL** yoo lohs

Celsius	**SEL** see us ¶25	ceremonial	
Celt	**KELT** or **SELT**		**SER** uh **MOH** nee ul ¶25
cement	si **MENT**	ceremony	**SER** uh moh nee
cemetery	**SEM** uh **TER** ee	Ceres	suh **RIR** eez
cenotaph	**SEN** uh taf	cerise	suh **REES** or suh **REEZ**
Cenozoic	**SEE** nuh **ZOH** ik or	certificate *(verb)*	sur **TIF** uh kayt
	SEN uh **ZOH** ik	certificate *(noun)*	sur **TIF** uh kit
censor	**SEN** sur ¶9	certify	**SUR** tuh fye
censorious	sen **SAWR** ee us ¶25	certitude	**SUR** tuh toohd ¶21
censure	**SEN** shur ¶9, 12	Cervantes	sur **VAN** teez or
census	**SEN** sus ¶9		ser **VAHN** tays
centaur	**SEN** tawr	cervical	**SUR** vuh kul
centenary	sen **TEN** ur ee or	cervix	**SUR** viks
	SEN tuh **NER** ee ¶23	cesium	**SEE** zee um
centennial	sen **TEN** ee ul ¶25	cessation	se **SAY** shun ¶1
centigrade	**SEN** tuh grayd	ceviche	suh **VEE** chee
centimeter	**SEN** tuh **MEET** ur	Ceylon	suh **LAHN** or say **LAHN** or
centipede	**SEN** tuh peed		see **LAHN**
centrifugal	sen **TRIF** yoo gul or	Chablis	sha **BLEE** ¶1
	sen **TRIF** uh gul	chaconne	shah **KOHN**
centrifuge	**SEN** truh fyoohj	chagrin	shuh **GRIN**
centripetal	sen **TRIP** uh tul	chaise	**SHEZ** or **SHAYZ**
centurion		chaise longue	shayz **LAWNG** or
	sen **TYOOR** ee un ¶17, 21, 25		shez **LAWNG**
century	**SEN** chur ee ¶9, 12		
cephalic	suh **FAL** ik		*The French* longue *(meaning*
ceramic	suh **RAM** ik		*long) has been confused with*
ceramist	suh **RAM** ist or **SER** uh mist		*English* lounge, *and so the term*
cereal	**SIR** ee ul ¶25		*is now often written* chaise
cerebellum	**SER** uh **BEL** um		lounge *and pronounced*
cerebral	**SER** uh brul or suh **REE** brul		shayz **LOWNJ**.
cerebrum	suh **REE** brum or	chalcedony	kal **SED** un ee or
	SER uh brum		**KAL** suh **DOH** nee
cerements	**SER** uh munts or	chalet	sha **LAY** ¶1, 2
	SIR munts	chalice	**CHAL** is
		chalk	**CHAWK**

SPELLED	PRONOUNCED
challenge	**CHAL** unj
challis	**SHAL** ee
chamber	**CHAYM** bur
chamberlain	**CHAYM** bur lin
chameleon	kuh **MEEL** yun ¶25
chamois	**SHAM** ee
chamomile	**KAM** uh myle *or* **KAM** uh meel
champagne	sham **PAYN**
champignon	sham peen **YOHN** *or* sham **PIN** yun
chancellery	**CHAN** suh lur ee ¶5, 18
chancellor	**CHAN** suh lur ¶5, 18
chancery	**CHAN** sur ee ¶18
chancre	**SHANG** kur

KANG kur, *perhaps by confusion with* canker, *is not standard.*

chandelier	shan duh **LIR**
channel	**CHAN** ul
chanson	shahn **SOHN** *or* **SHAN** sun
chanteuse	shan **TOOZ** *or* shahn **TOOHZ**
chantey	**SHAN** tee
Chantilly	shan **TIL** ee
chaos	**KAY** ahs
chaotic	kay **AHT** ik
chaparral	chap uh **RAL** ¶12
chapeau	sha **POH**
chaperon	**SHAP** uh rohn
chaplain	**CHAP** lun
chaps	**CHAPS** ¶12
character	**KAR** ik tur ¶23
charade	shuh **RAYD**
Chardonnay	shahr duh **NAY** ¶2

SPELLED	PRONOUNCED
chargé d'affaires	shahr **ZHAY** duh **FER**
chariot	**CHAR** ee ut ¶23
charioteer	**CHAR** ee uh **TIR** ¶23
charisma	kuh **RIZ** muh
charismatic	**KAR** iz **MAT** ik ¶14, 23
charity	**CHAR** uh tee ¶23
charivari	shuh **RIV** uh **REE** *or* shiv uh **REE** *or* **SHIV** uh ree: *see* shivaree
charlatan	**SHAHR** luh tun
Charlemagne	**SHAHR** luh mayn
chartreuse	shahr **TROOHZ** ¶14
chary	**CHAR** ee ¶23
Charybdis	kuh **RIB** dis
chasm	**KAZ** um
chassis	**CHAS** ee ¶12
chasten	**CHAYS** un
chastise	chas **TYZE** ¶2
chasuble	**CHAZ** yoo bul ¶14
château	sha **TOH**
chateaubriand	sha **TOH** bree **AHN**
chattel	**CHAT** ul
Chaucer	**CHAW** sur
chauffeur	**SHOH** fur ¶12
Chautauqua	shuh **TAW** kwuh
chauvinism	**SHOH** vuh niz um
Cheddar (cheese)	**CHED** ur
cheetah	**CHEET** uh
chef	**SHEF**
chemise	shuh **MEEZ** ¶14
chemistry	**KEM** is tree
chemotherapy	**KEE** moh **THER** uh pee *or* **KEM** oh **THER** uh pee

chenille .... shi NEEL

cherish .... CHER ish

Cherokee .... CHER uh kee

cheroot .... shuh ROOHT

cherub .... CHER ub

Cheshire (cat) .... CHESH ur *or* CHESH ir

chestnut .... CHES nut

chevalier .... shev uh LIR

When the word is used to mean a French nobleman or legionnaire, the pronunciation is often shuh VAL yay.

chevron .... SHEV run

Cheyenne .... shye EN

In Wyoming, the city is always shye AN.

Chianti .... kee AHN tee *or* kee AN tee

chiaroscuro ....
.... kee AHR uh SKYOOR oh ¶21

chic .... SHEEK

Chicago .... shuh KAH goh ¶19

chicanery .... shi KAY nur ee ¶12

Chickasaw .... CHIK uh saw ¶19

chicory .... CHIK ur ee ¶5

chieftain .... CHEEF tun

chiffon .... shi FAHN

occasionally SHIF ahn

chiffonier .... shif uh NEER

chignon .... SHEE nyahn *or* SHEE nyohn ¶2

Chihuahua .... chuh WAH wah

chilblain .... CHIL blayn

chimera .... kye MIR uh *or* ki MIR uh

chimerical .... ki MIR i kul *or* ki MER i kul

The first syllable may also be kye.

chimpanzee .... chim pan ZEE *or* chim PAN zee

chinchilla .... chin CHIL uh

Chinese .... chye NEEZ

rarely chye NEES; *for the adjective* CHYE neez *is often also heard.*

chino .... CHEE noh *or* SHEE noh

Chinook ..... chi NOOHK *or* chi NOOK

These pronunciations are for the Indian tribes and their languages, but the wind is usually shi NOOHK *or* shi NOOK.

chintz .... CHINTS

chiropractor .. KYE ruh PRAK tur ¶1

chitterlings .... CHIT lunz

The spelling pronunciation CHIT ur lingz *is sometimes heard.*

chivalric ..... shi VAL rik *or* SHIV ul rik

chivalry .... SHIV ul ree

chives .... CHYVZE

chlorine ..... KLAWR een *or* KLAWR in

chlorophyll .... KLAWR uh fil

chocolate .... CHAWK lut ¶5, 19

Choctaw .... CHAHK taw ¶19

choir .... KWYRE

cholera .... KAHL ur uh

choleric ...... KAHL ur ik *or* kuh LER ik

cholesterol .... kuh LES tuh RAWL *or* kuh LES tuh ROHL

Chopin .... SHOH pan ¶2

chop suey .... chahp SOOH ee

SPELLED	PRONOUNCED
choral	**KAWR** ul
chorale	kuh **RAL** or kaw **RAL**
chorea	kaw **REE** uh
choreography	**KAWR** ee **AH** gruh fee
chorister	**KAWR** is tur
chortle	**CHAWR** tul
chough	**CHUF**
chow mein	CHOW **MAYN**
Christ	**KRYSTE**
christen	**KRIS** un
Christian	**KRIS** chun
Christianity	KRIS chee **AN** uh tee ¶13
Christmas	**KRIS** mus
chromatic	kroh **MAT** ik ¶1
chromium	**KROH** mee um
chromosome	**KROH** muh sohm
chronic	**KRAH** nik
chronicle	**KRAH** nuh kul
chronological	KRAHN uh **LAHJ** i kul
chronology	kruh **NAHL** uh jee
chrysalis	**KRIS** uh lus
chrysanthemum	kri **SAN** thuh mum ¶14
chukka (boot)	**CHUK** uh
Chungking	choong **KING** or chung **KING** or joong **CHING**
churlish	**CHURL** ish
chyme	**KYME**
ciao	**CHOW**
cicada	si **KAY** duh or si **KAH** duh
Cicero	**SIS** ur oh
cigarette	sig uh **RET** ¶2
cigarillo	SIG uh **RIL** oh
cilia	**SIL** ee uh ¶25

SPELLED	PRONOUNCED
Cincinnati	SIN suh **NAT** ee or SIN suh **NAT** uh
cincture	**SING** chur ¶9
cinema	**SIN** uh muh
cinematography	SIN uh muh **TAHG** ruh fee
cinnabar	**SIN** uh bahr
cinnamon	**SIN** uh mun
cinquefoil	**SINGK** foyl
cipher	**SYE** fur
circa	**SUR** kuh
circadian	sur **KAY** dee un
Circe	**SUR** see
circlet	**SUR** klit
circuit	**SUR** kit
circuitous	sur **KYOOH** uh tus
circuitry	**SUR** kuh tree
circulate	**SUR** kyuh layt
circumambulate	SUR kum **AM** byuh layt
circumcise	**SUR** kum syze
circumcision	SUR kum **SIZH** un
circumference	sur **KUM** fur uns ¶5, 9
circumflex	**SUR** kum flex
circumlocution	SUR kum loh **KYOOH** shun
circumscribe	SUR kum skrybe ¶8
circumstance	**SUR** kum stans also, but decreasing in frequency, SUR kum stuns ¶8, 9
circumstantial	SUR kum **STAN** shul
circumvent	sur kum **VENT** ¶2
cirque	**SURK**
cirrhosis	suh **ROH** sis

cirrocumulus		clavier	kluh **VIR**
.... SIR oh **KYOOH** myuh lus		*sometimes* **KLAV** ee ur	
cirrus .... **SIR** us		cleanse .... **KLENZ**	
Cistercian .... sis **TUR** shun		cleavage .... **KLEE** vij	
cistern .... **SIS** turn		clematis .... **KLEM** uh tis	
citadel .... **SIT** uh dul *or* **SIT** uh del		kluh **MAT** is *has become a very*	
citizen ..... **SIT** uh zun *or* **SIT** uh sun		*common pronunciation.*	
citronella .... SIT ruh **NEL** uh		clemency .... **KLEM** un see ¶9	
citrus .... **SIT** rus		Cleopatra .... KLEE uh **PAT** ruh	
civilian .... suh **VIL** yun		clergy .... **KLUR** jee	
civility .... suh **VIL** uh tee		clerical .... **KLER** i kul	
civilization ...... SIV uh luh **ZAY** shun		clerk .... **KLURK**	
civilize .... SIV uh lyze		cliché .... klee **SHAY** ¶1	
clairvoyant .... kler **VOY** unt		client .... **KLYE** unt	
clamber .... **KLAM** bur		clientele .... klye un **TEL**	
clamor .... **KLAM** ur		*occasionally* klee ahn **TEL**, *which is*	
clandestine .... klan **DES** tun		*the usual British pronunciation*	
occasionally **KLAN** duh styne		climacteric .... klye **MAK** tur ik *or*	
clangor .... **KLANG** ur		KLYE mak **TER** ik ¶23	
clapboard .... **KLAB** urd		climactic .... klye **MAK** tik	
occasionally **KLAP** bawrd		climate .... **KLYE** mut	
claque .... **KLAK**		climatology ... KLYE muh **TAHL** uh jee	
claret .... **KLAR** it ¶23		climax .... **KLYE** maks	
clarify .... **KLAR** uh fye ¶23		climb .... **KLYME**	
clarinet .... klar uh **NET**		clinician .... kli **NISH** un	
occasionally **KLAR** uh nit ¶8, 23		clique .... **KLEEK** *or* **KLIK**	
clarion .... **KLAR** ee un ¶23		clitoris .... **KLIT** ur us	
clarity .... **KLAR** uh tee ¶23		*occasionally* kli **TAWR** us *or*	
classicism .... **KLAS** uh siz um		**KLYTE** ur us	
classify .... **KLAS** uh fye		cloaca .... kloh **AY** kuh	
clause .... **KLAWZ**		cloche .... **KLOHSH**	
claustrophobia		cloisonné .... kloy zuh **NAY**	
..... KLAWS truh **FOH** bee uh ¶4, 25		cloister .... **KLOYS** tur	
clavichord .... **KLAV** uh kawrd		cloning .... **KLOH** ning	
clavicle .... **KLAV** uh kul		close *(verb)* .... **KLOHZ**	

SPELLED	PRONOUNCED
close *(adjective)*	**KLOHS**
closemouthed	klohs **MOWDHD** *or* klohs **MOWTHT**
closet	**KLAHZ** it ¶19
closure	**KLOH** zhur
clothe	**KLOHDH**
clothier	**KLOHDH** yur ¶25
clothing	**KLOH** dhing
cloture	**KLOH** chur
clover	**KLOH** vur
clumber (spaniel)	**KLUM** bur
clumsy	**KLUM** zee
Clytemnestra	KLYTE um **NES** truh
coagulate	koh **AG** yuh layt
coalesce	koh uh **LES**
coalition	KOH uh **LISH** un
coati	koh **AHT** ee
coati–mundi	koh **AHT** i **MUN** dee
coax	**KOHKS**
coaxial	koh **AK** see ul ¶25
cobalt	**KOH** bawlt
COBOL	**KOH** bawl
cocaine	koh **KAYN** ¶2
coccus	**KAHK** uhs

The plural cocci *is* **KAHK** sye.

coccyx	**KAHK** siks
cochineal	**KAHCH** uh neel ¶19
cochlea	**KAHK** lee uh
cockamamie	**KAHK** uh **MAY** mee
cockateel	**KAHK** uh teel ¶2
cockatoo	**KAHK** uh tooh ¶2
cockatrice	**KAHK** uh tris
cockerel	**KAHK** ur ul ¶5
cocoa	**KOH** koh
cocoon	kuh **KOOHN**

SPELLED	PRONOUNCED
codeine	**KOH** deen

The earlier **KOH** *dee un is still sometimes heard.*

codex	**KOH** deks
codicil	**KAHD** i sul *or* **KAHD** i sil
codify	**KAHD** uh fye

occasionally **KOH** *duh fye*

coed	**KOH** ed
coerce	koh **URS**
coercion	koh **UR** shun *or* koh **UR** zhun
coeval	koh **EE** vul
coffee	**KAWF** ee ¶19
coffin	**KAWF** in ¶19
cogency	**KOH** jun see ¶9
cogent	**KOH** junt
cogitate	**KAHJ** uh tayt
cognac	**KOHN** yak ¶20
cognate	**KAHG** nayt
cognition	kahg **NISH** un
cognizance	**KAHG** nuh zuns ¶9
cognomen	kahg **NOH** mun
cognoscente	**KOH** nyoh **SHEN** tay
cognovit	kahg **NOH** vit
cohere	koh **HIR**
cohesion	koh **HEE** zhun
cohesive	koh **HEES** iv
cohort	**KOH** hawrt
coif	**KOYF**

This is the pronunciation for the word meaning a cap, *but the word formed from* coiffure *is usually* **KWAHF**.

coiffure	kwah **FYOOR** ¶24
coincide	koh in **SYDE**
coincidence	koh **IN** suh duns ¶9

SPELLED	PRONOUNCED	SPELLED	PRONOUNCED

coincidental .... koh IN suh DENT ul

Cointreau .... kwahn TROH

coitus .... KOH uh tus *or* koh EET us

colander .. KAHL un dur *or* KUL un dur

colectomy ...... kuh LEK tuh mee ¶1

Coleridge .... KOHL rij
*Although not the poet's own
pronunciation,* KOHL ur ij *is often
heard.*

coleus .... KOH lee us

colic .... KAHL ik

coliseum .... KAHL uh SEE um

colitis .... koh LYTE is ¶1

collaborate .... kuh LAB uh rayt

collage .... kuh LAHZH ¶1

collapse .... kuh LAPS

collard .... KAHL urd

collate .... KAH layt *or*
kuh LAYT ¶2, 20

collateral .... kuh LAT ur ul

collation .... kah LAY shun ¶20

colleague .... KAHL eeg

collection .... kuh LEK shun

collectivism .... kuh LEK ti viz um

colleen .... KAHL een *or* kuh LEEN

college .... KAHL ij

collegial .... kuh LEE jee ul

collegiality ...... kuh LEE jee AL uh tee

collegian .... kuh LEE jun

collegiate .... kuh LEE jit
kuh LEE jee ut *is no longer much
heard.*

collier .... KAHL yur ¶25

collision .... kuh LIZH un

colloid .... KAHL oyd

colloquial .... kuh LOH kwee ul

colloquy .... KAHL uh kwee

collusion .... kuh LOOH zhun

cologne .... kuh LOHN

colon .... KOH lun

colonel .... KUR nul

colonial .... kuh LOH nee ul

colonize .... KAHL uh nyze

colonnade .... kahl uh NAYD ¶2

colony .... KAHL uh nee

colophon .... KAHL uh fahn *or*
KAHL uh fun

Colorado .... KAHL uh RAD oh *or*
KAHL uh RAH doh

coloratura ...... KUL ur uh TOOR uh *or*
KAHL ur uh TOOR uh ¶21

colossal .... kuh LAHS ul

Colosseum .... KAHL uh SEE um

Colossians .... kuh LAHSH unz

colossus .... kuh LAHS us

colostomy .... kuh LAHS tuh mee

colter .... KOHL tur

columbine .... KAHL um byne

column .... KAHL um
KAHL yum *is generally frowned
upon by educated speakers.*

columnist .... KAHL um nist *or*
KAHL uh mist

coma .... KOH muh

Comanche ..... kuh MAN chee ¶1

comatose .... KOH muh tohs *or*
KAHM uh tohs

comb .... KOHM

combat *(verb)* .... kum BAT *or*
KAHM bat

42

combat *(noun)* .... **KAHM** bat
    KUM bat *has become rare.*

combatant .... kum **BAT** unt
    KAHM buh tunt *is now less common.*

combination ...... KAHM buh **NAY** shun

combine .... kum **BYNE**
    For the noun, and when the
    verb means to harvest, *the*
    pronunciation is KAHM byne.

combustion .... kum **BUS** chun

comedian .... kuh **MEE** dee un

comedic .... kuh **MEE** dik
    kuh **MED** ik *is occasionally heard.*

comedienne .... kuh **MEE** dee **EN**

comedy .... **KAHM** uh dee

come–hither .... kum **HIDH** ur

comely .... **KUM** lee

comestible .... kuh **MES** tuh bul

comet .... **KAHM** ut

comfit .... **KUM** fit *or* **KAHM** fit

comfort .... **KUM** furt ¶9

comfortable ...... **KUMF** tur bul *or*
    KUMF tuh bul *or* **KUM** fur tuh bul ¶3

comic .... **KAHM** ik

comity .... **KAHM** uh tee

comma .... **KAHM** uh

command .... kuh **MAND** ¶18

commandeer .... kahm un **DIR**

commando .... kuh **MAN** doh

commemorate .... kuh **MEM** uh rayt

commemorative .... kuh **MEM** ur uh tiv
    or kuh **MEM** uh rayt iv

commence .... kuh **MENS** ¶9

commend .... kuh **MEND**

commendation ... KAHM un **DAY** shun

commendatory ....
         kuh **MEN** duh **TAWR** ee

commensurate ....
         kuh **MEN** shur it ¶9, 11

comment .... **KAHM** ent

commentary .. **KAHM** un TER ee ¶23

commercial .... kuh **MUR** shul

commingle .... kuh **MING** gul

commiserate .... kuh **MIZ** uh rayt

commissar .... **KAHM** uh sahr

commissariat ....
         KAHM uh **SAR** ee ut ¶23

commissary ... **KAHM** uh **SER** ee ¶23

commission .... kuh **MISH** un

commit .... kuh **MIT**

committee .... kuh **MIT** ee

commode .... kuh **MOHD**

commodious .... kuh **MOH** dee us

commodity .... kuh **MAHD** uh tee

commodore .... **KAHM** uh dawr

commonweal .... **KAHM** un weel

commotion .... kuh **MOH** shun

communal .... **KAHM** yoo nul *or*
         kuh **MYOOH** nul

commune *(verb)* .... kuh **MYOOHN**

commune *(noun)* .... **KAHM** yoohn

communicable ....
         kuh **MYOOH** ni kuh bul

communicate ... kuh **MYOOH** nuh kayt

communicative ....
         kuh **MYOOH** nuh kayt iv *or*
         kuh **MYOOH** ni kuh tiv

communion .... kuh **MYOOHN** yun

communiqué ....
         kuh MYOOH nuh **KAY** ¶2

communism .... **KAHM** yuh niz um

community .... kuh **MYOOH** nuh tee

commutation ....

.... KAHM yuh **TAY** shun ¶1

commute .... kuh **MYOOHT**

commuter .... kuh **MYOOHT** ur

compact .... kum **PAKT**

KAHM pakt *is also heard for the*
adjective, and the noun is always
pronounced this way.

compadre .... kum **PAH** dray ¶1

companion .... kum **PAN** yun

company .... **KUM** puh nee ¶5

comparable .... **KAHM** pur uh bul

Although a disputed
pronunciation, kum **PAR** *uh bul is*
now also heard.

comparative ..... kum **PAR** uh tiv ¶23

comparison .... kum **PAR** uh sun ¶23

compartment .... kum **PAHRT** munt

compartmentalize ....

.... kum PAHRT **MEN** tuh **LYZE**

compass .... **KUM** pus

compassion .... kum **PASH** un

compatible .... kum **PAT** uh bul

compatriot .... kum **PAY** tree ut

compeer .... **KAHM** pir *or* kum **PIR**

compel .... kum **PEL**

compellation ..... KAHM puh **LAY** shun

compendium .... kum **PEN** dee um

compensate .... **KAHM** pun sayt

compete .... kum **PEET**

competent .... **KAHM** puh tunt

competition .... KAHM puh **TISH** un

competitive .... kum **PET** uh tiv

compilation ...... KAHM puh **LAY** shun

compile .... kum **PYLE**

complacent .... kum **PLAY** sunt

complain .... kum **PLAYN**

complaint .... kum **PLAYNT**

complaisant .... kum **PLAY** sunt *or*
.... kum **PLAY** zunt

complement *(verb)* ....
.... **KAHM** pluh ment

complement *(noun)* ....
.... **KAHM** pluh munt

complementary ....
.... KAHM pluh **MEN** tur ee ¶5

complete .... kum **PLEET**

completion .... kum **PLEE** shun

complex .... kum **PLEKS**

The adjective is also **KAHM** *pleks,*
and the noun is always
pronounced this way.

complexion .... kum **PLEK** shun

complexity .... kum **PLEK** suh tee

compliance .... kum **PLYE** uns ¶9

complicate .... **KAHM** pluh kayt

complicity .... kum **PLIS** uh tee

compliment *(verb)* .. **KAHM** pluh ment

compliment *(noun)* ....
.... **KAHM** pluh munt

complimentary ....
.... KAHM pluh **MEN** tur ee ¶5

comply .... kum **PLYE**

component .... kum **POH** nunt

comport .... kum **PAWRT**

compose .... kum **POHZ**

composite .... kum **PAHZ** it

composition .... KAHM puh **ZISH** un

SPELLED	PRONOUNCED
compositor	kum **PAHZ** uh tur
compost	**KAHM** pohst
composure	kum **POH** zhur
compote	**KAHM** poht
compound *(verb)*	kum **POWND** *or* kahm **POWND** *or* **KAHM** pownd
compound *(noun and adjective)*	**KAHM** pownd

*For the adjective, kahm **POWND** is also heard.*

comprehend	kahm pruh **HEND**
comprehensible	**KAHM** pruh **HEN** suh bul ¶9
comprehension	**KAHM** pruh **HEN** shun ¶9, 12
comprehensive	**KAHM** pruh **HEN** siv ¶9
compress *(verb)*	kum **PRES**
compress *(noun)*	**KAHM** pres
compression	kum **PRESH** un
comprise	kum **PRYZE**
compromise	**KAHM** pruh myze
comptroller	kun **TROH** lur

kahmp **TROH** lur *is a spelling pronunciation and is not generally recognized as a standard usage.*

compulsion	kum **PUL** shun
compulsive	kum **PUL** siv
compulsory	kum **PUL** sur ee ¶5
compunction	kum **PUNGK** shun ¶9
computation	**KAHM** pyoo **TAY** shun
compute	kum **PYOOHT**
computerese	kum PYOOHT ur **EEZ**
computerize	kum **PYOOHT** uh RYZE

SPELLED	PRONOUNCED
comrade	**KAHM** rad *or* **KAHM** rud ¶8
concatenate	kun **KAT** uh nayt ¶16
concave	kahn **KAYV** ¶16

*The adjective is also **KAHN** kayv, which is the usual pronunciation for the noun.*

conceal	kun **SEEL**
concede	kun **SEED**
conceit	kun **SEET**
conceited	kun **SEET** id
conceive	kun **SEEV**
concentrate	**KAHN** sun trayt
concentric	kun **SEN** trik
concept	**KAHN** sept
conception	kun **SEP** shun
conceptualize	kun **SEP** choo wuh LYZE ¶5, 12
concern	kun **SURN**
concert *(verb)*	kun **SURT** ¶9
concert *(noun)*	**KAHN** surt ¶9
concertina	KAHN sur **TEE** nuh ¶9
concertize	**KAHN** sur tyze
concerto	kun **CHER** toh
concession	kun **SESH** un
concessionaire	kun SESH uh **NER**
conch	**KAHNGK** *or* **KAHNCH**
concierge	kohn see **ERZH** *or* kohn **SYERZH** *or* kahn see **URZH**
conciliate	kun **SIL** ee ayt
conciliatory	kun **SIL** ee uh **TAWR** ee
concise	kun **SYSE**
concision	kun **SIZH** un
conclave	**KAHN** klayv ¶16
conclude	kun **KLOOHD** ¶16

conclusion ..... kun **KLOOH** zhun ¶16

conclusive .... kun **KLOOH** siv ¶16

concoct .... kun **KAHKT** ¶16

concomitance ....

.... kun **KAHM** uh tuns ¶9

Concord .... **KAHNG** kurd
*Thus for the town in
Massachusetts and the capital of
New Hampshire as well as the
wine and the grape, but for the
city in California, it is*
KAHNG kawrd. ¶16

concord .... **KAHN** kawrd ¶16

concordance ....

.... kun **KAWR** duns ¶1, 16

concordat ..... kun **KAWR** dat ¶1, 16

concourse .... **KAHN** kawrs ¶16

concrete .... kahn **KREET** ¶1, 16
also, and for the noun usually,
KAHN kreet

concretion .... kun **KREE** shun ¶1

concretize ...... **KAHN** kruh tyze ¶16

concubinage ....

.... kahn **KYOOH** buh nij ¶16

concubine .... **KAHNG** kyuh byne ¶16

concupiscence ....

.... kahn **KYOOHP** uh suns ¶9
KAHN kyuh **PIS** uns *is sometimes
heard but is not standard.*

concur .... kun **KUR** ¶16

concurrent .... kun **KUR** unt

concussion .... kun **KUSH** un ¶16

condemn .... kun **DEM**

condemnation ....

.... KAHN dem **NAY** shun ¶1

condemnatory ....

.... kun **DEM** nuh **TAWR** ee

condensate .... **KAHN** dun sayt
sometimes kun **DEN** sayt

condense .... kun **DENS** ¶9

condescend .... kahn duh **SEND** ¶2

condescension ....

.... KAHN duh **SEN** shun ¶9, 12

condiment .... **KAHN** duh munt

condition .... kun **DISH** un

condolences .... kun **DOH** lun siz

condom ..... **KAHN** dum *or* **KUN** dum

condominium ... KAHN duh **MIN** ee um

condone .... kun **DOHN**

conducive .... kun **DOOH** siv ¶21

conduct *(verb)* .... kun **DUKT**

conduct *(noun)* .... **KAHN** dukt

conduction .... kun **DUK** shun

conductivity ..... KAHN duk **TIV** uh tee

conduit .... **KAHN** doo wit
*This spelling pronunciation has
replaced earlier* **KAHN** dit *as the
prevailing one.*

Conestoga (wagon) ....

.... KAHN uh **STOH** guh

confection .... kun **FEK** shun

confederacy .... kun **FED** ur uh see

confederate *(verb)* ... kun **FED** uh rayt

confederate *(noun and adjective)* ...

.... kun **FED** ur it ¶5

confer .... kun **FUR**

conference .... **KAHN** fur uns ¶5, 9

confess .... kun **FES**

confession .... kun **FESH** un

confetti .... kun **FET** ee

SPELLED	PRONOUNCED	SPELLED	PRONOUNCED

confidant .... **KAHN** fuh dant *or* **KAHN** fuh dahnt ¶2

confide .... kun **FYDE**

confidence .... **KAHN** fuh duns ¶9

confidential ....
.... KAHN fuh **DEN** shul ¶9, 12

configuration .. kun FIG yuh **RAY** shun

confine .... kun **FYNE**
*The noun is usually in the
plural,* KAHN *fynze.*

confirm .... kun **FURM**

confirmation ...... KAHN fur **MAY** shun

confiscate .... **KAHN** fuh skayt

confiscatory ..... kun **FIS** kuh **TAWR** ee

conflagration .. KAHN fluh **GRAY** shun

conflation .... kun **FLAY** shun

conflict *(verb)* .... kun **FLIKT**

conflict *(noun)* .... **KAHN** flikt

confluence .... **KAHN** flooh uns
kun **FLOOH** uns *is now also heard
from time to time.*

conform .... kun **FAWRM**

conformation ... KAHN fawr **MAY** shun

conformity .... kun **FAWR** muh tee

confound .... kun **FOWND**
*When the word is used as a
mild oath meaning* damn, *it is
usually* kahn **FOWND**.

confrere .... **KAHN** frer *or* **KOHN** frer ¶2

confront .... kun **FRUNT**

Confucius .... kun **FYOOH** shus

confuse .... kun **FYOOHZ**

confusion .... kun **FYOOH** zhun

conga .... **KAHNG** guh

congeal .... kun **JEEL**

congenial .... kun **JEEN** yul ¶25

congenital .... kun **JEN** uh tul

conger (eel) .... **KANG** gur

congeries .... **KAHN** jur eez

congest .... kun **JEST**

congestion .... kun **JES** chun

conglomerate *(verb)* ....
.... kun **GLAHM** uh rayt ¶16

conglomerate *(noun and adjective)*
.... kun **GLAHM** ur it ¶5, 16

Congo .... **KAHNG** goh

congratulate ....
.... kun **GRACH** uh layt ¶17
kun **GRAJ** uh layt *is also heard.*

congregant .... **KAHNG** gruh gunt

congregate *(verb)* ....
.... **KAHNG** gruh gayt ¶16

congregate *(adjective)* ....
.... **KAHNG** gruh git ¶16

congress .... **KAHNG** grus ¶16

congressional ...... kun **GRESH** uh nul

congruent .... **KAHNG** groo wunt *or* kun **GROOH** unt ¶16

congruity .... kun **GROOH** uh tee

conic .... **KAHN** ik

conifer ..... **KAHN** uh fur *or* **KOH** nuh fur

coniferous .... kuh **NIF** ur us ¶5

conjecture .... kun **JEK** chur ¶12

conjoin .... kun **JOYN**

conjugal .... **KAHN** juh gul *or* kun **JOOH** gul

conjugate *(verb)* .... **KAHN** juh gayt

conjugate *(adjective)* ... **KAHN** juh gut

conjunction ... kun **JUNGK** shun ¶12

47

conjunctivitis ....
          .... kun JUNGK tuh **VYTE** is
conjure .... **KAHN** jur *or* **KUN** jur
    sometimes kun **JOOR**
connect .... kuh **NEKT**
connection .... kuh **NEK** shun
connive .... kuh **NYVE**
connoisseur .... kahn uh **SUR** *or*
            kahn uh **SOOR**
connotation .. KAHN uh **TAY** shun ¶1
connote .... kuh **NOHT**
connubial ..... kuh **NOOH** bee ul ¶25
conquer .... **KAHNG** kur
conquest .... **KAHNG** kwest ¶16
conquistador .... kahn KEES tuh DAWR
    or kahn KWIS tuh DAWR ¶16
CONRAIL .... **KAHN** rayl
consanguinity ....
         .... KAHN sang **GWIN** uh tee ¶16
conscience ...... **KAHN** shuns ¶9, 12
conscientious ....
          .... KAHN shee **EN** shus ¶9, 12
conscious .... **KAHN** shus ¶9, 12
conscript *(verb)* .... kun **SKRIPT**
conscript *(noun)* .... **KAHN** skript
consecrate .... **KAHN** suh krayt ¶9
consecutive .... kun **SEK** yuh tiv
consensus .... kun **SEN** sus ¶9
consequence ...... **KAHN** suh kwens *or*
       KAHN suh kwuns ¶8, 9
conservation ...... KAHN sur **VAY** shun
conservative .... kun **SUR** vuh tiv
conservatory ... kun **SUR** vuh TAWR ee
consider .... kun **SID** ur
consign .... kun **SYNE**

consistent .... kun **SIS** tunt
consistory .... kun **SIS** tur ee ¶5
consolation .... KAHN suh **LAY** shun
console *(verb)* .... kun **SOHL**
console *(noun)* .... **KAHN** sohl
consolidate .... kun **SAHL** uh dayt
consommé .... **KAHN** suh may ¶2
consonant .... **KAHN** suh nunt ¶9
consort *(verb)* .... kun **SAWRT**
consort *(noun)* .... **KAHN** sawrt
consortium .... kun SAWR shee um *or*
    kun SAWR tee um *or* kun SAWR shum
conspicuous .... kun **SPIK** yoo wus
conspiracy .... kun **SPIR** uh see
conspirator .... kun **SPIR** uh tur
conspire .... kun **SPYRE**
constable .... **KAHN** stuh bul
    KUN stuh bul, *the usual British*
    pronunciation, is also heard
    occasionally.
constabulary ....
          .... kun **STAB** yoo LER ee ¶23
constancy .... **KAHN** stun see ¶9
constant .... **KAHN** stunt
Constantine .... **KAHN** stun teen ¶22
constellation ..... KAHN stuh **LAY** shun
consternation ... KAHN stur **NAY** shun
constipation .... KAHN stuh **PAY** shun
constituent .... kun **STICH** oo wunt
constitute ...... **KAHN** stuh tooht ¶21
constitution ....
          .... KAHN stuh **TOOH** shun ¶9
constrain .... kun **STRAYN**
constrict .... kun **STRIKT**
constriction .... kun **STRIK** shun

construct *(verb)*	kun **STRUKT**	contest *(noun)*	**KAHN** test
construct *(noun)*	**KAHN** strukt	context	**KAHN** tekst
construction	kun **STRUK** shun	contextual	kun **TEKS** choo wul
construe	kun **STROOH**	contiguous	kun **TIG** yoo wus
consul	**KAHN** sul	continence	**KAHN** tuh nuns ¶9
consulate	**KAHN** sul it	continent	**KAHN** tuh nunt
consult	kun **SULT**	continental	KAHN tuh **NEN** tul
consultation	KAHN sul **TAY** shun	contingency	kun **TIN** jun see ¶9
consultative	kun **SUL** tuh tiv *or*	contingent	kun **TIN** junt
	KAHN sul tayt iv	continual	kun **TIN** yoo wul
consume	kun **SOOHM** ¶21	continuance	kun **TIN** yoo wuns
consumerism		continuation ...	kun **TIN** yoo **WAY** shun
....	kun **SOOHM** ur iz um ¶21	continue	kun **TIN** yooh *or*
consummate *(verb)* ..	**KAHN** suh mayt		kun **TIN** yoo
consummate *(adjective)* ..	kun **SUM** it	kun **TIN** yuh *is common in the*
consummation ...	KAHN suh **MAY** shun	*South.*
consumption	kun **SUMP** shun ¶6	continuity	
contact	**KAHN** takt ¶10	....	KAHN tuh **NOOH** uh tee ¶21
contagion	kun **TAY** jun	continuo	kun **TIN** yoo **WOH**
contaminate	kun **TAM** uh nayt	continuous	kun **TIN** yoo wus
contemplate	**KAHN** tum playt	continuum	kun **TIN** yoo wum
contemplative	kun **TEM** pluh tiv	contort	kun **TAWRT**
now occasionally		contortion	kun **TAWR** shun
KAHN tum **PLAY** tiv		contour	**KAHN** toor ¶21
contemporaneous		contra–	**KAHN** truh
....	kun **TEM** puh **RAY** nee us	*sometimes mistaken for*
contemporary		counter– **KOWN** tur
....	kun **TEM** puh **RER** ee ¶23	contraband	**KAHN** truh band
contempt	kun **TEMPT**	contrabass	**KAHN** truh bays
contemptuous ...	kun **TEMP** choo wus	contraception	KAHN truh **SEP** shun
content *(noun)*	**KAHN** tent	contract	kun **TRAKT**
content *(adjective)*	kun **TENT**	*When the verb means* to enter
contention	kun **TEN** shun ¶12	into *or* make a contract, *it is*
contest *(verb)*	kun **TEST**	*usually* **KAHN** trakt, *which is*
occasionally **KAHN** test		*standard for the noun.*

contraction	kun **TRAK** shun
contractor	kun **KAHN** trak tur

also kun **TRAK** tur, *generally when it means a thing, especially a muscle, that contracts*

contractual	.... kun **TRAK** choo wul ¶12
contradict	kahn truh **DIKT** ¶4
contradiction	.... kahn truh **DIK** shun ¶4
contralto	kun **TRAL** toh
contraption	kun **TRAP** shun
contrapuntal	KAHN truh **PUN** tul
contrariwise ...	**KAHN** trer ee WYZE *or* kun **TRER** ee WYZE ¶23
contrary *(noun)*	**KAHN** trer ee

For the adjective meaning perverse, it is usually kun **TRER** ee. ¶23

contrast *(noun)*	**KAHN** trast

The verb is nearly always kun **TRAST**.

contravene	kahn truh **VEEN** ¶4
contretemps	kohn truh **TAHN**

This French word is often Anglicized to various forms such as **KAHN** truh tahn *and* **KOHN** truh tahn.

contribute	kun **TRIB** yoot ¶1
contribution ..	KAHN truh **BYOOH** shun
contrite	kun **TRYTE**

occasionally **KAHN** tryte

contrition	kun **TRISH** un
contrivance	kun **TRYE** vuns ¶9
contrive	kun **TRYVE**

control	kun **TROHL**
controversial	
....	KAHN truh **VUR** shul ¶25
controversy	**KAHN** truh VUR see
controvert	**KAHN** truh vurt
contumacious	
....	KAHN too **MAY** shus ¶21
contumacy	**KAHN** too muh see *or* kun **TOOH** muh see ¶21
contumely	**KAHN** too muh lee *or* **KAHN** too MEE lee ¶21

kun **TOOH** muh lee *is now also heard.*

contusion	kun **TOOH** zhun ¶21
conundrum	kuh **NUN** drum
conurbation	KAHN ur **BAY** shun
convalesce	kahn vuh **LES**
convalescent	KAHN vuh **LES** unt
convection	kun **VEK** shun
convene	kun **VEEN**
convenience ..	kun **VEEN** yuns ¶9, 25
convent	**KAHN** vunt *or* **KAHN** vent

The second pronunciation is being heard more frequently these days ¶8.

convention	kun **VEN** shun ¶9, 12
converge	kun **VURJ**
convergence	kun **VUR** juns
conversant	kun **VUR** sunt

less frequently, **KAHN** vur sunt

conversation	KAHN vur **SAY** shun
converse *(verb)*	kun **VURS**
converse *(noun and adjective)*	
....	**KAHN** vurs
conversely	kun **VURS** lee

conversion	kun **VUR** zhun

kun **VUR** shun *is common in British English but is infrequent in American.*

convert *(verb)*	kun **VURT**
convert *(noun)*	**KAHN** vurt
convex	**KAHN** veks ¶2
convict *(verb)*	kun **VIKT**
convict *(noun)*	**KAHN** vikt
conviction	kun **VIK** shun
convince	kun **VINS** ¶9
convivial	kun **VIV** ee ul ¶25
convocation	
	KAHN vuh **KAY** shun ¶1
convoluted	**KAHN** vuh LOOHT id
convoy	**KAHN** voy
convulse	kun **VULS** ¶9
convulsion	kun **VUL** shun
coolant	**KOOHL** unt
cooperate	koh **AHP** uh rayt
cooperative	koh **AHP** ur uh tiv *or*
	koh **AHP** uh rayt iv *or* koh **AHP** ruh tiv
co–opt	koh **AHPT**
coordinate *(verb)*	koh **AWR** duh nayt
coordinate *(adjective and noun)*	
	koh **AWR** duh nit
coordination	koh AWR duh **NAY** shun
Copenhagen	KOH pun **HAY** gun *or*
	KOH pun **HAH** gun ¶2
Copernicus	kuh **PUR** ni kus ¶1
copier	**KAHP** ee ur
copious	**KOH** pee us ¶25
copulate	**KAHP** yuh layt
coquetry	**KOHK** uh tree *or*
	koh **KET** ree

coquette	koh **KET**
coral	**KAWR** ul ¶19
cordial	**KAWR** jul
cordiality	KAWR jee **AL** uh tee
cordon	**KAWR** dun
cordovan	**KAWR** duh vun
corduroy	**KAWR** duh roy

Some people say **KAWR** dyuh roy.

coriander	**KAWR** ee AN dur ¶2
Corinth	**KAWR** inth ¶9, 19
Corinthian	kuh **RIN** thee un ¶19
Coriolis (force)	KAWR ee **OH** lis
cormorant	**KAWR** mur unt
cornea	**KAWR** nee uh ¶25
cornice	**KAWR** nis
cornucopia	
	KAWR nuh **KOH** pee uh ¶25
corolla	kuh **RAHL** uh *or* kuh **ROHL** uh
corollary	**KAWR** uh LER ee ¶19, 23
corona	kuh **ROH** nuh
coronary	
	KAWR uh NER ee ¶19, 23
coronation	KAWR uh **NAY** shun ¶19
coroner	**KAWR** uh nur ¶19
corporal	**KAWR** pur ul ¶5
corporate	**KAWR** pur it ¶5
corporation	KAWR puh **RAY** shun
corporeal	kawr **PAWR** ee ul ¶25
corps	**KAWR**
corpse	**KAWRPS**
corpulent	**KAWR** pyoo lunt
corpuscle	**KAWR** PUS ul *or*
	KAWR pus ul
corpus delicti	KAWR pus di **LIK** tye *or*
	or di **LIK** tee

SPELLED	PRONOUNCED
corral	kuh **RAL** ¶1
correction	kuh **REK** shun
correlate *(verb)*	**KAWR** uh layt ¶19
The noun is usually **KAWR** uh lit.	
correlative	kuh **REL** uh tiv
correspond	kawr uh **SPAHND** ¶19
corridor	**KAWR** uh dur *or*
	KAWR uh dawr ¶8, 19
corrigendum	
	KAWR uh **JEN** dum ¶19
corroborate	kuh **RAHB** uh rayt
corroborative	kuh **RAHB** uh rayt iv
	or kuh **RAHB** ur uh tiv
corrode	kuh **ROHD**
corrosion	kuh **ROH** zhun
corrugate	**KAWR** uh gayt
corrupt	kuh **RUPT**
corruption	kuh **RUP** shun
corsage	kawr **SAHZH** ¶2, 15
corsair	**KAWR** ser
cortege	kawr **TEZH** *or* kawr **TAYZH**
Cortés	kawr **TEZ**
cortex	**KAWR** teks
cortical	**KAWR** ti kul
cortisone	**KAWR** tuh sohn ¶14
cosecant	koh **SEE** kant *or*
	koh **SEE** kunt ¶8
cosine	**KOH** syne
cosmetic	kahz **MET** ik
cosmetician	KAHZ muh **TISH** un
cosmetology	KAHZ muh **TAHL** uh jee
cosmography	kahz **MAH** gruh fee
cosmonaut	**KAHZ** muh nawt ¶19
cosmopolitan	
	KAHZ muh **PAHL** uh tun

SPELLED	PRONOUNCED
cosmos	**KAHZ** mohs *or*
	KAHZ mus ¶8
Cossack	**KAHS** ak *or* **KAHS** uk ¶19
now also **KOHS** ak	
Costa Rica	**KAHS** tuh **REE** kuh ¶19
costume	**KAHS** toohm ¶21
Côte d'Azur	KOHT dah **ZOOR**
coterie	**KOHT** ur ee
cotillion	koh **TIL** yun ¶1, 25
cotyledon	KAHT ul **EED** un
cougar	**KOOH** gur ¶8
council	**KOWN** sul ¶9
counsel	**KOWN** sul ¶9
countenance	**KOWN** tun uns ¶9
counter–	**KOWN** tur
counterfeit	**KOWN** tur fit
countess	**KOWN** tis
countrified	**KUN** tri fyde
country	**KUN** tree
county	**KOWN** tee
coup	**KOOH**
coup de grâce	kooh duh **GRAHS**
coup d'état	kooh day **TAH**
coupe	**KOOHP**
originally, but now rarely, **kooh PAY**	
coupon	**KOOH** pahn
KYOOH pahn *is common but is generally disapproved by those who say* **KOOH** pahn.	
courage	**KUR** ij
courageous	kuh **RAY** jus
courier	**KUR** ee ur ¶24
course	**KAWRS**
courteous	**KUR** tee us

courtesan .... **KAWR** tuh zun ¶14
  occasionally **KUR** tuh zun

courtesy .... **KUR** tuh see

courtier ... **KAWR** tee ur *or* **KAWR** tyur

court–martial ....
  .... **KAWRT** mahr shul ¶2

cousin .... **KUZ** un

couturier ...... kooh **TOOR** ee **AY** ¶21

covenant ....
  KUV uh nunt

Covent (Garden) .... **KUV** unt

cover .... **KUV** ur

covert .... **KOH** vurt ¶2

  *The earlier standard
  pronunciation* **KUV** urt *is heard less
  frequently now.*

covet .... **KUV** it

covetous .... **KUV** it us

covey .... **KUV** ee

coward .... **KOW** urd

cower .... **KOW** ur

cowl .... **KOWL** ¶7

Cowper's (glands) ...... **KOW** purz *or*
  KOOH purz

coxswain ... **KAHK** sun *or* **KAHK** swayn

coyote .... kye **OH** tee *or* **KYE** oht

craftsman ...... **KRAFTS** mun ¶10, 18

cranium .... **KRAY** nee um ¶25

crapulence .... **KRAP** yoo luns ¶9

cravat .... kruh **VAT**

craven .... **KRAY** vun

crayon ..... **KRAY** ahn *or* **KRAY** un ¶7
  also, in casual speech, **KRAN**

create .... kree **AYT**

creation .... kree **AY** shun

creativity ...... **KREE** ay **TIV** uh tee ¶1

creature .... **KREE** chur

crèche .... **KRESH**
  occasionally **KRAYSH**

credence .... **KREED** uns

credential ... kri **DEN** shul ¶9, 12

credenza .... kri **DEN** zuh

credible .... **KRED** uh bul

credo .... **KREE** doh *or* **KRAY** doh

credulity ..... kruh **DOOH** luh tee ¶21

credulous .... **KREJ** oo lus

creek .... **KREEK** *or* **KRIK**
  Until recently **KRIK** *predominated
  in the North and* **KREEK** *in the
  South, but now* **KREEK** *prevails
  everywhere.*

cremate .... **KREE** mayt
  occasionally kri **MAYT**

cremation .... kree **MAY** shun ¶1

crematory ...... **KREE** muh **TAWR** ee

crème de cacao ....
  .... KREM duh kuh **KAH** oh
  The crème *may also be* **KREEM**,
  and the cacao *may be* kuh **KAY** oh
  or **KOHK** oh, *the latter by confusion
  with* cocoa.

crème de menthe .. KREM duh **MAHNT**
  For crème *see preceding: for*
  menthe, **MENTH** *and* **MINT** *are also
  heard.*

Creole .... **KREE** ohl

creosote .... **KREE** uh soht

crepe .... **KRAYP**
  When the word means pancake,
  it may also be **KREP**, *and it is
  usually written* crêpe.

crêpe suzette	KRAYP **sooh** ZET *or* KREP **sooh** ZET
crepuscular	kri **PUS** kyoo lur
crescendo	kruh **SHEN** doh
crescent	**KRES** unt
Cressida	**KRES** i duh
crestfallen	**KREST** fawl un ¶10
cretaceous	kri **TAY** shus
cretin	**KREET** un
cretonne	**KREE** tahn *or* kri **TAHN**
crevasse	kri **VAS**
crevice	**KREV** is
crewel	**KROOH** ul ¶7
cribbage	**KRIB** ij
Crimea	krye **MEE** uh ¶1
criminal	**KRIM** uh nul ¶5
criminology	KRIM uh **NAHL** uh jee
crimson	**KRIM** zun ¶14
cringe	**KRINJ**
crinkle	**KRING** kul
crinoline	**KRIN** ul in
crisis	**KRYE** sis

The plural form crises *is* **KRYE** seez.

criterion	krye **TIR** ee un ¶25
criticism	**KRIT** uh siz um
criticize	**KRIT** uh syze
critique	kri **TEEK**
Croat	**KROH** at

The preceding is standard, but **KROHT** *is also heard.*

Croatia	kroh **AY** shuh
crochet	kroh **SHAY**
crocodile	**KRAHK** uh dyle
crocus	**KROH** kus

croissant	kruh **SAHNT** *or* kwah **SAHNT** ¶19

The French pronunciation has an r *in the first syllable and a nasalized vowel in the second,* krwah **SAHN**, *generally omitted by English speakers.*

Cro–Magnon	kroh **MAG** nun *or* kroh **MAN** yun
Cromwell	**KRAHM** wel *or* **KRAHM** wul *or* **KRUM** wul
crony	**KROH** nee
crooked	**KROOK** id

This is the pronunciation when the word means not straight *or* dishonest, *but when the meaning is* having a crook or hook (as a stick), *it is* **KROOKT**.

croquet	kroh **KAY**
croquette	kroh **KET**
crossbow	**KRAWS** boh ¶19
cross–legged	**KRAWS** leg id *or* **KRAWS** legd ¶19
crotchety	**KRAHCH** i tee
crouch	**KROWCH**
croupier	**KROOH** pee ay *or* **KROOH** pee ur *or* kroh **PYAY**
crouton	**KROOH** tahn ¶2, 8
crucial	**KROOH** shul
crucible	**KROOH** suh bul
crucifer	**KROOH** suh fur
crucifix	**KROOH** suh fiks
crucifixion	KROOH suh **FIK** shun
cruciform	**KROOH** suh fawrm
crucify	**KROOH** suh fye

SPELLED	PRONOUNCED	SPELLED	PRONOUNCED
crudités	krooh duh **TAY** or krooh dee **TAY**	–cule	**kyoohl** or **kyool**
crudity	**KROOH** duh tee	culinary	**KYOOH** luh **NER** ee or **KUL** uh **NER** ee ¶23
cruel	**KROOH** ul ¶7	culminate	**KUL** muh nayt
cruet	**KROOH** it	culotte	**KOOH** laht or koo **LAHT** ¶2, 21
cruise	**KROOHZ**		
cruller	**KRUL** ur	culpable	**KUL** puh bul
crumby	**KRUM** ee	culprit	**KUL** prit
crusade	krooh **SAYD**	cultivate	**KUL** tuh vayt
cruse	**KROOHZ** ¶14	culture	**KUL** chur
crustacean	krus **TAY** shun	culvert	**KUL** vurt
crux	**KRUKS**	cum	**KOOM** or **KUM**
		cumbersome	**KUM** bur sum
The alternative plural cruces *is* **KROOH** seez.		cum laude	koom **LOW** day or kum **LAW** dee
cryogenics	**KRYE** uh **JEN** iks ¶1	cummerbund	**KUM** ur bund ¶10
cryonics	krye **AHN** iks	cumulus	**KYOOHM** yuh lus
crypt	**KRIPT**	cuneiform	kyooh **NEE** uh fawrm or **KYOOH** nee uh **FAWRM** ¶21
cryptic	**KRIP** tik		
cryptography	krip **TAHG** ruh fee	cunnilingus	**KUN** uh **LING** gus
crystal	**KRIS** tul	cupboard	**KUB** urd
crystalline	**KRIS** tuh lin	Cupid	**KYOOH** pid
crystallize	**KRIS** tuh lyze	cupidity	kyoo **PID** uh tee
crystallography	**KRIS** tuh **LAHG** ruh fee	cupola	**KYOOH** puh luh
Cuba	**KYOOH** buh	Curaçao	kyoor uh **SOH** or koor uh **SOW** ¶21
cubic	**KYOOH** bik		
cubism	**KYOOH** biz um	curate	**KYOOR** it ¶24
cuckold	**KUK** uld	curative	**KYOOR** uh tiv ¶24
cuckoo	**KOOH** kooh or **KOOK** ooh	curator	kyoo **RAYT** ur or **KYOOR** ayt ur or **KYOOR** uh tur ¶24
cucumber	**KYOOH** kum bur		
cudgel	**KUJ** ul	curettage	kyoor uh **TAHZH**
cuirass	kwi **RAS**	*Though* kyoo **RET** ij *was frequent formerly, it is now rare.* ¶24	
cuisine	kwi **ZEEN**		
cul–de–sac	kul duh **SAK** or kool duh **SAK**	curfew	**KUR** fyooh
		curia	**KYOOR** ee uh ¶24

Curie .... kyoo **REE** *or* **KYOOR** ee

curio .... **KYOOR** ee oh

curiosa ... KYOOR ee **OH** suh ¶14, 24

curiosity ....

.... KYOOR ee **AHS** uh tee ¶24

curious .... **KYOOR** ee us ¶5, 24

curlew .... **KUR** looh ¶21

curlicue .... **KUR** li kyooh ¶1

curmudgeon .... kur **MUJ** un

currant .... **KUR** unt

currency .... **KUR** un see ¶9

current .... **KUR** unt

curriculum .... kuh **RIK** yuh lum

curry .... **KUR** ee

cursed .... **KUR** sid *or* **KURST**

  The first is heard only for the

  adjective.

cursive .... **KUR** siv

cursory .... **KUR** sur ee ¶5

curtail .... kur **TAYL**

curtain .... **KURT** un

curtsy .... **KURT** see

curvaceous .... kur **VAY** shus

curvature .... **KUR** vuh chur

cushion .... **KOOSH** un

Cushitic .... koo **SHIT** ik

cuspidor .... **KUS** puh dawr

cussed *(adjective)* .... **KUS** id

custodian .... kus **TOH** dee un

custody .... **KUS** tuh dee

custom .... **KUS** tum

cuticle .... **KYOOHT** i kul

cutlass .... **KUT** lus

cutlery .... **KUT** lur ee

cutlet .... **KUT** lit

cyanamide .... sye **AN** uh myde

sometimes sye **AN** uh mid; *also,*

especially formerly among

chemists, SYE uh **NAM** yde

cyanide .... **SYE** uh nyde

Cybele .... **SIB** uh lee

cybernetics .... SYE bur **NET** iks

cyclamate .... **SYKE** luh mayt

formerly also, but now rarely,

 SYKE luh mit

cycle .... **SYKE** ul

also, for the meaning

motorcycle, **SIK** ul

cyclic .... **SYKE** lik *or* **SIK** lik

cyclone .... **SYE** klohn

cyclonic .... sye **KLAHN** ik

Cyclops .... **SYE** klahps

cyclotron .... **SYKE** luh trahn

cylinder .... **SIL** un dur

cylindrical .... suh **LIN** dri kul

cymbal .... **SIM** bul

cynic .... **SIN** ik

cynicism .... **SIN** uh siz um

cypress .... **SYE** pruhs

Cypriot .... **SIP** ree ut

Cyprus .... **SYE** pruhs

Cyrillic .... suh **RIL** ik

cystic (fibrosis) .... **SIS** tik

cytology .... sye **TAHL** uh jee

cytoplasm .... **SYE** tuh plaz um

czar .... **ZAHR**

czarina .... zah **REE** nuh

Czech .... **CHEK**

Czechoslovakia ....

.... CHEK uh sloh **VAH** kee uh ¶1, 25

D

dachshund .... **DAHKS** hoond *or*
    DAHKS hoont *or* **DAHKS** unt
also occasionally, **DASH** hund
Dacron *(trademark)* .. **DAY** krahn *or*
    DAK rahn
dactyl .... **DAK** tul
Daedalus .... **DED** uh lus
also, especially British,
DEED uh lus
daffodil .... **DAF** uh dil
dahlia .... **DAL** yuh ¶18
daiquiri .... **DAK** ur ee ¶5
dais .... **DAY** is *or* **DYE** is
daisy .... **DAY** zee
Dakota .... duh **KOH** tuh
Dalai Lama .... **DAH** lye **LAH** muh
Dali .... **DAH** lee ¶2
dalliance .... **DAL** ee uns ¶9, 25
Dalmatian .... dal **MAY** shun
damage .... **DAM** ij
Damascus .... duh **MAS** kus
damask .... **DAM** usk
damnable .... **DAM** nuh bul
damnation .... dam **NAY** shun
damned .... **DAMD**
*also, in some preaching and
poetry,* **DAM** nid *or* **DAM** id
Damocles .... **DAM** uh kleez

Damon and Pythias ....
    .... **DAY** mun un **PITH** ee us
damsel .... **DAM** zul
dandelion .... **DAN** di **LYE** un ¶1
danger .... **DAYN** jur
Danish .... **DAY** nish
danseuse .. dahn **SOOZ** *or* dahn **SOOHZ**
Dante .... **DAHN** tay *or* **DAHN** tee ¶18
Danube .... **DAN** yoohb
Daphne .... **DAF** nee
Darjeeling .... dahr **JEE** ling
darnel .... **DAHR** nul
Dartmouth .... **DAHRT** muth
Darwinism .... **DAHR** win iz um
dashiki .... dah **SHEE** kee
data .... **DAYT** uh *or* **DAT** uh
occasionally **DAHT** uh
dative .... **DAYT** iv
datum .... **DAYT** um *or* **DAT** um
occasionally **DAHT** um
daub .... **DAWB** ¶19
daughter .... **DAWT** ur ¶19
dauntless .... **DAWNT** lis ¶19
dauphin .... **DAW** fin *or* doh **FAN**
davenport .... **DAV** un pawrt
da Vinci .... duh **VIN** chee ¶1
de– .... di *or* duh
*When the prefix is spoken with
a little force, it may be* dee.
deacon .... **DEEK** un
deaconess .... **DEEK** un is
dearth .... **DURTH**
debacle ..... di **BAHK** ul *or* day **BAHK** ul
debatable .... di **BAYT** uh bul ¶1
debauch .... di **BAWCH** ¶1

debauchee .... di baw **CHEE** or
             deb aw **CHEE** ¶12

debauchery ... di **BAWCH** ur ee ¶1, 5

debenture .... di **BEN** chur ¶1

debilitate .... di **BIL** uh tayt ¶1

debonair .... deb uh **NER** ¶23

debouch .... di **BOOHSH**

debrief .... dee **BREEF**

debris .... di **BREE** or day **BREE**

debt .... **DET**

debtor .... **DET** ur

debut ..... di **BYOOH** or day **BYOOH** or
             DAY byooh

debutante .... **DEB** yoo tahnt

decade ("ten years") .... **DEK** ayd
   In recent years, de **KAYD** *has*
   become rare; when the word is
   used to refer to a division of the
   rosary, it is usually **DEK** *ud.*

decadence .... **DEK** uh duns
   rarely de **KAYD** *uns* ¶9

decal .... di **KAL** or **DEE** kal

decalcomania ....
        di **KAL** kuh **MAY** nee uh ¶25

Decalogue .... **DEK** uh lawg ¶19

Decameron .... di **KAM** ur un ¶5

decant .... di **KANT** ¶1

decapitate .... di **KAP** uh tayt ¶1

decathlon .... di **KATH** lahn or
             di **KATH** lun

di **KATH** uh lahn *is heard sometimes*
but is not standard.

decease .... di **SEES** ¶1

deceit .... di **SEET** ¶1

deceive .... di **SEEV** ¶1

decelerate .... dee **SEL** uh rayt

decency .... **DEE** sun see ¶9

decent .... **DEE** sunt

deception .... di **SEP** shun ¶1

decibel .... **DES** uh bel or **DES** uh bul

deciduous .... di **SIJ** oo wus ¶1, 21

decimal .... **DES** uh mul

decimate .... **DES** uh mayt

decipher .... di **SYE** fur ¶1

decision .... di **SIZH** un ¶1

decisive .... di **SYE** siv ¶1

declamation .... **DEK** luh **MAY** shun

declamatory ..... di **KLAM** uh **TAWR** ee

declaration ..... **DEK** luh **RAY** shun

declarative .... di **KLAR** uh tiv ¶1, 23

déclassé .... day klahs **AY** ¶18

declension .. di **KLEN** shun ¶1, 9, 12

declination .... **DEK** luh **NAY** shun

decline .... di **KLYNE** ¶1

declivity .... di **KLIV** uh tee ¶1

decoder .... di **KOH** dur ¶1

décolletage .... day **KAHL** uh **TAHZH** or
            day kawl **TAHZH**

décolleté .... day **KAHL** uh **TAY** or
            day kawl **TAY**

decompose .... dee kum **POHZ**

decompress .... dee kum **PRESS**

decompression .... **DEE** kum **PRESH** un

decongestant .... **DEE** kun **JES** tunt

décor .... day **KAWR** ¶2

decorate .... **DEK** uh rayt

decoration .... **DEK** uh **RAY** shun

decorous .... **DEK** ur us
   de **KAWR** us *is now sometimes*
   heard.

decorum	di **KAWR** um
decoupage	day kooh **PAHZH**
decoy	di **KOY**

This is for the verb; the noun is now usually **DEE** koy.

decrease	di **KREES**

also, and for the noun usually, **DEE** krees ¶1

decrepit	di **KREP** it ¶1
decrepitude	di **KREP** uh toohd ¶21
decresendo	**DEE** kruh **SHEN** doh
dedicate	**DED** uh kayt
deduce	di **DOOHS** ¶1, 21
deduct	di **DUKT** ¶1
deduction	di **DUK** shun ¶1
de–escalate	dee **ES** kuh layt
deface	di **FAYS** ¶1
de facto	di **FAK** toh *or* day **FAK** toh ¶1
defamation	**DEF** uh **MAY** shun
defamatory	di **FAM** uh **TAWR** ee
defecate	**DEF** uh kayt
defect	**DEE** fekt

also, and for the verb always, di **FEKT** ¶1

defection	di **FEK** shun ¶1
defendant	di **FEN** dunt
defense	di **FENS** ¶1, 9

In sports, especially when contrasted with the offense, **DEE** fens *is very common.*

defer	di **FUR** ¶1
deference	**DEF** ur uns ¶5, 9
deferential	**DEF** uh **REN** shul ¶12
defiance	di **FYE** uns ¶1, 9

deficiency	di **FISH** un see ¶1, 9
deficit	**DEF** uh sit
define	di **FYNE** ¶1
definite	**DEF** uh nit ¶5
definition	**DEF** uh **NISH** un
definitive	di **FIN** uh tiv
deflate	di **FLAYT** ¶1
deflation	di **FLAY** shun ¶1
deflect	di **FLEKT** ¶1
deflection	di **FLEK** shun ¶1
defoliate	di **FOH** lee ayt ¶1
deform	di **FAWRM** ¶1
deformation	**DEE** fawr **MAY** shun
defy	di **FYE** ¶1
dégagé	day gah **ZHAY**
degenerate *(verb)*	di **JEN** uh rayt ¶1
degenerate *(noun and adjective)*	di **JEN** ur it ¶1
degenerative	di **JEN** ur uh tiv
degradation	**DEG** ruh **DAY** shun
degrade	di **GRAYD** ¶1
dehydrate	dee **HYE** drayt ¶1
deify	**DEE** uh fye
deign	**DAYN**
deism	**DEE** iz um
deity	**DEE** uh tee
déjà vu	day zhah **VOOH**
deject	di **JEKT** ¶1
dejection	di **JEK** shun ¶1
de jure	di **JOOR** ee *or* day **JOOR** ee ¶1, 15
delectable	di **LEK** tuh bul ¶1
delectation	di **LEK** **TAY** shun *or* **DEE** lek **TAY** shun ¶1

delegate .... DEL uh gayt
*This is for the verb, but the
noun is more often DEL uh git.*

delete .... di LEET

deleterious .... DEL uh TIR ee us

deletion .... di LEE shun

Delhi .... DEL ee

deliberate *(verb)* .... di LIB uh rayt

deliberate *(adjective)* ....
.... di LIB ur it ¶5

delicacy .... DEL i kuh see

delicate .... DEL i kit

delicatessen .... DEL i kuh TES un

delicious .... di LISH us ¶1

Delilah .... di LYE luh

delineate .... di LIN ee ayt ¶1

delinquency ....
.... di LING kwun see ¶1, 9

delirious .... di LIR ee us

delirium tremens
.... di LIR ee um TREE munz

deliver .... di LIV ur ¶1

deliverance .... di LIV ur uns ¶1, 5, 9

delivery .... di LIV ur ee ¶5

Delphi .... DEL fye

delphinium .... del FIN ee um ¶25

delude .... di LOOHD ¶1

deluge .... DEL yoohj

delusion .... di LOOH zhun ¶1

deluxe .... di LUKS ¶1
*di LOOKS and di LOOHKS are
becoming less and less frequent.*

demagogic .... DEM uh GAHG ik *or*
DEM uh GAHJ ik

demagogue .... DEM uh gahg ¶19

demagogy .... DEM uh GAH gee *or*
DEM uh GOH jee
sometimes DEM uh GAH jee ¶19

demarcation ...... DEE mahr KAY shun

demeanor .... di MEE nur

dementia .... di MEN shuh ¶9, 12, 25

demesne ... di MAYN *or* di MEEN

Demeter .... duh MEET ur
DEM uh tur *is now sometimes
heard.*

demigod .... DEM ee gahd

demise .... di MYZE

demitasse .... DEM ee tas *or*
DEM ee tahs

democracy .... di MAHK ruh see

democrat .... DEM uh krat

democratize .... di MAHK ruh TYZE

demography .... di MAHG ruh fee

demoiselle .... dem wuh ZEL

demolish .... di MAHL ish ¶1

demolition .... DEM uh LISH un

demon .... DEE mun

demoniac .... di MOH nee AK ¶1

demonology .... DEE muh NAHL uh jee

demonstrable ...... di MAHN struh bul

demonstrate .... DEM un strayt

demonstrative ...... di MAHN struh tiv

demure .... di MYOOR ¶1

demurrage .... di MUR ij

denatured .... dee NAY churd

dengue .... DENG gee
occasionally DENG gay

denial .... di NYE ul ¶1, 7

denier .... DEN yur

denigrate .... DEN uh grayt

denizen	**DEN** i zun
denomination	
	di NAHM uh **NAY** shun ¶1
denominator	
	di **NAHM** uh nayt ur ¶1
denotation	DEE noh **TAY** shun
denouement	day nooh **MAHN** or
	day **NOOH** mahn

*The n in mahn indicates that the
vowel is nasalized.*

denounce	di **NOWNS** ¶1, 9
density	**DEN** suh tee ¶9
dentifrice	**DEN** tuh fris
dentition	den **TISH** un
denture	**DEN** chur ¶9, 12
denude	di **NOOHD** ¶1, 21
denumerable	
	di **NOOH** mur uh bul ¶1, 21
denunciation	
	di NUN see **AY** shun ¶1, 9
deny	di **NYE** ¶1
deodorant	dee **OH** dur unt
deodorize	dee **OH** duh RYZE
departmental	di PAHRT **MEN** tul or
	DEE pahrt **MEN** tul
departure	di **PAHR** chur ¶1
depict	di **PIKT**
depilatory	di **PIL** uh TAWR ee ¶1
deplete	di **PLEET** ¶1
depletion	di **PLEE** shun ¶1
deportment	di **PAWRT** munt ¶1
depose	di **POHZ** ¶1
deposition	DEP uh **ZISH** un or
	DEE puh **ZISH** un
depository	di **PAHZ** uh TAWR ee

depot	**DEE** poh

in military and British usage,
DEP oh

deprave	di **PRAYV** ¶1
depravity	di **PRAV** uh tee ¶1
deprecate	**DEP** ruh kayt
deprecatory	**DEP** ruh kuh TAWR ee
depreciate	di **PREE** shee ayt ¶1
depredation	DEP ruh **DAY** shun
depressed	di **PREST** ¶1
depression	di **PRESH** un ¶1
deprivation	DEP ruh **VAY** shun
deprive	di **PRYVE** ¶1
deputize	**DEP** yuh tyze
deputy	**DEP** yuh tee
deracinate	di **RAS** uh nayt
derailleur	di **RAY** lur

*Attempts at the French produce
something like day rye **YUR**.*

derelict	**DER** uh likt
dereliction	DER uh **LIK** shun
deride	di **RYDE** ¶1
de rigueur	duh ree **GUR**
derision	di **RIZH** un
derisive	di **RYE** siv
derivation	DER uh **VAY** shun
derivative	di **RIV** uh tiv
dermatitis	DUR muh **TYTE** is
dermatology	DUR muh **TAHL** uh jee
derogate	**DER** uh gayt
derogatory	
	di **RAHG** uh TAWR ee ¶19
derrière	der ee **ER**
derringer	**DER** in jur
dervish	**DUR** vish

SPELLED	PRONOUNCED
desalination ..	DEE sal uh **NAY** shun *or* DEE say luh **NAY** shun
Descartes	day **KAHRT**
descend	di **SEND** ¶1
descendant	di **SEND** unt
descent	di **SENT** ¶1
describe	di **SKRYBE**
description	di **SKRIP** shun
desecrate	**DES** uh krayt
desegregation	dee SEG ruh **GAY** shun

Sometimes, by contrast with segregation, it is DEE seg ruh **GAY** shun.

desert *(verb)*	di **ZURT**
desert ("a sandy region")	**DEZ** urt
desert ("a reward or punishment")	di **ZURT**
desertification	di ZURT uh fi **KAY** shun
desertion	di **ZUR** shun ¶1
deserve	di **ZURV** ¶1
desiccate	**DES** i kayt
desideratum	di SID uh **RAYT** um *or* di SID uh **RAHT** um
design	di **ZYNE**
designate	**DEZ** ig nayt

also, for the adjective, **DEZ** ig nit

desire	di **ZYRE** ¶1, 7
desirous	di **ZYRE** us ¶7
desist	di **ZIST** ¶1, 14
Des Moines	di **MOYN**
desolate *(verb)*	**DES** uh layt
desolate *(adjective)*	**DES** uh lit
desolation	DES uh **LAY** shun

SPELLED	PRONOUNCED
despair	di **SPER**
desperado	DES puh **RAH** doh *or* DES puh **RAY** doh
desperate	**DES** pur it ¶5
desperation	DES puh **RAY** shun
despicable	**DES** pik uh bul *or* di **SPIK** uh bul
despise	di **SPYZE**
despondent	di **SPAHN** dunt
despot	**DES** put *or* DES paht
despotic	de **SPAHT** ik ¶1
dessert	di **ZURT** ¶1
destination	DES tuh **NAY** shun
destine	**DES** tin
destiny	**DES** tuh nee
destitute	**DES** tuh tooht ¶21
destroy	di **STROY**
destruction	di **STRUK** shun
desuetude	**DES** wi toohd ¶21
desultory	**DES** ul TAWR ee
detach	di **TACH** ¶1
detail	di **TAYL** *or* DEE tayl ¶1
detain	di **TAYN** ¶1
detect	di **TEKT** ¶1
detection	di **TEK** shun ¶1
détente	day **TAHNT**
detention	di **TEN** shun ¶1, 12
deter	di **TUR** ¶1
detergent	di **TUR** junt ¶1
deteriorate	di **TIR** ee uh rayt ¶1
determinant	di **TUR** mi nunt ¶1
determination	di TUR muh **NAY** shun ¶1
determine	di **TUR** mun ¶1
detest	di **TEST** ¶1

detestation	DEE tes **TAY** shun *or*
	di TES **TAY** shun
detonate	**DET** uh nayt
detour	DEE toor *or* di **TOOR**
detox	**DEE** tahks ¶2
detract	di **TRAKT** ¶1
detraction	di **TRAK** shun ¶1
detriment	**DET** ruh munt
detrimental	DET ruh **MEN** tul
detritus	di **TRYTE** us
deuce	**DOOHS** ¶21
deuced	**DOOH** sid *or* **DOOHST** ¶21
Deuteronomy	
....	DOOHT uh **RAHN** uh mee ¶21
deutsche mark	**DOY** chuh MAHRK
occasionally **DOYCH** mahrk	
devastate	**DEV** uh stayt
develop	di **VEL** up ¶1
devest	di **VEST** ¶1
deviate *(verb)*	**DEE** vee ayt
deviate *(noun and adjective)*	
....	**DEE** vee it
device	di **VYSE** ¶1
deviltry	**DEV** ul tree
devious	**DEE** vee us ¶5
devise	di **VYZE** ¶1
devolve	di **VAHLV** ¶1, 19
Devonian	di **VOH** nee un ¶25
devotee	dev uh **TEE** *or*
	dev uh **TAY** ¶2
devotion	di **VOH** shun ¶1
devour	di **VOWR** ¶1
devout	di **VOWT**
dew	**DOOH** ¶21
dexterity	dek **STER** uh tee

dexterous	**DEK** strus ¶5
diabetes	DYE uh **BEET** is *or*
	DYE uh **BEET** eez
The most common form of the	
disease is diabetes mellitus	
muh **LYTE** is.	
diabetic	DYE uh **BET** ik
diabolic	DYE uh **BAHL** ik
diabolism	dye **AB** uh liz um
diacritic	DYE uh **KRIT** ik
diadem	DYE uh dem *or*
	DYE uh dum ¶8
diagnose	DYE ug nohs ¶14
diagnosis	DYE ug **NOH** sis
diagnostic	DYE ug **NAHS** tik
diagnostician	DYE ug nahs **TISH** un
diagonal	dye **AG** uh nul
diagram	**DYE** uh gram
dial	**DYE** ul ¶7
dialect	**DYE** uh lekt ¶1
dialectic	DYE uh **LEK** tik
dialectician	DYE uh lek **TISH** un
dialogue	**DYE** uh lawg ¶19
dialysis	dye **AL** uh sis
diameter	dye **AM** uh tur
diametrical	DYE uh **MET** ri kul
diamond	**DYE** mund ¶5
diapason	DYE uh **PAY** zun ¶14
diaper	**DYE** pur ¶5
diaphanous	dye **AF** uh nus
diaphragm	**DYE** uh fram
diarrhea	DYE uh **REE** uh
diary	**DYE** uh ree ¶7
Diaspora	dye **AS** pur uh
diastole	dye **AS** tuh lee

diastolic	DYE uh **STAHL** ik	dignity	**DIG** nuh tee
diathermy	**DYE** uh THUR mee	digress	dye **GRES** ¶1
diatonic	DYE uh **TAHN** ik	digression	dye **GRESH** un ¶1
diatribe	**DYE** uh trybe	dilapidated	di **LAP** uh dayt id
dichotomy	dye **KAHT** uh mee	dilatation	DIL uh **TAY** shun *or*
dictate *(noun)*	**DIK** tayt		DYE luh **TAY** shun

The verb is also dik **TAYT** ¶2.

dictator	**DIK** tayt ur *or* dik **TAYT** ur	dilate	dye **LAYT** *or* **DYE** layt ¶1
dictatorial	DIK tuh **TAWR** ee ul	dilatory	**DIL** uh TAWR ee
dictionary	**DIK** shuh NER ee ¶23	dilemma	di **LEM** uh ¶1
dictum	**DIK** tum	dilettante	**DIL** uh tahnt ¶2

The Englishing of this Italian
word sometimes gives
DIL uh **TAHN** tee.

didactic	dye **DAK** tik	diligence	**DIL** uh juns ¶9
diesel	**DEE** zul ¶14	dilute	di **LOOHT** ¶1
diet	**DYE** ut	dimension	
dietary	**DYE** uh TER ee ¶23		duh **MEN** shun ¶1, 9, 12
dietetics	DYE uh **TET** iks	diminish	duh **MIN** ish
dietitian	DYE uh **TISH** un	diminution	DIM uh **NYOOH** shun
difference	**DIF** runs ¶5, 9		
differential	DIF uh **REN** shul ¶9, 12		

By reversing the two middle
syllables, some people produce
DIM yoo **NISH** un, *which is not*
standard. ¶4

differentiate		diminutive	duh **MIN** yoo tiv
	DIF uh **REN** shee ayt ¶9	dinar	di **NAHR**
difficult	**DIF** i kult ¶8	dinette	dye **NET**
diffidence	**DIF** uh duns ¶9	dinghy	**DING** ee *or* **DING** gee
diffraction	di **FRAK** shun	dingy	**DIN** jee
diffuse *(verb)*	di **FYOOHZ**	dinosaur	**DYE** nuh sawr
diffuse *(adjective)*	di **FYOOHS**	diocesan	dye **AHS** uh sun
diffusion	di **FYOOH** zhun	diocese	**DYE** uh sis *or* **DYE** uh sees
digest *(verb)*	di **JEST** ¶1	diode	**DYE** ohd
digest *(noun)*	**DYE** jest	Diogenes	dye **AHJ** uh NEEZ
digestive	di **JES** tiv	Dionysus	DYE uh **NYE** sus
digit	**DIJ** it	diopter	dye **AHP** tur ¶2
digital	**DIJ** it ul		
digitalis	DIJ uh **TAL** is		
dignify	**DIG** nuh fye		
dignitary	**DIG** nuh TER ee ¶23		

diorama .... DYE uh **RAM** uh ¶18

dioxin .... dye **AHK** sin

diphtheria .... dif **THIR** ee uh *or*
dip **THIR** ee uh ¶25

diphthong .... **DIF** thawng *or*
DIP thawng ¶19

diploma .... di **PLOH** muh

diplomacy .... di **PLOH** muh see

diplomat .... **DIP** luh mat

dipsomania ....
.... DIP suh **MAY** nee uh ¶1, 25

dipteran .... **DIP** tur un

diptych .... **DIP** tik

dire .... **DYRE** ¶7

direct .... di **REKT** ¶1

direction .... di **REK** shun ¶1

directly .... di **REKT** lee ¶1, 10

director .... di **REK** tur ¶1

directory .... di **REK** tur ee ¶1, 5

dirge .... **DURJ** ¶15

dirigible .... **DIR** i juh bul *or*
duh **RIJ** uh bul

dirndl .... **DURN** dul

disaster .... di **ZAS** tur ¶18

disastrous .... di **ZAS** trus

disburse .... dis **BURS** ¶6

discard *(verb)* .... dis **KAHRD**

discard *(noun)* .... **DIS** kahrd

discern .... di **SURN** ¶14

discharge .... dis **CHAHRJ**
The noun is usually
DIS chahrj ¶2.

disciple .... di **SYPE** ul

disciplinarian ....
.... DIS uh pli **NER** ee un ¶23, 25

discipline .... **DIS** uh plin

discography .... dis **KAHG** ruh fee

discombobulate ....
.... DIS kum **BAHB** yoo layt

discomfit .... dis **KUM** fit ¶19

discomfiture .... dis **KUM** fi chur

disconcert .... dis kun **SURT**

disconsolate .... dis **KAHN** suh lit

discord .... **DIS** kawrd

discordant .... dis **KAWR** dunt

discothèque .... **DIS** kuh tek ¶1, 2

discount .... **DIS** kownt
The verb is also dis **KOWNT.**

discourage .... dis **KUR** ij

discourse .... **DIS** kawrs
The noun is also dis **KAWRS,** *and
the verb is usually pronounced
this way* ¶2.

discourtesy .... dis **KUR** tuh see

discovery .... dis **KUV** ur ee ¶5

discredit .... dis **KRED** it

discreet .... dis **KREET**

discrepancy ..... dis **KREP** un see ¶9

discrete .... dis **KREET**

discretion .... dis **KRESH** un

discriminate .... dis **KRIM** uh nayt

discursive .... dis **KUR** siv

discus .... **DIS** kus

discuss .... dis **KUS**

discussion .... dis **KUSH** un

disdain .... dis **DAYN** ¶14

disease .... di **ZEEZ**

disembowel .... DIS im **BOW** ul

disgruntled .... dis **GRUN** tuld

disguise .... dis **GYZE**

SPELLED	PRONOUNCED	SPELLED	PRONOUNCED

disgust .... dis **GUST**
   by assimilation dis **KUST**, *the same*
   as discussed ¶6

dishabille .... dis uh **BEEL**

disheveled .... di **SHEV** uld

disintegrate .... di **SIN** tuh grayt

dislocate .... **DIS** loh kayt *or*
                     dis **LOH** kayt

dismal .... **DIZ** mul

dismantle .... dis **MAN** tul

dismay .... dis **MAY**

dismember .... dis **MEM** bur

dismiss .... dis **MIS**

disparage .... dis **PAR** ij ¶23

disparate .... **DIS** pur it

disparity .... dis **PAR** uh tee ¶23

dispel .... dis **PEL**

dispensary .... dis **PEN** suh ree

dispensation ... **DIS** pun **SAY** shun ¶1

dispense .... dis **PENS** ¶9

disperse .... dis **PURS**

dispersion .... dis **PUR** zhun *or*
                    dis **PUR** shun

dispirit .... di **SPIR** it

disport .... dis **PAWRT**

disposal .... dis **POH** zul

dispose .... dis **POHZ**

disposition .... **DIS** puh **ZISH** un

disputant .... dis **PYOOHT** unt *or*
                 DIS pyoo tunt

disputatious .... **DIS** pyoo **TAY** shus

disquisition .... **DIS** kwuh **ZISH** un

Disraeli .... diz **RAY** lee

disrupt .... dis **RUPT**

disruption .... dis **RUP** shun

dissect .... di **SEKT** ¶1

dissection .... di **SEK** shun ¶1

dissemble .... di **SEM** bul

disseminate .... di **SEM** uh nayt

dissension .... di **SEN** shun ¶9, 12

dissent .... di **SENT**

dissertation .... **DIS** ur **TAY** shun

dissident .... **DIS** uh dunt

dissimilation ...... di **SIM** uh **LAY** shun

dissipate .... **DIS** uh payt

dissipation .... **DIS** uh **PAY** shun

dissociate .... di **SOH** shee ayt ¶11

dissolute .... **DIS** uh looht

dissolution .... **DIS** uh **LOOH** shun

dissolve .... di **ZAHLV** ¶19

dissonance .... **DIS** uh nuns ¶9

dissuade .... di **SWAYD**

distaff .... **DIS** taf ¶18

distant .... **DIS** tunt

distaste .... dis **TAYST**

distemper .... dis **TEM** pur

distill .... dis **TIL**

distillate ...... **DIS** tuh layt *or* **DIS** tuh lit
   also dis **TIL** ut

distillation .... **DIS** tuh **LAY** shun

distinct .... dis **TINGKT**

distinction .... dis **TINGK** shun ¶9

distingué .... dis tang **GAY**

distinguish .... dis **TING** gwish

distort .... dis **TAWRT**

distortion .... dis **TAWR** shun

distract .... dis **TRAKT**

distraction .... dis **TRAK** shun

distraught .... dis **TRAWT**

distress .... dis **TRES**

SPELLED	PRONOUNCED
distribute	dis **TRIB** yoot ¶1
distribution	DIS truh **BYOOH** shun
distributor	dis **TRIB** yoo tur
district	**DIS** trikt
disturb	dis **TURB**
disuse *(noun)*	dis **YOOHS**
dither	**DIDH** ur
dithyramb	**DITH** uh ram *or* **DITH** uh ramb
diuretic	DYE yoo **RET** ik
diurnal	dye **UR** nul
diva	**DEE** vuh
divan	**DYE** van *or* di **VAN**
diverge	di **VURJ** ¶1
diverse	dye **VURS** ¶1, 2
diversion	di **VUR** zhun ¶1
divert	di **VURT** ¶1
divest	di **VEST** ¶1
divestiture	di **VEST** i chur
divide	di **VYDE**
dividend	**DIV** uh dend
DIV uh dund *is now less common.* ¶8	
divination	DIV uh **NAY** shun
divine	di **VYNE**
divinity	di **VIN** uh tee
divisible	di **VIZ** uh bul
division	di **VIZH** un
divisive	di **VYE** siv *or* di **VIS** iv
divorce	di **VAWRS**
divorcée	di vawr **SAY** *or* di vawr **SEE** ¶2
divot	**DIV** ut
divulge	di **VULJ**
Dixieland	**DIK** see land

SPELLED	PRONOUNCED
Doberman pinscher	**DOH** bur mun **PIN** shur ¶12
docent	**DOH** sunt *or* doh **TSENT**
docile	**DAHS** ul
doctorate	**DAHK** tur it ¶5
doctrinaire	dahk truh **NER**
doctrine	**DAHK** trun
docudrama	**DAHK** yuh **DRAH** muh ¶18
document *(verb)*	**DAHK** yuh ment
document *(noun)*	**DAHK** yuh munt
documentary	**DAHK** yuh **MEN** tur ee ¶5
documentation	**DAHK** yuh men **TAY** shun ¶1
doer	**DOOH** ur
doge	**DOHJ**
dogged	**DAW** gid ¶19
doggerel	**DAW** gur ul ¶5, 19
doggone	**DAWG GAWN** ¶10, 19
dogie	**DOH** gee
dogma	**DAWG** muh ¶19
dogmatic	dawg **MAT** ik ¶19
doily	**DOY** lee
dolce vita	**DOHL** chay **VEE** tah
doldrums	**DAHL** drumz ¶20
doleful	**DOHL** ful
dolman	**DAHL** mun ¶20
dolorous	**DOH** lur us ¶20
dolphin	**DAHL** fun ¶19
dolt	**DOHLT**
domain	doh **MAYN** ¶1
domestic	duh **MES** tik ¶1
domesticity	**DOH** mes **TIS** uh tee ¶1, 20

domicile .... **DAHM** uh syle ¶20
DAHM uh sil *is no longer common.*

dominant .... **DAHM** uh nunt

dominate .... **DAHM** uh nayt

domineering .... DAHM uh **NIR** ing

Dominican .... duh **MIN** i kun

dominion .... duh **MIN** yun ¶1

domino .... **DAHM** uh noh

donate .... **DOH** nayt ¶2

donation .... doh **NAY** shun ¶1

Donegal .... **DAHN** uh gawl *or*
dun uh **GAWL**

Don Juan .... DAHN **WAHN** *or*
DAHN **JOOH** un

donkey .... **DAWNG** kee *or*
DUNG kee ¶19

Don Quixote ... DOHN kee **HOH** tay *or*
DAHN kee **HOHT** ee ¶20
DAHN **KWIK** sut *is chiefly British.*

doomsday .... **DOOHMZ** day

doozy .... **DOOH** zee

dopamine .... **DOH** puh meen ¶22

doppelgänger .... **DAHP** ul GANG ur *or*
DAWP ul GENG ur

Doric .... **DAWR** ik ¶19

dormant .... **DAWR** munt

dorsal .... **DAWR** sul

dos-à-dos .... **DOH** see **DOH**

dosage .... **DOHS** ij

dossier .... **DAHS** ee ay ¶19

Dostoevski ....
.... DAWS taw **YEF** skee ¶19

dotage .... **DOHT** ij

dotard .... **DOHT** urd

Douay .... dooh **AY** ¶2

double-entendre ....
.... DOOH blahn **TAHN** druh
DOOH blahn **TAHND** *and*
DUB ul ahn **TAHND** *are also heard,*
the second being a thorough
Americanization.

doublet .... **DUB** lit

doubloon .... duh **BLOOHN**

doubly .... **DUB** lee ¶7

doubt .... **DOWT**

douche .... **DOOHSH**

dough .... **DOH**

doughty .... **DOWT** ee

doughy .... **DOH** ee

dour .. **DOOR** *or* **DOOHR** *or* **DOWR** ¶7

douse .... **DOWS**
Douse *meaning* to drench *is*
sometimes **DOWZ**.

dowager .... **DOW** uh jur

dowdy .... **DOW** dee

dowel .... **DOW** ul ¶7

dower .... **DOW** ur ¶7

Down's (syndrome) .... **DOWNZ**

dowry .... **DOW** ree ¶7

dowse .... **DOWZ**

doxology .... dahk **SAHL** uh jee

dozen .... **DUZ** un

drachm .... **DRAM**

drachma .... **DRAK** muh

Draconian .... dray **KOH** nee un *or*
dra **KOH** nee un ¶1

draftee .... draf **TEE** ¶18

draftsman ..... **DRAFTS** mun ¶10, 18

dragon .... **DRAG** un

dragoon .... druh **GOOHN**

drama .... DRAH muh ¶18

dramatic .... druh MAT ik

dramatis personae ....

.... DRAM uh tis pur SOH nee *or*
DRAHM uh tis pur SOH nee
druh MAT is *is now heard
sometimes.*

dramatize .... DRAM uh tyze ¶18

dramaturgy .... DRAM uh TUR jee

drapery .... DRAY pur ee ¶5

draughts .... DRAFTS ¶10, 18

drawer .... DRAW ur
*for the sliding box in a bureau,
desk, etc.,* DRAWR

dread .... DRED

dreadnought .... DRED nawt ¶19

dreary .... DRIR ee

Dreiser .... DRYE sur ¶14

Dresden .... DREZ dun

Dreyfus .... DRAY fus *or* DRYE fus

drivel .... DRIV ul

drogue .... DROHG

droll .... DROHL

dromedary .. DRAHM uh DER ee ¶23

dross .... DRAWS ¶19

drought .... DROWT *or* DROWTH

drowse .... DROWZ

drudgery .... DRUJ ur ee ¶5

drudville .... DROOH id

drunkard .... DRUNG kurd

drunkometer ..... DRUNG kuh MEET ur
or drung KAHM uh tur

druthers .... DRUDH urz

dryad .... DRYE ud ¶1

dual .... DOOH ul ¶7, 21

dubiety ...... dooh BYE uh tee ¶1, 21

dubious .... DOOH bee us ¶5, 21

ducal ....,..... DOOH kul ¶21

ducat .... DUK ut

duchess .... DUCH is

duchy .... DUCH ee

ductile .... DUK tul ¶22

dudgeon .... DUJ un

due .... DOOH ¶21

duel .... DOOH ul ¶7, 21

duet .... dooh ET ¶21

Dufy .... dooh FEE

dulcet .... DUL sit

dulcimer .... DUL suh mur

dullard .... DUL urd

duly .... DOOH lee ¶21

Dumas .... dooh MAH ¶2

dunce .... DUNS ¶9

dunderhead .... DUN dur hed

dune .... DOOHN ¶21

dungarees .... dung guh REEZ ¶2, 16

dungeon .... DUN jun

Dunkirk .... DUN kurk ¶16

duo .... DOOH oh ¶21

duodenum ...... DOOH uh DEE num *or*
dooh AHD uh num ¶21

dupe .... DOOHP ¶21

duple .... DOOH pul ¶21

duplex .... DOOH pleks ¶21

duplicate *(verb)* ....

.... DOOH pluh kayt ¶21

duplicate *(noun and adjective)* ......

.... DOOH pluh kit ¶21

duplicitous .... dooh PLIS uh tus ¶21

du Pont .... dooh PAHNT ¶2, 21

durable .... **DOOR** uh bul ¶21, 24
duration .... duh **RAY** shun ¶1, 21
Dürer .... **DYOOR** ur
duress .... doo **RES** ¶21
during .... **DOOR** ing ¶21, 24
durum .... **DOOR** um ¶21
dusky .... **DUS** kee
Düsseldorf .... **DOOS** ul dawrf
dutiful .... **DOOHT** uh ful ¶21
duty .... **DOOHT** ee ¶21
duumvirate .... dooh **UM** vuh rit
Dvořák .... **DVAWR** zhahk ¶19
dwarf .... **DWAWRF**
dwindle .... **DWIN** dul
dyad .... **DYE** ad ¶1
dybbuk .... **DIB** uk
dynamic .... dye **NAM** ik
dynamism .... **DYE** nuh miz um
dynamite .... **DYE** nuh myte
dynamo .... **DYE** nuh moh
dynamometer .. DYE nuh **MAHM** uh tur
dynasty .... **DYE** nus tee
dynel .... dye **NEL**
dysentery .... **DIS** un **TER** ee
dysfunction .... dis **FUNGK** shun ¶12
dyslexia .... dis **LEK** see uh ¶11
dysmenorrhea ..... DIS men uh **REE** uh
dyspepsia .... dis **PEP** shuh ¶11
dyspeptic .... dis **PEP** tik
dysphasia ... dis **FAY** zhuh ¶11
dysphoria .... dis **FAWR** ee uh
dysplasia .... dis **PLAY** zhuh ¶11
dystrophic .... dis **TRAHF** ik ¶20
dystrophy .... **DIS** truh fee
dysuria .... dis **YOOR** ee uh

E

eager .... **EE** gur
eagle .... **EE** gul
Earhart .... **ER** hahrt
earl .... **URL**
early .... **UR** lee
earnest .... **UR** nist
earth .... **URTH**
ease .... **EEZ**
easel .... **EE** zul
easement .... **EEZ** munt
easily .... **EE** zul ee ¶5
easterly .... **EES** tur lee
easy .... **EE** zee
eatery .... **EET** ur ee
eau de Cologne ..... OH duh kuh **LOHN**
eaves .... **EEVZ**
ebony .... **EB** uh nee
ebullient .... i **BOOL** yunt or i **BUL** yunt
ecce homo .... EK ay **HOH** moh or
.... EK see **HOH** moh

In Church Latin, the first word
is pronounced **E** *chay.*

eccentric .... ik **SEN** trik ¶1
eccentricity ... EK sen **TRIS** uh tee ¶1
Ecclesiastes .. i **KLEE** zee **AS** teez ¶1
ecclesiastical ....
.... i **KLEE** zee **AS** ti kul ¶1
echelon .... **ESH** uh lahn ¶5

echeveria .... ECH uh VER ee uh *or*
              EK uh VER ee uh

echinoderm .... i KYE nuh DURM *or*
              EK uh nuh DURM

echo .... EK oh

echoic .... e KOH ik ¶1

echolalia .... EK oh LAY lee uh ¶1

éclair .... ay KLER *or* ee KLER ¶1

éclat .... ay KLAH

eclectic .... i KLEK tik ¶1

eclecticism ..... i KLEK tuh siz um ¶1

eclipse .... i KLIPS ¶1

ecology .... ee KAHL uh jee ¶1

economic .... EE kuh NAHM ik *or*
              EK uh NAHM ik

economize .... i KAHN uh myze ¶1

economy .... i KAHN uh mee ¶1

ecosphere .... EE koh sfir ¶1

ecru .... EK rooh *or* AY krooh ¶2

ecstasy .... EK stuh see

ecstatic .... ik STAT ik ¶1

ectoderm .... EK tuh durm

ectoplasm .... EK tuh plaz um ¶1

Ecuador .... EK wuh dawr

ecumenical .... EK yoo MEN uh kul

ecumenism .... e KYOOH mun iz um *or*
              EK yoo mun iz um

eczema .... EK suh muh *or* EG zuh muh
              or ig ZEE muh

Edam (cheese) ..... EE dum *or* EE dam

edelweiss .... AY dul vyse
   ED ul wyse *is an Englished*
   pronunciation that is sometimes
   heard.

edema .... i DEE muh

edible .... ED uh bul

edict .... EE dikt

edification .... ED uh fi KAY shun

edifice .... ED uh fis

edify .... ED uh fye

Edinburgh .... ED un BUR uh *or*
              ED un BUR oh

edition .... i DISH un ¶1

editor .... ED i tur

editorial ...... ED uh TAWR ee ul ¶25

educable .... EJ uh kuh bul

educate .... EJ uh kayt

educe .... i DOOHS ¶1, 21

Edwardian ....
          ed WAHR dee un ¶19, 25

e'er .... ER
   This word will be heard most
   often in poetry.

eerie .... IR ee

efface .... i FAYS ¶1

effect .... i FEKT ¶1

effectual .... i FEK choo wul ¶1

effectuate .... i FEK choo wayt ¶1

effeminacy .... i FEM uh nuh see ¶1

effeminate .... i FEM uh nit ¶1

effervesce .... ef ur VES

effete .... e FEET ¶1

efficacious .... EF uh KAY shus

efficacy .... EF i kuh see

efficiency .... i FISH un see ¶1, 9

efficient .... i FISH unt ¶1

effigy .... EF uh jee

effluence .... EF loo wuns ¶9

effluvium .... i FLOOH vee um ¶1

effort .... EF urt

effrontery	i **FRUN** tur ee ¶1	elaborate *(adjective)*	
effulgence	i **FUL** juns ¶1, 9		i **LAB** uh rit ¶5
effuse	i **FYOOHZ** ¶1	élan	ay **LAHN**
effusion	i **FYOOH** zhun ¶1	elapse	i **LAPS** ¶1
effusive	i **FYOOH** siv ¶1	elastic	i **LAS** tik ¶1
egalitarian		elasticity	i **LAS TIS** uh tee *or*
	i **GAL** uh **TAR** ee un ¶1, 23		EE las **TIS** uh tee ¶1
ego	**EE** goh	elasticize	i **LAS** tuh syze ¶1
egocentric	**EE** goh **SEN** trik	elate	i **LAYT** ¶1
egoist	**EE** goh ist	Elbe	**EL** buh *or* **ELB**
egotism	**EE** guh tiz um	El Dorado	**EL** duh **RAH** doh *or*
egotist	**EE** guh tist		EL duh **RAY** doh ¶18
egregious	i **GREE** jus	elect	i **LEKT** ¶1
egress	**EE** gres	election	i **LEK** shun ¶1
egret	**EE** grit	elector	i **LEK** tur ¶1, 8
Egypt	**EE** jipt	electoral	i **LEK** tur ul ¶1, 5
Egyptian	i **JIP** shun ¶1	electorate	i **LEK** tur it ¶1, 5
eider	**EYE** dur	Electra	i **LEK** truh ¶1
Eiffel (Tower)	**EYE** ful	electric	i **LEK** trik ¶1
eighteen	ay **TEEN** ¶6	electrician	i LEK **TRISH** un *or*
eighteenth	ay **TEENTH** ¶9		EE lek **TRISH** un
eighth	**AYTTH** ¶6	electricity	i LEK **TRIS** uh tee ¶1
eightieth	**AYT** ee ith	electrify	i **LEK** truh fye ¶1
eighty	**AYT** ee	electrocardiogram	
Einstein	**EYNE** styne	... i LEK troh **KAHR** dee uh GRAM ¶1	
Eisenhower	**EYE** zun **HOW** ur	electrocute	i **LEK** truh KYOOHT ¶1
either	**EE** dhur	electrode	i **LEK** trohd ¶1
EYE dhur, *the usual British pronunciation, is also frequently heard in America.*		electroencephalogram	
		... i LEK troh en **SEF** uh luh GRAM ¶1	
ejaculate	i **JAK** yuh layt	electrolysis	i LEK **TRAHL** uh sis *or*
eject	i **JEKT** ¶1		EE lek **TRAHL** uh sis
eke	**EEK**	electrolyte	i **LEK** truh LYTE ¶1
elaborate *(verb)*	i **LAB** uh rayt	electron	i **LEK** trahn ¶1
		electronics	i LEK **TRAHN** iks *or*
			EE lek **TRAHN** iks

SPELLED	PRONOUNCED	SPELLED	PRONOUNCED
eleemosynary		elope .... i LOHP ¶1
.... EL uh MAHS uh NER ee *or*		eloquence .... EL uh kwuns ¶9
EL ee uh MAHS uh NER ee ¶23		El Salvador .... el SAL vuh dawr
elegant .... EL uh gunt		elucidate .... i LOOH suh dayt ¶1
elegiac .... EL uh JYE uk		elude .... i LOOHD ¶1
i LEE jee ak *is also heard*		elusion .... i LOOH zhun ¶1
occasionally.		elusive .... i LOOH siv ¶1
elegy .... EL uh jee		Elysian (fields) .... i LIZH un ¶25
element .... EL uh munt		emaciate .... i MAY shee ayt ¶11
elemental .... EL uh MEN tul		emanate .... EM uh nayt
elementary ..... EL uh MEN tur ee ¶5		emancipate .... i MAN suh payt ¶1, 9
elephant .... EL uh funt		emasculate .... i MAS kyuh layt ¶1
elephantiasis .... EL uh fun TYE uh sis		embalm .... im BAHM
elephantine ..... EL uh FAN teen ¶22		im BAHLM *is a spelling*
Eleusinian ..... EL yoo SIN ee un ¶25		*pronunciation.* ¶1
elevate .... EL uh vayt		embankment .... im BANGK munt
eleven .... i LEV un ¶1		embarcadero ....
Elgin (marbles) .... EL gun		.... em BAHR kuh DER oh ¶1
El Greco .... el GREK oh		embargo .... im BAHR goh ¶1
elicit .... i LIS it ¶1		embark .... im BAHRK ¶1
elide .... i LYDE ¶1		embarrass .... im BAR us ¶23
eligible .... EL i juh bul		embassy .... EM buh see
Elijah .... i LYE juh		embellish .... im BEL ish ¶1
elision .... i LIZH un ¶1		embezzle .... im BEZ ul
elite .... i LEET *or* ay LEET ¶1		emblazon .... im BLAY zun
elixir .... i LIK sur		emblem .... EM blum
Elizabethan .... i LIZ uh BEE thun		emblematic .... EM bluh MAT ik
ellipse .... i LIPS ¶1		embodiment ... im BAHD ee munt ¶1
ellipsis .... i LIP sis ¶1		embolism .... EM buh liz um
elliptical .... i LIP ti kul		emboss .... im BAWS ¶19
El Niño .... el NEE nyoh		embouchure ... ahm boo SHOOR ¶2
elocution .... EL uh KYOOH shun		embrace .... im BRAYS ¶1
elongate .... i LAWNG gayt ¶1, 19		embrasure .... im BRAY zhur ¶1
elongation ...... i LAWNG GAY shun *or*		embroider .... im BROY dur ¶1
EE lawng GAY shun ¶19		embryo .... EM bree oh

73

SPELLED	PRONOUNCED	SPELLED	PRONOUNCED

embryology .... EM bree AHL uh jee

embryonic .... EM bree AHN ik

emcee .... EM SEE

emend .... i MEND ¶1

emendation .... EE men DAY shun
  rarely EM un DAY shun ¶1

emerald .... EM ur uld ¶5

emerge .... i MURJ ¶1

emergency .... i MUR jun see ¶1, 9

emeritus .... i MER uh tus ¶1

emersion .... i MUR zhun *or* i MUR shun

emery .... EM ur ee ¶5

emetic .... i MET ik ¶1

emigrate .... EM uh grayt

émigré .... EM uh gray *or* ay muh GRAY

eminence .... EM uh nuns ¶9

emir .... i MIR *or* e MIR

emissary .... EM uh SER ee ¶23

emission .... i MISH un ¶1

emit .... i MIT ¶1

Emmanuel .... i MAN yoo wul ¶1

emollient .... i MAHL yunt ¶25

emolument ..... i MAHL yoo munt ¶1

emote .... i MOHT ¶1

emotion .... i MOH shun ¶1

empathize .... EM puh thyze

empathy .... EM puh thee

emperor .... EM pur ur ¶5

emphasis .... EM fuh sis ¶6, 9

emphatic .... im FAT ik ¶1, 6

emphysema ..... EM fuh SEE muh ¶6

empire *(noun)* .... EM pyre
  The adjective Empire, *referring
  to styles of the first French
  Empire, is usually* ahm PIR.

empirical .... im PIR i kul ¶1

empiricism .... im PIR uh siz um ¶1

employee .... im PLOY ee *or*
  im ploy EE ¶1

emporium .... em PAWR ee um

empty .... EM tee ¶1

emu .... EE myooh ¶21

emulate .... EM yuh layt

emulsify .... i MUL suh fye ¶1

emulsion .... i MUL shun ¶1

enamel .... i NAM ul ¶1

enamor .... i NAM ur ¶1

encapsulate .. in KAP suh layt ¶1, 21

encephalitis ... en SEF uh LYTE is ¶1

enchant .... in CHANT ¶1, 18

enchilada .... EN chuh LAH duh

enclave .... EN klayv *or* AHN klayv

encomium .... en KOH mee um

encompass .... in KUM pus ¶1

encore .... AHNG kawr ¶2, 16

encumber .... in KUM bur ¶1

encyclical .... in SIK li kul

encyclopedia ....
  .... in SYE kluh PEE dee uh ¶1

endearment .... in DIR munt ¶1

endeavor .... in DEV ur ¶1

endemic .... en DEM ik

endive ....EN dyve
  AHN deev *is becoming rare.*

endocrine .... EN duh krin ¶22

endorphin .... en DAWR fin

endorse .... in DAWRS ¶1

endorsee .... in dawr SEE *or*
  en dawr SEE

endow .... in DOW ¶1

endurance ... in **DOOR** uns ¶1, 9, 21

endure .... in **DOOR** ¶1, 21

enema .... **EN** uh muh

enemy .... **EN** uh mee

energize .... **EN** ur jyze

enervate .... **EN** ur vayt

enfilade .... **EN** fuh layd ¶2

en garde .... ahn **GAHRD**

engender .... in **JEN** dur ¶1

engine .... **EN** jun

engineer .... en juh **NIR**

England .... **ING** glund

English .... **ING** glish

engrave .... in **GRAYV** ¶1

engross .... in **GROHS** ¶1

enhance .... in **HANS** ¶1, 9, 18

enigma .... uh **NIG** muh

enigmatic .... **EN** ig **MAT** ik

en masse .... en **MAS**

ahn **MAHS** *is closer to the French
pronunciation.*

enmity .... **EN** muh tee

ennoble .... i **NOH** _bul_ ¶1

ennui .... **AHN** wee *or* ahn **WEE**

enormity .... i **NAWR** muh tee ¶1

enormous .... i **NAWR** mus ¶1

enough .... i **NUF** ¶1

enquire .... in **KWYRE**

en route ..... ahn **ROOHT** *or* en **ROOHT**

ensconce .... in **SKAHNS** ¶1

ensemble .... ahn **SAHM** bul

ensign .... **EN** syne

*also, and for the naval officer
always,* **EN** sun

ensilage .... **EN** sul ij

ensue .... en **SOOH** ¶1, 21

ensure .... in **SHOOR** ¶1

entablature ...... en **TAB** luh chur ¶1

entail .... in **TAYL** ¶1

entente .... ahn **TAHNT**

enteritis .... **EN** tuh **RYTE** is

enterprise .... **EN** tur pryze ¶3

entertain .... en tur **TAYN**

enthuse .... in **THOOHZ** ¶1, 21

enthusiasm ....

.... in **THOOH** zee az um ¶1

enthusiast .... in **THOOH** zee **AST** *or*

in **THOOH** zee ust ¶1

entice .... in **TYSE** ¶1

entire .... in **TYRE** ¶1

entirety .... in **TYRE** tee ¶1

entitle .... in **TYTE** ul ¶1

entity .... **EN** tuh tee

entomology .... **EN** tuh **MAHL** uh jee

entourage .... ahn too **RAHZH**

entrails .... **EN** traylz *or* **EN** trulz

entrance *(noun)* .... **EN** truns ¶9

entrance *(verb)* .... in **TRANS** ¶1, 18

entree .... **AHN** tray ¶2

entrepôt .... **AHN** truh poh

entrepreneur ....

.... **AHN** truh pruh **NOOR** ¶21, 24

entropy .... **EN** truh pee

enumerate .. i **NOOH** muh rayt ¶1, 21

enunciate ...... i **NUN** see ayt ¶1, 11

envelop .... in **VEL** up ¶1

envelope .... **EN** vuh lohp *or*

AHN vuh lohp

environment ...... in **VYE** run munt ¶1

in **VYE** urn munt ¶1, 4

75

SPELLED	PRONOUNCED	SPELLED	PRONOUNCED
environs	in **VYE** runz ¶4	epoch	**EP** uk
envisage	en **VIZ** ij	eponym	**EP** uh nim
envoy	**EN** voy *or* **AHN** voy	epoxy	e **PAHK** see
enzyme	**EN** zyme	Epsom	**EP** sum
eon	**EE** ahn *or* **EE** un	equable	**EK** wuh bul
–eous	ee us *or* yus ¶25	equal	**EE** kwul
epaulet	**EP** uh let ¶1, 2	equality	i **KWAHL** uh tee ¶1, 19
epee	e **PAY** *or* ay **PAY**	equalize	**EE** kwuh lyze
epergne	i **PURN** *or* ay **PURN**	equanimity	EK wuh **NIM** uh tee *or*
ephemeral	i **FEM** ur ul ¶1		EE kwuh **NIM** uh tee
epi–	ep uh *or* ep i	equate	i **KWAYT** ¶1
epic	**EP** ik	equation	i **KWAY** zhun ¶1
epicure	**EP** i kyoor ¶24	equator	i **KWAYT** ur ¶1
Epicurean	EP i kyoo **REE** un *or*	equatorial	EE kwuh **TAWR** ee ul *or*
	EP i **KYOOR** ee un ¶24		EK wuh **TAWR** ee ul
epidemic	**EP** uh **DEM** ik	equerry	**EK** wuh ree
epidemiology		*The British pronunciation is*	
	EP uh **DEE** mee **AHL** uh jee	i **KWER** ee.	
epidermis	**EP** uh **DUR** mus	equestrian	i **KWES** tree un ¶1
epiglottis	**EP** uh **GLAHT** is	equilateral	EE kwuh **LAT** ur ul
epigram	**EP** uh gram	equilibrium	EE kwuh **LIB** ree um
epigraph	**EP** uh graf ¶18	equine	**EE** kwyne *or* **EK** wyne
epilepsy	**EP** uh **LEP** see	equinox	**EE** kwuh nahks *or*
epilogue	**EP** uh lawg ¶19		**EK** wuh nahks
epiphany	i **PIF** uh nee ¶1	equip	i **KWIP** ¶1
episcopal	i **PIS** kuh pul ¶1	equitable	**EK** wuh tuh bul
Episcopalian		equity	**EK** wuh tee
	i **PIS** kuh **PAYL** yun ¶25	equivalence	i **KWIV** uh luns ¶1, 9
episode	**EP** uh sohd ¶14	equivocal	i **KWIV** uh kul ¶1
episodic	EP uh **SAHD** ik	equivocate	i **KWIV** uh kayt ¶1
epistle	i **PIS** ul ¶1	era	**IR** uh *or* **ER** uh
epistolary	i **PIS** tuh **LER** ee ¶23	eradicate	i **RAD** uh kayt ¶1
epithet	**EP** uh thet	erase	i **RAYS** ¶1
epitome	i **PIT** uh mee ¶1	Erasmus	i **RAZ** mus
epitomize	i **PIT** uh myze ¶1	erasure	i **RAY** shur ¶1

SPELLED	PRONOUNCED
ere	**ER**

This word will be heard most often in poetry, religious contexts, and the like.

erect	i **REKT** ¶1
erectile ... i **REK** tul *or* i **REK** tyle ¶22

The second is chiefly British.

erection	i **REK** shun ¶1
erg	**URG**
ergo	**ER** goh *or* **UR** goh
Erie	**IR** ee
ermine	**UR** mun
erode	i **ROHD** ¶1
erogenous	i **RAHJ** uh nus
Eros	**ER** ahs *or* **IR** ahs

ER ohs *and* **IR** ohs *are now also heard.*

erosion	i **ROH** zhun ¶1
erotic	i **RAHT** ik ¶1
eroticism	i **RAHT** uh siz um ¶1
erotogenic	i **RAHT** uh **JEN** ik *or* **ER** uh tuh **JEN** ik
err	**UR**

Though **ER** *is now common, it is still objected to by some.*

errand	**ER** und
errant	**ER** unt
errata	e **RAHT** uh *or* e **RAYT** uh ¶1, 18
erratic	i **RAT** ik ¶1
erroneous	i **ROH** nee us ¶1, 25
error	**ER** ur
ersatz	**UR** zahts *or* **ER** zahts *or* er **ZAHTS** ¶18
erstwhile	**URST** wyle: *see* wh–

SPELLED	PRONOUNCED
erudite	**ER** yoo dyte ¶21
erudition	**ER** yoo **DISH** un ¶21
erupt	i **RUPT** ¶1
eruption	i **RUP** shun
erythromycin	i **RITH** ruh **MYE** sun ¶1
escadrille	**ES** kuh dril
escalate	**ES** kuh layt
escapade	**ES** kuh payd
escapee	e skay **PEE** ¶1
escargot	es kahr **GOH**
escarole	**ES** kuh rohl ¶1
escarpment	e **SKAHRP** munt ¶1
eschatology	**ES** kuh **TAHL** uh jee
escheat	es **CHEET**
eschew	es **CHOOH**
escort *(verb)*	i **SKAWRT**

occasionally **ES** kawrt

escort *(noun)*	**ES** kawrt
escritoire	es kruh **TWAHR**
escrow	**ES** kroh
escutcheon	i **SKUCH** un ¶1
Eskimo	**ES** kuh moh ¶1
esophagus	i **SAHF** uh gus
esoteric	**ES** uh **TER** ik ¶1
espalier	es **PAL** yur ¶25
especially	i **SPESH** ul ee ¶5
Esperanto	**ES** puh **RAHN** toh ¶18
espionage	**ES** pee uh **NAHZH**

Formerly **ES** pee uh **NIJ** *was a frequent variant but is now less common.*

esplanade	es pluh **NAYD** *or* es pluh **NAHD**
espouse	e **SPOWZ** ¶1

espresso	es **PRES** oh	ethical	**ETH** i kul

The pronunciation ek **SPRES** *oh, which is now sometimes heard, is a blend of this Italian word with its English cognate,* express.

espresso	es **PRES** oh
esprit de corps	es **PREE** duh **KAWR**
esquire	**ES** kwyre

i **SKWYRE** *is now old–fashioned in the U.S. but is usual in Britain.*

essay *(verb)*	e **SAY**
essay *(noun)*	**ES** ay
essence	**ES** uns ¶9
Essene	**ES** een *or* e **SEEN** ¶1
essential	i **SEN** shul ¶1, 9, 12
establish	i **STAB** lish ¶1
establishmentarian	
...	i STAB lish mun **TER** ee un ¶1, 23
estate	i **STAYT** ¶1
esteem	i **STEEM** ¶1
estimable	**ES** tuh muh bul
estimate *(verb)*	**ES** tuh mayt
estimate *(noun)*	**ES** tuh mit
estrange	e **STRAYNJ** ¶1
estrogen	**ES** truh jun
estrus	**ES** trus
estuary	**ES** choo **WER** ee ¶17, 23
et cetera	et **SET** ur uh ¶5

ek **SET** ur uh, *heard increasingly nowadays, is not considered standard.*

eternal	i **TUR** nul ¶1
eternity	i **TUR** nuh tee ¶1
ethane	**ETH** ayn
ether	**EE** thur
ethereal	i **THIR** ee ul ¶1

ethical	**ETH** i kul
ethics	**ETH** iks
Ethiopia	EE thee **OH** pee uh ¶125
ethnic	**ETH** nik
ethnicity	eth **NIS** uh tee
ethnocentrism	ETH noh **SEN** triz um
ethnology	eth **NAHL** uh jee
ethos	**EE** thahs ¶19
ethyl	**ETH** ul
etiological	EET ee uh **LAHJ** i kul
etiology	EET ee **AHL** uh jee
etiquette	**ET** i kut

occasionally ET uh ket ¶8

Etruscan	i **TRUS** kun ¶1
étude	**AY** toohd ¶2, 21
etymology	ET uh **MAHL** uh jee
etymon	**ET** uh mahn
eucalyptus	YOOH kuh **LIP** tus
Eucharist	**YOOH** kur ist
euchre	**YOOH** kur
eugenics	yoo **JEN** iks
eulogize	**YOOH** luh jyze
eulogy	**YOOH** luh jee
eunuch	**YOOH** nuk ¶1
euphemism	**YOOH** fuh miz um
euphonious	yoo **FOH** nee us ¶25
euphony	**YOOH** fuh nee
euphoria	yoo **FAWR** ee uh ¶25
euphuistic	YOOH fyoo **WIS** tik
Eurasian	yoo **RAY** zhun
eureka	yoo **REE** kuh ¶1
Europe	**YOOR** up ¶24
European	YOOR uh **PEE** un ¶24
Eurydice	yoo **RID** uh see ¶1
eurythmics	yoo **RIDH** miks

euthanasia ....

.... YOOH thuh **NAY** zhuh ¶25

euthenics .... yoo **THEN** iks

evacuate .... i **VAK** yoo wayt ¶1

evacuee .... i **VAK** yoo **WEE** ¶1, 2

evade .... i **VAYD** ¶1

evaluate .... i **VAL** yoo wayt ¶1

evanescent .... EV uh **NES** unt

evangelical .... EE van **JEL** i kul or

EV un **JEL** i kul ¶1

evangelism ...... i **VAN** juh liz um ¶1

evaporate .... i **VAP** uh rayt ¶1

evasion .... i **VAY** zhun ¶1

evasive .... i **VAY** siv ¶1

evening .... **EEV** ning

event .... i **VENT** ¶1

eventuality ....

.... i **VEN** choo **WAL** uh tee ¶1, 12

eventually ....

.... i **VEN** choo wul ee ¶1, 9, 12

every .... **EV** ree ¶5

everybody .... **EV** ree BUD ee or

EV ree BAHD ee

everyone .... **EV** ree wun ¶8

evict .... i **VIKT** ¶1

evidence .... **EV** uh duns ¶9

evidential .... EV uh **DEN** shul ¶9, 12

evil .... **EE** vul

evince .... i **VINS** ¶1

eviscerate .... i **VIS** uh rayt ¶1

evocative .... i **VAHK** uh tiv ¶1

evoke .... i **VOHK** ¶1

evolution .... EV uh **LOOH** shun

evolve .... i **VAHLV** ¶1, 19

ewe .... **YOOH**

ewer .... **YOOH** ur

ex– .... iks or igz or eks or egz

The prefix is pronounced
variously, depending on the
meaning of the word it has
become a part of, and on the
stress pattern ¶1.

exacerbate .... ig **ZAS** ur bayt ¶1

exact .... ig **ZAKT**

exactly .... ig **ZAKT** lee ¶10

exaggerate .... ig **ZAJ** uh rayt ¶1

exalt .... ig **ZAWLT** ¶19

exaltation .... EG zawl **TAY** shun or

EK sawl **TAY** shun ¶1

examination ...... ig ZAM uh **NAY** shun

examine .... ig **ZAM** un

example .... ig **ZAM** pul ¶18

exasperate .... ig **ZAS** puh rayt ¶1

ex cathedra .... EKS kuh **THEE** druh

also, but now somewhat
old–fashioned, eks **KATH** uh druh

excavate .... **EKS** kuh vayt

exceed .... ik **SEED** ¶1

excel .... ik **SEL** ¶1

excellence .... **EK** sul uns ¶9

excelsior .... ek **SEL** see awr

So for the exclamation meaning
higher, upward; *the noun*
meaning wood shavings is
ik **SEL** see ur ¶1.

except .... ik **SEPT** ¶1

excerpt *(verb)* .. ik **SURPT** or ig **ZURPT**

or **EK** surpt

The last is the only
pronunciation for the noun. ¶1

excess *(noun)* .... ik **SES** *or* **EK** ses
The latter is usual for the
adjective.

exchequer .... iks **CHEK** ur *or*
EKS chek ur

excise *(noun)* ...... **EK** syze *or* **EK** syse

excise *(verb)* .... ik **SYZE** ¶1

excitation .... **EK** sye **TAY** shun

excite .... ik **SYTE**

exclaim .... iks **KLAYM** ¶1

exclamation .... **EKS** kluh **MAY** shun

exclamatory ....
.... iks **KLAM** uh **TAWR** ee ¶1

exclude .... iks **KLOOHD** ¶1

exclusion .... iks **KLOOH** zhun ¶1

exclusive .... ik **SKLOOH** siv ¶1

excoriate .... ik **SKAWR** ee ayt ¶1

excrement .... **EKS** kruh munt

excresence .... ik **SKRES** uns ¶1, 9

excrete .... ik **SKREET** ¶1

excretion .... ik **SKREE** shun ¶1

excretory .... **EKS** kruh **TAWR** ee

excruciating ....
.... ik **SKROOH** shee ayt ing ¶1

exculpate .... **EKS** kul payt *or*
iks **KUL** payt

excursion .... ik **SKUR** zhun ¶1

excursus .... ik **SKUR** sus ¶1

excuse *(verb)* .... ik **SKYOOHZ** ¶1

excuse *(noun)* .... ik **SKYOOHS** ¶1

execrable .... **EK** si kruh bul

execration .... **EK** suh **KRAY** shun

execute .... **EK** suh kyooht

execution .... **EK** suh **KYOOH** shun

executive .... ig **ZEK** yuh tiv

executor .... **EK** suh **KYOOT** ur
When the word means one who
administers a will, *it is*
ig **ZEK** yuh tur.

exegesis .... **EK** suh **JEE** sis

exemplar .. ig **ZEM** plahr *or* ig **ZEM** plur

exemplary .... ig **ZEM** plur ee

exemplify .... ig **ZEM** pluh fye

exempt .... ig **ZEMPT**

exemption .... ig **ZEMP** shun ¶9

exercise .... **EK** sur syze

exert .... ig **ZURT**

exertion .... ig **ZUR** shun

exfoliate .... iks **FOH** lee ayt ¶1

exhalation .... **EKS** huh **LAY** shun *or*
EK suh **LAY** shun

exhale ...... eks **HAYL** *or* ek **SAYL** ¶2

exhaust .... ig **ZAWST**

exhaustion .... ig **ZAWS** chun

exhibit .... ig **ZIB** it

exhibition .... **EK** suh **BISH** un

exhilarate .... ig **ZIL** uh rayt

exhort .... ig **ZAWRT**

exhortation ...... **EG** zawr **TAY** shun *or*
EK sur **TAY** shun

exhume ... ig **ZYOOHM** *or* iks **HYOOHM**

exigency .... **EK** suh jun see *or*
ik **SIJ** un see ¶9

exile .... **EG** zyle *or* **EK** syle

exist .... ig **ZIST**

existential .... **EG** zis **TEN** shul *or*
EK sis **TEN** shul ¶9, 12

exit .... **EG** zit *or* **EK** sit

ex libris .... eks **LEE** brus ¶22

exodus .... **EK** suh dus

ex officio .... EKS uh FISH ee oh

exonerate .... ig ZAHN uh rayt

exorbitant .... ig ZAWR buh tunt

exorcise .... EK sawr syze ¶1

exotic .... ig ZAHT ik

expand .... ik SPAND ¶1

expansion ... ik SPAN shun ¶1, 9, 12

expatiate .... ik SPAY shee ayt ¶1

expatriate *(verb)* ..... eks PAY tree ayt
for the noun and adjective,
usually eks PAY tree it

expect .... ik SPEKT ¶1

expectation .... EK spek TAY shun

expectorate ...... ik SPEK tuh rayt ¶1

expedient .... ik SPEE dee unt ¶1

expedite .... EK spuh dyte

expedition .... EK spuh DISH un

expel .... ik SPEL ¶1

expend .... ik SPEND ¶1

expenditure .... ik SPEN duh chur ¶1

expense .... ik SPENS ¶9

experience .... ik SPIR ee uns ¶9, 25

experiment *(noun)* .. ik SPER uh munt
or ik SPIR uh munt ¶1
For the verb, the last syllable
may also be MENT.

expert *(noun)* .... EK spurt
The adjective is also
ik SPURT ¶1.

expertise .... ek spur TEEZ

expiate .... EK spee ayt

expiration .... EK spuh RAY shun

expire .... ik SPYRE ¶1

explain .... ik SPLAYN ¶1

explanation .... EKS pluh NAY shun

explanatory ....
.... ik SPLAN uh TAWR ee ¶1

expletive .... EKS pluh tiv

explicable .... EKS pli kuh bul *or*
iks PLIK uh bul ¶1

explicate .... EKS pli kayt

explicit .... ik SPLIS it ¶1

explode .... ik SPLOHD ¶1

exploit *(noun)* .... EKS ployt
The verb is usually
ik SPLOYT. ¶1

exploration .... EKS pluh RAY shun

exploratory ....
.... ik SPLAWR uh TAWR ee ¶1

explore .... ik SPLAWR ¶1

explosion .... ik SPLOH zhun ¶1

explosive .... ik SPLOH siv ¶1

exponent .... ik SPOH nunt ¶1
As a term in mathematics, it is
EKS POH nunt.

exponential ....
.... EKS puh NEN shul ¶9, 12

export *(noun)* .... EKS pawrt
The verb is often ik SPAWRT.

expose .... ik SPOHZ ¶1

exposé .... eks poh ZAY

exposition .... EKS puh ZISH un

expository ....
.... ik SPAHZ uh TAWR ee ¶1

expostulate ....
.... ik SPAHS chuh layt ¶1, 17

exposure .... ik SPOH zhur ¶1

expound .... ik SPOWND ¶1

express .... ik SPRES ¶1

expression .... ik SPRESH un ¶1

expressive .... ik **SPRES** iv ¶1

expropriate .... eks **PROH** pree ayt

expulsion .... ik **SPUL** shun ¶1

expunge .... ik **SPUNJ** ¶1, 15

expurgate .... **EKS** pur gayt

exquisite ... ik **SKWIZ** it *or* **EKS** kwi zit

extant .... **EKS** tunt *or* ik **STANT**

extemporaneous ....

.... ik STEM puh **RAY** nee us ¶1

extempore .... ik **STEM** pur ee ¶1

extemporize .... ik **STEM** puh RYZE

extend .... ik **STEND** ¶1

extension .... ik **STEN** shun ¶9, 12

extensive .... ik **STEN** siv ¶1, 9

extent .... ik **STENT** ¶1

extenuating ....

.... ik **STEN** yoo wayt ing ¶1

exterior .... ik **STIR** ee ur ¶1

exterminate ... ik **STUR** muh nayt ¶1

external .... ik **STUR** nul ¶1

extinct .... ik **STINGKT** ¶1

extinction ...... ik **STINGK** shun ¶1, 9

extinguish .... ik **STING** gwish ¶1

extirpate .... **EKS** tur payt *or*
               ik **STUR** payt

extol .... ik **STOHL** ¶1

extort .... ik **STAWRT** ¶1

extortion .... ik **STAWR** shun ¶1

extract *(verb)* .... ik **STRAKT** ¶1

extract *(noun)* .... **EKS** trakt

extraction .... ik **STRAK** shun ¶1

extracurricular ....

.... **EKS** truh kuh **RIK** yuh lur

extradite .... **EKS** truh dyte

extradition .... **EKS** truh **DISH** un

extraneous .. ik **STRAY** nee us ¶1, 25

extraordinary ....

.... ik **STRAWR** duh **NER** ee

*When applied to someone with
special authority, as an envoy, it
is* EKS **truh** AWR **duh** NER **ee** ¶1, 23

extrapolate ..... ik **STRAP** uh layt ¶1

extravagance ....

.... ik **STRAV** uh guns ¶1, 9

extravaganza ....

.... ik STRAV uh **GAN** zuh ¶1

extreme .... ik **STREEM** ¶1

extremity .... ik **STREM** uh tee ¶1

extricate .... **EKS** truh kayt

extrinsic .... ek **STRIN** sik

extrovert .... **EKS** truh vurt

extrude .... ik **STROOHD** ¶1

exuberant ... ig **ZOOH** bur unt ¶5, 21

exude .... ig **ZOOHD** ¶21

exult .... ig **ZULT**

exultation .... EG zul **TAY** shun *or*
               EK sul **TAY** shun

exurbia .... eks **UR** bee uh

F

fabricate .... **FAB** ruh kayt

fabulous .... **FAB** yoo lus

façade .... fuh **SAHD** ¶1

SPELLED	PRONOUNCED
facet	**FAS** it
facetious	fuh **SEE** shus
facial	**FAY** shul
facile	**FAS** ul
facilitate	fuh **SIL** uh tayt
facility	fuh **SIL** uh tee
facsimile	fak **SIM** uh lee
faction	**FAK** shun
factitious	fak **TISH** us
factor	**FAK** tur
factorial	fak **TAWR** ee ul ¶25
factory	**FAK** tur ee ¶5
factotum	fak **TOHT** um
factual	**FAK** choo wul ¶5, 12
faculty	**FAK** ul tee
Faeroese	fer uh **WEEZ** ¶1
Fahrenheit	**FER** un hyte ¶23
sometimes **FAHR** un hyte	
faience .. fye **AHNS** *or* fay **AHNS** ¶2, 9	
faille	**FYLE** *or* **FAYL**
fairy	**FER** ee
fait accompli ... FET uh kohm **PLEE** *or*	
	FAYT uh kahm **PLEE**
faithful	**FAYTH** ful
falafel	fuh **LAHF** ul
falcon .... FAL kun *or* FAWL kun *or*	
	FAW kun
falderal .... **FAWL** duh rawl *or*	
	FAL duh ral
fallacious	fuh **LAY** shus
fallacy	**FAL** uh see
fallible	**FAL** uh bul
Fallopian (tube)	
	fuh **LOH** pee un ¶25
fallow	**FAL** oh
false	**FAWLS** ¶9, 19
falsetto	fawl **SET** oh
falsify	**FAWL** suh fye
familial	fuh **MIL** yul ¶25
familiar	fuh **MIL** yur
familiarity .. fuh **MIL** **YER** uh tee ¶23
family	**FAM** uh lee ¶5
famine	**FAM** un
famish	**FAM** ish
famous	**FAY** mus
fanatic	fuh **NAT** ik
fanaticism	fuh **NAT** uh siz um
fanciful	**FAN** si ful ¶9
fandango	fan **DANG** goh
Faneuil (Hall)	**FAN** ul *or* **FAN** yul
fantasia	fan **TAY** zhuh
fantastic	fan **TAS** tik
fantasy	**FAN** tuh see ¶14
farad	**FAR** ad *or* **FAR** ud ¶23
farcical	**FAHR** si kul
farina	fuh **REE** nuh
faro	**FAR** oh
farrago ... fuh **RAY** goh *or* fuh **RAH** goh
farrier	**FAR** ee ur ¶23
farrow	**FAR** oh ¶23
farthing	**FAHR** dhing
fascicle	**FAS** i kul
fascinate	**FAS** uh nayt
fascism	**FASH** iz um
fascist	**FASH** ist
fashion	**FASH** un
fasten	**FAS** un ¶18
fastidious	fas **TID** ee us ¶1, 25
fatal	**FAYT** ul
fatality	fuh **TAL** uh tee ¶1

SPELLED	PRONOUNCED
fathom	**FADH** um
fatigue	fuh **TEEG**
Fatima	**FAT** i muh *or* fuh **TEE** muh ¶18
fatuous	**FACH** oo wus
faucet	**FAW** sit
fauna	**FAW** nuh
Faust	**FOWST**

In Marlowe's play he is called Faustus, usually pronounced **FAWS** tus.

fauvism	**FOH** viz um
faux pas	**FOH PAH** ¶19
favorite	**FAY** vur it ¶5
fealty	**FEE** ul tee ¶7
feasance	**FEE** zuns ¶9
feasible	**FEE** zuh bul
feature	**FEE** chur
febrile	**FEE** brul *or* **FEE** bryle *or* **FEE** rul
February	**FEB** ruh **WER** ee *or* **FEB** yoo **WER** ee

Although objected to by some, **FEB** yoo **WER** ee *is the prevailing pronunciation of educated speakers.* ¶3, 23

feces	**FEE** seez
fecund	**FEE** kund *or* **FEK** und
federal	**FED** ur ul ¶5
federation	FED uh **RAY** shun
fedora	fuh **DAWR** uh
feign	**FAYN**
feint	**FAYNT**
feisty	**FYSE** tee
feldspar	**FELD** spahr ¶10

SPELLED	PRONOUNCED
felicitation	fuh LIS uh **TAY** shun
felicity	fuh **LIS** uh tee
feline	**FEE** lyne
fellatio	fuh **LAHT** ee oh *or* fuh **LAY** shee oh ¶25
felon	**FEL** un
felonious	fuh **LOH** nee us ¶25
felony	**FEL** uh nee
female	**FEE** mayl
feminine	**FEM** uh nin
femininity	FEM uh **NIN** uh tee
feminism	**FEM** uh niz um
femme fatale	FAHM fuh **TAHL** *or* FEM fuh **TAL**
femur	**FEE** mur
fenestration	FEN uh **STRAY** shun
Fenian	**FEE** nee un ¶25
feral	**FIR** ul *or* **FER** ul
ferment *(verb)*	fur **MENT**
ferment *(noun)*	**FUR** ment ¶1
fermentation	FUR men **TAY** shun ¶1
Fermi	**FER** mee
ferocious	fuh **ROH** shus
ferocity	fuh **RAHS** uh tee
ferret	**FER** it
ferrule	**FER** ul *or* **FER** ool ¶21
fertile	**FUR** tul ¶22
fertility	fur **TIL** uh tee
fertilize	**FUR** tuh lyze
ferule	**FER** ul *or* **FER** ool
fervent	**FUR** vunt
fervid	**FUR** vud
fervor	**FUR** vur
fescue	**FES** kyooh

festival .... **FES** tuh vul

festive .... **FES** tiv

festivity .... fes **TIV** uh tee

festoon .... fes **TOOHN**

feta (cheese) .....·........... **FET** uh

fetal .... **FEET** ul

fete .... **FAYT** *or* **FET**

fetid .... **FET** id
  FEET id *has become less common.*

fetish .... **FET** ish
  FEET ish *has become less common.*

fettuccini .... FET uh **CHEE** nee

fetus .... **FEET** us

feudal .... **FYOOHD** ul

fever .... **FEE** vur

fiancé, fiancée .... FEE ahn **SAY** *or*
  fee **AHN** say

fiasco .... fee **AS** koh ¶25

fiat .... **FYE** ut *or* **FYE** at ¶8

fibrillation .... FIB ruh **LAY** shun *or*
  FYE bruh **LAY** shun

fibrosis .... fye **BROH** sis

fibula .... **FIB** yoo luh

fiction .... **FIK** shun

fictitious .... fik **TISH** us

fidelity .... fuh **DEL** uh tee ¶1

fiduciary .... fi **DOOH** shee ER ee *or*
  fi **DOOH** shuh ree ¶11, 21, 23

fief .... **FEEF**

fiend .... **FEEND**

fierce .... **FIRS**

fiery .... **FYE** ur ee ¶7

fiesta .... fee **ES** tuh

fifth .... **FIFTH** ¶10

figment .... **FIG** munt

figurative .... **FIG** yur uh tiv

figure .... **FIG** yur

figurine .... fig yuh **REEN**

figwort .... **FIG** wurt

Fiji .... **FEE** jee

filament .... **FIL** uh munt

filet .... fi **LAY** *or* **FIL** ay

filet mignon ..... fi **LAY** min **YOHN** *or*
  fi lay min **YAHN**

filial .... **FIL** ee ul ¶25

filibuster .... **FIL** uh **BUS** tur

filigree .... **FIL** uh gree

Filipino .... FIL uh **PEE** noh

fillet .... **FIL** it
  *When used in its cooking or
  food preparation meanings, it is
  usually* fuh **LAY** *or* **FIL** ay.

fillip .... **FIL** up

finagle .... fuh **NAY** gul

finale .... fuh **NAH** lee *or*
  fuh **NAH** lay ¶1, 18

finality .... fye **NAL** uh tee ¶1

finally .... **FYE** nuh lee ¶5

finance .... fuh **NANS** *or* **FYE** nans ¶9

financial ...... fuh **NAN** shul ¶1, 9, 12

financier ..... fin un **SIR** *or* fye nan **SIR**
  The standard British fi **NAN** see ur
  is not unknown in the U.S.

finder .... **FYNE** dur

finery .... **FYNE** ur ee ¶5

fines herbes .. feen **ZERB** *or* feen **URBZ**

finesse .... fi **NES**

fingerling .... **FING** gur ling

finial .... **FIN** ee ul

finicky .... **FIN** i kee

finis .... **FIN** is
  rarely **FYE** nis; *often taken as*
  French, hence fee **NEE**

finite .... **FYE** nyte

fiord ...... **FYAWRD** *or* fee **AWRD** ¶7

firkin .... **FUR** kin

firmament .... **FUR** muh munt

fiscal .... **FIS** kul

fishery .... **FISH** ur ee

fissile .... **FIS** ul ¶22

fission .... **FISH** un

fissure .... **FISH** ur

fistula .... **FIS** choo luh ¶17

fixate .... **FIK** sayt

fixation .... fik **SAY** shun

fixative .... **FIK** suh tiv

fixture .... **FIKS** chur ¶17

flaccid .... **FLAK** sid
  occasionally **FLAS** id

flagellate .... **FLAJ** uh layt

flagellum .... fluh **JEL** um

flagon .... **FLAG** un

flagrant .... **FLAY** grunt

flagrante delicto ....
  .... fluh **GRAN** tee duh **LIK** toh

flambé .... flahm **BAY** ¶18

flambeau .... flahm **BOH** ¶18

flamboyant .... flam **BOY** unt

flamenco .... fluh **MENG** koh

flamingo .... fluh **MING** goh

flammable .... **FLAM** uh bul

flange .... **FLANJ** ¶15

flannelette .... flan uh **LET**

flask .... **FLASK** ¶18

flatulent .... **FLACH** oo lunt ¶21

flatus .... **FLAYT** us

Flaubert .... floh **BER**

flaunt .... **FLAWNT**

flautist .... **FLAWT** ist *or* **FLOWT** ist

flavor .... **FLAY** vur

flaxen .... **FLAK** sun

fleur–de–lis .... **FLUR** duh **LEE** *or*
  FLUR duh **LEES** ¶24

flibbertigibbit ...... **FLIB** ur tee **JIB** it

flimsy .... **FLIM** zee

flippant .... **FLIP** unt

flirt .... **FLURT**

flirtation .... flur **TAY** shun

flog .... **FLAHG** ¶19

floozy .... **FLOOH** zee

floribunda .... **FLAWR** uh **BUN** duh

florid .... **FLAWR** id ¶19

floss .... **FLAWS** ¶19

flotation .... floh **TAY** shun

flotilla .... floh **TIL** uh ¶1

flotsam .... **FLAHT** sum

flounce .... **FLOWNS** ¶9

flounder .... **FLOWN** dur

flour .... **FLOWR** ¶7

flourish .... **FLUR** ish ¶24

flout .... **FLOWT**

flower .... **FLOW** ur ¶5
  Originally the same word as
  flour, it is commonly
  pronounced like it, **FLOWR**.

fluctuate .... **FLUK** choo wayt ¶12

fluegelhorn .... **FLOOH** gul hawrn

fluency .... **FLOOH** un see ¶9

fluid .... **FLOOH** id

flummery .... **FLUM** ur ee ¶25

SPELLED	PRONOUNCED	SPELLED	PRONOUNCED

fluorescent .... floo **RES** unt *or*
flaw **RES** unt

FLOOH uh **RES** unt *is no longer
much heard.*

fluoridate .... **FLAWR** uh dayt
FLOOR uh dayt *is becoming rare.*

fluorine ..... **FLAWR** een *or* **FLOOR** een
FLOOH uh reen *and* FLOOH uh rin *are
now rare;* FLOOR een *prevails
among chemists.*

fluoroscope .... **FLAWR** uh skohp *or*
FLOOR uh skohp

flutist .... **FLOOHT** ist

focus .... **FOH** kus

foggy .... **FAW** gee ¶19

fogy .... **FOH** gee

foible .... **FOY** bul

foliage .... **FOH** lee ij
FOH lij *is heard occasionally, but is
considered careless speech.*

folic (acid) .... **FOH** lik

folio .... **FOH** lee oh ¶25

folk .... **FOHK**
The spelling pronunciation FOHLK
has some frequency.

follicle .... **FAHL** i kul ¶19

follow .... **FAHL** oh
FAHL uh *is common in some
contexts, as in* I'll follow you.

foment .... foh **MENT** ¶2

fondue .... fahn **DOOH** ¶2

font .... **FAHNT**

foppery .... **FAHP** ur ee

for– .... fawr *or* fur *variously*

forage .... **FAWR** ij ¶19

foray .... **FAWR** ay

forbearance ..... fawr **BER** uns ¶1, 9

forceps .... **FAWR** seps *or*
FAWR sups ¶8

forebear .... **FAWR** ber

foreboding .... fawr **BOHD** ing

forecast .... **FAWR** kast
The verb is sometimes
fawr **KAST** ¶18.

forecastle .... **FOHK** sul
FAWR kas ul *is a spelling
pronunciation.* ¶18

foreclose .... fawr **KLOHZ** ¶2

forehead .... **FAWR** hed
FAWR id *and* **FAHR** id *are fast
losing ground.* ¶8, 19

foreign .... **FAWR** in ¶19

forensic .... fuh **REN** sik ¶19

forest .... **FAWR** ist ¶19

foreword .... **FAWR** WURD *or*
FAWR wurd

forfeit .... **FAWR** fit

forfeiture .... **FAWR** fuh chur

forgery .... **FAWR** jur ee ¶5

forlorn .... fawr **LAWRN** ¶1

formal .... **FAWR** mul

formaldehyde ..... fawr **MAL** duh hyde

formality .... fawr **MAL** uh tee ¶1

formally .... **FAWR** muh lee

format .... **FAWR** mat

formation .... fawr **MAY** shun ¶1

formidable .... **FAWR** muh duh bul
fawr **MID** uh bul *is now also heard,
but often objected to.*

formula .... **FAWRM** yuh luh

SPELLED	PRONOUNCED	SPELLED	PRONOUNCED
formulate	**FAWRM** yuh layt	fractious	**FRAK** shus
fornicate	**FAWR** nuh kayt	fracture	**FRAK** chur
forsake	fur **SAYK** ¶1	fragile	**FRAJ** ul ¶22
forsythia	fur **SITH** ee uh ¶1	fragment *(noun)*	**FRAG** munt
forte ("a person's strong point")		*The verb is also* frag **MENT**.	
	FAWRT	fragmentary	
now often **FAWR** tay, *which is*			**FRAG** mun **TER** ee ¶23
generally considered nonstandard		fragrance	**FRAY** gruns ¶9
forte ("loud, in music")	**FAWR** tay	frailty	**FRAYL** tee
	or **FAWR** tee	franc	**FRANGK**
fortify	**FAWR** tuh fye	franchise	**FRAN** chyze
fortissimo	fawr **TIS** uh MOH *or*	Franciscan	fran **SIS** kun
	fawr **TEES** ee MOH ¶1	frangible	**FRAN** juh bul
fortitude	**FAWR** tuh toohd ¶21	frangipani	FRAN juh **PAN** ee ¶18
fortnight	**FAWRT** nyte	Frankenstein	**FRANG** kun styne
sometimes, in rapid speech,		frankfurter	**FRANGK** fur tur
FAWRT nit		frankincense	**FRANG** kun sens ¶9
FORTRAN	**FAWR** tran	frappé	fra **PAY**
fortress	**FAWR** trus	fraternal	fruh **TUR** nul
fortuitious		fraternity	fruh **TUR** nuh tee
	fawr **TOOH** uh tus ¶1, 13, 21	fraternize	**FRAT** ur nyze ¶3
fortune	**FAWR** chun	fratricide	**FRAT** ruh syde
forum	**FAWR** um	Frau	**FROW**
forward	**FAWR** wurd	fraud	**FRAWD**
fossil	**FAHS** ul ¶19	fraudulent	**FRAW** juh lunt ¶17
foster	**FAWS** tur ¶19	fraught	**FRAWT**
foulard	fooh **LAHRD**	Fräulein	**FROY** lyne
foundation	fown **DAY** shun	**FROW** lyne *is a spelling*	
foundry	**FOUN** dree	*pronunciation.*	
fountain	**FOWNT** un	frazzle	**FRAZ** ul
fowl	**FOWL** ¶7	free–lance	**FREE** lans ¶9, 18
foyer	**FOY** ur *or* **FOY** ay *or* foy **YAY**	freight	**FRAYT**
fracas	**FRAY** kus	frenetic	fruh **NET** ik
also, especially formerly, **FRAK** us		frenzy	**FREN** zee
fraction	**FRAK** shun	frequency	**FREE** kwun see ¶9

SPELLED	PRONOUNCED
frequent *(adjective)*	**FREE** kwunt
The verb is usually	
free **KWENT**. ¶1	
fresco	**FRES** koh
Freud	**FROYD**
friable	**FRYE** uh bul
friar	**FRYE** ur ¶7
fricassee	**FRIK** uh see ¶2, 14
Friday	**FRYE** dee *or* **FRYE** day
friendly	**FREND** lee ¶10
frieze	**FREEZ**
frigate	**FRIG** ut
frijoles	free **HOH** lays *or*
	free **HOH** leez
frisé	fri **ZAY** ¶1
Frisian	**FRIZH** un *or* **FREE** zhun
frivolity	fri **VAHL** uh tee
frivolous	**FRIV** uh lus ¶5
frolic	**FRAH** lik
frontage	**FRUN** tij
frontier	frun **TIR**
frontispiece	**FRUN** tis pees
fronton	**FRAHN** tahn
frothy	**FRAW** thee ¶19
froufrou	**FROOH** frooh
froward	**FROH** urd *or* **FROH** wurd
fructose	**FRUK** tohs *or* **FROOK** tohs
frugal	**FROOH** gul
fruition	frooh **ISH** un
frustrate	**FRUS** trayt
now also frus **TRAYT**	
fuchsia	**FYOOH** shuh
fuel	**FYOOH** ul ¶7
fugitive	**FYOOH** juh tiv
fugue	**FYOOHG**

SPELLED	PRONOUNCED
–ful	ful
a suffix used in such words as	
joyful, helpful, *etc.*	
–ful	fool
a suffix used in such words as	
handful, cupful, *etc.*	
fulcrum	**FOOL** krum *or* **FUL** krum
fulminate	**FUL** muh nayt
fulsome	**FOOL** sum *or* **FUL** sum
fumigate	**FYOOH** muh gayt
function	**FUNGK** shun
fundamental	**FUN** duh **MEN** tul
funeral	**FYOOH** nur ul ¶5
funereal	fyoo **NIR** ee ul
fungi	**FUN** jye *or* **FUNG** gye
fungicide	**FUN** juh syde *or*
	FUNG guh syde
fungus	**FUNG** gus
funicular	fyoo **NIK** yuh lur *or*
	fuh **NIK** yoo lur
furbelow	**FUR** buh loh
furious	**FYOOR** ee us ¶5, 24
furlough	**FUR** loh
furnace	**FUR** nus
furniture..	**FUR** ni chur
furrier	**FUR** ee ur ¶25
furrow	**FUR** oh
further	**FUR** dhur
furtive	**FUR** tiv
fuselage ..	**FYOOH** suh lahzh ¶14, 15
fusillade	**FYOOH** suh layd *or*
	FYOOH suh lahd ¶2, 14
fusion	**FYOOH** zhun
fustian	**FUS** chun ¶13
futile	**FYOOHT** ul ¶22

futility	fyoo **TIL** uh tee ¶1	Gallic	**GAL** ik
future	**FYOOH** chur	Gallicism	**GAL** uh siz um
futurity	fyoo **TOOR** uh tee ¶13, 21	gallimaufry	**GAL** uh **MAW** free
		gallium	**GAL** ee um ¶5
		gallivant	**GAL** uh vant
		gallows	**GAL** ohz
		galoot	guh **LOOHT**

G

		galore	guh **LAWR**
		galoshes	guh **LAHSH** uz
		galumph	guh **LUMF** ¶9
		galvanic	gal **VAN** ik
gabardine	**GAB** ur deen ¶2	galvanize	**GAL** vuh nyze
gadgetry	**GAJ** uh tree	gambol	**GAM** bul
Gaelic	**GAY** lik	gamete	**GAM** eet ¶2
gaiety	**GAY** uh tee	gamin	**GAM** in
gainsay	gayn **SAY** ¶2	gamut	**GAM** ut
gala	**GAY** luh *or* **GAL** uh ¶18	gamy	**GAY** mee
galactic	guh **LAK** tik	Gandhi	**GAHN** dee *or* **GAN** dee
Galahad	**GAL** uh had	Ganges	**GAN** jeez
Galápagos	guh **LAH** puh gohs	ganglion	**GANG** glee un
GAL uh **PAY** gohs *is heard but is not*		gangrene	**GANG** green ¶2
considered standard.		gangrenous	**GANG** gruh nus
Galatians	guh **LAY** shunz ¶1	gantlet	**GAWNT** lit *or* **GANT** lit
galaxy	**GAL** uk see	Ganymede	**GAN** uh meed
Galilee	**GAL** uh lee	garage	guh **RAHJ** ¶15
Galileo	GAL uh **LAY** oh *or*	garbanzo	gahr **BAHN** zoh *or*
GAL uh **LEE** oh		gahr **BAN** zoh
gallant *(adjective)*	**GAL** unt	gardenia	gahr **DEEN** yuh
When the meaning is polite *or*		gargantuan	gahr **GAN** choo wun
amorous, *it is usually* guh **LANT**		gargoyle	**GAHR** goyl
as it is for the noun, which is not		garish	**GAR** ish ¶23
much used today ¶1, 18.		garnet	**GAHR** nit
galleon	**GAL** ee un ¶25	garnishee	gahr nuh **SHEE**
gallery	**GAL** ur ee ¶5	garret	**GAR** it ¶23
		garrison	**GAR** uh sun ¶23

garrote .... guh **RAHT**
occasionally guh **ROHT**

garrulity .... guh **ROOH** luh tee

garrulous .... **GAR** uh lus ¶21, 23

gaseous ...... **GAS** ee us *or* **GAS** yus *or* **GASH** us

gasohol .... **GAS** uh hawl ¶19

gasoline .... gas uh **LEEN** ¶2

gastrectomy .... gas **TREK** tuh mee

gastritis .... gas **TRYTE** is

gastronomy .... gas **TRAHN** uh mee

gather .... **GADH** ur

gauche .... **GOHSH**

gaucherie .... goh shuh **REE** ¶2

gaucho .... **GOW** choh

gaudeamus .... **GOW** day **AH** moohs *or* **GAW** dee **AY** mus

gaudy .... **GAW** dee

gauge .... **GAYJ**

Gauguin .... goh **GAN**

gauntlet .... **GAWNT** lit ¶19

gauze .... **GAWZ**

gavage .... guh **VAHZH**

gavotte .... guh **VAHT** ¶19

Gaza .... **GAH** zuh *or* **GAZ** uh
occasionally **GAY** zuh

gazebo .... guh **ZEE** boh *or* guh **ZAY** boh

gazelle .... guh **ZEL**

gazette .... guh **ZET**

gazetteer .... gaz uh **TIR**

gazpacho .... gahz **PAH** choh ¶14

Gdansk ... guh **DAHNSK** *or* guh **DANSK**

gefilte (fish) .... guh **FIL** tuh

Gehenna .... guh **HEN** uh

Geiger (counter) .... **GYE** gur

geisha .... **GAY** shuh
GEE shuh *is now often heard.*

gelatin .... **JEL** uh tun

gelatinous .... juh **LAT** uh nus

geld .... **GELD**

gelding .... **GEL** ding

Gemini ..... **JEM** uh nye *or* **JEM** uh nee

gemsbok .... **GEMZ** bahk

gendarme .... **ZHAHN** dahrm ¶2

gender .... **JEN** dur

genealogy .... JEE nee **AHL** uh jee *or* JEE nee **AL** uh jee

general .... **JEN** ur ul ¶5

generalissimo ....
.... JEN ur uh **LIS** uh moh ¶5

generality .... JEN uh **RAL** uh tee

generally .... **JEN** ur uh lee *or* **JEN** ruh lee *or* **JEN** ur lee ¶5

generate .... **JEN** uh rayt

generation .... JEN uh **RAY** shun

generative .... **JEN** ur uh tiv *or* **JEN** uh rayt iv

generic .... juh **NER** ik

generosity .... JEN uh **RAHS** uh tee

generous .... **JEN** ur us ¶5

genesis .... **JEN** uh sis

genetics .... juh **NET** iks

Geneva .... juh **NEE** vuh

Genghis Khan .... **GENG** gis **KAHN** *or* **JENG** gis **KAHN**

genial .... **JEEN** yul ¶5

genital .... **JEN** uh tul

genitalia .... JEN uh **TAYL** yuh ¶25

genitive .... **JEN** uh tiv

genius .... **JEEN** yus ¶5

SPELLED	PRONOUNCED	SPELLED	PRONOUNCED

SPELLED	PRONOUNCED
Genoa	**JEN** uh wuh
genocide	**JEN** uh syde
genre	**ZHAHN** ruh ¶19
genteel	jen **TEEL**
gentian	**JEN** shun
gentile	**JEN** tyle
gentility	jen **TIL** uh tee
gentleman	**JEN** tul mun
gentrification	
	JEN truh fuh **KAY** shun
genuflect	**JEN** yuh flekt ¶1
genuine	**JEN** yoo wun

JEN yoo wyne *is occasionally said, usually in a joking way.*

genus	**JEE** nus
geode	**JEE** ohd
geodesic	JEE uh **DES** ik *or*
	JEE uh **DEE** sik
geodesy	jee **AHD** uh see
geodetic	JEE uh **DET** ik
Geoffrey	**JEF** ree
geographical	JEE uh **GRAF** uh kul
geography	jee **AHG** ruh fee
geology	jee **AHL** uh jee
geometric	JEE uh **MET** rik
geometry	jee **AHM** uh tree
geotropism	jee **AHT** ruh piz um
geranium	juh **RAY** nee um ¶5
gerbil	**JUR** bul
geriatrician	JER ee uh **TRISH** un
geriatrics	JER ee **AT** riks
germicide	**JUR** muh syde
germinate	**JUR** muh nayt
Geronimo	juh **RAHN** uh **MOH**
gerontology	JER un **TAHL** uh jee

SPELLED	PRONOUNCED
gerrymander	**JER** ee **MAN** dur *or*
	GER ee **MAN** dur
gerund	**JER** und
gerundive	juh **RUN** div
gesso	**JES** oh
gestalt	guh **SHTAHLT** *or*
	guh **STAHLT** ¶19
Gestapo	guh **STAH** poh

*When the term was common, guh **STAP** oh was occasionally heard.*

gestation	jes **TAY** shun
gesticulate	jes **TIK** yuh layt ¶1
gesture	**JES** chur ¶6
Gesundheit	guh **ZOONT** hyte
Gethsemane	geth **SEM** uh nee
Gettysburg	**GET** iz burg *or*
	GET eez burg
gewgaw	**GYOOH** gaw ¶21
geyser	**GYE** zur ¶14
Ghana	**GAHN** uh
ghastly	**GAST** lee ¶18
gherkin	**GUR** kin
ghetto	**GET** oh
Ghibelline	GIB uh lin *or* GIB uh leen
ghost	**GOHST**
ghoul	**GOOHL**
GI	JEE **EYE**
giant	**JYE** unt
gibberish	**JIB** ur ish

GIB ur ish *is also heard and is usual in British speech.*

gibbet	**JIB** it
gibbon	**GIB** un
gibbous	**GIB** us

92

SPELLED	PRONOUNCED
giblet	**JIB** lit
Gibraltar	juh **BRAWL** tur ¶19
gigahertz	**JIG** uh hurts
GIG uh hurts *is now also heard.*	
gigantic	jye **GAN** tik
GIGO	**GIG** oh
gigolo	**JIG** uh loh ¶15
gigot	**JIG** ut *or* zhee **GOH**
Gila (monster)	**HEE** luh
gilding	**GIL** ding
Gilead	**GIL** ee ud
gill ("fish organ")	**GIL**
gill ("measurement")	**JIL**
gilt–edged	**GILT EJD**
gimbals	**GIM** bulz *or* **JIM** bulz
gimcrack	**JIM** krak
gimlet	**GIM** lit
gimmick	**GIM** ik
ginger	**JIN** jur
gingerly	**JIN** jur lee
gingham	**GING** um
gingivitis	**JIN** juh **VYTE** is
ginkgo	**GING** koh
ginseng	**JIN** seng
giraffe	juh **RAF** ¶18
girandole	**JIR** un dohl
girth	**GURTH**
gist	**JIST**
gizmo	**GIZ** moh
gizzard	**GIZ** urd
glabrous	**GLAY** brus
glacé	gla **SAY**
glacial	**GLAY** shul
glaciate	**GLAY** shee ayt ¶11
glacier	**GLAY** shur

SPELLED	PRONOUNCED
gladiator	**GLAD** ee ayt ur
gladiola	**GLAD** ee **OH** luh
gladiolus	**GLAD** ee **OH** lus
Gladstone	**GLAD** stohn
glandular	**GLAN** juh lur ¶17
Glasgow	**GLAS** koh *or* **GLAZ** goh
Glaswegian	glas **WEE** jun ¶25
glaucoma	glaw **KOH** muh
glazier	**GLAY** zhur
Glengarry	glen **GAR** ee ¶23
glissade	gli **SAHD** *or* gli **SAYD**
glissando	gli **SAHN** doh
glisten	**GLIS** un
glitzy	**GLIT** see
global	**GLOH** bul
globular	**GLAHB** yuh lur ¶1
glockenspiel	**GLAHK** un speel *or* **GLAHK** un shpeel
glorify	**GLAWR** uh fye ¶19
glorious	**GLAWR** ee us ¶19, 25
glory	**GLAWR** ee
glossary	**GLAHS** ur ee ¶19
glossy	**GLAWS** ee ¶19
glottis	**GLAHT** is
Gloucester	**GLAHS** tur ¶19
glove	**GLUV**
glower	**GLOW** ur
gloxinia	glahk **SIN** ee uh
Gluck	**GLOOK**
glucose	**GLOOH** kohs
gluon	**GLOOH** ahn
gluteal	glooh **TEE** ul *or* **GLOOHT** ee ul
gluten	**GLOOHT** un
glycerin	**GLIS** ur in ¶5
glycogen	**GLYE** kuh jun

SPELLED	PRONOUNCED
glycol	**GLYE** kawl *or* **GLYE** kohl
glyph	**GLIF**
gnarled	**NAHRLD**
gnash	**NASH**
gnat	**NAT**
gnaw	**NAW**
gneiss	**NYSE**
gnocchi	**NYAWK** ee *or* **NAH** kee ¶19
gnome	**NOHM**
gnosticism	**NAHS** tuh siz um
gnu	**NOOH** ¶21
goad	**GOHD**
goatee	goh **TEE**
Gobelin	**GAHB** uh lin
Gobi	**GOH** bee
Godiva	guh **DYE** vuh ¶1
Gog and Magog	**GAHG** un **MAY** gahg
goiter	**GOYT** ur
golem	**GOH** lum
Golgotha	**GAHL** guh thuh
Goliath	guh **LYE** uth
Gomorrah	guh **MAWR** uh
gonad	**GOH** nad
gondola	**GAHN** duh luh *or* gahn **DOH** luh

The first is usual for the boat, but the second is more common for other meanings.

SPELLED	PRONOUNCED
gondolier	gahn duh **LIR**
gonfalon	**GAHN** fuh lun *or* **GAHN** fuh lahn
gonococcus	GAHN uh **KAHK** us
gonorrhea	GAHN uh **REE** uh
googol	**GOOH** gawl
gooney	**GOOH** nee

SPELLED	PRONOUNCED
gooseberry	**GOOHS** ber ee *or* **GOOHS** bur ee ¶14
gopher	**GOH** fur
Gordian (knot)	**GAWR** dee un
gorgeous	**GAWR** jus
Gorgon	**GAWR** gun
Gorgonzola	GAWR gun **ZOH** luh
gorilla	guh **RIL** uh
gormandize	**GAWR** mun dyze
goshawk	**GAHS** hawk
Goshen	**GOH** shun
gosling	**GAHZ** ling ¶14
gossamer	**GAHS** uh mur
Gotham	**GAHTH** um *or* **GOH** thum

An English village with the same name is **GAHT** um.

SPELLED	PRONOUNCED
Gothic	**GAHTH** ik
gouache	**GWAHSH**
Gouda (cheese)	**GOOH** duh *or* **GOW** duh
gouge	**GOWJ**
goulash	**GOOH** lahsh ¶18
gourami	guh **RAH** mee

formerly also **GOOR** uh mee

SPELLED	PRONOUNCED
gourd	**GAWRD** *or* **GOORD**
gourmand	**GOOR** mund *or* goor **MAHND**
gourmet	**GOOR** may *or* **GAWR** may ¶2
gout	**GOWT**
govern	**GUV** urn
government	**GUV** ur munt ¶3
governor	**GUV** uh nur ¶3
Graafian (follicle)	**GRAHF** ee un ¶18, 25

SPELLED	PRONOUNCED	SPELLED	PRONOUNCED
gracile	**GRAS** ul	gravamen	gruh **VAY** mun
gracious	**GRAY** shus	gravel	**GRAV** ul
gradation	gray **DAY** shun ¶1	graven	**GRAY** vun
gradient	**GRAY** dee unt ¶5	gravid	**GRAV** id
gradual	**GRAJ** oo wul	gravitate	**GRAV** uh tayt
graduate	**GRAJ** oo wit	gravity	**GRAV** uh tee

occasionally, for the noun,
GRAJ *oo wayt, which is the only*
pronunciation for the verb

		gravure ... gruh **VYOOR** *or* **GRAY** vyoor	
		gravy	**GRAY** vee
		graze	**GRAYZE**
graffiti	gruh **FEET** ee	greasy	**GREES** ee
graham	**GRAY** um	*in some areas,* **GREEZ** *ee*	
gramercy	gruh **MUR** see *or*	grebe	**GREEB**
	GRAM ur see	Grecian	**GREE** shun
grammar	**GRAM** ur	Greco–Roman	GREK oh **ROH** mun
grammatical	gruh **MAT** i kul	GREE koh **ROH** mun *is also heard,*	
Granada	gruh **NAH** duh	*especially for the style of*	
granary ... **GRAN** ur ee *or* **GRAY** nur ee		*wrestling.*	
grandeur	**GRAN** jur *or*	greengage	**GREEN** gayj
	GRAN joor ¶17	Greenland	**GREEN** lund
grandiloquent	gran **DIL** uh kwunt	greensward	**GREEN** swawrd
grandiose	**GRAN** dee ohs ¶2	Greenwich	**GREN** ich
grand mal .. gran **MAL** *or* grahn **MAHL**		*In British usage,* **GRIN** *ij is usually*	
grand prix	grahn **PREE**	*heard.*	
granite	**GRAN** it	gregarious	gruh **GAR** ee us ¶23
granola	gruh **NOH** luh	Gregorian	gruh **GAWR** ee un
granular	**GRAN** yuh lur	greige	**GRAYZH**
granulate	**GRAN** yuh layt	Grenada	gruh **NAY** duh
granule	**GRAN** yool	grenade	gruh **NAYD**
graph	**GRAF** ¶18	grenadier	gren uh **DIR**
graphite	**GRAF** yte	grenadine	**GREN** uh deen ¶2
graphology	gra **FAHL** uh jee	Gresham's (law)	**GRESH** umz
gratification	GRAT uh fi **KAY** shun	gridiron	**GRID** eye urn
gratify	**GRAT** uh fye	grievance	**GREE** vuns ¶9
gratuitous	gruh **TOOH** uh tus ¶21	grieve	**GREEV**
gratuity	gruh **TOOH** uh tee ¶21	grievous	**GREE** vus

SPELLED	PRONOUNCED	SPELLED	PRONOUNCED

grimace .... gri **MAYS** or **GRIM** us
*The second is being heard more
frequently today than formerly.*

grimalkin .... gri **MAL** kun or
gri **MAWL** kun

grimy .... **GRYE** mee

grippe .... **GRIP**

grisaille .... gri **ZYE** or gri **ZAYL**

grisette .... gri **ZET**

gris–gris .... **GREE** gree

grisly .... **GRIZ** lee

gristle .... **GRIS** ul

grocery .... **GROH** sur ee ¶5, 11

groggy .... **GRAHG** ee

grogram .... **GRAHG** rum ¶19

Grolier .... **GROH** lee ur ¶25

grommet .... **GRAHM** it or **GRUM** it

grosbeak .... **GROHS** beek

grosgrain .... **GROH** grayn

grotesque .... groh **TESK**

grotto .... **GRAHT** oh

grouse .... **GROWS**

grout .... **GROWT**

grovel .... **GRUV** ul or **GRAH** vul

gruel .... **GROOH** ul ¶7

grueling .... **GROOH** ul ing ¶7

gruesome .... **GROOH** sum

grungy .... **GRUN** jee

grunion .... **GRUN** yun

Gruyère (cheese) ...... grooh **YER** or
gree **YER**

guacamole ..... **GWAH** kuh **MOH** lee or
GWAH kuh **MOH** lay

Guadeloupe .... gwah duh **LOOHP**

Guam .... **GWAHM**

Guantánamo ..... gwahn **TAH** nuh moh

guarantee .... gar un **TEE** or
gahr un **TEE** ¶23
*The second pronunciation is
considered unsophisticated by
many.*

guaranty .... **GAR** un tee or
GAHR un tee ¶23: *see preceding*

guardian .... **GAHR** dee un ¶5

Guarnerius .... gwahr **NER** ee us

Guatemala .... **GWAH** tuh **MAH** luh

guava .... **GWAH** vuh

gubernatorial ....
... **GOOH** bur nuh **TAWR** ee ul ¶3, 25

Guernsey .... **GURN** zee

guerrilla .... guh **RIL** uh

guesstimate *(verb)* ..... **GES** tuh mayt

guesstimate *(noun)* ...... **GES** tuh mit

guffaw .... guh **FAW**

Guggenheim .... **GOOG** un hyme or
GOOH gun hyme

guidance .... **GYDE** uns ¶9

guild .... **GILD**

guile .... **GYLE** ¶7

guillotine .... **GIL** uh teen or
GEE uh teen
*The stress pattern is usually
reversed to* gil uh **TEEN** *or*
gee uh **TEEN** *for the verb* ¶2.

guimpe .... **GIMP** or **GAMP**

guinea .... **GIN** ee

Guinevere .... **GWIN** uh vir

guise .... **GYZE**

guitar .... gi **TAHR**

gulag .... **GOOH** lahg

Gullah .... **GUL** uh
gullet .... **GUL** ut
gullible .... **GUL** uh bul
Gulliver .... **GUL** uh vur
gully .... **GUL** ee
gumption .... **GUMP** shun ¶9
gunwale .... **GUN** ul
guru .... **GOOR** ooh *or* **GOOH** rooh *or*
goo **ROOH**
gustatory .... **GUS** tuh **TAWR** ee
Gutenberg .... **GOOHT** un burg
gutta percha .... **GUT** uh **PUR** chuh
guttural .... **GUT** ur ul
Guyana .... gye **AN** uh ¶18
gymkhana .... jim **KAH** nuh
gymnasium .... jim **NAY** zee um
gymnastic .... jim **NAS** tik
gynecology ...... **GYE** nuh **KAHL** uh jee
JYE nuh **KAHL** uh jee *and*
JIN uh **KAHL** uh jee *are still*
sometimes heard, especially
among older speakers.

gyp .... **JIP**
gypsum .... **JIP** sum
Gypsy .... **JIP** see
gyrate .... **JYE** rayt
gyre .... **JYRE**
gyrfalcon .... **JUR** fal kun *or*
JUR fawl kun *or* **JUR** faw kun
gyro ("gyroscope") .... **JYE** roh
gyro ("sandwich") ... **YIR** oh *or* **JIR** oh
or **JYE** roh
gyrocompass ... **JYE** roh **KUM** pus ¶1
gyros .... **YIR** aws
gyroscope .... **JYE** ruh skohp

H

habeas corpus ....
.... **HAY** bee us **KAWR** pus
haberdasher ..... **HAB** ur **DASH** ur ¶3
habergeon .... **HAB** ur jun
habiliment .... huh **BIL** uh munt
habitat .... **HAB** uh tat
habitation .... **HAB** uh **TAY** shun
habitual .... huh **BICH** oo wul ¶5
habituate .... huh **BICH** oo wayt
habitué .... huh **BICH** oo way
hacienda .... **HAH** see **EN** duh ¶18
hackneyed .... **HAK** need
Hades .... **HAY** deez
haggard .... **HAG** urd
haggis .... **HAG** is
hagiology .... **HAG** ee **AHL** uh jee *or*
HAY jee **AHL** uh jee
Hague .... **HAYG**
haiku .... **HYE** kooh
Haiti .... **HAYT** ee
Haitian .... **HAY** shun *or* **HAYT** ee un
halcyon .... **HAL** see un
half .... **HAF** ¶18
halite .... **HAL** yte *or* **HAY** lyte
halitosis .... **HAL** uh **TOH** sis
hallelujah .... **HAL** uh **LOOH** yuh
hallow .... **HAL** oh
Halloween .... hal uh **WEEN** ¶18

97

hallucinate .... huh **LOOH** suh nayt

hallucinogen .. huh **LOOH** suh nuh **JEN**

halve .... **HAV** ¶18

halyard .... **HAL** yurd

Hambletonian ... HAM bul **TOH** nee un

hammock .... **HAM** uk

hamster .... **HAM** stur ¶19

handful .... **HAND** fool ¶10

handicap .... **HAN** dee kap

handkerchief .... **HANG** kur chif *or* **HANG** kur cheef

The plural ends in chifs *or* chivz *or* cheefs *or* cheevz.

handler .... **HAN** dlur ¶15

handsel .... **HAN** sul ¶9

handsome .... **HAN** sum

hangar .... **HANG** ur

Hanoi .... hah **NOY** *or* ha **NOY**

Hanuka .... **HAH** noo kah *or* **HAH** nuh kuh

haphazard .... hap **HAZ** urd

haf **HAZ** urd *results from mistaking the* ph *as representing the Greek* phi.

hara–kiri .... HAH ruh **KIR** ee

popularly HAR ee **KER** ee

harangue .... huh **RANG**

harass .... huh **RAS** *or* HAR us ¶23

harbinger .... **HAHR** bin jur

Hare (Krishna) .... **HAH** ree

harem .... HAR um ¶23

harlequin .... **HAHR** luh kwin *or* **HAHR** luh kin

harlot .... **HAHR** lut

harmonica .... hahr **MAHN** i kuh

harmonious .... hahr **MOH** nee us

harmonium .... hahr **MOH** nee um

harmonize .... **HAHR** muh nyze

harmony .... **HAHR** muh nee

harpsichord .... **HAHRP** si kawrd

harridan .... HAR i dun ¶23

harrier .... HAR ee ur ¶23

harrow ....,........ HAR oh ¶23

hartebeest .... **HAHR** tuh beest *or* **HAHRT** beest

haruspex .... huh **RUS** peks *or* HAR us peks ¶23

Harz .... **HAHRTS**

hasenpfeffer .... **HAHS** un FEF ur ¶14

hashish .... **HASH** eesh *or* **HASH** ish

hassock .... **HAS** uk

hasten .... **HAYS** un

hasty .... **HAYS** tee

hatred .... **HAY** trid ¶1

Hatteras .... **HAT** ur us

hauberk .... **HAW** burk

haughty .... **HAWT** ee ¶19

haulm .... **HAWM**

haunch .... **HAWNCH** ¶19

haunt .... **HAWNT** ¶19

Hausa .... **HOW** suh *or* **HOW** sah

hausfrau .... **HOWS** frow

haute couture .... OHT kooh **TOOR**

haute cuisine ...... OHT kwee **ZEEN** *or* OHT kwi **ZEEN**

hauteur .... hoh **TUR** *or* oh **TUR**

haut monde .... oh **MOHND**

haven .... **HAY** vun

haversack .... **HAV** ur sak

havoc .... **HAV** uk

Hawaii .. huh **WAH** ee *or* huh **WAH** yee
huh **WAH** yuh *is also sometimes
heard.*

Hawaiian .... huh **WAH** yun

hawser .... **HAW** zur

hawthorn .... **HAW** thawrn

Haydn .... **HYDE** un

haymow .... **HAY** mow

hazard .... **HAZ** urd

hazy .... **HAY** zee

headland .... **HED** lund

*When the word is used in its
agricultural meaning, it may
also be* **HED** land.

health .... **HELTH**

hearken .... **HAHR** kun

hearse .... **HURS**

hearth .... **HAHRTH**

heath .... **HEETH**

heathen .... **HEE** dhun

heather .... **HEDH** ur

heaume .... **HOHM**

heaven .... **HEV** un

heavily .... **HEV** uh lee

hebetude .... **HEB** uh toohd ¶21

Hebraic .... hi **BRAY** ik

Hebrew .... **HEE** brooh

Hebrides .... **HEB** ruh deez

Hecate .... **HEK** uh tee

HEK it *is sometimes also heard.*

hectare .... **HEK** ter ¶23

hectic .... **HEK** tik

Hecuba .... **HEK** yoo buh

hedonism .... **HEED** un iz um

Hegel .... **HAY** gul

Hegelian .... hay **GAY** lee un *or*
hi **JEE** lee un ¶25

hegemony .... hi **JEM** uh nee *or*
HEJ uh **MOH** nee *or* **HEE** juh **MOH** nee

hegira .... hi **JYE** ruh *or* **HEJ** uh ruh

Heidelberg .... **HYE** dul burg

heifer .... **HEF** ur

height .... **HYTE**

HYTTHE *is sometimes heard by
false analogy with* length *and*
width *but is not standard.*

Heimlich (maneuver) .... **HYME** lik

heinous .... **HAY** nus

heir .... **ER**

heist .... **HYSTE**

helianthus .... HEE lee **AN** thus

helical .... **HEL** i kul *or* **HEE** luh kul

helicopter .... **HEL** uh kahp tur *or*
HEE luh **KAHP** tur

heliotrope .... **HEE** lee uh **TROHP** ¶25

heliotropism
.... **HEE** lee **AHT** ruh piz um

heliport .... **HEL** uh pawrt

helium .... **HEE** le um ¶25

helix .... **HEE** liks

The plural helices *is either*
HEL uh seez *or* **HEE** luh seez.

Hellenic .... huh **LEN** ik ¶1

Hellenism .... **HEL** un iz um

Hellespont .... **HEL** us pahnt

hellion .... **HEL** yun

helot .... **HEL** ut *or* **HEE** lut

Helsinki .... **HEL** sing kee

hematin .... **HEE** muh tin *or* **HEM** uh tin

hematology ..... HEE muh **TAHL** uh jee

SPELLED	PRONOUNCED
hematoma	HEE muh **TOH** muh ¶2
hemi–	**HEM** i *or* **HEM** uh *or* **HEM** ee
hemidemisemiquaver	
	HEM ee **DEM** ee **SEM** ee **KWAY** vur
hemisphere	**HEM** uh sfir
hemistich	**HEM** uh stik
hemoglobin	HEE muh **GLOH** bun *or* **HEM** uh **GLOH** bun
hemophilia	HEE muh **FIL** ee uh *or* HEM uh **FIL** ee uh ¶25
hemorrhage	**HEM** uh rij ¶5
hemorrhoid	**HEM** uh royd ¶5
hepatitis	HEP uh **TYTE** is
heptameter	hep **TAM** uh tur
Heptateuch	**HEP** tuh toohk ¶21
Hera	**HIR** uh
herald	**HER** uld
heraldic	huh **RAL** dik
herb	URB
HURB *is also heard and is usual in British usage.*	
herbaceous	hur **BAY** shus *or* ur **BAY** shus
herbalist	**HUR** bul ist *or* **UR** bul ist
herbicide	**HUR** buh syde *or* **UR** buh syde
herbivorous	hur **BIV** ur us
Herculean	HUR kyuh **LEE** un *or* hur **KYOOH** lee un
Hercules	**HUR** kyuh leez
hereditary	huh **RED** uh **TER** ee
heredity	huh **RED** uh tee
heresy	**HER** uh see
heretic	**HER** uh tik
heretical	huh **RET** i kul

SPELLED	PRONOUNCED
heritable	**HER** it uh bul
heritage	**HER** uh tij
hermaphrodite	hur **MAF** ruh dyte
Hermes	**HUR** meez
hermetic	hur **MET** ik
hermitage	**HUR** muh tij
hernia	**HUR** nee uh ¶25
herniate	**HUR** nee ayt
hero	**HIR** oh
Herodotus	huh **RAHD** uh tus
heroic	hi **ROH** ik
heroin	**HER** uh win
heroine	**HER** uh win
heroism	**HER** uh wiz um
heron	**HER** un
herpes	**HUR** peez
herpetology	HUR puh **TAHL** uh jee
herring	**HER** ing
hertz	**HURTS**
hesitancy	**HEZ** uh tun see ¶9
hesitant	**HEZ** uh tunt
hesitate	**HEZ** uh tayt
hesitation	HEZ uh **TAY** shun
Hessian	**HESH** un
hetaera	hi **TIR** uh
heterodox	**HET** ur uh **DAHKS**
heterogeneous	
	HET ur uh **JEE** nee us ¶5, 25
heterosexual	
	HET ur uh **SEK** shoo wul
heuristic	hyoo **RIS** tik
hexachlorophene	
	HEK suh **KLAWR** uh feen
hexagon	**HEK** suh gahn
hexagonal	hek **SAG** uh nul

SPELLED	PRONOUNCED
hexameter	HEK **SAM** uh tur
Hexateuch	HEK suh toohk ¶21
hiatal (hernia)	hye **AYT** ul
hiatus	hye **AYT** us
Hiawatha	HYE uh **WAW** thuh *or*
	HEE uh **WAW** thuh ¶19
hibachi	hi **BAH** chee
hibernal	hye **BUR** nul
hibernate	**HYE** bur nayt
hibiscus	hye **BIS** kus ¶1
hiccough	**HIK** up
hiccup	**HIK** up
hickory	**HIK** ur ee ¶5
hidalgo	hi **DAL** goh *or* ee **DHAHL** goh
hideous	**HID** ee us
hierarchy	**HYE** uh RAHR kee ¶5
hieroglyphic	HYE ur uh **GLIF** ik ¶5
highfalutin	HYE fuh **LOOHT** un
highland	**HYE** lund
hilarious	hi **LAR** ee us *or*
	hye **LAR** ee us ¶23
hilarity	hi **LAR** uh tee *or*
	hye **LAR** uh tee ¶23
hillock	**HIL** uk
Himalayas	HIM uh **LAY** uz
rarely	hi **MAHL** yuz
hinder ("restrain")	**HIN** dur
hinder ("rear")	**HYNE** dur
Hindi	**HIN** dee
hindrance	**HIN** druns ¶9
Hindu	**HIN** dooh
Hindustani	HIN doo **STAN** ee *or*
	HIN doo **STAH** nee
hinterland	**HIN** tur land
Hippocrates	hi **PAHK** ruh teez
Hippocratic	HIP uh **KRAT** ik
hippodrome	**HIP** uh drohm
Hippolyta	hi **PAHL** i tuh
hippopotamus	HIP uh **PAHT** uh mus
hircine	**HUR** syne ¶22
Hiroshima	HIR uh **SHEE** muh
hi **ROH** shi muh *is also sometimes heard.*	
hirsute	**HUR** sooht *or* **HIR** sooht ¶2
Hispanic	his **PAN** ik
histamine	**HIS** tuh meen ¶22
histology	his **TAHL** uh jee
historian	his **TAWR** ee un ¶25
historic	his **TAWR** ik
historiography	
	his TAWR ee **AHG** ruh fee
history	**HIS** tuh ree ¶5
histrionics	HIS tree **AHN** iks
hither	**HIDH** ur
Hittite	**HIT** tyte
hoagy	**HOH** gee
hoax	**HOHKS**
hobbit	**HAHB** it
hobgoblin	**HAHB** gahb lin
hocus–pocus	HOH kus **POH** kus
hoi polloi	HOY puh **LOY**
holiday	**HAHL** uh day
holiness	**HOH** lee nis
holistic	hoh **LIS** tik
hollandaise	**HAHL** un dayz
holocaust	**HOH** luh kawst ¶20
holocrine	**HAHL** uh krin ¶20, 22
holograph	**HAHL** uh graf ¶18, 20
holography	huh **LAHG** ruh fee ¶1
Holstein	**HOHL** steen *or* **HOHL** styne

SPELLED	PRONOUNCED	SPELLED	PRONOUNCED
homage	**HAHM** ij *or* **AHM** ij	hoodlum	**HOOHD** lum
hombre	**AHM** bray ¶20	hoof	**HOOF** *or* **HOOHF**
homburg	**HAHM** burg	*The plural is* **HOOFS** *or* **HOOHVZ.**	
homeopathic		hooligan	**HOOH** li gun
.... HOH mee uh **PATH** ik ¶20		hoopla	**HOOHP** lah ¶21
homeopathy		hoosegow	**HOOHS** gow
.... HOH mee **AHP** uh thee ¶20		Hoosier	**HOOH** zhur
Homeric	hoh **MER** ik	Hopi	**HOH** pee
homicide	**HAHM** uh syde ¶20	horizon	huh **RYE** zun
homiletics	HAHM uh **LET** iks	horizontal ... HAWR uh **ZAHN** tul ¶19	
homily	**HAHM** uh lee	hormone	**HAWR** mohn
hominid	**HAHM** uh nid	horology	haw **RAHL** uh jee ¶1
hominy	**HAHM** uh nee	horoscope	**HAWR** uh skohp ¶19
homogeneous		horrendous	haw **REN** dus ¶1
.... HOH muh **JEE** nee us ¶1, 20, 25		horrible	**HAWR** uh bul ¶19
homogenize	huh **MAHJ** uh nyze	horrid	**HAWR** id ¶19
homograph .. HAHM uh graf ¶18, 20		horrify	**HAWR** uh fye ¶19
homologous .... hoh **MAHL** uh gus ¶1		horror	**HAWR** ur ¶19
homonym .... **HAHM** uh nim ¶20		hors d'oeuvre	awr **DURV**
Homo sapiens		*occasionally* awr **DUV**	
.... HOH moh **SAY** pee unz *or*		horseshoe	**HAWR** shooh ¶6
HOH moh **SAP** ee unz ¶1		hortatory	**HAWR** tuh **TAWR** ee
homosexual .. HOH muh **SEK** shoo wul		horticulture	**HAWR** tuh KUL chur
honcho	**HAHN** choh	hosanna	hoh **ZAN** uh
Honduras	hahn **DOOR** us ¶24	hosiery .... HOH zhur ee *or* HOH zur ee	
honest	**AHN** ust	hospice	**HAHS** pis
honeyed	**HUN** eed	hospitable	**HAHS** pi tuh bul *or*
honky–tonk		hahs **PIT** uh bul	
.... **HAWNG** kee tawnk ¶19		hospital	**HAHS** pi tul
Honolulu .. HAHN uh **LOOH** looh ¶20		hospitality .... HAHS puh **TAL** uh tee	
honor	**AHN** ur	hostage	**HAHS** tij
honorarium		hostel	**HAHS** tul
.... AHN uh **RAR** ee um ¶23		hostess	**HOHS** tis
honorary .... **AHN** uh RER ee ¶23		hostile	**HAHS** tul ¶22
honorific	AHN uh **RIF** ik	hostility	hahs **TIL** uh tee

SPELLED	PRONOUNCED	SPELLED	PRONOUNCED
hostler	**HAHS** lur *or* **AHS** lur	humidity	hyooh **MID** uh tee *or*
hotelier	hoh tel **YAY** *or* oht ul **YAY**		yooh **MID** uh tee ¶1
Hottentot	**HAHT** un taht	humidor	**HYOOH** muh dawr *or*
houri	**HOOR** ee *or* **HOW** ree		**YOOH** muh dawr
house *(noun)*	**HOWS**	humiliate	hyooh **MIL** ee ayt *or*
house *(verb)*	**HOWZ**		yooh **MIL** ee ayt ¶1
housewife	**HOWS** wyfe	humility	hyooh **MIL** uh tee *or*
When this word means sewing			yooh **MIL** uh tee
kit, *it is usually* **HUZ** if.		hummock	**HUM** uk
housing	**HOW** zing	humongous	hyooh **MAHNG** gus *or*
Houston	**HYOOHS** tun		hyooh **MUNG** gus
This is for the city in Texas, but		humor	**HYOOH** mur *or* **YOOH** mur
elsewhere it is often **HOWS** tun.		humoresque	hyooh muh **RESK**
Houyhnhnm	hooh **IN** um *or*	humus	**HYOOH** mus *or* **YOOH** mus
	HWIN um	hundred ...	**HUN** drud *or* **HUN** durd ¶4
hovel	**HUV** ul *or* **HAHV** ul	hurrah	huh **RAH** *or* huh **RAW**
hover	**HUV** ur *or* **HAHV** ur	hurricane	**HUR** uh kayn *or*
howitzer	**HOW** it sur		**HUH** ruh kayn ¶1
hoyden	**HOY** dun	hurry	**HUR** ee *or* **HUH** ree
huaraches	huh **RAH** cheez *or*	husband	**HUZ** bund
	wuh **RAH** cheez	husbandry	**HUZ** bun dree
hubris	**HYOOH** bris	hussar	hoo **ZAHR** ¶1
Huguenot	**HYOOH** guh naht ¶19	hussy	**HUZ** ee ¶14
hula	**HOOH** luh	hustle	**HUS** ul
hullabaloo	HUL uh buh **LOOH** ¶2	hyacinth	**HYE** uh sinth ¶9
human	**HYOOH** mun *or* **YOOH** mun	hybrid	**HYE** brid
humane ...	hyooh **MAYN** *or* yooh **MAYN**	hydrangea	hye **DRAYN** juh *or*
humanitarian			hye **DRAN** juh ¶25
....	hyooh **MAN** uh **TAR** ee un *or*	hydraulic	hye **DRAW** lik ¶19
	yooh **MAN** uh **TAR** ee un ¶23	hydrocephalous	
humanity	hyooh **MAN** uh tee *or*	....	**HYE** druh **SEF** uh lus ¶1
	yooh **MAN** uh tee ¶1	hydroelectric	**HYE** droh i **LEK** trik
humectant	hyooh **MEK** tunt ¶1	hydrofoil	**HYE** druh foyl
humerus	**HYOOH** mur us	hydrogen	**HYE** druh jun
humid	**HYOOH** mid *or* **YOOH** mid	hydrology	hye **DRAHL** uh jee

hydrolysis .... hye **DRAHL** uh sis

hydrophobia ....
.... HYE druh **FOH** bee uh ¶25

hydroplane .... **HYE** druh playn

hydroponics .... HYE druh **PAHN** iks

hydrotherapy ....
.... HYE druh **THER** uh pee ¶1

hydroxide .... hye **DRAHK** syde

hyena .... hye **EE** nuh

hygiene .... **HYE** jeen

hygienic .. HYE jee **EN** ik *or* hye **JEE** nik
or hye **JEN** ik

hymen .... **HYE** mun

hymenopteran ....
.... HYE muh **NAHP** tur un

hymn .... **HIM**

hymnal .... **HIM** nul

hyperactive .... HYE pur **AK** tiv

hyperbola .... hye **PUR** buh luh

hyperbole .... hye **PUR** buh lee

hyperbolic .... HYE pur **BAHL** ik

hyperborean .... HYE pur **BAWR** ee un
or HYE pur buh **REE** un

Hyperion .... hye **PIR** ee un

hyperkinesis .... HYE pur ki **NEE** sis

hypermetropia ....
.... HYE pur mi **TROH** pee uh

hypertension ....
.... HYE pur **TEN** shun ¶9, 12

hyphen .... **HYE** fun

hypnosis .... hip **NOH** sis

hypnotic .... hip **NAHT** ik

hypnotize .... **HIP** nuh tyze

hypochondria ....
.... HYE puh **KAHN** dree uh

hypocrisy .... hi **PAHK** ruh see

hypocrite .... **HIP** uh krit

hypodermic .... HYE puh **DUR** mik

hypostatize .... hye **PAHS** tuh tyze

hypotenuse ....
.... hye **PAHT** uh noohs ¶21

hypothesis .... hye **PAHTH** uh sis

hypothetical .... HYE puh **THET** i kul

hyrax .... **HYE** raks

hyssop .... **HIS** up

hysterectomy ... HIS tuh **REK** tuh mee

hysteria .... his **TER** ee uh *or*
his **TIR** ee uh ¶25

hysterical .... his **TER** i kul

I

–ia .... ee uh *or* yuh ¶25

Iago .... ee **AH** goh

iambic .... eye **AM** bik

iatrogenic .... eye AT ruh **JEN** ik

Iberian .... eye **BIR** ee un

ibex .... **EYE** beks

ibis .... **EYE** bis

Icarus .... **IK** ur us

Iceland .... **EYSE** lund ¶8

Icelandic .... eyse **LAN** dik

ichor .... **EYE** kawr *or* **EYE** kur

ichthyology .... IK thee **AHL** uh jee

SPELLED	PRONOUNCED
icicle	**EYE** si kul
icon	**EYE** kahn
iconic	eye **KAHN** ik
iconoclast	eye **KAHN** uh KLAST
iconography	EYE kuh **NAHG** ruh fee
ideal	eye **DEE** ul ¶7
idealistic	EYE dee uh **LIS** tik or
	eye DEE uh **LIS** tik
ideation	EYE dee **AY** shun
idée fixe	ee day **FEEKS**
identical	eye **DEN** ti kul
identify	eye **DEN** tuh fye
ideogram	**ID** ee uh GRAM or
	EYE dee uh GRAM
ideologue	**EYE** dee uh LAWG or
	ID ee uh LAWG ¶19
ideology	EYE dee **AHL** uh jee or
	ID ee **AHL** uh jee
idiocy	**ID** ee uh see
idiom	**ID** ee um
idiomatic	ID ee uh **MAT** ik
idiosyncrasy	
	ID ee uh **SING** kruh see ¶1, 16
idiosyncratic	**ID** ee oh sin **KRAT** ik
idiot	**ID** ee ut
idiotic	ID ee **AHT** ik
idol	**EYE** dul
idolater	eye **DAHL** uh tur
idyll	**EYE** dul
igloo	**IG** looh
igneous	**IG** nee us
ignite	ig **NYTE**
ignition	ig **NISH** un
ignoble	ig **NOH** bul
ignominious	IG nuh **MIN** ee us

SPELLED	PRONOUNCED
ignominy	**IG** nuh min ee
ignoramus	IG nuh **RAY** mus or
	IG nuh **RAM** us
ignorance	**IG** nur uns ¶9
iguana	i **GWAH** nuh
–ile	il or ul or eyle *variously* ¶22
ileitis	IL ee **YTE** is
ileum	**IL** ee um
Iliad	**IL** ee ud
illegal	i **LEE** gul
illicit	i **LIS** it
Illinois	il uh **NOY**
il uh **NOYZ** *is sometimes still heard.*	
illiterate	i **LIT** ur it
illuminate	i **LOOH** muh nayt
illusion	i **LOOH** zhun
illusive	i **LOOH** siv
illusory	i **LOOH** sur ee
illustrate	**IL** uh strayt or i **LUS** trayt
illustrative	i **LUS** truh tiv or
	IL us trayt iv
illustrious	i **LUS** tree us
image	**IM** ij
imagery	**IM** ij ree ¶5
imaginary	i **MAJ** uh **NER** ee
imagination	i MAJ uh **NAY** shun
imagine	i **MAJ** in
imagism	**IM** uh jiz um
imago	i **MAY** goh
imbecile	**IM** buh sul
imbecility	**IM** buh **SIL** uh tee
imbibe	im **BYBE**
imbroglio	im **BROHL** yoh ¶25
imbue	im **BYOOH**
imitate	**IM** uh tayt

105

immaculate	i **MAK** yuh lit	imperturbable	IM pur **TUR** buh bul
immanent	**IM** uh nunt	impervious	im **PUR** vee us
immediate	i **MEE** dee it	impetigo	IM puh **TYE** goh
immense	i **MENS** ¶9	impetuosity	
immerse	i **MURS**		im PECH oo **WAHS** uh tee
immersion	i **MUR** shun *or* i **MUR** zhun	impetuous	im **PECH** oo wus
immigrate	**IM** uh grayt	impetus	**IM** puh tus
imminent	**IM** uh nunt	impinge	im **PINJ**
immolate	**IM** uh layt	impious	**IM** pee us
immoral	i **MAWR** ul ¶19	im **PYE** us *is now also sometimes*

heard.

immortalize	i **MAWR** tuh lyze	implacable	im **PLAK** uh bul *or*
immune	i **MYOOHN**		im **PLAY** kuh bul
immunity	i **MYOOH** nuh tee	implement *(verb)*	**IM** pluh ment
immunize	**IM** yoo nyze	implement *(noun)*	**IM** pluh munt
immunology	IM yoo **NAHL** uh jee	implicate	**IM** pluh kayt
immure	i **MYOOR**	implicit	im **PLIS** it
impact *(verb)*	im **PAKT**	implode	im **PLOHD**

occasionally, but for the noun
always, **IM** pakt

		implosion	im **PLOH** zhun
impala	im **PAH** luh ¶18	import *(verb)*	im **PAWRT**
impasse	**IM** pas *or* im **PAS**	*also, and for the noun always,*
impatience	im **PAY** shuns ¶9	**IM** pawrt
impatiens	im **PAY** shunz *or*	importunate	im **PAWR** chuh nit
	im **PAY** shee enz	importune	IM pawr **TOOHN**
impeach	im **PEECH**	im **PAWR** chun *is also sometimes*

heard. ¶21

impeccable	im **PEK** uh bul	imposition	IM puh **ZISH** un
impecunious	im pi **KYOOH** nee us	imposter	im **PAHS** tur
impedance	im **PEED** uns ¶9	impotent	**IM** puh tunt
impede	im **PEED**	imprecate	**IM** pruh kayt
impediment	im **PED** uh munt	impregnable	im **PREG** nuh bul
impedimenta	im PED uh **MEN** tuh	impregnate	im **PREG** nayt
imperative	im **PER** uh tiv	impresario	IM pruh **SAHR** ee oh *or*
imperial	im **PIR** ee ul		IM pruh **SER** ee oh ¶23
imperious	im **PIR** ee us	impress *(verb)*	im **PRES**
impersonate	im **PUR** suh nayt		

impress *(noun)* .... **IM** pres

impressionism ... im **PRESH** uh niz um

imprimatur .... IM pruh **MAHT** ur *or*
IM pruh **MAYT** ur

imprint *(verb)* .... im **PRINT**

imprint *(noun)* .... **IM** print

impromptu ....
.... im **PRAHMP** tooh ¶10, 21

improvisation ....
.... im PRAHV uh **ZAY** shun *or*
IM pruh vuh **ZAY** shun

improvise .... im **pruh** vyze

impudence .... **IM** pyoo duns ¶9

impugn .... im **PYOOHN**

impulse .... **IM** puls

impulsive .... im **PUL** siv

impunity .... im **PYOO** nuh tee

impute .... im **PYOOHT**

in absentia ....
.... IN ub **SEN** shuh ¶9, 12, 25

inadvertent .... IN ud **VUR** tunt ¶1

inalienable .... in **AYL** yun uh bul ¶25

inamorata .... in **AM** uh **RAHT** uh ¶18

inane .... in **AYN**

inanity .... in **AN** uh tee

inaugurate .... in **AWG** yoo rayt *or*
in **AW** guh rayt

in camera ., ... in **KAM** ur uh

incandescent ...... IN kun **DES** unt ¶1

incantation .... IN kan **TAY** shun

incapacitate .... IN kuh **PAS** uh tayt

incarcerate .... in **KAHR** suh rayt

incarnate *(adjective)* ...... in **KAHR** nit
also, and for the verb always,
in **KAHR** nayt

incendiary .... in **SEN** dee **ER** ee

incense *(verb)* .... in **SENS** ¶9

incense *(noun)* .... **IN** sens ¶9

incentive .... in **SEN** tiv

inception .... in **SEP** shun

incessant .... in **SES** unt

incest .... **IN** sest

incestuous .... in **SES** choo wus

inchoate .... in **KOH** it *or* in **KOH** ayt

inchoative .... in **KOH** uh tiv

incidence .... **IN** suh duns ¶9

incidental .... IN suh **DEN** tul

incinerate .... in **SIN** uh rayt

incipient .... in **SIP** ee unt

incise .... in **SYZE**

incision .... in **SIZH** un

incisive .... in **SYE** siv

incisor .... in **SYE** zur

incite .... in **SYTE**

inclement .... in **KLEM** unt ¶3

inclination .... IN kluh **NAY** shun

incline *(verb)* .... in **KLYNE**
The noun is usually **IN** klyne.

incognito .... IN kahg **NEET** oh *or*
in **KAHG** ni toh

incommunicado ....
.... IN kuh **MYOOH** nuh **KAH** doh

incomparable ..... in **KAHM** pur uh bul
occasionally
IN kum **PAR** uh bul ¶23

incongruity ...... IN kun **GROOH** uh tee

incongruous .... in **KAHNG** groo wus

incontinent .... in **KAHN** tuh nunt

incorporate .... in **KAWR** puh rayt

incorporeal .... IN kawr **PAWR** ee ul

incorrigible ... in **KAWR** i juh bul ¶19

increase *(verb)* .... in **KREES**
also, and for the noun always,
IN krees

incredulity ....

.... IN kruh **DOOH** luh tee ¶21

incredulous ...... in **KREJ** oo lus ¶13

increment .... **IN** kruh munt ¶16

incriminate .... in **KRIM** uh nayt

incrustation .... IN krus **TAY** shun

incubate .... **ING** kyoo bayt ¶16

incubus .... **ING** kyoo bus ¶16

inculcate .... in **KUL** kayt *or* **IN** kul kayt

incumbency ...... in **KUM** bun see ¶9

incumbent .... in **KUM** bunt

incumbrance .... in **KUM** bruns ¶9

incur .... in **KUR**

incursion .... in **KUR** zhun

indecency .... in **DEE** sun see ¶9

indefatigable .... IN di **FAT** i guh bul

indelible .... in **DEL** uh bul

indemnify .... in **DEM** nuh **FYE**

indenture .... in **DEN** chur ¶9

indeterminate .... IN di **TUR** muh nit

index .... **IN** deks

indicate .... **IN** duh kayt

indicative .... in **DIK** uh tiv

indices .... **IN** duh seez

indict .... in **DYTE**

indictment .... in **DYTE** munt

indigenous .... in **DIJ** uh nus

indigent .... **IN** di junt

indignant .... in **DIG** nunt

indignation .... IN dig **NAY** shun

indigo .... **IN** di goh

indiscriminate ...... **IN** dis **KRIM** uh nit

individual .... **IN** di **VIJ** oo wul

individuality .. **IN** di **VIJ** oo **WAL** uh tee

indoctrinate .... in **DAHK** truh nayt

indolent .... **IN** duh lunt

indomitable .... in **DAHM** uh tuh bul

Indonesia ...... **IN** duh **NEE** zhuh *or*
IN duh **NEE** shuh

indubitable .... in **DOOH** bi tuh bul

induce .... in **DOOHS** ¶21

induction .... in **DUK** shun

indulge .... in **DULJ**

indurate .... **IN** doo rayt ¶21

industrial .... in **DUS** tree ul

industry .... **IN** dus tree

–ine .... eyne *or* in *or* een *or* un
variously ¶22

inebriate *(verb)* .... in **EE** bree ayt
*The noun and adjective are
usually* in **EE** bree it.

ineffable .... in **EF** uh bul

ineluctable .... **IN** i **LUK** tuh bul

ineptitude ...... in **EP** tuh **TOOHD** ¶21

inertia .... in **UR** shuh

inevitable .... in **EV** uh tuh bul

inexorable .... in **EK** sur uh bul

inexpiable .... in **EK** spee uh bul

inexplicable ...... in **EKS** pli kuh bul *or*
IN iks **PLIK** uh bul ¶1

inextricable .... in **EKS** tri kuh bul *or*
IN ik **STRIK** uh bul ¶1

infamous .... **IN** fuh mus

infamy .... **IN** fuh mee

infanticide .... in **FAN** tuh syde

infantile .... **IN** fun tyle ¶22

infatuate .... in **FACH** oo wayt

infectious .... in **FEK** shus

inference .... **IN** fur uns ¶5, 9

inferior .... in **FIR** ee ur

infernal .... in **FUR** nul

inferno .... in **FUR** noh

infidel .... **IN** fuh dul

infiltrate ..... in **FIL** trayt *or* **IN** fil trayt

infinite .... **IN** fuh nit

infinitesimal ... **IN** fin uh **TES** uh mul *or*
in **FIN** uh **TES** uh mul

infinitive .... in **FIN** uh tiv

infinitude ...... in **FIN** uh **TOOHD** ¶21

infinity .... in **FIN** uh tee

infirmary .... in **FUR** mur ee ¶5

infirmity .... in **FUR** muh tee

inflammable .... in **FLAM** uh bul

inflation .... in **FLAY** shun

inflection .... in **FLEK** shun

influence .... **IN** floo wuns ¶9

influential .. **IN** floo **WEN** shul ¶9, 12

influenza .... **IN** floo **WEN** zuh

information .... **IN** fur **MAY** shun

infrastructure ..... **IN** fruh **STRUK** chur

infuriate .... in **FYOOR** ee ayt ¶24

–ing .... ing
in context often in *or* un

ingenious .... in **JEEN** yus ¶25

ingénue .... **AN** zhuh nooh *or*
AHN juh nooh ¶2, 15, 21

ingenuity .... **IN** juh **NOOH** uh tee ¶21

ingenuous .... in **JEN** yoo wus

ingest .... in **JEST**

ingot .... **ING** gut

ingrate .... **IN** grayt

ingratiate ....

.... in **GRAY** shee ayt ¶11, 16

ingredient .... in **GREE** dee unt

inhalant .... in **HAYL** unt

inhalator .... **IN** huh layt ur

inherent .... in **HIR** unt *or* in **HER** unt

inherit .... in **HER** it

inhibit .... in **HIB** it

inhibition .... **IN** hi **BISH** un *or*
IN uh **BISH** un

inimical .... in **IM** i kul

inimitable .... in **IM** uh ti bul

iniquitous .... in **IK** wuh tus

iniquity .... in **IK** wuh tee

initial .... i **NISH** ul

initiate *(verb)* .... i **NISH** ee ayt
The adjective and noun are usually i **NISH** ee it.

initiative .... i **NISH** uh tiv *or*
i **NISH** ee uh tiv

injunction .... in **JUNGK** shun ¶9

injurious .... in **JOOR** ee us ¶24

injury .... **IN** jur ee ¶5

in loco parentis ....
.... in **LOH** koh puh **REN** tis

innate .... i **NAYT** *or* **IN** ayt

innervate ...... i **NUR** vayt *or* **IN** ur vayt

innocent .... **IN** uh sunt

innocuous .... i **NAHK** yoo wus

innovate .... **IN** uh vayt ¶1

innuendo .... **IN** yoo **WEN** doh

inoculate .... i **NAHK** yoo layt

inoperable .... in **AHP** ur uh bul

inordinate .... in **AWR** duh nit ¶5

inquest .... **IN** kwest

SPELLED	PRONOUNCED
inquire	in **KWYRE**
inquiry	**IN** kwur ee *or*
	in **KWYRE** ee ¶16
inquisition	**IN** kwuh **ZISH** un
inquisitive	in **KWIZ** uh tiv
insanity	in **SAN** uh tee
insatiable	in **SAY** shuh bul
in **SAY** shee uh bul *has become*	
much less common.	
inscription	in **SKRIP** shun
inscrutable	in **SKROOHT** uh bul
insecticide	in **SEK** tuh syde
insectivore	in **SEK** tuh vawr
inseminate	in **SEM** uh nayt
insensate	in **SEN** sayt *or* in **SEN** sit
inseparable	in **SEP** ur uh bul ¶5
insert *(verb)*	in **SURT**
insert *(noun)*	**IN** surt
insertion	in **SUR** shun
insidious	in **SID** ee us
insignia	in **SIG** nee uh ¶25
insinuate	in **SIN** yoo wayt
insipid	in **SIP** id
insolate	**IN** suh layt
insole	**IN** sohl
insolent	**IN** suh lunt
insomnia	in **SAHM** nee uh
insouciant	in **SOOH** see unt
inspiration	**IN** spuh **RAY** shun
installation	**IN** stuh **LAY** shun
instance	**IN** stuns ¶9
instantaneous	
	IN stun **TAY** nee us ¶25
instead	in **STED**
instigate	**IN** stuh gayt

SPELLED	PRONOUNCED
instinct *(noun)*	**IN** stingkt
instinct *(adjective)*	in **STINGKT**
institute	**IN** stuh tooht ¶21
institution	**IN** stuh **TOOH** shun ¶21
instrument	**IN** struh munt
instrumental	**IN** struh **MEN** tul
insufferable	in **SUF** ur uh bul ¶5
insular	**IN** suh lur ¶1, 21
insulate	**IN** suh layt ¶1, 21
insulin	**IN** suh lin ¶1, 21
insult *(verb)*	in **SULT**
insult *(noun)*	**IN** sult
insuperable	
	in **SOOH** pur uh bul ¶5, 21
insurance	in **SHOOR** uns ¶9, 24
insurgent	in **SUR** junt
insurrection	**IN** suh **REK** shun
intaglio	in **TAL** yoh ¶18
intarsia	in **TAHR** see uh
integer	**IN** tuh jur
integral	**IN** tuh grul
also in **TEG** rul, *except in*	
mathematics	
integrate	**IN** tuh grayt
integration	**IN** tuh **GRAY** shun
integrity	in **TEG** ruh tee
integument	in **TEG** yoo munt
intellect	**IN** tuh lekt
intellectual	**IN** tuh **LEK** choo wul
intelligent	in **TEL** uh junt
intelligentsia	in **TEL** uh **JENT** see uh
or in **TEL** uh **GENT** see uh	
intense	in **TENS** ¶9
inter	in **TUR**
intercalary	in **TUR** kuh **LER** ee

intercede	in tur **SEED**	intern	**IN** turn
intercept *(verb)*	in tur **SEPT**		*This is for the noun and the*
intercept *(noun)*	**IN** tur sept		*verb meaning* to serve as a
intercession	**IN** tur **SESH** un		medical intern, *but for the verb*
intercom	**IN** tur kahm		*meaning* to detain, *it is usually*
interdict *(verb)*	in tur **DIKT**		in **TURN**.
interdict *(noun)*	**IN** tur dikt	internecine	**IN** tur **NEE** sin *or*
interdiction	**IN** tur **DIK** shun		**IN** tur **NES** in
interest *(noun)*	**IN** trist ¶5		*Various other combinations are*
for the verb, also **IN** tuh rest; *both*			*heard with a final syllable of*
t's *are sounded in standard*			syne *or* seen *or with the main*
English, *that is, not* **IN** uh rest.			*stress on the second syllable.*
interfere	in tur **FIR**	internist	**IN** tur nist *or*
interferon	**IN** tur **FIR** ahn		in **TUR** nist ¶2
interim	**IN** tur im	Interpol	**IN** tur pohl
interior	in **TIR** ee ur	interpolate	in **TUR** puh layt
interject	in tur **JEKT**	interpret	in **TUR** prit
interlocutor	**IN** tur **LAHK** yuh tur	interpretation	in **TUR** pruh **TAY** shun
often **IN** tur **LAHK** uh tur *for the*		interpretive	in **TUR** pruh tiv
master of ceremonies in a		interregnum	**IN** tur **REG** num
minstrel show ¶3		interrogate	in **TER** uh gayt
interloper	**IN** tur **LOH** pur	interrogative	**IN** tuh **RAHG** uh tiv
interlude	**IN** tur loohd	interrupt	in tuh **RUPT**
intermediary	**IN** tur **MEE** dee **ER** ee	intersect	in tur **SEKT**
intermediate *(verb)*		intersperse	in tur **SPURS**
	IN tur **MEE** dee ayt	interstice	in **TUR** stis
intermediate *(adjective)*		*The plural is either*	
	IN tur **MEE** dee it ¶5	in **TUR** stuh seez *or* in **TUR** stis iz.	
interment	in **TUR** munt	interval	**IN** tur vul
intermezzo	**IN** tur **MET** soh	intervene	in tur **VEEN**
IN tur **MED** zoh *is still heard*		intervention	
sometimes.			**IN** tur **VEN** shun ¶9, 12
interminable	in **TUR** mi nuh bul	intestate	in **TES** tayt *or* in **TES** tit
intermission	**IN** tur **MISH** un	intestine	in **TES** tin
intermittent	**IN** tur **MIT** unt	intimacy	**IN** tuh muh see

intimate *(verb)* .... IN tuh mayt

intimate *(adjective)* .... IN tuh mit

intimidate .... in TIM uh dayt

intonation .... IN tuh NAY shun

intoxicate .... in TAHK suh kayt

intractable .... in TRAK tuh bul

intrados .... IN truh dahs *or*
  in TRAY dohs ¶20

intramural .... IN truh MYOOR ul ¶24

intransigent ....
  .... in TRAN suh junt ¶9, 14

intravenous .... IN truh VEE nus

intrepid .... in TREP id

intricacy .... IN tri kuh see

intricate .... IN tri kit

intrigue *(verb)* .... in TREEG
  The noun is also IN treeg ¶2.

intrinsic .... in TRIN sik ¶9, 14

introduce .... in truh DOOHS ¶21

introduction .... IN truh DUK shun

introit .... in TROH it *or* IN troh it *or*
  IN troyt

introspective .... IN truh SPEK tiv ¶1

introversion .... IN truh VUR zhun

introvert *(noun)* .... IN truh vurt
  The verb is also in truh VURT ¶2.

intrusion .... in TROOH zhun

intuit .... in TOOH it ¶21

intuition .... IN too WISH un ¶21

intuitive .... in TOOH i tiv ¶21

inundate .... IN un dayt
  in UN dayt *is occasionally heard.*

inure .... in YOOR

in utero .... in YOOHT ur oh

inutile .... in YOOHT ul ¶22

invalid *(noun)* .... IN vuh lid

invalid *(adjective)* .... in VAL id

invasion .... in VAY zhun

invective .... in VEK tiv

inveigh .... in VEY

inveigle .... in VEE gul *or* in VAY gul

inventory .... IN vun TAWR ee

inverse .... in VURS
  also, especially for the noun,
  IN vurs

invert *(verb)* .... in VURT

invert *(noun, adjective)* .... IN vurt

investigate .... in VES tuh gayt

investiture .... in VES tuh chur

inveterate .... in VET ur ut

invidious .... in VID ee us

invigorate .... in VIG uh rayt

invincible .... in VIN suh bul ¶9

inviolable .... in VYE uh luh bul

inviolate .... in VYE uh lit

invitation .... IN vuh TAY shun

in vitro .... in VEE troh

in vivo .... in VEE voh

invocation .... IN vuh KAY shun ¶1

invoice .... IN voys

involve .... in VAHLV ¶19

inward .... IN wurd

iodine .... EYE uh dyne ¶22
  Among chemists and in British
  usage, EYE uh deen *is usual.*

ion .... EYE un *or* EYE ahn ¶8

Ionian .... eye OH nee un ¶25

Ionic .... eye AHN ik

ionize .... EYE uh nyze

ionosphere .... eye AHN uh sfir

iota .... eye **OHT** uh *or* ee **OHT** uh

Iowa .... **EYE** uh wuh
   In rural areas of Iowa,
   EYE uh way *is sometimes heard.*

ipecac .... **IP** uh kak

ipse dixit .... **IP** see **DIK** sit

ipso facto .... **IP** soh **FAK** toh

Iran .... i **RAHN** *or* i **RAN** *or* eye **RAN**

irascible .... i **RAS** uh bul

irate .. eye **RAYT** *or* **EYE** rayt *or* i **RAYT**

iridescent .... **IR** uh **DES** unt

iris .... **EYE** ris

iron .... **EYE** urn

ironic .... eye **RAHN** ik

irony .... **EYE** ruh nee ¶4

Iroquois .... **IR** uh kwoy

irradiate .... i **RAY** de ayt

irredentist .... **IR** i **DEN** tist

irrefragable .... i **REF** ruh guh bul

irrefutable .... i **REF** yoo tuh bul *or*
             IR i **FYOOHT** uh bul

irreparable .... i **REP** ur uh bul
  IR i **PAR** uh bul *is now sometimes*
  heard. ¶23.

irrevocable .... i **REV** uh kuh bul
  IR i **VOHK** uh bul *is now sometimes*
  heard.

irritable .... **IR** uh tuh bul

irritate .... **IR** uh tayt

Isis .... **EYE** sis

Islam .... **IS** lahm ¶2, 14, 18

island .... **EYE** lund

isle .... **EYLE**

islet .... **EYE** lit

ism .... **IZ** um

isobar .... **EYE** suh bahr ¶1

Isocrates .... eye **SAHK** ruh teez

isogloss .... **EYE** suh glaws ¶19

isolate *(verb)* .... **EYE** suh layt
  IS uh layt *is also still heard*
  sometimes for the verb.
  EYE suh lit *is more frequent*
  for the noun.

isolation .... **EYE** suh **LAY** shun

Isolde ...... i **SOHL** duh *or* ee **ZOHL** duh

isomer .... **EYE** suh mur

isometric .... **EYE** suh **MET** rik

isomorph .... **EYE** suh morf

isosceles .... eye **SAHS** uh leez

isotope .... **EYE** suh tohp

Israel .... **IZ** ree ul *or* **IZ** ray ul

Israeli .... iz **RAY** lee

Israelite .... **IZ** ree uh **LYTE** *or*
            IZ ray uh **LYTE**

issue .... **ISH** ooh

Istanbul .... **IS** tan **BOOL** *or*
      is tahn **BOOL** ¶2

isthmus .... **IS** mus

Italian .... i **TAL** yun
  eye **TAL** yun *is not a standard*
  pronunciation.

italic .... i **TAL** ik *or* eye **TAL** ik

italicize .... i **TAL** uh **SYZE** *or*
      eye **TAL** uh **SYZE**

iterate .... **IT** uh rayt

iterative ..... **IT** ur uh tiv *or* **IT** uh rayt iv

itinerant .... eye **TIN** ur unt *or*
      i **TIN** ur unt ¶1

itinerary .... eye **TIN** uh **RER** ee *or*
      i **TIN** uh **RER** ee ¶1

SPELLED	PRONOUNCED	SPELLED	PRONOUNCED

ivory .... **EYE** vuh ree *or* **EYE** vree ¶5

–ization ... i **ZAY** shun *or* eye **ZAY** shun

J

jabot .... zha **BOH** ¶15

jacaranda .... JAK uh **RAN** duh

jackal .... **JAK** ul

jackanapes .... **JAK** uh nayps

Jacobean .... JAK uh **BEE** un

Jacobin .... **JAK** uh bin

Jacobite .... **JAK** uh byte

jaguar .... **JAG** wahr

 JAG yoo wahr *is occasionally heard.*

jai alai .... **HYE** lye *or* **HYE** uh lye

Jainism .... **JYNE** iz um

Jakarta .... juh **KAHR** tuh

jalopy .... juh **LAHP** ee

jalousie .... **JAL** uh see

Jamaica .... juh **MAY** kuh

jamb .... **JAM**

jambalaya .... JUM buh **LYE** uh

jamboree .... jam buh **REE** ¶2

janitor .... **JAN** uh tur

janizary .... **JAN** uh **ZER** ee

January .... **JAN** yoo **WER** ee

Janus .... **JAY** nus

japan .... juh **PAN**

japonica .... juh **PAHN** i kuh

jardiniere .... jahr duh **NIR** *or*
zhahr duh **NYER** ¶15

jargon .... **JAHR** gun

jasmine .... **JAZ** mun

jaundice .... **JAWN** dis ¶19

javelin ...... **JAV** lin *or* JAV uh lun ¶5

jealous .... **JEL** us

jejune .... ji **JOOHN**

je ne sais quoi .... zhuh nuh say **KWAH**

jeopardize .... **JEP** ur dyze

jeopardy .... **JEP** ur dee

jeroboam .... JER uh **BOH** um

Jerusalem .... juh **ROOH** suh lum ¶14

Jesuit .... **JEZH** oo wit *or*
JEZ oo wit ¶21

Jesus .... **JEE** zus *or* JEE zuz

jeté .... zhuh **TAY**

jetsam .... **JET** sum

jettison .... **JET** uh sun ¶14

jewel .... **JOOH** ul ¶7

jewelry .... **JOOH** ul ree ¶4, 7

jew's–harp .... **JOOHZ** hahrp ¶6, 14

jibe .... **JYBE**

jingo .... **JING** goh

jinrikisha .... jin **RIK** shaw ¶5, 19

jocose .... joh **KOHS** ¶1

jocosity .... joh **KAHS** uh tee

jocular .... **JAHK** yoo lur

jocund ...... **JAHK** und *or* **JOH** kund

jocundity .... joh **KUN** duh tee
occasionally jah **KUN** duh tee

jodhpur .... **JAHD** pur

joie de vivre ...... zhwah duh **VEEV** ruh
*Sometimes the last word is
shortened to* **VEEV.**

jollity .... **JAHL** uh tee

jonquil .... **JAHNG** kwul ¶9, 16

jostle .... **JAHS** ul

joule .... **JOOHL**
  JOWL, *once common for this word, is now rare.*

journal .... **JUR** nul

journey .... **JUR** nee

joust .... **JOWST**
  This spelling pronunciation has taken over from earlier **JUST** *and* **JOOHST**.

jovial .... **JOH** vee ul ¶5

jubilant .... **JOOH** buh lunt

jubilation .... **JOOH** buh **LAY** shun

jubilee .... **JOOH** buh lee ¶2

Judaic .... jooh **DAY** ik

Judaism .... **JOOH** duh iz um *or*
  JOOH dee iz um

Judea .... jooh **DEE** uh

judgment .... **JUJ** munt

judicatory ...... **JOOH** di kuh **TAWR** ee

judicial .... jooh **DISH** ul ¶1

judiciary .... jooh **DISH** ee **ER** ee *or*
  jooh **DISH** ur ee ¶1

judicious .... jooh **DISH** us ¶1

judo .... **JOOH** doh

Juggernaut .... **JUG** ur nawt ¶19

jugular .... **JUG** yoo lur *or*
  JOOHG yoo lur

jujitsu .... jooh **JIT** sooh

jujube (tree) .... **JOOH** joohb

jujube (candy) .... **JOOH** jooh bee

jukebox .... **JOOHK** bahks

julep .... **JOOH** lup

julienne ... jooh lee **EN** *or* zhooh **LYEN**

junco .... **JUNG** koh

junction .... **JUNGK** shun ¶9

juncture .... **JUNGK** chur ¶9

junior .... **JOOHN** yur

juniper .... **JOOH** nuh pur

Junker .... **YOONG** kur

junta .... **HOON** tuh *or* **JUN** tuh

Jupiter .... **JOOH** puh tur

Jurassic .... joo **RAS** ik

juridical .... joo **RID** i kul

jurisdiction ... **JOOR** is **DIK** shun ¶24

jurisprudence ....
  .... **JOOR** is **PROOHD** uns ¶24

jurist .... **JOOR** ist ¶24

juror .... **JOOR** ur ¶24

jury .... **JOOR** ee ¶24

justice .... **JUS** tis

justification ...... **JUS** tuh fi **KAY** shun

justify .... **JUS** tuh fye

Jute .... **JOOHT**

juvenile .... **JOOH** vuh nul ¶22

juxtapose .... juk stuh **POHZ**

juxtaposition .... **JUK** stuh puh **ZISH** un

K

Kabuki .... kah **BOOH** kee ¶1

kaddish .... **KAHD** ish

SPELLED	PRONOUNCED
kaffeeklatsch	KAH fay klahch or KAW fee klach
kaiser	KYE zur
kaleidoscope	kuh LYE duh SKOHP
Kamasutra	KAH muh SOOH truh
kamikaze	KAH muh KAH zee
kangaroo	kang guh ROOH
kaolin	KAY uh lin
Kapellmeister	kah PEL myse tur
kapok	KAY pahk
kaput ...	kuh POOHT or kuh POOT ¶1
karat	KAR ut ¶23
karate	kuh RAHT ee
karma	KAHR muh or KUR muh
Kashmir	KASH mir ¶2
katydid	KAYT ee did
katzenjammer	KAT sun JAM ur
kayak	KYE ak
kazoo	kuh ZOOH
kebab	kuh BAHB
keeshond	KAYS hawnt or KEES hawnt
The second syllable may also be hund.	
Kenya	KEN yuh or KEEN yuh
Keogh (plan)	KEE oh
keratin	KER uh tun
kerchief	KUR chif
kernel	KUR nul
kerosene	KER uh seen ¶2
kestral	KES trul
ketone	KEE tohn
Kewpie (doll)	KYOOH pee
Keynes	KAYNZ
Keynesian	KAYN zee un

SPELLED	PRONOUNCED
khaki	KAK ee
formerly also KAH kee; the usual Canadian pronunciation is KAHR kee.	
Khmer	kuh MER
Khyber (Pass)	KYE bur
kibbe	KIB ee or KIB uh
kibbutz	ki BOOTS or ki BOOHTS
The plural is kibbutzim kee boot SEEM.	
kibitz	KIB its
now often ki BITS	
kibosh	KYE bahsh or ki BAHSH
kielbasa	keel BAH suh
Kierkegaard	KIR kuh gahrd
kiln	KILN
The earlier, standard KIL is now less frequent.	
kilo	KEE loh
KIL oh is rare, except when used as a combining form.	
kilogram	KIL uh gram
kiloliter	KIL uh LEET ur
kilometer	ki LAHM uh tur or KIL uh MEET ur
kimono	kuh MOH nuh or kuh MOH noh
kindergarten	KIN dur GAHRT un
kindly	KYNDE lee
kindred	KIN drid
kinescope	KIN uh skohp
kinesics	ki NEE siks ¶1
kinesthesia	KIN is THEE zhuh ¶25
kinetic	ki NET ik
kinin	KYE nin

SPELLED	*PRONOUNCED*
kinkajou	**KING** kuh jooh
kiosk	**KEE** ahsk ¶2
Kirov	**KEE** rawf *or* **KIR** awf
kirschwasser	**KIRSH** vahs ur
kismet	**KIZ** met ¶14
kitsch	**KICH**
kiwi	**KEE** wee
kleptomania	
	KLEP tuh **MAY** nee uh ¶25
klieg (light)	**KLEEG**
knackwurst	**NAHK** wurst *or* kuh **NAHK** voorst
knavery	**NAYV** ur ee ¶5
Knickerbockers	**NIK** ur **BAHK** urz
knight–errant	**NYTE ER** unt
knish	kuh **NISH**
knoll	**NOHL**
know	**NOH**
knowledge	**NAHL** ij
koala	kuh **AH** luh
kodiak	**KOH** dee ak
kohlrabi	**KOHL** rah bee *or* kohl **RAH** bee
Komodo (dragon)	kuh **MOH** doh
kookaburra	**KOOK** uh **BUR** uh
kopeck	**KOH** pek
Koran	koh **RAN** *or* kaw **RAN** ¶1, 18
Korea	kuh **REE** uh *or* kaw **REE** uh ¶1
Kosciusko	kawsh **CHOOHSH** koh *sometimes Americanized to* **KAHS** ee **OOHS** koh *or* **KAHS** ee **US** koh
kosher	**KOH** shur

SPELLED	*PRONOUNCED*
kowtow	**KOW TOW** *earlier* **KOH TOW** *has become rare.*
kraal	**KRAHL** ¶19
kraft	**KRAFT** *or* **KRAHFT**
Kremlin	**KREM** lin
kreplach	**KREP** lahkh
kreutzer	**KROYT** sur
kriegspiel	**KREEG** speel *or* **KREEG** shpeel
Krishna	**KRISH** nuh
krypton	**KRIP** tahn
Kuala Lumpur	
	KWAH luh loom **POOR** *or* kooh **AH** luh loom **POOR**
Kublai Khan	**KOOH** blye **KAHN** *or* **KOOH** bluh **KAHN**
kuchen	**KOOH** kun *or* **KOOH** khun
kudos	**KOOH** dahs ¶20, 21 **KOOH** dohz *is nonstandard, because kudos is not a plural.*
kudu	**KOOH** dooh
Ku Klux Klan	
	KOOH KLUKS **KLAN** ¶21 **KLOOH** KLUKS **KLAN** *is a euphonious "mistake."*
Kultur	kool **TOOHR**
kümmel	**KIM** ul
kumquat	**KUM** kwaht ¶19
kung fu	kung **FOOH** *rarely* koong **FOOH**
Kurd	**KURD** ¶24
Kuwait	kooh **WAYT** *also, especially formerly,* kooh **WYTE**
Kyoto	**KYOH** toh *or* kee **OH** toh

laissez faire .. les ay FER *or* lez ay FER
or lay zay FER

laity .... LAY uht ee

lama .... LAH muh

Lamaze .... luh MAHZ

lambaste .... lam BAYST *or*
lam BAST ¶2

L

lamé .... la MAY

lament .... luh MENT

lamentable .... LAM un tuh bul *or*
luh MEN tuh bul

lamentation .... LAM un TAY shun

laminate .... LAM uh nayt

labial .... LAY bee ul ¶25

laboratory .... LAB ruh TAWR ee
The British pronunciation is
luh BAHR uh tur ee. ¶5

lampoon .... lam POOHN

lamprey .... LAM pree
occasionally LAM pray

laborious .... luh BAWR ee us

lanai .... lah NYE *or* luh NYE

laborite .... LAY buh ryte

lance .... LANS ¶9, 18

Labrador .... LAB ruh dawr

labyrinth .... LAB ur inth ¶5, 9

landau .... LAN dow
also, especially formerly, LAN daw

labyrinthine .... LAB uh RIN thin ¶22

landscape .... LAND skayp ¶10

lacerate .... LAS uh rayt

language .... LANG gwij

lachrymose .... LAK ruh mohs

languid .... LANG gwid

lackadaisical .... LAK uh DAY zi kul

languish .... LANG gwish

lackey .... LAK ee

languor .... LANG gur

laconic .... luh KAHN ik

lanolin .... LAN uh lin

lacquer .... LAK ur

lanugo .... luh NOOH goh ¶21

lacrosse .... luh KRAWS ¶19

lanyard .... LAN yurd

lacteal .... LAK tee ul ¶25

Laos .... LAH ohs *or* LOWS *or* LAY ahs

lactose .... LAK tohs

Laotian .... lay OH shun

lacuna .... luh KYOOH nuh ¶21

Lao–tse .... LOWD ZUH

laden .... LAYD un

lapel .... luh PEL

la–di–da .... LAH dee DAH

lapidary .... LAP uh DER ee ¶23

Ladino .... luh DEE noh ¶1

lapis lazuli ...... LAP is LAZ yoo lee *or*
LAP is LAZH yoo lye

ladle .... LAY dul

laetrile .... LAY uh tril

Lafayette .... lah fee ET ¶18

lager .... LAH gur

laggard .... LAG urd

lagniappe .... lan YAP ¶2

Lapland .... **LAP** land

larboard .... **LAHR** burd

larceny .... **LAHR** suh nee ¶5

largess .... lahr **JES** *or* **LAHR** jis

lariat .... **LAR** ee ut ¶23

larva .... **LAHR** vuh

   The plural larvae *is* **LAHR** vee.

laryngitis .... LAR un **JYTE** is ¶23

larynx .... **LAR** ingks

   LAHR niks, *which reverses the*
   order of the y *and the* n, *is heard,*
   but is not standard. ¶4

lasagna .... luh **ZAHN** yuh

lascivious .... luh **SIV** ee us ¶1

laser .... **LAY** zur

lassitude .... **LAS** uh toohd ¶21

lasso ... **LAS** oh *or* **LAS** ooh *or* la **SOOH**

lateen .... la **TEEN** ¶1

latent .... **LAYT** unt

lateral .... **LAT** ur ul

latex .... **LAY** teks

lath .... **LATH** ¶18

lathe .... **LAYDH**

lather .... **LADH** ur

latitude .... **LAT** uh toohd ¶21

latrine .... luh **TREEN**

lattice .... **LAT** is

laudable .... **LAWD** uh bul

laudanum .... **LAWD** un um ¶5

laugh .... **LAF** ¶18

launch .... **LAWNCH** ¶19

launder .... **LAWN** dur ¶19

laureate .... **LAWR** ee it ¶19

laurel .... **LAWR** ul ¶19

lava .... **LAH** vuh *or* **LAV** uh

lavabo .... luh **VAH** boh *or* luh **VAY** boh

lavage .... luh **VAHZH** *or* **LAV** ij

lavaliere .... lav uh **LIR** ¶18

lavatory .... **LAV** uh TAWR ee

lavender .... **LAV** un dur

lavish .... **LAV** ish

lawyer .... **LAW** yur

   now also **LOY** ur

laxative .... **LAK** suh tiv

laxity .... **LAK** suh tee

layette .... lay **ET**

layman .... **LAY** mun

Lazarus .... **LAZ** ur us

league .... **LEEG**

lean–to .... **LEEN** tooh

leapfrog .... **LEEP** frawg ¶19

learned .... **LUR** nid

   When the meaning is acquired
   by study or experience, *as in "a*
   learned response," *it is* **LURND**.

leather .... **LEDH** ur

leaven .... **LEV** un

Lebanon .... **LEB** uh nahn

   also **LEB** uh nun, *which prevailed*
   until recently ¶8

lecherous .... **LECH** ur us

lecithin .... **LES** uh thin

lectern .... **LEK** turn

lecture .... **LEK** chur ¶12

ledger .... **LEJ** ur

leeward .... **LEE** wurd

   among sailors **LOOH** urd

legacy .... **LEG** uh see

legal .... **LEE** gul

legalese .... lee guh **LEEZ**

SPELLED	PRONOUNCED
legality	li **GAL** uh tee ¶1
legate	**LEG** it
legatee	leg uh **TEE**
legend	**LEJ** und
legendary	**LEJ** un **DER** ee ¶23
legerdemain	**LEJ** ur di **MAYN**
legged	**LEG** id or **LEGD**
legible	**LEJ** uh bul
legion	**LEE** jun
legionnaire	lee juh **NER**
legislate	**LEJ** is layt
legislature	**LEJ** is **LAY** chur
legitimate *(verb)*	luh **JIT** uh mayt
legitimate *(adjective)*	luh **JIT** uh mit
legume	**LEG** yoohm or li **GYOOHM**
leguminous	li **GYOOHM** i nus
Le Havre	luh **HAHV** ruh or luh **AH** vruh
lei	**LAY** or **LAY** ee
Leibniz	**LYPE** nits
sometimes **LEEB** nits	
Leicester	**LES** tur
leisure	**LEE** zhur or **LEZH** ur
leitmotif	**LYTE** moh teef
lemming	**LEM** ing
lemon	**LEM** un
lemur	**LEE** mur
length	**LENGTH** or **LENGKTH**
LENTH *has wide currency, but is not heard in standard speech* ¶9.	
leniency	**LEE** ni un see ¶15
lenient	**LEE** ni unt ¶15
lentil	**LEN** tul
leonine	**LEE** uh nyne ¶22
leopard	**LEP** urd

SPELLED	PRONOUNCED
leotard	**LEE** uh tahrd
leper	**LEP** ur
leprechaun	**LEP** ruh kahn or **LEP** ruh kawn
leprosy	**LEP** ruh see
leprous	**LEP** rus
lesbian	**LEZ** bee un ¶5
lese majesty	**LEEZ** **MAJ** is tee
lesion	**LEE** zhun
Lesotho	le **SUT** hoh or le **SOH** thoh
The official pronunciation is luh **SOOH** thooh.	
lessee	les **EE**
lesson	**LES** un
lessor	**LES** awr or les **AWR**
lethal	**LEE** thul
lethargic	li **THAHR** jik
lethargy	**LETH** ur jee
leukemia	looh **KEE** mee uh ¶25
leukocyte	**LOOH** kuh syte
levee ("embankment")	**LEV** ee
levee ("reception")	**LEV** ee or luh **VEE** or luh **VAY**
lever	**LEV** ur or **LEE** vur
leverage	**LEV** ur ij ¶5
leviathan	luh **VYE** uh thun
levitate	**LEV** uh tayt
Leviticus	luh **VIT** i kus
levity	**LEV** uh tee
levy	**LEV** ee
lewd	**LOOHD**
lexicography	**LEK** suh **KAHG** ruh fee ¶19
lexicon	**LEK** si kahn or **LEK** suh kun ¶8

120

Lhasa apso .... LAH suh AP soh
liability .... LYE uh BIL uh tee
liable .... LYE uh bul
also, especially when the
meaning is likely, LYE bul

liaison ..... LEE uh zahn *or* lee AY zahn
LAY uh zahn *and* lee uh ZOHN *are*
also heard.

libation .... lye BAY shun
libel .... LYE bul
libelous .... LYE bul us
liberal .... LIB ur ul   ¶5
liberalize .... LIB ur uh lyze
liberate .... LIB uh rayt
Liberia .... lye BIR ee uh
libertarian .... LIB ur TER ee un
libertine .... LIB ur teen
also, especially formerly,
LIB ur tin   ¶8

libidinous .... li BID un us
libido .... li BEE doh
li BYE doh *is now rare.*

Libra .... LYE bruh *or* LEE bruh
Some horoscope followers,
especially those with this sign,
object to LYE bruh, *others to*
LEE bruh.

librarian .... lye BRER ee un   ¶23
library .... LYE brer ee *or* LYE bruh ree
libretto .... li BRET oh
Libya .... LIB ee uh   ¶25
license .... LYE suns   ¶9
licentiate .... lye SEN shee it
occasionally lye SEN shee ayt   ¶12
licentious .... lye SEN shus   ¶9, 12

lichen .... LYE kun
licit .... LIS it
licorice .... LIK ur ish
sometimes LIK ur is   ¶5
lido .... LEE doh
lidocaine .... LYE duh kayn
lied ("song") .... LEET *or* LEED
lief .... LEEF
liege .... LEEJ   ¶15
lien .... LEEN *or* LEE un
lieu .... LOOH
lieutenant .... looh TEN unt
In British and Canadian Army
usage, it is lef TEN unt.

ligament .... LIG uh munt
ligature .... LIG uh chur
lightning .... LYTE ning
lilac .... LYE lak *or* LYE lahk
The earlier LYE luk *is becoming*
rarer.   ¶8

Lilliputian .... LIL uh PYOOH shun
limber .... LIM bur
limerick .... LIM ur ik   ¶5
limitation .... LIM uh TAY shun
limn .... LIM
Limoges .... lee MOHZH   ¶1
limousine .... LIM uh zeen   ¶2
lineage .... LIN ee ij   ¶25
When this spelling is a variant
of linage, *meaning* number of
lines, *it is* LYNE ij.

lineal .... LIN ee ul   ¶25
linear .... LIN ee ur   ¶25
linen .... LIN in
linger .... LING gur

121

lingerie	lahn zhuh **RAY** or	literature	**LIT** ur uh chur ¶5, 24
	lahn zhuh **REE** ¶2, 15	lithe	**LYDHE**
The first syllable is often also		lithium	**LITH** ee um ¶25
lan.		lithograph	**LITH** uh graf ¶18
lingo	**LING** goh	lithography	li **THAHG** ruh fee
lingua franca	**LING** gwuh **FRANG** kuh	Lithuania	**LITH** oo **WAY** nee uh ¶25
linguine	ling **GWEE** nee	litigant	**LIT** uh gunt
linguistics	ling **GWIS** tiks	litigate	**LIT** uh gayt
liniment	**LIN** uh munt	litigious	li **TIJ** us
Linnaeus	li **NEE** us	litmus	**LIT** mus
linnet	**LIN** it	littoral	**LIT** ur ul
linoleum	li **NOH** lee um ¶5	liturgical	li **TUR** ji kul
linsey–woolsey	**LIN** zee **WOOL** zee	liturgy	**LIT** ur jee
lintel	**LIN** tul	–lived	**LYVDE** or **LIVD**
lipid	**LIP** id or **LYE** pid	*The second pronunciation stems*	
Lippizaner	**LIP** ut **SAHN** ur	*from the notion that the form*	
popularly **LIP** uh **ZAHN** ur		*(as in* long–lived*) comes from*	
liquefy	**LIK** wuh fye	*the verb* live, *but it is formed*	
liqueur	li **KUR**	*from the noun* life *plus the*	
liquid	**LIK** wid	*suffix* –ed.	
liquidate	**LIK** wuh dayt	livelihood	**LYVE** lee hood
liquor	**LIK** ur	livelong	**LIV** lawng
lira	**LIR** uh	lively	**LYVE** lee
The plural form lire *is*		liven	**LYE** vun
pronounced **LIR** ay.		liver	**LIV** ur
lisle	**LYLE**	liverwurst	**LIV** ur wurst
lissome	**LIS** um	livery	**LIV** ur ee ¶5
listen	**LIS** un	livid	**LIV** id
listless	**LIST** lis ¶10	lizard	**LIZ** urd
litany	**LIT** un ee	llama	**LAH** muh
litchi	**LEE** chee	loath	**LOHTH**
liter	**LEET** ur	loathe	**LOHDH**
literacy	**LIT** ur uh see ¶5	loathsome	**LOHDH** sum or
literal	**LIT** ur ul ¶5		**LOHTH** sum
literary	**LIT** uh **RER** ee ¶23	lobotomy	loh **BAHT** uh mee ¶1

lobster .... **LAHB** stur
locale .... loh **KAL**
locality .... loh **KAL** uh tee
localize .... **LOH** kuh lyze
locate .... **LOH** kayt ¶2
loch .... **LAHK** *or* **LAHKH**
Lochinvar .... **LAHK** in vahr
locomotion .... LOH kuh **MOH** shun
locomotive .... LOH kuh **MOH** tiv
locus .... **LOH** kus
The plural loci *is* **LOH** sye.
locust .... **LOH** kust
locution .... loh **KYOOH** shun
loess .... **LES** *or* **LOH** es
logarithm ..... **LAWG** uh ridh um ¶19
loge .... **LOHZH**
loggia .... **LAH** jee uh ¶5, 15, 20
logic .... **LAH** jik
logistics .... loh **JIS** tiks ¶1
logo .... **LOH** goh
The earlier **LAW** goh *is becoming rare.*
logorrhea ...... LAWG uh **REE** uh ¶19
logy .... **LOH** gee
loiter .... **LOY** tur
loneliness .... **LOHN** lee nis
longevity .... lahn **JEV** uh tee ¶19
longitude .... **LAHN** juh toohd ¶21
long–lived .... **LAWNG LYVDE** *or*
  LAWNG LIVD: *see* –lived
loose .... **LOOHS**
loquacious .... loh **KWAY** shus ¶1
loquacity .... loh **KWAS** uh tee ¶1
lorgnette .... lawrn **YET**
lorry .... **LAWR** ee ¶19

Los Angeles .... laws **AN** juh lus *or*
  lahs **AN** juh lus *or* lahs **ANG** guh lus
  or laws **AN** juh **LEEZ**
The sound of the letter l *is the only one certain to be heard. Any pronunciation is apt to be scorned by someone who pronounces it another way.*
lose .... **LOOHZ**
lothario .... loh **THER** ee oh ¶1
lotion .... **LOH** shun
lottery .... **LAHT** ur ee
lotus .... **LOHT** us
Louisiana .... loo **WEE** zee **AN** uh *or*
  LOOH uh zee **AN** uh
sometimes LOOH zee **AN** uh
Louisville .... **LOOH** ee vil
in the local area and, often, elsewhere in the central U.S., **LOOH** uh vul
lounge .... **LOWNJ** ¶15
louse .... **LOWS**
lousy .... **LOW** zee
Louvre .... **LOOH** vruh *or* **LOOHV**
lover .... **LUV** ur
lower ("scowl") .... **LOW** ur
This word should not be confused with lower, **LOH** ur, *meaning* below *or* let down.
lowland *(noun)* .... **LOH** lund *or*
  LOH land
The adjective is always **LOH** lund.
lox .... **LAHKS**
lozenge .... **LAHZ** unj
luau .... **LOOH** ow ¶2

lubricant .... **LOOH** bruh kunt
lubricate .... **LOOH** bruh kayt
lucent .... **LOOH** sunt
lucid .... **LOOH** sid
Lucifer .... **LOOH** suh fur
lucrative .... **LOOH** kruh tiv
lucre .... **LOOH** kur
lucubration .... LOOH kyoo **BRAY** shun
ludicrous .... **LOOH** di krus
luge .... **LOOHZH**
lugsail .... **LUG** sul or **LUG** sayl
lugubrious ... loo **GOOH** bree us ¶21
lullaby .... **LUL** uh bye
lumbago .... lum **BAY** goh
lumbar ..... **LUM** bahr or **LUM** bur ¶8
lumen .... **LOOH** mun
luminary ..... LOOH muh **NER** ee ¶23
luminescence ....
.... LOOH muh **NES** uns ¶9
luminosity ...... looh muh **NAHS** uh tee
luminous .... **LOOH** muh nus
lummox .... **LUM** uks
lunacy .... **LOOH** nuh see
lunar .... **LOOH** nur
lunatic .... **LOOH** nuh tik
luncheon .... **LUN** chun ¶9, 12
lunge .... **LUNJ** ¶15
lunula .... **LOOH** nyoo luh
lupine ("of wolves") ....
.... **LOOH** pyne ¶22
lurid .... **LOOR** id ¶24
luscious .... **LUSH** us
lustrous .... **LUS** trus
lutein .... **LOOHT** ee in
Lutheran .... **LOOH** thur un ¶5

luxurious .... lug **ZHOOR** ee us or
luk **SHOOR** ee us ¶24
luxury .... **LUK** shur ee or **LUG** zhur ee
lycanthropy .... lye **KAN** thruh pee
lyceum ..... lye **SEE** um or **LYE** see um
lymph .... **LIMF** ¶9
lymphatic .... lim **FAT** ik ¶6
lymphoma .... lim **FOH** muh ¶6
lynx .... **LINGKS**
lyonnaise .... lye uh **NAYZ** ¶2
lyre .... **LYRE** ¶7
lyric .... **LIR** ik
lyricism .... **LIR** uh siz um
Lysander .... lye **SAN** dur ¶1
lysergic (acid) .... lye **SUR** jik ¶1

M

macabre .... muh **KAHB** ruh or
muh **KAHB** or muh **KAH** bur
macadam .... muh **KAD** um
macadamia (nut) ....
.... MAK uh **DAY** mee uh
Macao .... muh **KOW**
macaque ...... muh **KAK** or muh **KAHK**
macaroni .... MAK uh **ROH** nee
macaroon .... mak uh **ROOHN**
macaw .... muh **KAW**
Maccabees .... **MAK** uh beez

Macedonia		Magellan .... muh **JEL** un
.... MAS uh **DOH** nee uh ¶25		magenta .... muh **JEN** tuh
macerate .... MAS uh rayt		Magi .... MAY jye
Mach (number) .... MAHK		magic .... MAJ ik
machete .... muh **SHET** ee ¶12		magician .... muh **JISH** un
Machiavelli		magisterial .... MAJ is **TIR** ee ul
.... MAK ee uh **VEL** ee ¶18, 25		magistrate .. MAJ is trayt or MAJ is trit
machination .... MAK uh **NAY** shun		Magna Carta (or Charta) ....
now often MASH uh **NAY** shun		.... MAG nuh **KAHR** tuh
machinery ..... muh **SHEEN** ur ee ¶5		magna cum laude .. MAHG nuh ¶18:
machismo .... mah **CHEEZ** moh ¶1		see cum laude
macho .... MAH choh		magnanimity ..... MAG nuh **NIM** uh tee
mackerel .... MAK ur ul ¶5		magnanimous .... mag **NAN** uh mus
mackintosh ...... MAK in tahsh ¶19		magnate .... MAG nayt or MAG nit
macramé .... MAK ruh may		magnesia .... mag **NEE** zhuh or
macrocosm .... MAK ruh KAHZ um		mag **NEE** shuh
macron .. MAY krahn or MAY krun ¶8		magnesium ...... mag **NEE** zee um or
Madagascar .... MAD uh **GAS** kur		mag **NEE** zhee um or mag **NEE** zhum
now also MAD uh **GAS** kahr ¶8		magnet .... MAG nit
madame .... MAD um or ma DAM or		magnetic .... mag **NET** ik
muh DAHM		magneto .... mag **NEET** oh
Madeira .... muh DIR uh		magnificent ..... mag **NIF** uh sunt ¶1
mademoiselle .... MAD uh muh **ZEL** or		magnifico .... mag **NIF** uh koh
MAD mwuh **ZEL** or mam **ZEL**		magnify .... MAG nuh fye
madonna .... muh **DAHN** uh ¶20		magnitude ...... MAG nuh toohd ¶21
madras .. MAD rus or muh **DRAS** ¶18		magnolia .... mag **NOH** lee uh ¶25
madrigal .... MAD ri gul		maharajah .... MAH huh **RAH** juh ¶15
maelstrom .... MAYL strum		maharishi .... MAH hah **RISH** ee
maestro .... MYSE troh		mahatma .... muh **HAT** muh ¶18
especially among musicians,		mah–jongg .... mah **JAWNG** ¶15, 19
often mah **ES** troh		mahogany ... muh **HAHG** uh nee ¶19
Mafia .... MAH fee uh		maillot .... mah **YOH**
also, but more British than		mainmast .... MAYN must or
American, MAF ee uh		MAYN mast ¶18
magazine .... mag uh **ZEEN** ¶2		mainsail .... MAYN sul or MAYN sayl

SPELLED	PRONOUNCED	SPELLED	PRONOUNCED
maintain	mayn **TAYN** ¶1	malicious	muh **LISH** us
maintenance	**MAYN** tuh nuns ¶5, 9	malign	muh **LYNE**
maisonette	may zun **NET**	malignant	muh **LIG** nunt
maitre d'	mayt ur **DEE**	malinger	muh **LING** gur
majestic	muh **JES** tik	mall	**MAWL**
majesty	**MAJ** is tee	mallard	**MAL** urd
majolica	muh **JAHL** i kuh or	malleable	**MAL** ee uh bul ¶25
	muh **YAHL** i kuh	mallet	**MAL** it
major	**MAY** jur	Malta	**MAWL** tuh
Majorca	muh **JAWR** kuh	Malthusian	mal **THOOH** zhun ¶25
A half–Spanish pronunciation,		mambo	**MAHM** boh
mah **YAWR** *kuh, is often heard,*		mammalian	muh **MAY** lee un ¶25
based on its Spanish name		mammary	**MAM** ur ee
Mallorca *mahl* **YAWR** *kah.*		mammon	**MAM** un
major–domo	**MAY** jur **DOH** moh	mammoth	**MAM** uth
majority	muh **JAWR** uh tee ¶19	manacle	**MAN** uh kul
Malachi	**MAL** uh kye	manage	**MAN** ij
maladroit	mal uh **DROYT**	managerial	**MAN** uh **JIR** ee ul ¶25
malady	**MAL** uh dee	mañana	mahn **YAH** nuh ¶1
Malaga	**MAL** uh guh	manatee	**MAN** uh tee ¶2
malaise	ma **LAYZ**	mandamus	man **DAY** mus
sometimes ma **LEZ** ¶1		mandarin	**MAN** dur in
malamute	**MAL** uh myooht ¶21	mandatory	**MAN** duh **TAWR** ee
malaprop	**MAL** uh prahp ¶20	mandible	**MAN** duh bul
malaria	muh **LAR** ee uh ¶23	mandolin	**MAN** duh lin ¶2
Malay	**MAY** lay or muh **LAY**	mandrill	**MAN** drul
Malaysia	muh **LAY** zhuh or	manège	ma **NEZH** or ma **NAYZH**
	muh **LAY** shuh	maneuver	muh **NOOH** vur ¶21
mal de mer	**MAL** duh **MER** ¶18	manganese	
malediction	**MAL** uh **DIK** shun		**MANG** guh neez ¶14, 16
malefactor	**MAL** uh **FAK** tur	mange	**MAYNJ** ¶15
maleficent	muh **LEF** uh sunt	mangrove	**MANG** grohv ¶16
malevolence	muh **LEV** uh luns ¶9	mangy	**MAYN** jee
malfeasance	mal **FEE** zuns ¶9	mania	**MAY** nee uh ¶25
malice	**MAL** is	maniacal	muh **NYE** uh kul

SPELLED	PRONOUNCED	SPELLED	PRONOUNCED
manic	**MAN** ik	marchesa	mahr **KAY** zah
manicotti	MAN i **KAHT** ee	marchioness	**MAHR** shuh nis *or*
manicure	**MAN** uh kyoor ¶24		mahr shuh **NES**
manifest	**MAN** uh fest	Mardi gras	**MAHR** dee **GRAH**
manifestation		margarine	**MAHR** jur in ¶5
	MAN uh fes **TAY** shun ¶1	margin	**MAHR** jun
manifesto	MAN uh **FES** toh	marijuana	MAR uh **WAH** nuh ¶23
manikin	**MAN** uh kin	marimba	muh **RIM** buh
Manila	muh **NIL** uh	marina	muh **REE** nuh
manipulate	muh **NIP** yuh layt	marinade	mar uh **NAYD** ¶2, 23
manna	**MAN** uh	marinara	MAH ruh **NAH** ruh *or*
mannequin	**MAN** uh kin		MAR uh **NAR** uh ¶23
mansard	**MAN** sahrd	marinate	**MAR** uh nayt ¶23
mansion	**MAN** shun ¶9, 12	mariner	**MAR** uh nur ¶23
mansuetude	**MAN** swi toohd ¶21	marionette	MAR ee uh **NET** ¶23
mantilla	man **TIL** uh *or* man **TEE** uh	marital	**MAR** uh tul ¶23
mantissa	man **TIS** uh	maritime	**MAR** uh tyme ¶23
mantra	**MUN** truh *or* **MAN** truh	marjoram	**MAHR** jur um
manual	**MAN** yoo wul ¶1, 5	marmalade	**MAHR** muh layd
manufacture		marmoset	**MAHR** muh set ¶14
	MAN yuh **FAK** chur ¶12	marmot	**MAHR** mut
manure	muh **NOOR** ¶7, 21	maroon	muh **ROOHN**
manuscript	**MAN** yuh skript	marquee	mahr **KEE**
Maori	**MOW** ree *or* **MAH** awr ee ¶7	marquess	**MAHR** kwis
Mao Tse-tung	**MOWD** zuh **DOONG**	marquis	**MAHR** kwis *or* mahr **KEE**
	or **MOWT** suh **TOONG**	marquise	mahr **KEEZ**
maraschino	MAR uh **SKEE** noh	marriage	**MAR** ij ¶23
	The common pronunciation	Marsala	mahr **SAH** lah
	MAR uh **SHEE** noh *apparently arose*	Marseillaise	mahr suh **LAYZ**
	from a misreading of Italian sch	marshmallow	**MAHRSH** mel oh *or*
	as the German cluster		**MAHRSH** mal oh
	pronounced SH. ¶23	marsupial	mahr **SOOH** pee ul ¶25
marathon	**MAR** uh thahn ¶23	martial	**MAHR** shul
maraud	muh **RAWD**	Martian	**MAHR** shun
marcel	mahr **SEL**	martinet	mahr tuh **NET** ¶2

SPELLED	PRONOUNCED	SPELLED	PRONOUNCED

martingale .... **MAHR** tun gayl

martini .... mahr **TEE** nee

Martinique .... mahr tuh **NEEK**

martyr .... **MAHR** tur

marvelous .... **MAHR** vuh lus ¶5

Marxism .... **MAHRK** siz um

marzipan .... **MAHR** zi pan

mascara .... mas **KAR** uh ¶23

mascot .... **MAS** kaht

  MAS kut *is becoming rare.* ¶8

masculine .... **MAS** kyuh lin

maser .... **MAY** zur

masochism ...... **MAS** uh kiz um ¶14

mason .... **MAY** sun

masque .... **MASK** ¶18

masquerade .... mas kuh **RAYD**

massacre .... **MAS** uh kur

  MAS uh kree *is facetious.*

massage .... muh **SAHZH** ¶15

massé .... ma **SAY**

masseur .... ma **SUR** ¶1, 24

masseuse ..... ma **SOOZ** *or* muh **SOOHZ**

massif .... ma **SEEF** *or* **MAS** if

mastectomy ... mas **TEK** tuh mee ¶1

mastery .... **MAS** tur ee ¶5, 18

masticate .... **MAS** tuh kayt

mastiff .... **MAS** tif

mastodon .... **MAS** tuh dahn

masturbate .... **MAS** tur bayt

matador .... **MAT** uh dawr

material .... muh **TIR** ee ul ¶25

materiality .... muh TIR ee **AL** uh tee

materiel .... muh TIR ee **EL**

maternal .... muh **TUR** nul

maternity .... muh **TUR** nuh tee

mathematician ....

  .... MATH uh muh **TISH** un *or*
           MATH muh **TISH** un

mathematics ..... MATH uh **MAT** iks *or*
           math **MAT** iks

matinee .... mat uh **NAY** ¶2

matins .... **MAT** inz

matriarch .... **MAY** tree ahrk

matricide .... **MAT** ruh syde

  MAY truh syde *is now rare.*

matriculate .... muh **TRIK** yoo layt

matrimony .... **MAT** ruh **MOH** nee

matrix .... **MAY** triks

matron .... **MAY** trun

maturate .... **MACH** uh rayt

mature .... muh **TOOR** ¶13, 21

matzo .... **MAHT** suh *or* **MAHT** saw

maudlin .... **MAWD** lin

maul .... **MAWL**

maunder .... **MAWN** dur

Maundy (Thursday) ..... **MAWN** dee

mausoleum ... MAW suh **LEE** um ¶14

mauve .... **MOHV** *or* **MAWV**

maven .... **MAY** vun

maverick .... **MAV** ur ik ¶5

mawkish .... **MAW** kish

maxim .... **MAK** sim

maximum .... **MAK** suh mum

Maya .... **MAH** yuh

  The popular form today is
  MYE uh.

mayhem .... **MAY** hem *or* **MAY** um ¶8

mayonnaise .... may uh **NAYZ** ¶2

mayor .... **MAY** ur

  MER *is also commonly heard.*

SPELLED	PRONOUNCED
mayoral	**MAY** ur ul

may **AWR** ul, *which is heard increasingly, is not yet considered standard.*

SPELLED	PRONOUNCED
mazel tov	**MAH** zul tawf *or* **MAH** zul tohv
mazurka	muh **ZUR** kuh ¶24
meadow	**MED** oh
meager	**MEE** gur
meander	mee **AN** dur
measles	**MEE** zulz
measly	**MEEZ** lee
measure	**MEZH** ur
mechanic	muh **KAN** ik
mechanism	**MEK** uh niz um
medallion	muh **DAL** yun
Medea	mi **DEE** uh
media	**MEE** dee uh
median	**MEE** dee un
mediate	**MEE** dee ayt
Medicaid	**MED** i kayd
medical	**MED** i kul
medicate	**MED** i kayt
Medici	**MED** uh chee
medicinal	muh **DIS** uh nul
medicine	**MED** uh sin
medieval	**MEE** dee **EE** vul *or* **MED** ee **EE** vul

also MID ee **EE** vul *and* mi **DEE** vul

SPELLED	PRONOUNCED
mediocre	**MEE** dee **OH** kur ¶2
mediocrity	**MEE** dee **AHK** ruh tee
meditate	**MED** uh tayt
Mediterranean	**MED** i tuh **RAY** nee un ¶25
medium	**MEE** dee um ¶25

SPELLED	PRONOUNCED
medulla	mi **DUL** uh
Medusa	muh **DOOH** suh ¶14, 21
meerschaum	**MIR** shum *or* **MIR** shawm ¶8
megalomania	**MEG** uh loh **MAY** nee uh ¶1, 25
megalopolis	**MEG** uh **LAHP** uh lus
megaton	**MEG** uh tun
megilla	muh **GIL** uh
meiosis	mye **OH** sis
Meistersinger	**MYSE** tur **SING** ur *or* **MYSE** tur **ZING** ur
melancholia	**MEL** un **KOH** lee uh ¶25
melancholy	**MEL** un **KAHL** ee
Melanesia	**MEL** uh **NEE** zhuh
mélange	may **LAHNZH** ¶15
melee	**MAY** lay ¶2
mellifluous	muh **LIF** loo wus
melodeon	muh **LOH** dee un
melodic	muh **LAHD** ik
melodious	muh **LOH** dee us
melodrama	**MEL** uh **DRAH** muh ¶1, 18
melodramatic	**MEL** uh druh **MAT** ik ¶1
melody	**MEL** uh dee
memento	mi **MEN** toh

Though one sees "momento" occasionally and hears moh **MEN** toh, *neither has become a part of standard English.*

SPELLED	PRONOUNCED
memoir	**MEM** wahr
memorabilia	**MEM** ur uh **BIL** ee uh *or* **MEM** ur uh **BEEL** ee uh ¶25

memorable	**MEM** ur uh bul ¶5	mercenary	**MUR** suh NER ee ¶23
memorandum	**MEM** uh **RAN** dum	merchandise *(verb)*	**MUR** chun dyze
memorial	muh **MAWR** ee ul	*For the noun,* **MUR** chun dyse *is*	
memory	**MEM** ur ee ¶5	*also common.*	
menace	**MEN** is	merchant	**MUR** chunt
ménage	may **NAHZH** ¶1	merci	mer **SEE**
menagerie	muh **NAJ** ur ee ¶15, 25	merciful	**MUR** si ful
mendacious	men **DAY** shus	mercurial	
mendacity	men **DAS** uh tee		mur **KYOOR** ee ul ¶24, 25
Mendel	**MEN** dul	Mercury	**MUR** kyoor ee ¶24
Mendelssohn	**MEN** dul sun *or*	mercy	**MUR** see
	MEN dul zohn *or* **MEN** dul sohn	merde	**MERD**
mendicant	**MEN** di kunt	meretricious	MER uh **TRISH** us
Menelaus	**MEN** uh **LAY** us	merganser	mur **GAN** sur ¶9
menial	**MEE** nee ul ¶5	merge	**MURJ**
meningitis	**MEN** in **JYTE** is	meridian	muh **RID** ee un
Mennonite	**MEN** uh nyte	meringue	muh **RANG**
menopause	**MEN** uh pawz	merino	muh **REE** noh
menorah	muh **NOH** ruh *or*	meritorious	
	muh **NAWR** uh		MER uh **TAWR** ee us ¶25
menses	**MEN** seez	merriment	**MER** i munt ¶1
menstruate	**MEN** stroo wayt	mesa	**MAY** suh
MEN strayt *is now at least as*		mescal	mes **KAL**
common ¶5.		mescaline	**MES** kuh leen ¶22
–ment	munt *or* mint	mesdames	may **DAHM**
mentality	men **TAL** uh tee	mesmerize	**MEZ** muh ryze *or*
menthol	**MEN** thawl ¶19, 20		**MES** muh ryze
mention	**MEN** shun ¶9, 12	meson	**MEZ** ahn *or* **MES** ahn
mentor	**MEN** tur *or* **MEN** tawr	**MAY** sahn *and* **MEE** zahn *are also*	
menu	**MEN** yooh	*heard.*	
occasionally **MAYN** yooh		Mesopotamia	
Mephistopheles			MES uh puh **TAY** mee uh ¶25
	MEF uh **STAHF** uh **LEEZ**	Mesozoic	**MES** uh **ZOH** ik *or*
mercantile	**MUR** kun tyle ¶22		MEZ uh **ZOH** ik
Mercator (projection)	mur **KAYT** ur	mesquite	mes **KEET** ¶2

SPELLED	PRONOUNCED
messenger	**MES** un jur
Messiah	muh **SYE** uh
mestizo	mes **TEE** zoh
metabolic	MET uh **BAHL** ik
metabolism	muh **TAB** uh liz um
metallic	muh **TAL** ik
metallurgy	**MET** uh LUR jee
metamorphosis	
	MET uh **MAWR** fuh sis
metaphor	**MET** uh fawr
MET uh fur *has become rare* ¶8.	
metaphysical	MET uh **FIZ** i kul
metaphysics	MET uh **FIZ** iks ¶2
metastasis	muh **TAS** tuh sis
metatarsal	MET uh **TAHR** sul
metathesis	muh **TATH** uh sis
mete	**MEET**
meteor	**MEET** ee ur
meteoric	MEET ee **AWR** ik
meteorite	**MEET** ee uh RYTE
meteorological	
	MEET ee ur uh **LAHJ** i kul ¶5
meteorology	
	MEET ee uh **RAHL** uh jee
methadone	**METH** uh dohn
methane	**METH** ayn
methanol	**METH** uh nawl ¶20
methaqualone	meth **AK** wuh LOHN
method	**METH** ud
methodical	muh **THAHD** i kul
methodology	METH uh **DAHL** uh jee
Methuselah	
	muh **THOOH** zuh luh ¶5, 21
meticulous	muh **TIK** yoo lus
métier	may **TYAY** ¶2

SPELLED	PRONOUNCED
metonymy	muh **TAHN** uh mee
metric	**MET** rik
metrication	MET ruh **KAY** shun
metrology	muh **TRAHL** uh jee ¶1
metronome	**MET** ruh nohm
metropolis	muh **TRAHP** uh lis
metropolitan	MET ruh **PAHL** i tun
meunière	moo **NYER**
mezzanine	**MEZ** uh neen ¶2
mezzo	**MET** soh
occasionally **MED** zoh; *rarely*	
MEZ oh	
miasma ... mye **AZ** muh *or* mee **AZ** muh	
mica	**MYE** kuh
Michelangelo	MYE kuh **LAN** juh loh
	or MIK uh **LAN** juh loh
microbe	**MYE** krohb
microbiology	
	MYE kroh bye **AHL** uh jee ¶1
microcosm	**MYE** kruh kahz um ¶1
microfiche	**MYE** kruh feesh
now often **MYE** kruh fish	
micrometer	mye **KRAHM** uh tur
micron	**MYE** krahn
Micronesia	MYE kruh **NEE** zhuh
microscope	**MYE** kruh skohp
microscopic	MYE kruh **SKAHP** ik
microscopy	mye **KRAHS** kuh pee
microwave	**MYE** kruh wayv
Midas	**MYE** dus
middleman	**MID** ul man
middling	**MID** ling *or* **MID** lun ¶5
midget	**MIJ** it
midriff	**MID** rif
midst	**MIDST** ¶6

SPELLED	PRONOUNCED
midwifery	mid **WYE** fur ee
also, especially formerly,	
mid **WIF** ur ee ¶5	
mien	**MEEN**
mignon	**MIN** yahn ¶20
migraine	**MYE** grayn
migrant	**MYE** grunt
migrate	**MYE** grayt
migration	mye **GRAY** shun
migratory	**MYE** gruh **TAWR** ee
mikado	mi **KAH** doh
milady	mi **LAY** dee
mildew	**MIL** dooh ¶21
Milhaud	mee **YOH**
milieu	mil **YOOH** *or* meel **YOO**
militant	**MIL** i tunt
militarism	**MIL** uh tur iz um
military	**MIL** uh **TER** ee ¶23
militate	**MIL** uh tayt
militia	muh **LISH** uh
millennium	mi **LEN** ee um ¶25
millet	**MIL** it
milligram	**MIL** uh gram
milliliter	**MIL** uh **LEET** ur
millinery	**MIL** uh **NER** ee
millipede	**MIL** uh peed
milquetoast	**MILK** tohst
mime	**MYME**
mimeograph	
.... **MIM** ee uh graf ¶5, 18	
mimetic ...... mi **MET** ik *or* mye **MET** ik	
mimicry	**MIM** ik ree
mimosa	mi **MOH** suh
minaret	min uh **RET** ¶2
mineral	**MIN** ur ul ¶5

SPELLED	PRONOUNCED
mineralogy	
.... min uh **RAHL** uh jee ¶18	
Minerva	mi **NUR** vuh
minestrone	**MIN** uh **STROH** nee
occasionally MIN uh **STROHN,**	
probably by false association with	
other words ending in –one	
miniature	**MIN** ee uh chur *or*
	MIN i chur ¶24
For art senses, the unsyncopated	
(four–syllable) pronunciation is	
favored; for general senses, the	
syncopated (three–syllable)	
pronunciation is common ¶5.	
minim	**MIN** im
minimum	**MIN** uh mum
minion	**MIN** yun
minister	**MIN** is tur
ministerial	**MIN** is **TIR** ee ul
Minoan	mi **NOH** un
MIN uh win *is not standard.*	
minority ..... muh **NAWR** uh tee ¶19	
Minotaur	**MIN** uh tawr
minstrel	**MIN** strul ¶9
minuend	**MIN** yoo wend
minuet	min yoo **WET**
minuscule	mi **NUS** kyoohl *or*
	MIN uh skyoohl
minute *(noun)*	**MIN** it
minute *(adjective)*	
.... mye **NOOHT** ¶21	
minutiae	mi **NOOH** shi ee
now sometimes	
mi **NOOH** shee **EYE** ¶21	
Miocene	**MYE** uh seen

SPELLED	PRONOUNCED	SPELLED	PRONOUNCED
miosis	mye **OH** sis	Missouri	mi **ZOOR** ee

The usual pronunciation in Missouri is mi ZOOR uh.

SPELLED	PRONOUNCED
miosis	mye **OH** sis
miracle	**MIR** uh kul
miraculous	mi **RAK** yoo lus
mirage	mi **RAHZH** ¶15
Miranda	muh **RAN** duh
mirror	**MIR** ur
mirth	**MURTH**
misanthrope	**MIS** un throhp ¶14
miscegenation	**MIS** i juh **NAY** shun
	or mi **SEJ** uh **NAY** shun
miscellaneous	
	MIS uh **LAY** nee us ¶25
miscellany	**MIS** uh LAY nee
mi **SEL** uh nee *is British.*	
mischief	**MIS** chif
mischievous	**MIS** chi vus
mis **CHEE** vee us *is heard but is not standard.*	
miscible	**MIS** uh bul
miscreant	**MIS** kree unt
misdemeanor	**MIS** di **MEEN** ur
miser	**MYE** zur
miserable	**MIZ** ur uh bul ¶5
misery	**MIZ** ur ee ¶5
misfeasance	mis **FEE** zuns ¶9
mishap	**MIS** hap
misnomer	mis **NOH** mur *or*
	MIS noh mur
misogamy	mi **SAHG** uh mee
misogyny	mi **SAHJ** uh nee
misprision	mis **PRIZH** un
missal	**MIS** ul
missile	**MIS** ul
mission	**MISH** un
missive	**MIS** iv

SPELLED	PRONOUNCED
Missouri	mi **ZOOR** ee
mistletoe	**MIS** ul toh
mistral	**MIS** trul *or* mi **STRAHL**
misuse *(verb)*	mis **YOOHZ**
misuse *(noun)*	mis **YOOHS**
miter	**MYTE** ur
mitigate	**MIT** uh gayt
mitosis	mye **TOH** sis ¶1
mixture	**MIKS** chur
mnemonic	ni **MAHN** ik
mobile	**MOH** bul *or* **MOH** byle *or*
	MOH beel ¶22

When the art object is meant, it is always MOH beel.

SPELLED	PRONOUNCED
mobilize	**MOH** buh lyze
moccasin	**MAHK** uh sin
mocha	**MOH** kuh
mockery	**MAHK** ur ee ¶5
modal	**MOHD** ul
modality	moh **DAL** uh tee ¶1
modem	**MOH** dem
moderate *(verb)*	**MAHD** uh rayt
moderate *(noun and adjective)*	
	MAHD ur it
modern	**MAHD** urn
modest	**MAHD** ist
modify	**MAHD** uh fye
modish	**MOHD** ish
modulate	**MAHJ** uh layt
module	**MAHJ** oohl ¶17
modus operandi	
	MOH dus **AHP** uh **RAHN** dee *or*
	MOH dus AHP uh **RAN** dye

SPELLED	PRONOUNCED	SPELLED	PRONOUNCED
mogul	**MOH** gul	monetary	**MAHN** uh **TER** ee
mohair	**MOH** her	monger	**MUNG** gur *or* **MAHNG** gur
Mohammed	moh **HAM** id ¶1		*Younger speakers have taken to*
moiety	**MOY** uh tee		**MAHNG** gur.
moire	**MWAHR** *or* **MAWR**	Mongol	**MAHNG** gul *or* **MAHN** gohl
moiré	mwah **RAY** *or* maw **RAY**	mongoose	**MAHNG** goohs ¶16
moisture	**MOYS** chur	mongrel	**MUNG** grul *or* **MAHNG** grul
Mojave (Desert)	moh **HAH** vee	moniker	**MAHN** i kur
molar	**MOH** lur	monism	**MOH** niz um ¶20
molasses	muh **LAS** iz	monitor	**MAHN** uh tur
molecular	muh **LEK** yuh lur	mono–	**MAHN** uh *or* **MAHN** oh
molecule	**MAHL** uh kyoohl		*occasionally* **MOH** noh
molest	muh **LEST** ¶1	monocle	**MAHN** i kul
Molière	mohl **YER** *or* moh lee **ER**	monocular	muh **NAHK** yuh lur
mollify	**MAHL** uh fye	monogamy	muh **NAHG** uh mee
mollusk	**MAHL** usk	monograph	**MAHN** uh graf ¶18
molybdenum	muh **LIB** duh num	monolith	**MAHN** uh lith
moment	**MOH** munt	monologue	**MAHN** uh lawg ¶19
memento	*See* memento.	mononucleosis	
momentum	moh **MEN** tum ¶1		**MAHN** oh **NOOH** klee **OH** sis ¶1, 21
Monaco	**MAHN** uh koh *or*	monopoly	muh **NAHP** uh lee ¶5
	muh **NAH** koh	monotone	**MAHN** uh tohn
monad	**MOH** nad ¶20	monotonous	muh **NAHT** un us
Mona Lisa	MOH nuh **LEE** suh ¶14	monsieur	muh **SYUR**
monarch	**MAHN** ahrk	Monsignor	mahn **SEEN** yur
	MAHN urk *is now less common*	monsoon	mahn **SOOHN**
	than formerly ¶8.	monstrosity	mahn **STRAHS** uh tee
monarchy	**MAHN** ur kee *or*	monstrous	**MAHN** strus
	MAHN ahr kee	montage	mahn **TAHZH** ¶20
monastery	**MAHN** uh **STER** ee	Montesquieu	**MAHN** tus kyooh
monastic	muh **NAS** tik	Montessori	MAHN tuh **SAWR** ee
monaural	mahn **AWR** ul ¶1	Montezuma	MAHN tuh **ZOOH** muh
Monday	**MUN** dee *or* **MUN** day	month	**MUNTH** ¶9
Mondrian	**MAWN** dree ahn ¶19	Monticello	MAHN tuh **SEL** oh *or*
Monet	moh **NAY**		MAHN tuh **CHEL** oh

134

SPELLED	PRONOUNCED	SPELLED	PRONOUNCED

SPELLED	PRONOUNCED
Montreal	mahn tree **AWL** or mun tree **AWL**
monument	**MAHN** yuh munt
monumental	**MAHN** yuh **MEN** tul
mooncalf	**MOOHN** kaf ¶18
moor	**MOOR**
moot	**MOOHT**
moraine	muh **RAYN** ¶1
moral	**MAWR** ul ¶19
morale	muh **RAL** ¶1
morality	muh **RAL** uh tee ¶1
morass	muh **RAS** ¶1
moratorium	**MAWR** uh **TAWR** ee um
moray (eel)	**MAWR** ay ¶2
morbidity	mawr **BID** uh tee
mordant	**MAWR** dunt
morel	muh **REL** or maw **REL**
mores	**MAWR** ayz or **MAWR** eez
morgue	**MAWRG**
moribund	**MAWR** uh bund
Morocco	muh **RAH** koh
moron	**MAWR** ahn
morose	muh **ROHS** ¶1
morpheme	**MAWR** feem
morphine	**MAWR** feen
morphology	mawr **FAHL** uh jee
morsel	**MAWR** sul
mortal	**MAWR** tul
mortality	mawr **TAL** uh tee
mortar	**MAWR** tur
mortgage	**MAWR** gij
mortician	mawr **TISH** un
mortify	**MAWR** tuh fye
mortise	**MAWR** tis
mortuary	**MAWR** choo **WER** ee ¶23

SPELLED	PRONOUNCED
mosaic	moh **ZAY** ik ¶1
Moscow	**MAHS** kow or **MAHS** koh
Moselle	moh **ZEL**
Moslem	**MAHZ** lum or **MUZ** lum ¶14
mosque	**MAHSK** ¶19
mosquito	mus **KEET** oh ¶1
moth	**MAWTH**
The plural moths *is* **MAWDHZ** *or* **MAWTHS**.	
motif	moh **TEEF**
motile	**MOHT** ul ¶22
motion	**MOH** shun
motivate	**MOHT** uh vayt
motive	**MOHT** iv
motley	**MAHT** lee
mountebank	**MOWN** tuh bangk
mourn	**MAWRN**
mouse *(noun)*	**MOWS**
The verb is usually **MOWZ**.	
moussaka	mooh **SAH** kuh
mousse	**MOOHS**
mouth *(noun)*	**MOWTH**
mouth *(verb)*	**MOWDH**
mouthy	**MOW** dhee or **MOW** thee
mouton	mooh **TAHN**
mow ("to cut")	**MOH**
mow ("part of a barn")	**MOW**
Mozambique	moh zum **BEEK** or moh zam **BEEK** ¶8
Mozart	**MOHT** sahrt
MOH zahrt *is not standard.*	
mozzarella	**MAHT** suh **REL** uh
Mr.	**MIS** tur
Mrs.	**MIS** iz

135

SPELLED	PRONOUNCED	SPELLED	PRONOUNCED
Ms.	MIZ	muscatel	mus kuh TEL
muchacha	mooh CHAH chah	muscle	MUS ul
The masculine is muchacho		Muscovite	MUS kuh vyte
mooh CHAH choh.		muscular	MUS kyuh lur
mucilage	MYOOH suh lij ¶5	muse	MYOOHZ
mucous	MYOOH kus	museum	myooh ZEE um ¶1
mucus	MYOOH kus	mushroom	MUSH roohm *or*
Muenster	MUN stur *or* MOON stur		MUSH room
muezzin	myooh EZ in	musician	myooh ZISH un ¶1
mufti	MUF tee	musicology	MYOOH zi KAHL uh jee
mulberry	MUL ber ee *or* MUL bur ee	muskellunge	MUS kuh lunj
mulch	MULCH	musket	MUS kit
mulct	MULKT	muskmelon	MUSK mel un ¶10
mulish	MYOOHL ish	Muslim	MUZ lum *or* MOOZ lum
mulligan	MUL i gun	muslin	MUZ lin
mullion	MUL yun	mussel	MUS ul
multi–	MUL ti *or* MUL tuh *or* MUL tee	mustache	muh STASH *or* MUS tash
	or MUL tye	mustachio	mus TAH shoh ¶25
multifarious		mustang	MUS tang
	MUL tuh FAR ee us ¶23	mustard	MUS turd
multiple	MUL tuh pul	mutant	MYOOHT unt
multiplex	MUL tuh pleks	mutate	MYOOH tayt
multitude	MUL tuh toohd ¶21	mute	MYOOHT
multitudinous		mutilate	MYOOHT uh layt
	MUL tuh TOOHD un us ¶21	mutiny	MYOOHT un ee ¶5
mundane	mun DAYN ¶2	mutual	MYOOH choo wul ¶5
municipal	myoo NIS uh pul	myelogram	MYE uh loh GRAM ¶1
municipality		myna	MYE nuh
	myoo NIS uh PAL uh tee	myopia	mye OH pee uh ¶25
munificent	myoo NIF uh sunt	myopic	mye AHP ik
munitions	myoo NISH unz	myriad	MIR ee ud
muon	MYOOH ahn	myrrh	MUR
mural	MYOOR ul ¶24	mysterious	mis TIR ee us ¶25
muriatic (acid)		mystery	MIS tur ee ¶5
	MYOOR ee AT ik ¶24	mystic	MIS tik

SPELLED	PRONOUNCED	SPELLED	PRONOUNCED

mysticism .... **MIS** tuh siz um

mystify .... **MIS** tuh fye

mystique .... mis **TEEK**

mythological .... MITH uh **LAHJ** i kul

mythology .... mi **THAHL** uh jee

N

Na–Dene .... nah di **NEE** or
nah day **NAY**

nadir .... **NAY** dur or **NAY** dir

naiad .... **NYE** ad or **NAY** ad

Nairobi .... nye **ROH** bee

naive .... nah **EEV**
or, sometimes, nye **EEV**

naiveté .... nah eev **TAY** or nah **EEV** tay

naked .... **NAY** kid

napalm .... **NAY** pahm
sometimes **NAY** pahlm

naphtha .... **NAF** thuh or **NAP** thuh

Napoleon .... nuh **POH** lee un ¶25

narcissism .... **NAHR** suh siz um

narcissus .... nahr **SIS** us

narcotic .... nahr **KAHT** ik

narghile .... **NAHR** guh lee or
NAHR guh lay

narrate ..... **NAR** ayt or na **RAYT** ¶23

narration .... na **RAY** shun ¶1

narrative .... **NAR** uh tiv ¶23

narrator .. **NAR** ayt ur or **NAR** uh tur or
na **RAYT** ur ¶23

narwhal ...... **NAHR** wul or **NAHR** hwul

nasal .... **NAY** zul

nasality .... nay **ZAL** uh tee

nascent .... **NAS** unt or **NAY** sunt

Nashville .... **NASH** vil
in parts of the south central
U.S., **NASH** vul

Nassau .... **NAS** aw

nasturtium .... nuh **STUR** shum ¶1

natal .... **NAYT** ul

natatorium ..... NAYT uh **TAWR** ee um

Natchez .... **NACH** iz

nation .... **NAY** shun

national .... **NASH** uh nul ¶5

nationality .... NASH uh **NAL** uh tee

native .... **NAYT** iv

nativity .... nuh **TIV** uh tee ¶1

natural .... **NACH** ur ul ¶5

nature .... **NAY** chur

naughty .... **NAWT** ee

nausea ... **NAW** zee uh or **NAW** shuh or
NAW zhuh ¶11, 14, 25

nauseate .... **NAW** zee ayt or
NAW shee ayt
sometimes **NAW** zhee ayt ¶11, 14

nautical .... **NAWT** i kul

nautilus .... **NAWT** i lus

Navaho .... **NAV** uh hoh
sometimes **NAH** vuh hoh

navigable .... **NAV** i guh bul

navigate .... **NAV** uh gayt

Nazarene .... naz uh **REEN** ¶2

Nazi .... **NAHT** see

137

SPELLED	PRONOUNCED
Neanderthal ...	nee **AN** dur THAWL or nee **AN** dur TAHL
Neapolitan	NEE uh **PAHL** uh tun
Nebuchadnezzar	NEB yuh kud **NEZ** ur or NEB uh kud **NEZ** ur
nebula	**NEB** yuh luh
necessarily	NES uh **SER** uh lee ¶2, 23
necessary	NES uh **SER** ee ¶23
necessity	nuh **SES** uh tee
necrology	ne **KRAHL** uh jee ¶1
necromancy	**NEK** ruh MAN see ¶9
necrosis	ne **KROH** sis ¶1
nectar	**NEK** tur
nectarine	nek tuh **REEN** ¶2
nee	**NAY** now often NEE
ne'er–do–well	**NAR** doo wel
nefarious	ni **FAR** ee us ¶1
Nefertiti	NEF ur **TEE** tee
negate	ni **GAYT** ¶1
negative	**NEG** uh tiv
Negev	**NEG** ev
neglect	ni **GLEKT** ¶1
negligee	neg luh **ZHAY** ¶2
negligent	**NEG** li junt
negligible	**NEG** li juh bul
negotiable	ni **GOH** shuh bul or ni **GOH** shee uh bul ¶1
negotiate	ni **GOH** shee ayt
negritude	**NEG** ruh toohd or NEE gruh toohd ¶21
Negro	**NEE** groh
Nehemiah	NEE uh **MYE** uh

SPELLED	PRONOUNCED
neighbor	**NAY** bur
neither	**NEE** dhur or **NYE** dhur: see either
nemesis	**NEM** uh sis
neo–	**NEE** oh or **NEE** uh
Neocene	**NEE** uh seen
neolithic	NEE uh **LITH** ik ¶1
neologism	nee **AHL** uh jiz um
neon	**NEE** ahn
neophyte	**NEE** uh fyte ¶1
neoprene	**NEE** uh preen ¶1
Nepal	ni **PAWL** ¶1, 19
nephew	**NEF** yooh chiefly British **NEV** yooh
nephritis	ne **FRYTE** is ¶1
nephrosis	ne **FROH** sis ¶1
nepotism	**NEP** uh tiz um
Neptune	**NEP** toohn ¶13, 21
nervous	**NUR** vus
nescient	**NESH** unt ¶5
–ness	nis or nus Words formed with this noun suffix (preciseness, sulkiness, etc.) are not generally entered in this book.
nestle	**NES** ul
nestling	**NEST** ling ¶10
nether	**NEDH** ur
Neufchâtel	nooh shuh **TEL** ¶21
neural	**NOOR** ul ¶21
neuralgia	noo **RAL** juh ¶21
neurasthenia	NOOR us **THEE** nee uh ¶21
neuritis	noo **RYTE** us ¶1, 21
neurology ...	noo **RAHL** uh jee ¶1, 21

neuron .... **NOOR** ahn ¶21

neurosis .... noo **ROH** sis ¶1, 21
  The plural is neuroses
  noo **ROH** seez.

neurotic .... noo **RAHT** ik ¶1, 21

neuter .... **NOOHT** ur ¶21

neutral .... **NOOH** trul ¶21

neutrality ..... nooh **TRAL** uh tee ¶21

neutralize .... **NOOH** truh lyze ¶21

neutron .... **NOOH** trahn ¶21

nevus .... **NEE** vus

Newfoundland ... **NOOH** fund land *or*
  NOOH fund lund
  nooh **FOWND** lund *is also heard, but*
  for the province, Canadians favor
  NOOH fund land ¶2.
  NOOH fund lund *is usual for the*
  dog. ¶21

New Orleans .... nooh **AWR** lee unz *or*
  NOOH awr **LEENZ**
  nooh **AWR** lunz *is the prevailing*
  pronunciation in the South.

newspaper .. **NOOHZ** pay pur ¶14, 21

nexus .... **NEK** sus

niacin .... **NYE** uh sin

Niagara .... nye **AG** ruh ¶5

Nicaragua .... NIK uh **RAH** gwuh

Nice ("city in France") .... **NEES**

nicety .... **NYSE** uh tee

niche .... **NICH**

nickelodeon .. NIK uh **LOH** dee un ¶5

nicotine .... **NIK** uh teen
  also, especially formerly,
  NIK uh tin ¶8

Nietzsche .... **NEE** chuh

Niger .... **NYE** jur

Nigeria .... nye **JIR** ee uh

niggardly .... **NIG** urd lee

nigh .... **NYE**

nightingale .... **NYTE** in gayl *or*
  NYTE ing gayl

nihilism .... **NYE** uh liz um *or*
  NEE uh liz um *or* NI huh liz um

nimble .... **NIM** bul

nimbus .... **NIM** bus

nincompoop ..... **NIN** kum poohp ¶16

ninth .... **NYNTHE** ¶9

nirvana ... nir **VAH** nuh *or* nur **VAH** nuh
  occasionally nir **VAN** uh

nitrate .... **NYE** trayt

nitric .... **NYE** trik

nitrify .... **NYE** truh fye

nitrite .... **NYE** tryte

nitrogen .... **NYE** truh jun

nitroglycerin ....
  .... NYE truh **GLIS** ur in ¶1, 5

Nobel .... noh **BEL**

nobility .... noh **BIL** uh tee

noblesse oblige ....
  .... noh **BLES** oh **BLEEZH**

nobody ... **NOH** bud ee *or* **NOH** bahd ee

nocturnal .... nahk **TUR** nul

nocturne .... **NAHK** turn

nodule .... **NAHJ** oohl ¶17

noisome .... **NOY** sum

nolo contendere ....
  .... **NOH** loh kun **TEN** dur ee

nomad .... **NOH** mad

nom de plume ....
  .... NAHM duh **PLOOHM** ¶20

nomenclature .... **NOH** mun KLAY chur
noh **MEN** kluh chur *is the usual*
British pronunciation.

nominal .... **NAHM** i nul

nominate .... **NAHM** uh nayt

nominative .... **NAHM** uh nuh tiv *or*
NAHM uh nayt iv
in grammar, only **NAHM** uh nuh tiv

nominee .... nahm uh **NEE**

non– .... **NAHN**
occasionally **NUN**

nonagenarian .. NAHN uh ji **NER** ee un

nonce .... **NAHNS** ¶19

nonchalant .... nahn shuh **LAHNT** ¶2

non compos mentis ....
.... NAHN KAHM pus **MEN** tis

nondescript ...... nahn di **SKRIPT** ¶2

nonentity .... nahn **EN** tuh tee

nonfeasance .... nahn **FEE** zuns ¶19

nonpareil .... nahn puh **REL**

nonplus .... nahn **PLUS** ¶2

nonsense .... **NAHN** sens *or*
NAHN suns ¶19

nonsensical .... nahn **SEN** si kul ¶19

non sequitur .... nahn **SEK** wi tur

Norfolk .... **NAWR** fuk

normal .... **NAWR** mul

normality .... nawr **MAL** uh tee

northeast .... nawrth **EEST**
among sailors nawr **EEST**

northerly .... **NAWR** dhur lee

Northumbria ..... nawr **THUM** bree uh

northwest .... nawrth **WEST**
among sailors nawr **WEST**

Norwegian .... nawr **WEE** jun

nostalgia .... nahs **TAL** juh *or*
nus **TAL** juh ¶19, 25

nostril .... **NAHS** trul

notable .... **NOHT** uh bul

notarize .... **NOHT** uh ryze

notary .... **NOHT** ur ee

notation .... noh **TAY** shun

nothing .... **NUTH** ing

notice .... **NOHT** is

notify .... **NOHT** uh fye

notoriety .... NOHT uh **RYE** uh tee

notorious .... noh **TAWR** ee us ¶1

Notre Dame ...... NOH truh **DAHM** *or*
NOHT ur **DAYM**
Thus for the cathedral in Paris,
but colleges and universities in
the U.S. are nearly always
NOHT ur **DAYM**.

nougat .... **NOOH** gut

nourish .... **NUR** ish ¶24

nouveau riche ...... NOOH voh **REESH**

nova .... **NOH** vuh

Nova Scotia ...... NOH vuh **SKOH** shuh

novel .... **NAHV** ul

novella .... noh **VEL** uh ¶1

novelty .... **NAHV** ul tee

novena .... noh **VEE** nuh

novice .... **NAHV** is

novitiate .... noh **VISH** ee it *or*
noh **VISH** ee ayt *or* noh **VISH** it

noxious .... **NAHK** shus

nth .... **ENTH** ¶9

nuance .... **NOOH** ahns ¶2, 9, 21

nubile .... **NOOH** byle *or*
NOOH bul ¶8, 21

nuclear .... **NOOH** klee ur ¶4, 21
NOOH kyuh lur *is quite common, even among public figures, but it is generally not approved.*

nucleic (acid) .... nooh **KLEE** ik *occasionally* nooh **KLAY** ik ¶21

nucleus .... **NOOH** klee us
The plural is nuclei
NOOH klee eye. ¶21

nudity .... **NOOH** duh tee ¶21

nugatory ... **NOOH** guh TAWR ee ¶21

nuisance .... **NOOH** suns ¶9, 21

nuke .... **NOOHK** ¶21

nullify .... **NUL** uh fye

numeral .... **NOOH** mur ul ¶5, 21

numerator ... **NOOH** muh rayt ur ¶21

numerical .... nooh **MER** i kul ¶21

numerology ....
.... **NOOH** muh **RAHL** uh jee ¶21

número uno ... NOOH mur oh **OOH** noh

numerous ... **NOOH** mur us ¶5, 21

numismatic ....
.... NOOH miz **MAT** ik ¶14, 21

numismatist ....
.... NOOH **MIZ** muh tist ¶14, 21

nuncio .... **NUN** shee oh ¶11

nuptials .... **NUP** shulz ¶12
NUP choo wulz *is not standard.*

nursery .... **NUR** sur ee ¶5

nurture .... **NUR** chur

nutrient .... **NOOH** tree unt ¶21

nutriment ..... **NOOH** truh munt ¶21

nutrition .... noo **TRISH** un ¶1, 21

nutritious .... noo **TRISH** us ¶21

nymph .... **NIMF** ¶6, 9

nymphet .... nim **FET** *or* **NIM** fut

nymphomania ....
.... NIM fuh **MAY** nee uh ¶1, 6, 25

O

Oahu .... oh **AH** hooh

oakum .... **OH** kum

oasis .... oh **AY** sis

obbligato .... AHB luh **GAHT** oh

obdurate .... **AHB** door ut ¶21

obedient ...... oh **BEE** dee unt ¶1, 25

obeisance .... oh **BAY** suns *or*
oh **BEE** suns ¶1, 9

obelisk .... **AHB** uh lisk ¶20

Oberammergau .. OH bur **AHM** ur **GOW**

obese .... oh **BEES**

obfuscate .... **AHB** fus kayt *or*
ub **FUS** kayt

obiter dictum ... OH bi tur **DIK** tum *or*
AHB i tur **DIK** tum

obituary .. oh **BICH** oo **WER** ee ¶1, 23

object *(verb)* .... ub **JEKT** ¶1

object *(noun)* .... **AHB** jikt

objection .... ub **JEK** shun ¶1

objectivity .... AHB jek **TIV** uh tee ¶1

objet d'art .... AHB zhay **DAHR** ¶1

objurgate .... **AHB** jur gayt *or*
ub **JUR** gayt

oblate	**AHB** layt ¶2	obtrude	ub **TROOHD** ¶1
oblation	ah **BLAY** shun or	obtrusive	ub **TROOH** siv ¶1
	oh **BLAY** shun ¶1	obtuse	ahb **TOOHS** ¶1, 21
obligate	**AHB** luh gayt	obverse *(noun)*	**AHB** vurs
obligatory	uh **BLIG** uh **TAWR** ee or	*The adjective is usually*	
	AHB li guh **TAWR** ee	ahb **VURS.** ¶1, 2	
oblige	uh **BLYJE**	obviate	**AHB** vee ayt
oblique	uh **BLEEK** ¶1	obvious	**AHB** vee us
in military usage, oh **BLYKE**		ocarina	AHK uh **REE** nuh
obliquity	uh **BLIK** wuh tee ¶1	occasion	uh **KAY** zhun ¶1
obliterate	uh **BLIT** uh rayt ¶1	occident	**AHK** suh dunt
oblivion	uh **BLIV** ee un ¶1, 5	occidental	AHK suh **DEN** tul
obloquy	**AHB** luh kwee	occipital	ahk **SIP** uh tul
obnoxious	ub **NAHK** shus	occlude	uh **KLOOHD** ¶1
oboe	**OH** boh	occlusion	uh **KLOOH** zhun ¶1
obscene	ub **SEEN** ¶1	occult	uh **KULT** or **AH** kult ¶20
obscenity	ub **SEN** uh tee ¶1	occupant	**AHK** yuh punt
obscure	ub **SKYOOR** ¶1, 24	occupation	AHK yuh **PAY** shun
obsequies	**AHB** suh kweez	occupy	**AHK** yuh pye
obsequious	ub **SEE** kwee us	ocean	**OH** shun
observation	AHB zur **VAY** shun ¶14	Oceania	OH shee **AN** ee uh
observe	ub **ZURV** ¶1	oceanic	OH shee **AN** ik ¶11
obsess	ub **SES** ¶1	oceanography	
obsession	ub **SESH** un ¶1		OH shuh **NAHG** ruh fee
obsidian	ub **SID** ee un ¶1	ocelot	**AHS** uh laht
obsolescent	AHB suh **LES** unt	*occasionally* OH suh laht ¶1	
obsolete	ahb suh **LEET**	ocher	**OH** kur
obstacle	**AHB** sti kul	octagon	**AHK** tuh gahn
obstetrician	AHB stuh **TRISH** un	octagonal	ahk **TAG** uh nul
obstetrics	ub **STET** riks ¶1	octane	**AHK** tayn
obstinacy	**AHB** stuh nuh see	octave	**AHK** tiv
obstinate	**AHB** stuh nit	*also, in senses other than music,*	
obstreperous	ub **STREP** ur us ¶1, 5	**AHK** tayv	
obstruct	ub **STRUKT** ¶1	octavo	ahk **TAY** voh or ahk **TAH** voh
obstruction	ub **STRUK** shun	octet	ahk **TET**

octopus .... **AHK** tuh pus
　also now **AHK** tuh poos ¶8

octoroon .... ahk tuh **ROOHN**

octuple .... **AHK** too pul *or*
　　　　　　ahk **TOOH** pul ¶21

ocular .... **AHK** yuh lur

odalisque .... **OHD** ul isk

oddity .... **AHD** uh tee

odious .... **OH** dee us

odium .... **OH** dee um

odometer .... oh **DAHM** uh tur

odor .... **OH** dur

odoriferous .... OH duh **RIF** ur us

Odysseus .... oh **DIS** ee us
　oh **DIS** yoos *has become relatively*
　rare ¶7.

Odyssey .... **AHD** uh see

Oedipus ...... **ED** uh pus *or* **EE** duh pus

offal .... **AWF** ul ¶20

offense .... uh **FENS**
　also **AW** fens, *especially in sports*
　usage ¶9, 19

offertory ... **AWF** ur **TAWR** ee ¶6, 19

officer .... **AWF** uh sur ¶19

official .... uh **FISH** ul ¶1

officiate .... uh **FISH** ee ayt ¶1

officious .... uh **FISH** us ¶1

often .... **AWF** un *or* **AWF** tun

ogee .... **OH** jee ¶2

ogive .... **OH** jyve ¶2

ogle .... **OH** gul ¶20

ogre .... **OH** gur

ohm .... **OHM**

Ojibwa .... oh **JIB** way

okapi .... oh **KAH** pee

Okeechobee .... OH kee **CHOH** bee

Okefenokee .... OH kuh fuh **NOH** kee
　OH kee fuh **NOH** kee *is also heard.*

okra .... **OH** kruh

oldster .... **OHLD** stur

oleaginous .... OH lee **AJ** i nus

oleander .... OH lee **AN** dur ¶2

oleomargarine ....
　　　　　 OH lee oh **MAHR** juh rin

olfactory ... ahl **FAK** tur ee ¶2, 5, 20

oligarch .... **AHL** uh gahrk

Oligocene .... **AHL** uh goh **SEEN**

oligopoly .... **AHL** uh **GAHP** uh lee

Olympiad .... uh **LIM** pee ad ¶1

Olympic .... uh **LIM** pik ¶1

Olympus .... uh **LIM** pus ¶1

Omaha .... **OH** muh haw ¶19

ombudsman .... **AHM** budz mun

omega ...... oh **MAY** guh *or* oh **MEG** uh
　oh **MEE** guh *has become rare.*

omelet .... **AHM** lit ¶5

omen .... **OH** mun

omicron .... **AHM** uh krahn ¶20

ominous .... **AHM** uh nus

omission .... oh **MISH** un

omit .... oh **MIT**

omnibus .... **AHM** nuh bus

omnipotent .... ahm **NIP** uh tunt

omnipresent .... AHM ni **PREZ** unt ¶2

omniscient .... ahm **NISH** unt

omnivore .... **AHM** nuh vawr

omnivorous .... ahm **NIV** ur us ¶5

onanism .... **OH** nuh niz um

once .... **WUNS** ¶9

oncology ...... ahng **KAHL** uh jee ¶16

SPELLED	PRONOUNCED
onerous	**AH** nur us ¶20
onion	**UN** yun
onomatopoeia	
	AHN uh MAT uh **PEE** uh *or*
	AHN uh MAHT uh **PEE** uh
Onondaga	
	AHN un **DAW** guh ¶19, 20
Ontario	ahn **TER** ee oh ¶23
ontogeny	ahn **TAHJ** uh nee
ontological	AHN tuh **LAHJ** i kul
ontology	ahn **TAHL** uh jee
onus	**OH** nus
onyx	**AHN** iks
occasionally **OH** niks	
oocyte	**OH** uh syte
oolong	**OOH** lawng
oomph	**OOMF** ¶9
oosphere	**OH** uh sfir
opacity	oh **PAS** uh tee ¶18
opal	**OH** pul
opalescent	OH puh **LES** unt
opaline	**OH** pul in ¶22
opaque	oh **PAYK**
OPEC	**OH** pek
OP–ED	AHP **ED**
opera	**AHP** ur uh ¶5
operable	**AHP** ur uh bul ¶5
operand	**AHP** uh rand
operant	**AHP** ur unt
operate	**AHP** uh rayt
operatic	AHP uh **RAT** ik
operation	AHP uh **RAY** shun
operative	**AHP** uh RAY tiv *or*
	AHP ur uh tiv ¶5
operetta	AHP uh **RET** uh

SPELLED	PRONOUNCED
ophthalmic	ahf **THAL** mik *or*
	ahp **THAL** mik
ophthalmology	
	AHF thul **MAHL** uh jee *or*
	AHP thul **MAHL** uh jee
thuh *is also heard as the second*	
syllable. ¶3	
–opia	**OH** pee uh ¶25
opiate	**OH** pee it ¶25
opinion	uh **PIN** yun ¶1
opium	**OH** pee um ¶25
opossum	uh **PAHS** um
PAHS um *is also heard, but is*	
usually then spelled possum.	
opponent	uh **POH** nunt
opportune	ahp ur **TOOHN** ¶21
oppose	uh **POHZ**
opposite	**AHP** uh zit ¶14
opposition	AHP uh **ZISH** un
oppress	uh **PRES** ¶1
oppression	uh **PRESH** un ¶1
opprobrium	uh **PROH** bree um
optical	**AHP** ti kul
optician	ahp **TISH** un
optimism	**AHP** tuh miz um
optimum	**AHP** tuh mum
optometry	ahp **TAHM** uh tree
opulent	**AHP** yuh lunt
opus	**OH** pus
oracle	**AWR** uh kul ¶19
oracular	aw **RAK** yoo lur ¶1
oral	**AWR** ul
orange	**AWR** inj ¶7, 19
orangutan	uh **RANG** uh TAN *or*
	uh **RANG** uh TANG ¶1

SPELLED	PRONOUNCED
orate	aw RAYT *or* AWR ayt
oration	aw RAY shun ¶1
orator	AWR uh tur ¶19
oratorio	AWR uh TAWR ee oh ¶19
oratory	AWR uh TAWR ee ¶19
orchard	AWR churd
orchestra	AWR kis truh
occasionally AWR KES truh	
orchestral	awr KES trul
orchestrate	AWR kis trayt
orchid	AWR kid
ordain	awr DAYN
ordeal	awr DEEL ¶2, 7
ordinal	AWR dun ul ¶5
ordinance	AWR dun uns ¶5, 9
ordinary	AWR duh NER ee ¶23
ordinate	AWR duh nit *or*
	AWR duh nayt
ordination	AWR duh NAY shun
ordnance	AWRD nuns ¶9
Ordovician	AWR duh VISH un ¶1
ordure	AWR jur *or* AWR dyoor
oregano	uh REG uh noh ¶1
Oregon	AWR i gun
also AWR uh gahn, *a pronunciation*	
not used by Oregonians	
AWR uh GOH nee unz ¶19	
Orestes	aw RES teez ¶1
organdy	AWR gun dee
organic	awr GAN ik
organism	AWR guh niz um
organize	AWR guh nyze
organza	awr GAN zuh
orgasm	AWR gaz um
orgiastic	AWR jee AS tik

SPELLED	PRONOUNCED
orgy	AWR jee
Orient	AWR ee unt *or*
	AWR ee ent ¶25
orient	AWR ee ent
occasionally AWR ee unt	
oriental	AWR ee EN tul
orientate	AWR ee un tayt ¶1, 25
orifice	AWR uh fis ¶19
origami	AWR uh GAH mee
origin	AWR uh jin ¶19
original	uh RIJ uh nul ¶1
originality	uh RIJ uh NAL uh tee ¶1
originate	uh RIJ uh nayt ¶1
oriole	AWR ee ohl
Orion	oh RYE un ¶19
ornament *(noun)*	AWR nuh munt
ornament *(verb)*	AWR nuh ment
ornamental	AWR nuh MEN tul
ornate	awr NAYT ¶2
ornithology	AWR nuh THAHL uh jee
orotund	AWR uh tund
orphan	AWR fun
Orpheus	AWR fee us
Orphic	AWR fik
orthodontics	
	AWR thuh DAHN tiks ¶1
orthodox	AWR thuh dahks
orthographic	
	AWR thuh GRAF ik ¶1, 18
orthopedics	AWR thuh PEE diks ¶1
oryx	AWR iks ¶19
Osage	oh SAYJ ¶2
oscillate	AHS uh layt
oscilloscope	uh SIL uh skohp ¶1
osculate	AHS kyuh layt

osier	**OH** zhur
osmium	**AHZ** mee um
osmosis	ahs **MOH** sis *or* ahz **MOH** sis
osprey	**AHS** pree
sometimes **AHS** pray	
ossify	**AHS** uh fye
ostensible	ahs **TEN** suh bul ¶1, 9
ostentatious	AHS tun **TAY** shus ¶1
osteomyelitis	
	AHS tee oh MYE uh **LYTE** is
osteopath	**AHS** tee uh PATH
osteopathy	AHS tee **AHP** uh thee
ostracize	AHS truh syze
ostrich	**AWS** trich ¶19
Othello	uh **THEL** oh ¶1
otherwise	**UDH** ur wyze
otiose	**OH** shee ohs
OH tee ohs *is now also heard.*	
otitis	oh **TYTE** us
otolaryngology	
OHT uh LAR ing **GAHL** uh jee ¶1, 16	
Ottawa	**AHT** uh wuh *or*
	AHT uh wah ¶19
Ottoman	**AHT** uh mun
Ouija	**WEE** juh *or* **WEE** jee
our	**OWR** *or* **AHR**
ouster	**OW** stur
outage	**OWT** ij
outdoorsman	owt **DAWRZ** mun
outlandish	owt **LAN** dish
outlive	owt **LIV**
outrage	**OWT** rayj
outrageous	owt **RAY** jus
outré	ooh **TRAY**
outstanding	owt **STAN** ding

outward	**OWT** wurd
ouzel	**OOH** zul
ouzo	**OOH** zoh
oval	**OH** vul
ovary	**OH** vur ee ¶5
ovation	oh **VAY** shun
overage ("surplus")	**OH** vur ij ¶5
to be distinguished from	
overage, oh vur **AYJ**, *meaning* "over	
a certain age"	
overalls	**OH** vur awlz
overseer	**OH** vur SEE ur
overt	oh **VURT** ¶2
overture	**OH** vur chur ¶3
overweening	OH vur **WEE** ning
overwhelm	oh vur **WELM**: *see* wh—
overwrought	oh vur **RAWT**
oviduct	**OH** vi dukt
ovine	**OH** vyne ¶22
oviparous	oh **VIP** ur us ¶5
ovipositor	OH vi **PAHZ** i tur ¶2
ovoid	**OH** voyd
ovulate	**AHV** yuh layt *or* **OH** vyuh layt
ovum	**OH** vum
oxalic	ahk **SAL** ik
Oxford	**AHKS** furd
oxidation	AHK suh **DAY** shun
oxidize	**AHK** suh dyze
Oxonian	ahk **SOH** nee un
oxygen	**AHK** si jun
oxymoron	AHK si **MAWR** ahn
oyez	**OH YAY** *or* **OH YEZ** *or* **OH YES**
oyster	**OY** stur
Ozarks	**OH** zahrks
ozone	**OH** zohn

P

pabulum	**PAB** yoo lum
pachyderm	**PAK** uh durm
pachysandra	PAK uh **SAN** druh
pacific	pa **SIF** ik ¶1
pacifism	**PAS** uh fiz um
pacify	**PAS** uh fye
package	**PAK** ij
paddock	**PAD** uk
Paderewski	PAD uh **REF** skee
padre	**PAH** dray *or* **PAH** dree
paean	**PEE** un
paella	pah **YEL** uh
paesan	pye **SAHN** ¶2, 14
paesano	pye **SAH** noh ¶14
pagan	**PAY** gun
Paganini	PAH gah **NEE** nee *or* PAG uh **NEE** nee
pageant	**PAJ** unt
paginate	**PAJ** uh nayt
pagoda	puh **GOH** duh
Pago Pago	**PAHNG** oh **PAHNG** oh *or* PAH goh **PAH** goh
painterly	**PAYNT** ur lee
paisan	pye **SAHN** ¶2, 14
paisano	pye **SAH** noh ¶14
paisley	**PAYZ** lee
Paiute	**PYE** yooht ¶2
pajamas	puh **JAM** uz ¶18

Pakistani	PAH ki **STAH** nee ¶18
palace	**PAL** is
paladin	**PAL** uh din
palanquin	pal un **KEEN**
palatal	**PAL** i tul
palate	**PAL** it
palatial	puh **LAY** shul
palaver	puh **LAV** ur
palazzo	puh **LAHT** soh
Paleocene	**PAY** lee uh **SEEN**
paleography	**PAY** lee **AHG** ruh fee
paleolithic	**PAY** lee uh **LITH** ik
paleontology	PAY lee ahn **TAHL** uh jee ¶1
Paleozoic	**PAY** lee uh **ZOH** ik
Palermo	puh **LER** moh *or* puh **LUR** moh
Palestine	**PAL** us tyne
palestra	puh **LES** truh
palette	**PAL** it
palimony	**PAL** uh **MOH** nee
palindrome	**PAL** in drohm
paling	**PAYL** ing
palisades	pal uh **SAYDZ** ¶2
pall	**PAWL**
Palladium	puh **LAY** dee um
pallet	**PAL** it
palliate	**PAL** ee ayt
palliative	**PAL** ee **AYT** iv *or* **PAL** ee uh tiv ¶25
Pall Mall	PEL **MEL** *or* PAL **MAL** PAWL **MAWL** *is a spelling pronunciation often heard in the U.S.*
pallor	**PAL** ur

palm .... **PAHM**
also **PAHLM**, *which is a spelling*
pronunciation

palmetto .... pal **MET** oh

palmistry .... **PAHM** is tree

palomino .... **PAL** uh **MEE** noh

palooka .... puh **LOOH** kuh

palpable .... **PAL** puh bul

palpitate .... **PAL** puh tayt

palsy .... **PAWL** zee ¶19

paltry .... **PAWL** tree

pampas .... **PAM** puz *or* **PAHM** puz
when used as an adjective,
usually **PAM** puhs

pamphlet .... **PAM** flit ¶9

panacea .... **PAN** uh **SEE** uh

panache .... puh **NASH** ¶1, 18

Panama .... **PAN** uh mah ¶19

panatella .... **PAN** uh **TEL** uh

pancreas .... **PAN** kree us ¶16

pancreatic .... **PAN** kree **AT** ik

pandemonium ....
.... **PAN** duh **MOH** nee um ¶25

Pandora .... pan **DAWR** uh

panegyric .... **PAN** uh **JIR** ik *or*
.... **PAN** uh **JYE** rik

pannier .... **PAN** yur ¶5

panoply .... **PAN** uh plee

panorama .... **PAN** uh **RAM** uh ¶18

pansy .... **PAN** zee

pantaloon .... pan tuh **LOOHN** ¶2

pantheism .... **PAN** thee iz um

pantheon .... **PAN** thee ahn *or*
.... **PAN** thee un

panther .... **PAN** thur

pantomime .... **PAN** tuh myme

pantomimic .... **PAN** tuh **MIM** ik

pantothenic .... **PAN** tuh **THEN** ik

panzer .... **PAN** zur *or* **PAHNT** sur

papacy .... **PAY** puh see

papal .... **PAY** pul

papaya .... puh **PAH** yuh *or* puh **PYE** uh

papier–mâché ...... **PAY** pur muh **SHAY**

papilla .... puh **PIL** uh ¶1
The plural is papillae puh **PIL** ee.

papillary .... **PAP** uh **LER** ee *or*
.... puh **PIL** ur ee ¶23

papillon .... **PAP** uh lahn

papist .... **PAY** pist

papoose .... pa **POOHS** ¶1

paprika .... pa **PREE** kuh ¶1
PAP ri kuh *is no longer common.*

Papua ... **PAP** yoo wuh *or* **PAH** poo wuh

papule .... **PAP** yoohl ¶21

papyrus .... puh **PYE** rus

parable .... **PAR** uh bul ¶23

parabola .... puh **RAB** uh luh

parabolic .... **PAR** uh **BAHL** ik ¶23

parachute .... **PAR** uh shooht ¶23

paraclete .... **PAR** uh kleet ¶23

paradigm .... **PAR** uh dyme
Fewer and fewer are
saying **PAR** uh dim ¶23.

paradigmatic ....
.... **PAR** uh dig **MAT** ik ¶23

paradise .... **PAR** uh dyse ¶14, 23

paradisiacal ....
.... **PAR** uh di **SYE** uh kul ¶23

paradox .... **PAR** uh dahks ¶23

paraffin .... **PAR** uh fin ¶23

paragon .... **PAR** uh gahn *or*
      PAR uh gun ¶8, 23

paragraph ..... **PAR** uh graf ¶18, 23

Paraguay .... **PAR** uh gway *or*
      PAR uh gwye ¶23

parakeet .... **PAR** uh keet ¶23

parallax .... **PAR** uh laks ¶23

parallel .... **PAR** uh lel *or*
      PAR uh lul ¶8, 23

paralysis .... puh **RAL** uh sis

paralytic .... PAR uh **LIT** ik ¶23

paralyze .... **PAR** uh lyze ¶23

paramecium ....
      .... PAR uh **MEE** shee um ¶11, 23

parameter .... puh **RAM** uh tur

paramount ...... **PAR** uh mownt ¶23

paramour .... **PAR** uh moor ¶23

paranoia .... PAR uh **NOY** uh ¶23

paranoid .... **PAR** uh noyd ¶23

parapet .... **PAR** uh pet *or*
      PAR uh put ¶8, 23

paraphernalia ... PAR uh fuh **NAYL** yuh
or
    PAR uh fur **NAYL** ee uh ¶3, 23, 25

paraphrase .... **PAR** uh frayz ¶23

paraphrastic .. PAR uh **FRAS** tik ¶23

paraplegic ...... PAR uh **PLEE** jik ¶23
    rarely PAR uh **PLEJ** ik

parasite .... **PAR** uh syte ¶23

parasitic .... PAR uh **SIT** ik ¶23

parasol .... **PAR** uh sawl ¶19, 23

paratroops ...... **PAR** uh troohps ¶23

parboil .... **PAHR** boyl

Parcheesi *(trademark)* ....
      .... pahr **CHEE** zee

pardon .... **PAHR** dun

paregoric .. PAR uh **GAWR** ik ¶19, 23

parentage .... **PAR** un tij

parental .... puh **REN** tul
    PAR un tul *is not standard.* ¶23

parenteral .... puh **REN** tur ul

parenthesis .... puh **REN** thuh sis
The plural is parentheses
  puh **REN** thuh seez.

parenthetical ....
      .... PAR un **THET** i kul ¶23

paresis ..... puh **REE** sis *or* PAR uh sis

pareve .... **PAHR** uh vuh

par excellence ....
      .... PAHR EK suh **LAHNS** ¶5, 9

parfait .... pahr **FAY**

pariah .... puh **RYE** uh

parietal .... puh **RYE** uh tul

parimutuel .. PAR uh **MYOOH** choo wul

Paris .... **PAR** is
  pah REE *is French.* ¶23

parishioner .... puh **RISH** uh nur

Parisian .... puh **RIZH** un *or*
      puh **REE** zhun

parity .... **PAR** uh tee

parka .... **PAHR** kuh

Parkinson's (disease or Law) ....
      .... **PAHR** kin sunz

parlance .... **PAHR** luns ¶9

parlay *(noun)* .. **PAHR** lay *or* **PAHR** lee
The verb is also pahr **LAY** ¶2.

parley .... **PAHR** lee

parliament .... **PAHR** luh munt

parliamentarian ....
     ..... PAHR luh mun **TER** ee un ¶1, 23

Parmesan .... **PAHR** muh zahn *or*
　　　　　　　　　PAHR muh zun

　PAHR muh zahn, *through the
　influence of* parmigiana, *is now
　also heard.* ¶2, 18

parmigiana ....
　.......... PAHR muh **JAH** nuh ¶15

Parnassus .... pahr **NAS** us

parochial .... puh **ROH** kee ul ¶25

parody .... **PAR** uh dee ¶23

parole .... puh **ROHL**

parolee .... puh roh **LEE**
　now sometimes puh **ROH** lee

paronomasia ....
　........ PAR uh noh **MAY** zhuh ¶1, 25

parotid .... puh **RAHT** id

paroxysm .... **PAR** uk siz um ¶23
　One hears puh **RAHK** siz um
　occasionally.

parquet .... pahr **KAY**

parquetry .... **PAHR** kuh tree

parricide .... **PAR** uh syde ¶23

parsimonious ....
　.......... PAHR suh **MOH** nee us ¶25

parsimony .... **PAHR** suh MOH nee

parsley .... **PAHRS** lee

parson .... **PAHR** sun

parthenogenesis ....
　.......... PAHR thuh noh **JEN** uh sis

Parthenon .... **PAHR** thuh nahn
　also, especially formerly,
　PAHR thuh nun ¶8

partial .... **PAHR** shul

partiality ...... PAHR shee **AL** uh tee *or*
　　　　　　　pahr **SHAL** uh tee ¶5

participant ...... pahr **TIS** uh punt ¶1

participate .... pahr **TIS** uh payt ¶1

participial .... PAHR tuh **SIP** ee ul

participle .... **PAHR** tuh SIP ul

particle .... **PAHR** ti kul

particular .... pur **TIK** yuh lur ¶1, 3

partisan .... **PAHR** tuh zun ¶14

partition .... pahr **TISH** un ¶1

partitive .... **PAHRT** uh tiv

parturition .. PAHR choo **RISH** un ¶13

parvenu .... **PAHR** vuh nooh ¶21

Pascal .... pas **KAL**

paschal .... **PAS** kul

pasha .... puh **SHAH** *or* **PAH** shuh *or*
　　　　　　　　　　　PASH uh

passé .... pa **SAY** ¶2

passenger .... **PAS** un jur

passerine .... **PAS** ur in ¶22

passion .... **PASH** un

passivity .... pa **SIV** uh tee

pasta .... **PAHS** tuh

pastel .... pas **TEL**

pastern .... **PAS** turn

Pasteur .... pas **TUR**

pasteurize .... **PAS** chuh ryze ¶13

pastiche .... pas **TEESH** ¶18

pastor .... **PAS** tur ¶18

pastoral .... **PAS** tur ul ¶5, 18

pastorale .... pas tuh **RAL** ¶18
　PAS tuh **RAH** lee *is now rare.*

pastorate .... **PAS** tur it ¶18

pastrami .... puh **STRAH** mee

pastry .... **PAYS** tree

pasture .... **PAS** chur ¶18

Patagonia ... PAT uh **GOH** nee uh ¶25

SPELLED	PRONOUNCED	SPELLED	PRONOUNCED

pâté .... pah **TAY**

pâté de foie gras ....
.... pah **TAY** duh **FWAH GRAH**

patent *(verb and noun)* ...... **PAT** unt
also for the adjective, except in
meanings obvious, accessible, *or*
unobstructed, *when it usually*
becomes **PAYT** unt

pater .... **PAYT** ur

paternal .... puh **TUR** nul

paternity .... puh **TUR** nuh tee

pathetic .... puh **THET** ik

pathogen .... **PATH** uh jun

pathological .... PATH uh **LAHJ** i kul

pathology ...... puh **THAHL** uh jee ¶1

pathos .... **PAY** thahs ¶19

patience .... **PAY** shuns ¶9

patina ...... **PAT** uh nuh *or* puh **TEE** nuh

patio .... **PAT** ee oh ¶18

patois .... **PAT** wah ¶2

patriarch .... **PAY** tree ahrk

patrician .... puh **TRISH** un

patricide .... **PAT** ruh syde

patrimony .... **PAT** ruh **MOH** nee

patriot .... **PAY** tree ut *or* **PAY** tree aht

patrol .... puh **TROHL**

patron .... **PAY** trun

patronize .... **PAY** truh nyze *or*
PAT ruh nyze

patronymic .... PAT ruh **NIM** ik

paucity .... **PAW** suh tee

pauper .... **PAW** pur

pause .... **PAWZ**

pavilion .... puh **VIL** yun

Pavlov .... **PAHV** lawf ¶18

Pawnee .... **paw NEE**

payola .... pay **OH** luh

peaked ("weak and wan") ... **PEE** kid
to be distinguished from peaked,
PEEKT, *meaning* having a peak

pear .... **PER**

pearl .... **PURL**

peasant .... **PEZ** unt

pecan ..... pi **KAN** *or* **PEE** kan ¶2, 18

peccadillo .... PEK uh **DIL** oh

peccary .... **PEK** ur ee

Pecos .... **PAY** kohs ¶1

pectoral .... **PEK** tur ul

peculiar .... pi **KYOOHL** yur

peculiarity .... pi KYOOH lee **AR** uh tee
or pi KYOOHL **YAR** uh tee ¶23

pecuniary pi **KYOOH** nee **ER** ee ¶23

pedagogical ....
.... PED uh **GAHJ** i kul ¶20

pedagogue .... **PED** uh gahg ¶19

pedagogy .... **PED** uh **GOH** jee ¶20

pedal .... **PED** ul
So for both adjective and noun,
but when the adjective refers to
the foot or feet, it may also be
PEE dul.

pedant .... **PED** unt

pederast .... **PED** uh rast
rarely **PEE** duh rast

pedestal .... **PED** is tul

pedestrian .... puh **DES** tree un

pediatrician ..... PEE dee uh **TRISH** un

pediatrics .... PEE dee **AT** riks

pedicure .... **PED** i kyoor ¶24

pedigree .... **PED** uh gree

SPELLED	PRONOUNCED	SPELLED	PRONOUNCED

pediment	**PED** uh munt	penetrable	**PEN** i truh bul
pedometer	pi **DAHM** uh tur	penetrate	**PEN** uh trayt
peduncle	pi **DUNG** kul *or*	penguin	**PENG** gwin ¶16
	PEE dung kul	penicillin	**PEN** uh **SIL** un
Pegasus	**PEG** uh sus	peninsula	puh **NIN** suh luh ¶21
peignoir	payn **WAHR** *or*	penis	**PEE** nis
	pen **WAHR** ¶2	penitence	**PEN** uh tuns ¶9
pejorative	pi **JAWR** uh tiv ¶19	penitentiary	
PEE juh rayt iv *and* **PEJ** uh rayt iv *are*		....	**PEN** uh **TEN** shur ee ¶12
infrequent.		penniless	**PEN** i lus
Pekingese	pee king **EEZ**	pennywort	**PEN** ee wurt
Thus when referring to Peking,		penology	pee **NAHL** uh jee ¶1
but for the breed of dog, it is		pension	**PEN** shun ¶12
nearly always pee kuh **NEEZ**.		pensive	**PEN** siv ¶9
pekoe	**PEE** koh	pentagon	**PEN** tuh gahn
pelican	**PEL** uh kun	pentagonal	pen **TAG** uh nul
pellagra	puh **LAG** ruh *or*	pentameter	pen **TAM** uh tur
	puh **LAY** gruh	Pentateuch	**PEN** tuh toohk ¶21
pellucid	puh **LOOH** sid	pentathlon	pen **TATH** lahn *or*
Peloponnesian ..	**PEL** uh puh **NEE** zhun		pen **TATH** lun
or **PEL** uh puh **NEE** shun		pen **TATH** uh **LAHN** *is not standard.*	
penal	**PEE** nul	Pentecost	**PEN** tuh kawst ¶19
penalize ..	**PEE** nuh lyze *or* **PEN** uh lyze	penultimate	pi **NUL** ti mit
penalty	**PEN** ul tee	penumbra	pi **NUM** bruh
pence	**PENS**	penurious	
in compounds, puns, with no		....	puh **NYOOR** ee us ¶21, 24
stress, as in sixpence		penury	**PEN** yur ee
SIKS puns ¶9		peon	**PEE** ahn
penchant	**PEN** chunt	**PEE** uhn *is not as common as it*	
pendant	**PEN** dunt	*once was.* ¶8	
pendulous	**PEN** joo lus ¶17	peonage	**PEE** uh nij
pendulum	**PEN** joo lum ¶17	peony	**PEE** uh nee
PEN dul um *is heard but is not*		Pepys	**PEEPS**
common.		*occasionally* **PEPS**, **PEP** is, *or*	
Penelope	puh **NEL** uh pee	**PEE** pis	

per– .... pur
*Some people "correct" this prefix
to* pruh *(perspire becomes*
pruh SPYRE), *worrying about the
reverse mistake of professor
pronounced as* pur FES ur ¶4:
see also pre–

peradventure .... PUR ud VEN chur

perambulator ..... pur AM byuh layt ur

percale .... pur KAYL
pur KAL *is now infrequent.*

per capita .... pur KAP uh tuh

perceive .... pur SEEV

percent .... pur SENT

percentile .... pur SEN tyle

percept .... PUR sept

perceptible .... pur SEP tuh bul

perception .... pur SEP shun

perchance .... pur CHANS ¶9, 18

percipient .... pur SIP ee unt ¶25

percolate .... PUR kuh layt

percussion .... pur KUSH un

per diem .... pur DEE um
occasionally pur DYE um

perdition .... pur DISH un

peregrine .... PER uh grin ¶22

peremptory ..... puh REMP tur ee ¶5

perennial .... puh REN ee ul ¶25

perfect *(verb)* .... pur FEKT

perfect *(adjective)* .... PUR fikt

perfection .... pur FEK shun

perfidious .... pur FID ee us

perfidy .... PUR fuh dee

perforate .... PUR fuh rayt

perforce .... pur FAWRS

perfume *(noun)* .... PUR fyoohm
also, and for the verb always,
pur FYOOHM

perfunctory ... pur FUNGK tur ee ¶5

Pericles .... PER uh kleez

perigee .... PER uh jee

perihelion .... PER uh HEE lee un ¶25

perilous .... PER ul us

perimeter .... puh RIM uh tur

perineum .... PER uh NEE um

period .... PIR ee ud

periodic .... PIR ee AHD ik

periodicity .... PIR ee uh DIS uh tee

periodontics ..... PER ee uh DAHN tiks

peripatetic .... PER i puh TET ik

peripheral .... puh RIF ur ul

periscope .... PER uh skohp

peristalsis .... PER uh STAWL sis *or*
PER uh STAL sis

peritoneum .... PER i tuh NEE um

peritonitis .... PER i tuh NYTE is

periwinkle .... PER i WING kul ¶1

perjure .... PUR jur

perjury .... PUR jur ee ¶5

permanent .... PUR muh nunt

permeable ...... PUR mee uh bul ¶25

permeate .... PUR mee ayt

permission .... pur MISH un

permit *(verb)* .... pur MIT
The noun is usually PUR mit, *but*
pur MIT *is sometimes also heard.*

permutation ...... PUR myoo TAY shun

pernicious .... pur NISH us

peroration .... PER uh RAY shun

perpendicular .... PUR pun DIK yuh lur

SPELLED	*PRONOUNCED*
perpetrate	**PUR** puh trayt
perpetual	pur **PECH** oo wul
perpetuate	pur **PECH** oo wayt
perpetuity	
	PUR puh **TOOH** uh tee ¶13, 21
perplexity	pur **PLEK** suh tee
perquisite	**PUR** kwuh zit
per se	**PUR SAY**
occasionally	**PUR SEE**
persecute	**PUR** suh kyooht
Persephone	pur **SEF** uh nee
perseverance	**PUR** suh **VIR** uns ¶9
persevere	pur suh **VIR**
Persia	**PUR** zhuh
persiflage	**PUR** suh flahzh
persimmon	pur **SIM** un
persist	pur **SIST** ¶14
persnickety	pur **SNIK** uh tee
persona	pur **SOH** nuh
personage	**PUR** suh nij
personality	**PUR** suh **NAL** uh tee
persona non grata	
	pur **SOH** nuh nahn **GRAHT** uh
For the final word, **GRAT** uh *and*	
GRAYT uh *are also heard.*	
personify	pur **SAHN** uh FYE
personnel	pur suh **NEL**
perspective	pur **SPEK** tiv
perspicacious	**PUR** spuh **KAY** shus
perspicuous	pur **SPIK** yoo wus
perspiration	**PUR** spuh **RAY** shun
perspire	pur **SPYRE**: *see* per–
persuade	pur **SWAYD**
persuasion	pur **SWAY** zhun
pertinacity	**PUR** tuh **NAS** uh tee
pertinent	**PUR** tuh nunt
perturb	pur **TURB**
perturbation	**PUR** tur **BAY** shun ¶3
pertussis	pur **TUS** is
peruse	puh **ROOHZ**
Peruvian	puh **ROOH** vee un
pervasive	pur **VAY** siv
perverse	pur **VURS**
perversion	pur **VUR** zhun
pervert *(verb)*	pur **VURT**
pervert *(noun)*	**PUR** vurt
peseta	puh **SAYT** uh ¶1
peso	**PAY** soh
pessary	**PES** ur ee
pessimism	**PES** uh miz um
pessimistic	PES uh **MIS** tik
pesticide	**PES** tuh syde
pestilence	**PES** tuh luns ¶9
pestilential	
	PES tuh **LEN** shul ¶9, 12
pestle	**PES** ul *or* **PES** tul
petard	pi **TAHRD**
petite	puh **TEET**
petit four	**PET** ee **FAWR** *or*
	puh tee **FOOHR**
petition	puh **TISH** un
petit *(jury or larceny)*	**PET** ee
petit mal	**PET** ee mal *or*
	puh tee **MAHL**
Petrarchan	pi **TRAHR** kun
petrel	**PET** rul
petri *(dish)*	**PEE** tree
petrify	**PET** ruh fye
petrodollars	**PET** roh DAHL urz ¶1
petroleum	puh **TROH** lee um ¶25

petrology .... pi **TRAHL** uh jee ¶1

petticoat .... **PET** ee koht

pettifogger ...... **PET** ee FAHG ur ¶19

petulant .... **PECH** oo lunt ¶17

petunia ..... puh **TOOHN** yuh ¶21, 25

pewter .... **PYOOHT** ur

peyote .... pay **OHT** ee

phaeton .... **FAY** uh tun

phalanx .... **FAY** langks

The regular plural is phalanxes, *but the alternative,* phalanges, *always used in anatomy, is* fuh **LAN** jeez.

phalarope .... **FAL** uh rohp

phallic .... **FAL** ik

phantasm .... **FAN** taz um

phantasmagoria ....

.... fan **TAZ** muh **GAWR** ee uh

phantom .... **FAN** tum

Pharaoh .... **FAR** oh ¶23

Pharisee .... **FAR** uh see ¶23

pharmaceutical ....

.... FAHR muh **SOOHT** i kul ¶21

pharmacist .... **FAHR** muh sist

pharmacology ....

.... FAHR muh **KAHL** uh jee

pharmacopeia ....

.... FAHR muh kuh **PEE** uh

pharmacy .... **FAHR** muh see

pharyngeal .... fuh **RIN** jee ul *or* FAR un **JEE** ul ¶25

pharynx .... **FAR** ingks ¶23

pheasant .... **FEZ** unt

phenobarbital ....

.... FEE nuh **BAHR** buh TAWL ¶1

phenol .... **FEE** nohl ¶19, 20

phenomenology ....

.... fi NAHM uh **NAHL** uh jee

phenomenon .... fi **NAHM** uh NAHN

fi **NAHM** uh nun *is now less frequent* ¶8; *the usual plural* phenomena *is* fi **NAHM** uh nuh.

phial .... **FYE** ul

Phi Beta Kappa ....

.... FYE BAYT uh **KAP** uh

philanderer .... fi **LAN** dur ur

philanthropic ..... FIL un **THRAHP** ik

philanthropist .... fi **LAN** thruh pist

philatelic .... FIL uh **TEL** ik

philately .... fi **LAT** uh lee

philharmonic .... FIL hahr **MAHN** ik *or* FIL ur **MAHN** ik

Philistine .... **FIL** is teen

The earlier fuh **LIS** tin *is now less common, but* **FIL** is tyne *and* fuh **LIS** teen *are now also heard.*

philodendron .... FIL uh **DEN** drun

philology .... fi **LAHL** uh jee

philosopher .... fi **LAHS** uh fur

philosophic .... FIL uh **SAHF** ik

philosophy .... fi **LAHS** uh fee

phlebitis .... fli **BYTE** is

phlegm .... **FLEM**

phlegmatic .... fleg **MAT** ik

phobia .... **FOH** bee uh ¶25

phoebe .... **FEE** bee

Phoenicia .... fuh **NISH** uh *or* fuh **NEE** shuh

phoenix .... **FEE** niks

phoneme .... **FOH** neem

phonemics .... fuh **NEE** miks ¶1

phonetics .... fuh **NET** iks ¶1

phonics .... **FAHN** iks

phonograph ..... **FOH** nuh graf ¶18

phonology .... fuh **NAHL** uh jee ¶1

phony .... **FOH** nee

phosphate .... **FAHS** fayt

phosphorescent ..... **FAHS** fuh **RES** unt

phosphorus .... **FAHS** fur us ¶5

photic .... **FOHT** ik

photocopy ..... **FOHT** uh **KAHP** ee ¶1

photogenic ...... **FOHT** uh **JEN** ik ¶1

photograph .... **FOHT** uh graf ¶18

photographer .... fuh **TAHG** ruh fur

photogravure

.... **FOHT** uh gruh **VYOOR** ¶1

photometer ...... foh **TAHM** uh tur ¶1

photon .... **FOH** tahn

Photostat *(trademark)* ....

.... **FOHT** uh stat

phototropism .... foh **TAHT** ruh piz um

phraseology ..... **FRAY** zee **AHL** uh jee

phrenology .... fri **NAHL** uh jee ¶1

phylactery .... fi **LAK** tur ee ¶5

phylogeny .... fye **LAHJ** uh nee

phylum .... **FYE** lum

physical .... **FIZ** i kul

physics .... **FIZ** iks

physiognomy ... **FIZ** ee **AHG** nuh mee

physiological ..... **FIZ** ee uh **LAHJ** i kul

physiology .... **FIZ** ee **AHL** uh jee

physique .... fi **ZEEK**

pi .... **PYE**

pianist .... pee **AN** ist *or* **PYAN** ist *or*

PEE un ist

piano .... pee **AN** oh *or* **PYAN** oh

pianoforte .... pee **AN** uh fawrt *or*

PYAN uh fawrt *or*

pee **AN** uh **FAWR** tee *or*

pee **AN** uh **FAWR** tay ¶1

piaster .... pee **AS** tur

piazza ... pee **AZ** uh *or* pee **AHT** suh *or*

pee **AT** suh ¶5

The first is usual when the word

means a covered gallery *or* a

covered porch.

pica .... **PYE** kuh

picador .... **PIK** uh dawr

picaresque .... pik uh **RESK**

Picasso .... pi **KAH** soh

picayune .... pik ee **OOHN** *or*

pik uh **YOOHN**

piccolo .... **PIK** uh loh

pickerel .... **PIK** ur ul ¶5

pictograph .... **PIK** tuh graf ¶18

pictorial .... pik **TAWR** ee ul

picture .... **PIK** chur ¶12

picturesque .... pik chuh **RESK**

pidgin .... **PIJ** un

piebald .... **PYE** bawld

Pietà .... pyay **TAH** *or* pee ay **TAH**

pee **AYT** ah *is also heard.*

piety .... **PYE** uh tee

pigeon .... **PIJ** un

pilaf .... **PEE** lahf

The prevailing pronunciation

until recently was pi **LAHF**.

pilaster .... pi **LAS** tur

pileated .... **PIL** ee ayt id *or*

PYE lee ayt id

SPELLED	PRONOUNCED	SPELLED	PRONOUNCED
pilferage	PIL fur ij ¶5	pistol	PIS tul
pilgrimage	PIL grum ij	pita (bread)	PEET uh or PEE tah
pillage	PIL ij	Pitcairn	PIT kern
pillory	PIL ur ee	piteous	PIT ee us
Pilsener	PILZ nur or PILS nur	pithy	PITH ee
pimento	pi MEN toh	pitiable	PIT ee uh bul
pimpernel	PIM pur nel or PIM pur nul	pitiful	PIT i ful
pince–nez	pans NAY or pins NAY	pittance	PIT uns ¶9
	pins NEZ is a spelling pronunciation and is not standard. ¶9	pituitary	pi TOOH uh TER ee ¶21, 23
pincers	PIN surz ¶9 sometimes folk–etymologized to PINCH urz	Pius	PYE us
		pixilated	PIK suh layt id
pinion	PIN yun	pizazz	puh ZAZ
pinnacle	PIN uh kul	pizza	PEET suh
pinochle	PEE NUK ul Enthusiasts often say PEE NAHK ul.	pizzacato	PIT suh KAHT oh
		pizzeria	PEET suh REE uh
pinto	PIN toh	placable	PLAK uh bul or PLAY kuh bul
pioneer	pye uh NIR ¶2		
pious	PYE us	placard	PLAK ahrd or PLAK urd ¶8
piquant	PEE kahnt or PEE kunt or PEE kwahnt ¶8	placate	PLAY kayt or PLAK ayt
		placebo	pluh SEE boh
pique ("resentment")	PEEK	placenta	pluh SEN tuh
piqué ("fabric")	pee KAY	placid	PLAS id
piracy	PYE ruh see	plage	PLAHZH or PLAZH
piranha	pi RAHN uh or pi RAHN yuh ¶18	plagiarism	PLAY jur iz um PLAY jee uh riz um is now rarely heard.
pirate	PYE rut		
pirogi	pi ROH gee	plague	PLAYG
pirouette	pir oo WET	plaid	PLAD
Pisa	PEE zuh ¶14	plaintiff	PLAYN tif
Pisces	PYE seez	plaintive	PLAYN tiv
pistachio	pi STAH shee OH ¶18, 25	plait	PLAYT
pistil	PIS tul	planet	PLAN it
		planetarium	PLAN uh TAR ee um ¶23

157

planetary ...... **PLAN** uh **TER** ee ¶23

plankton .... **PLANGK** tun
now occasionally **PLANGK** tahn ¶8

Plantagenet .... plan **TAJ** uh nit

plantain .... **PLAN** tin

plantar .... **PLAN** tur

plantation .... plan **TAY** shun

plaque .... **PLAK**

plasma .... **PLAZ** muh

plasticize .... **PLAS** tuh syze

plateau .... pla **TOH**

platelet .... **PLAYT** lit

platen .... **PLAT** un

platinum .... **PLAT** un um

platitude .... **PLAT** uh toohd ¶21

Plato .... **PLAY** toh

Platonic .... pluh **TAHN** ik *or*
play **TAHN** ik

platoon .... pluh **TOOHN**

Platte .... **PLAT**

platypus .... **PLAT** uh pus
now also **PLAT** uh poos ¶8

plaudit .... **PLAW** dit

plausible .... **PLAW** zuh bul

plaza .... **PLAH** zuh ¶18

plead .... **PLEED**

pleasant .... **PLEZ** unt

pleasurable ...... **PLEZH** ur uh bul ¶5

pleasure .... **PLEZH** ur

pleat .... **PLEET**

plebeian .... pli **BEE** un

plebiscite .... **PLEB** uh syte

plectrum .... **PLEK** trum

Pleiades .... **PLEE** uh deez

Pleistocene .... **PLYSE** tuh seen

plenary .... **PLEE** nur ee
PLEN ur ee *is now heard at least as
often as* **PLEE** nur ee.

plenipotentiary ....
.... PLEN i puh **TEN** shee **ER** ee *or*
PLEN i puh **TEN** shur ee ¶12, 23

plenitude .... **PLEN** uh toohd ¶21

plenteous .... **PLEN** tee us

plethora .... **PLETH** ur uh

pleurisy .... **PLOOR** uh see ¶24

plexus .... **PLEK** sus

pliable .... **PLYE** uh bul

pliant .... **PLYE** unt

plight .... **PLYTE**

Pliocene .... **PLYE** uh seen

plover .... **PLUV** ur
PLOH vur, *a spelling
pronunciation, is common.*

plumage .... **PLOOH** mij

pluperfect .... plooh **PUR** fikt

plural .... **PLOOR** ul ¶24

plurality .... ploo **RAL** uh tee

Plutarch .... **PLOOH** tahrk

plutocracy .... plooh **TAHK** ruh see

plutocrat .... **PLOOHT** uh krat

plutonium .... plooh **TOH** nee um

pneumatic ...... nooh **MAT** ik ¶1, 21

pneumonia ....
.... noo **MOHN** yuh ¶1, 21, 25

Pocahontas .... POH kuh **HAHN** tus

pococurante ....
...... POH koh koo **RAN** tee ¶18, 21

podiatry .... puh **DYE** uh tree
less frequently poh **DYE** uh tree ¶1

podium .... **POH** dee um

SPELLED	PRONOUNCED	SPELLED	PRONOUNCED
poem	**POH** um	politics	**PAHL** uh tiks

poem .... **POH** um
The one–syllable **POHM** *is not*
generally considered standard.

poesy .... **POH** uh see ¶14
poet .... **POH** ut
poetaster .... **POH** uh TAS tur
poetic .... poh ET ik
poetry .... **POH** uh tree
pogrom .. poh **GRAHM** *or* **POH** grum *or*
poh **GRUM** ¶2, 20
poignant .... **POYN** yunt
poinsettia .... poyn **SET** uh *or*
poyn **SET** ee uh

The first clearly prevails,
although it is objected to by
some.

pointillism ...... **PWAHN** tuh liz um *or*
PWAN tee iz um *or* **POYN** tuh liz um
poison .... **POY** zun
polar .... **POH** lur
polarity .... poh **LAR** uh tee ¶1, 23
polarization .... **POH** lur i **ZAY** shun
polemics .... puh **LEM** iks ¶1
policy .... **PAHL** uh see
poliomyelitis ....
.... POH lee oh MYE uh **LYTE** us
Polish .... **POH** lish
polish .... **PAHL** ish
Politburo .... **PAHL** it BYOOR oh *or*
puh **LIT** byoor oh ¶20
politic .... **PAHL** uh tik
political .... puh **LIT** i kul
politician .... PAHL uh **TISH** un
politicize .... puh **LIT** uh SYZE
politico .... puh **LIT** i KOH

politics .... **PAHL** uh tiks
polity .... **PAHL** uh tee
polka .... **POHL** kuh
POH kuh *sometimes for the dance*
and always for the dot
poll .... **POHL**
pollinate .... **PAHL** uh nayt
polliwog .... **PAHL** ee wahg ¶19
pollutant .... puh **LOOHT** unt
pollute .... puh **LOOHT**
Pollyanna .... PAHL ee **AN** uh
polonaise .... pahl uh **NAYZ** ¶20
polonium .... puh **LOH** nee um
poltergeist .... **POHL** tur gyste
poltroon .... pahl **TROOHN**
poly– .. **PAHL** i *or* **PAHL** uh *or* **PAHL** ee
polyandry ...... **PAHL** ee AN dree ¶2
polyclinic .... PAHL i **KLIN** ik ¶1
polyester .... **PAHL** ee ES tur
polygamy .... puh **LIG** uh mee
polyglot .... **PAHL** i glaht ¶1
polygon .... **PAHL** i gahn ¶1
polygraph .... **PAHL** i graf ¶1, 18
polymer .... **PAHL** i mur
polymerization ....
.... puh **LIM** ur i **ZAY** shun *or*
PAHL i mur i **ZAY** shun
Polynesia .... PAHL uh **NEE** zhuh
polynomial ....PAHL i **NOH** mee ul
polyp .... **PAHL** ip
polyphonic .... PAHL i **FAHN** ik ¶1
polyphony .... puh **LIF** uh nee
polytechnic .... PAHL i **TEK** nik
polyunsaturated ....
.... PAHL ee un **SACH** uh rayt id

159

pomace .... **PUM** is

pomade ... pah **MAYD** or poh **MAYD** or
 puh **MAYD**
 The second syllable may also be
 MAHD.

pomegranate .... **PAHM** gran it or
 PAHM uh **GRAN** it or **PUM** gran it

Pomeranian
 .... **PAHM** uh **RAY** nee un ¶25

pommel *(verb)* .... **PUM** ul
 The noun may be **PUM** ul or
 PAHM ul.

pompadour .... **PAHM** puh dawr

pompano .... **PAHM** puh noh

Pompeii ... pahm **PAY** or pahm **PAY** ee

pompon .... **PAHM** pahm ¶6
 sometimes **PAHM** pahn

pomposity .... pahm **PAHS** uh tee

pompous .... **PAHM** pus

poncho .... **PAHN** choh

ponderosa .... PAHN duh **ROH** suh

ponderous .... **PAHN** dur us ¶5

pongee .... pahn **JEE**

pontiff .... **PAHN** tif

pontificate .... pahn **TIF** uh kayt ¶1

pontoon .... pahn **TOOHN**

popery .... **POHP** ur ee

popinjay .... **PAHP** in jay

popish .... **POHP** ish

poplar .... **PAHP** lur

populace .... **PAHP** yuh lis

popular .... **PAHP** yuh lur

popularity ....
 .... PAHP yuh **LAR** uh tee ¶23

popularize .... **PAHP** yuh luh **RYZE**

populate .... **PAHP** yuh layt

populous .... **PAHP** yuh lus

porcelain .... **PAWR** suh lin ¶5

porcine .... **PAWR** syne ¶22

porcupine .... **PAWR** kyuh pyne

pornographic ....
 .... PAWR nuh **GRAF** ik ¶18

pornography ...... pawr **NAHG** ruh fee

porosity .... paw **RAHS** uh tee ¶1

porphyry .... **PAWR** fur ee

porpoise .... **PAWR** pus

porridge .... **PAWR** ij ¶19

portage .... **PAWR** tij

portend .... pawr **TEND**

portent .... **PAWR** tent

portentous .... pawr **TEN** tus

portfolio .... pawrt **FOH** lee OH

portico .... **PAWR** tuh koh

portmanteau .... pawrt **MAN** toh or
 pawrt man **TOH**

portrait .... **PAWR** trit or
 PAWR trayt ¶8

portraiture .... **PAWR** tri chur

portray .... pawr **TRAY** ¶1

Portsmouth .... **PAWRTS** muth

Portugal .... **PAWR** chuh gul

Portuguese ...... pawr chuh **GEEZ**

portulaca ... PAWR chuh **LAK** uh ¶18

poseur .... poh **ZUR**

posit .... **PAHZ** it

position .... puh **ZISH** un

positive .... **PAHZ** uh tiv

posse .... **PAHS** ee

possess .... puh **ZES**

possession .... puh **ZESH** un

SPELLED	PRONOUNCED	SPELLED	PRONOUNCED

SPELLED	PRONOUNCED
possibility	**PAHS** uh **BIL** uh tee
possible	**PAHS** uh bul
posterior	pahs **TIR** ee ur ¶20
posterity	pahs **TER** uh tee
postern	**POHS** turn ¶20
posthumous	**PAHS** choo mus ¶17

Some people manage a tongue–twisting spelling pronunciation **PAHS** thyoo mus. *That and another spelling pronunciation,* pohst **HYOO** mus, *are not standard.*

postiche	paws **TEESH**
post–mortem	
	pohst **MAWR** tum ¶10
postpartum	pohst **PAHR** tum ¶10
postpone	pohst **POHN** ¶10
postscript	**POHS** skript ¶10
postulate *(verb)*	**PAHS** chuh layt

The noun is usually **PAHS** chuh lit ¶17.

posture	**PAHS** chur
posy	**POH** zee
potable	**POHT** uh bul
potash	**PAHT** ash
potassium	puh **TAS** ee um ¶14, 25
potato	puh **TAYT** oh *or* puh **TAYT** uh
potency	**POHT** un see
potent	**POHT** unt
potentate	**POHT** un tayt
potential	puh **TEN** shul ¶9, 12
Potomac	puh **TOH** muk
potpourri	poh poo **REE** ¶2

The spelling pronunciation paht **POOR** ee *is heard often.*

SPELLED	PRONOUNCED
potsherd	**PAHT** shurd
pottage	**PAHT** ij
pottery	**PAHT** ur ee
pouch	**POWCH**
Poughkeepsie	puh **KIP** see
poultice	**POHL** tis
poultry	**POHL** tree
poverty	**PAHV** ur tee
practicable	**PRAK** ti kuh bul
practical	**PRAK** ti kul
practice	**PRAK** tis
practitioner	prak **TISH** un ur
praetorian	pri **TAWR** ee un
pragmatic	prag **MAT** ik
pragmatism	**PRAG** muh tiz um
Prague	**PRAHG**
prairie	**PRER** ee
praline	**PRAY** leen

chiefly Southern **PRAH** leen

prance	**PRANS** ¶9, 18
prate	**PRAYT**
prayer	**PRER** ¶23

One who prays is a **PRAY** ur.

pre–	pree *or* pri *or* pruh

also, by metathesis, sometimes pur, *but, in general, standard speakers have little tolerance for this "mistake": see also* per– ¶4

preamble	**PREE** am bul *or* pree **AM** bul
precarious	pri **KAR** ee us ¶23
precaution	pri **KAW** shun ¶19
precede	pri **SEED** ¶1
precedence	**PRES** uh duns *or* pri **SEED** uns ¶9

SPELLED	*PRONOUNCED*
precept	**PREE** sept
precinct	**PREE** singkt
preciosity	PRESH ee **AHS** uh tee
precious	**PRESH** us
precipice	**PRES** uh pis
precipitate *(verb)*	pri **SIP** uh tayt

For the noun and adjective,
pri **SIP** uh tit *is also heard.*

precipitous	pri **SIP** uh tus
précis	pray **SEE** ¶2
precise	pri **SYSE** ¶1
precision	pri **SIZH** un ¶1
preclude	pri **KLOOHD** ¶1
precocious	pri **KOH** shus ¶1
precocity	pri **KAHS** uh tee
precursor	pri **KUR** sur ¶1
predator	**PRED** uh tur
predatory	**PRED** uh TAWR ee
predecessor	**PRED** uh SES ur ¶2

PREE duh SES ur *is chiefly British.*

predicament	pri **DIK** uh munt ¶1
predicate *(verb)*	**PRED** uh kayt
predicate *(noun and adjective)*	
	PRED uh kit
predilection	PRED uh **LEK** shun or
	PREE duh **LEK** shun
prednisone	**PRED** nuh sohn ¶14
preempt	pree **EMPT** ¶10
preemption	pree **EMP** shun ¶10
preface	**PREF** is
prefatory	**PREF** uh TAWR ee
prefect	**PREE** fekt ¶10
prefecture	**PREE** fek chur
prefer	pri **FUR** ¶1
preferable	**PREF** ur uh bul

SPELLED	*PRONOUNCED*
preference	**PREF** runs ¶5, 9
preferential	
	PREF uh **REN** shul ¶9, 12
prefix *(noun)*	**PREE** fiks

The verb may also be pree **FIKS.**

pregnant	**PREG** nunt
prehensile	pri **HEN** sul ¶1, 9, 22
prejudice	**PREJ** uh dis
prejudicial	PREJ uh **DISH** ul
prelate	**PREL** it
preliminary	
	pri **LIM** uh **NER** ee ¶1, 23
prelude	**PREL** yoohd or **PRAYL** yood
	or **PRAY** loohd or **PREE** loohd
premature	
	pree muh **TOOR** ¶13, 21
premier	pri **MIR** or pri **MYIR**

PREE mee ur *is no longer common.*

première	pri **MYER** or pri **MYIR** or
	pri **MIR** or prem ee **ER**
premise *(noun)*	**PREM** is

The plural is **PREM** uh siz, *not*
PREM uh seez; *the verb is*
sometimes pri **MYZE.**

premium	**PREE** mee um ¶5
premonition	PREM uh **NISH** un or
	PREE muh **NISH** un
preparation	PREP uh **RAY** shun
preparatory	
	pri **PAR** uh **TAWR** ee ¶1, 23
preponderant	
	pri **PAHN** dur unt ¶1, 5
preposition	PREP uh **ZISH** un
preposterous	pri **PAHS** tur us ¶5
prepuce	**PREE** pyoohs

prerequisite ....

.... pri **REK** wuh zit ¶1, 14

prerogative .... pri **RAHG** uh tiv ¶3

presage *(noun)* .... **PRES** ij

The verb is usually pri **SAYJ.**

presbyter .... **PREZ** bi tur ¶14

presbyterian ....

.... PREZ buh **TIR** ee un ¶14

prescience .... **PREE** shee uns

Also heard are **PREE** shuns,

PRESH ee uns, *and* **PRESH** uns. ¶9

prescind .... pri **SIND**

prescribe .... pri **SKRYBE**

prescription ...... pri **SKRIP** shun ¶1

presence .... **PREZ** uns ¶9

present *(noun and adjective)* ....

.... **PREZ** unt

present *(verb)* .... pri **ZENT** ¶1

presentation ... PREE zen **TAY** shun *or*

PREZ un **TAY** shun

presentiment ... pri **ZEN** tuh munt ¶1

preservation .... PREZ ur **VAY** shun

preservative ...... pri **ZUR** vuh tiv ¶1

preside .... pri **ZYDE** ¶1

presidency ..... **PREZ** i dun see ¶1, 9

president .... **PREZ** i dunt

presidio .... pri **SID** ee oh

presidium .... pri **SID** ee um

pressure .... **PRESH** ur

prestidigitation ....

.... PRES tuh **DIJ** i **TAY** shun

prestige .... pres **TEEZH** ¶1, 15

prestigious .... pres **TIJ** us *or*

pres **TEE** jus

presume .... pri **ZOOHM** ¶21

presumption ..... pri **ZUMP** shun ¶10

presumptuous ....

.... pri **ZUMP** choo wus ¶10

pretense ... pri **TENS** *or* **PREE** tens ¶9

pretension ...... pri **TEN** shun ¶9, 12

pretentious ..... pri **TEN** shus ¶9, 12

preterit .... **PRET** ur it

preternatural ....

.... PREE tur **NACH** ur ul ¶5

pretext .... **PREE** tekst

pretty .... **PRIT** ee

by metathesis, often **PUR** tee ¶4

prevail .... pri **VAYL**

prevalent .... **PREV** uh lunt

prevaricate ..... pri **VAR** uh kayt ¶23

prevention .... pri **VEN** shun ¶9, 12

preview .... **PREE** vyooh

previous .... **PREE** vee us ¶5

Priam .... **PRYE** um

primacy .... **PRYE** muh see

prima donna .. PREE muh **DAHN** uh *or*

PRIM uh **DAHN** uh

prima facie ....

.... PRYE muh **FAY** shuh ¶25

also, especially in legal contexts,

PRYE muh **FAY** shi ee *or*

PRYE muh **FAY** shee

primal .... **PRYE** mul

primary .... **PRYE** mer ee *or*

PRYE mur ee ¶5, 23

primate ("mammal") ..... **PRYE** mayt

primate ("church official") ....

.... **PRYE** mayt *or* **PRYE** mit

primer ("something that primes") ..

.... **PRYE** mur

primer ("first teaching book") .... **PRIM** ur

The British pronunciation for the book is **PRYE** mur.

primeval .... prye **MEE** vul

primipara .... prye **MIP** ur uh

primitive .... **PRIM** uh tiv

primogenitor ...... **PRYE** muh **JEN** i tur

primordial .... prye **MAWR** dee ul

princess ..... **PRIN** sis *or* **PRIN** ses ¶9

principal .... **PRIN** suh pul ¶9

principality .... **PRIN** suh **PAL** uh tee

principium .... prin **SIP** ee um

principle .... **PRIN** suh pul ¶9

prior .... **PRYE** ur

prioress .... **PRYE** ur is

prioritize .... prye **AWR** uh tyze

priority .... prye **AWR** uh tee

priory .... **PRYE** ur ee

Priscilla .... pri **SIL** uh

prismatic .... priz **MAT** ik

prison .... **PRIZ** un

prisoner .... **PRIZ** nur ¶5

pristine .... **PRIS** teen ¶2

formerly also **PRIS** tin ¶8

privacy .... **PRYE** vuh see

PRIV uh see *is mainly a British variant.*

private .... **PRYE** vit

privation .... prye **VAY** shun

privative .... **PRIV** uh tiv

privet .... **PRIV** it

privilege .... **PRIV** uh lij ¶5

privity .... **PRIV** uh tee

privy .... **PRIV** ee

pro– .... proh *or* pruh

Such nonstandard spellings as "perfessor" *or* "perduction" *make us aware of a comparable pronunciation of this prefix, thus* pur, *but it is generally considered nonstandard.*

probability .... PRAHB uh **BIL** uh tee

probable .... **PRAHB** uh bul

probate .... **PROH** bayt

probation .... proh **BAY** shun ¶1

probity .... **PROH** buh tee

problem .... **PRAHB** lum

problematic .... PRAHB luh **MAT** ik

proboscis .... pruh **BAHS** is ¶1

procedure .... pruh **SEE** jur ¶1

proceed .... pruh **SEED** ¶1

proceeds .... **PROH** seedz

process .... **PRAHS** es ¶20

The plural is **PRAHS** es uz, *not* **PRAHS** uh seez.

procession .... pruh **SESH** un ¶1

proclaim .... proh **KLAYM** ¶1

proclamation ... PRAHK luh **MAY** shun

proclivity .... proh **KLIV** uh tee

procrastinate .... proh **KRAS** tuh nayt ¶1

procreate .... **PROH** kree ayt

Procrustean ... proh **KRUS** tee un ¶1

proctology .... prahk **TAHL** uh jee

proctor .... **PRAHK** tur

procurator .... **PRAHK** yoo ray tur

procure .... pruh **KYOOR** ¶1

prodigal .... **PRAHD** i gul

prodigious .... pruh **DIJ** us ¶1

prodigy	**PRAHD** uh jee	progression	pruh **GRESH** un ¶1
produce *(verb)*	pruh **DOOHS** ¶21	progressive	pruh **GRES** iv ¶1
produce *(noun)*	**PRAHD** oohs or	prohibit	proh **HIB** it ¶1
	PROH doohs ¶21	prohibition	PROH uh **BISH** un
product	**PRAHD** ukt	project *(noun)*	**PRAHJ** ekt or
production	pruh **DUK** shun		**PRAHJ** ikt
profanation	PRAHF uh **NAY** shun	project *(verb)*	pruh **JEKT**
profane	pruh **FAYN** ¶1	projectile	pruh **JEK** tul ¶1, 22
profanity	pruh **FAN** uh tee ¶1	projection	pruh **JEK** shun ¶1
profess	pruh **FES** ¶1	proletarian	
profession	pruh **FESH** un ¶1		PROH luh **TAR** ee un ¶23
professor	pruh **FES** ur	proletariat	
professorial	PROH fuh **SAWR** ee ul		PROH luh **TAR** ee ut ¶23
proffer	**PRAHF** ur	proliferate	pruh **LIF** uh rayt ¶1
proficient	pruh **FISH** unt ¶1	prolific	pruh **LIF** ik ¶1
profile	**PROH** fyle	prolix	proh **LIKS** ¶2
profit	**PRAHF** it	prologue	**PROH** lawg ¶19
profiteer	prahf uh **TIR**	prolong	pruh **LAWNG** ¶1
profligate	**PRAHF** luh git	promenade	prahm uh **NAYD** or
profound	pruh **FOWND** ¶1		prahm uh **NAHD**
profundity	pruh **FUN** duh tee ¶1	Prometheus	pruh **MEE** thee us or
profuse	pruh **FYOOHS** ¶1		pruh **MEE** thyoohs
profusion	pruh **FYOOH** zhun ¶1	prominence	**PRAHM** uh nuns ¶9
progenitor	proh **JEN** uh tur ¶1	promiscuity	
progeny	**PRAHJ** uh nee		PRAHM is **KYOOH** uh tee or
progesterone	proh **JES** tuh rohn ¶1		PROH mis **KYOOH** uh tee
prognosis	prahg **NOH** sis	promiscuous	
prognosticate	prahg **NAHS** tuh kayt		pruh **MIS** kyoo wus ¶1
program	**PROH** gram	promise	**PRAHM** is
PROH grum *is now heard less frequently* ¶8.		promissory	**PRAHM** i **SAWR** ee
		promontory	**PRAHM** un **TAWR** ee
progress *(verb)*	pruh **GRES** ¶1	promote	pruh **MOHT** ¶1
progress *(noun)*	**PRAH** gres or	promotion	pruh **MOH** shun ¶1
	PRAHG rus	promulgate	**PRAHM** ul gayt or
PROH gres *is chiefly British.*			proh **MUL** gayt ¶1

SPELLED	PRONOUNCED
pronounce	pruh **NOWNS** ¶9
pronunciation	
.... pruh **NUN** see **AY** shun ¶9	
propaganda	
.... PRAHP uh **GAN** duh ¶20	
propagandize .... PRAHP uh **GAN** dyze	
propagate ...... **PRAHP** uh **gayt**	
propane .... **PROH** payn	
propel .... pruh **PEL** ¶1	
propensity ... pruh **PEN** suh tee ¶1, 9	
property .... **PRAHP** ur tee	
prophecy .... **PRAHF** uh see	
prophesy .... **PRAHF** uh sye	
prophet .... **PRAHF** it	
prophetic .... pruh **FET** ik ¶1	
prophylactic .... PROH fuh **LAK** tik	
prophylaxis .... PROH fuh **LAK** sis	
propinquity	
.... pruh **PING** kwuh tee ¶1, 16	
propitiate .... pruh **PISH** ee ayt ¶1	
propitious .... pruh **PISH** us ¶1	
proponent .... pruh **POH** nunt	
proportion .... pruh **PAWR** shun	
proposal .... pruh **POH** zul	
proposition .... PRAHP uh **ZISH** un	
propound .... pruh **POWND** ¶1	
proprietary	
.... pruh **PRYE** uh TER ee ¶1, 23	
proprietor ...... pruh **PRYE** uh tur ¶1	
propriety .... pruh **PRYE** uh tee ¶1	
propulsion .... pruh **PUL** shun ¶1	
propylene .... **PROH** puh leen	
pro rata .... proh **RAYT** uh *or*	
proh **RAHT** uh *or* proh **RAT** uh	
prosaic .... proh **ZAY** ik ¶1	

SPELLED	PRONOUNCED
proscenium ..... pruh **SEE** nee um ¶1
prosciutto .... pruh **SHOOHT** oh
proscribe .... proh **SKRYBE**
proscription .... proh **SKRIP** shun
prose .... **PROHZ**
prosecute .... **PRAHS** uh kyooht
proselyte .... **PRAHS** uh lyte
proselytize .... **PRAHS** uh li **TYZE**
Proserpina .... proh **SUR** pi nuh
prosodic .... pruh **SAHD** ik
prosody .... **PRAHS** uh dee ¶14
prospect .... **PRAHS** pekt
prospectus .... pruh **SPEK** tus ¶1
prosperity ...... prahs **PER** uh tee ¶1
prosperous ...... **PRAHS** pur us ¶5
prostate .... **PRAHS** tayt
This word is sometimes confused
with prostrate **PRAHS** trayt.
prostatitis .... PRAHS tuh **TYTE** is
prosthesis .... prahs **THEE** sis
The earlier **PRAHS** thuh sis *is now*
less frequently heard.
prosthetics .... prahs **THET** iks
prosthodontics ....
.... PRAHS thuh **DAHN** tiks
prostitute ...... **PRAHS** tuh tooht ¶21
prostrate .... **PRAHS** trayt:
see prostate
prosy .... **PROH** zee
protagonist ..... pruh **TAG** uh nist ¶1
protean .. **PROHT** ee un *or* proh **TEE** un
protect .... pruh **TEKT** ¶1
protection .... pruh **TEK** shun ¶1
protectorate .... pruh **TEK** tur it ¶5
protégé .... **PROHT** uh zhay ¶2

protein .... **PROH** teen
Earlier **PROHT** *ee in* has *become
relatively rare.*

pro tempore .... proh **TEM** pur ee

protest *(verb)* .... pruh **TEST**
also, and for the noun always,
PROH test

Protestant .... **PRAHT** is tunt

protestant .... **PRAHT** is tunt *or*
pruh **TES** tunt

protestation ....
.... **PRAHT** is **TAY** shun ¶20

protocol .... **PROHT** uh kawl ¶19, 20

proton .... **PROHT** tahn

protoplasm .. **PROHT** uh **PLAZ** um ¶1

prototype ..... **PROHT** uh type ¶1

protozoan .... PROHT uh **ZOH** un

protract .... proh **TRAKT** ¶1

protractor .... **PROH** trak tur *or*
proh **TRAK** tur

protrude .... proh **TROOHD** ¶1

protrusile .... proh **TROOH** sul

protrusion ...... proh **TROOH** zhun ¶1

protuberance ....
.... proh **TOOH** bur uns ¶1, 5, 9

prove .... **PROOHV**

provenance .... **PRAHV** uh nuns ¶9

Provençal .... proh vahn **SAHL** ¶20

provender .... **PRAHV** un dur

provenience ....
.... pruh **VEE** nee uns ¶1, 25

proverb .... **PRAHV** urb

proverbial .. pruh **VUR** bee ul ¶1, 25

provide .... pruh **VYDE** ¶1

providence .... **PRAHV** uh duns ¶9

providential ....
.... PRAHV uh **DEN** shul ¶9, 12

province .... **PRAHV** ins ¶9

provincial ...... pruh **VIN** shul ¶9, 12

provision .... pruh **VIZH** un ¶1

proviso .... pruh **VYE** zoh ¶1

provocation ...... PRAHV uh **KAY** shun

provocative ..... pruh **VAHK** uh tiv ¶1

provoke .... pruh **VOHK** ¶1

provolone .... PROH vuh **LOH** nee *or*
PRAHV uh **LOH** nee

provost ..... **PROH** vohst *or* **PRAHV** ust
also, especially in the military,
PROH voh

prowess .... **PROW** is *or* **PROH** is

proximate .... **PRAHK** suh mit

proximity .... prahk **SIM** uh tee

proxy .... **PRAHK** see

prudent .... **PROOHD** unt

prudential ..... proo **DEN** shul ¶9, 12

prudery .... **PROOHD** ur ee

prurient .... **PROOR** ee unt
*Sometimes, perhaps by
dissimilation, this tongue–twister
is* pronounced **PYOOR** *ee unt,
which is not accepted as standard.*

psalm .... **SAHM**
occasionally **SAHLM** ¶19

psaltery .... **SAWL** tur ee ¶5

pseudonym ...... **SOOH** duh nim ¶21

pseudonymous ....
.... sooh **DAHN** uh mus ¶21

pseudoscience ....
.... **SOOH** doh **SYE** uns ¶9, 21

pshaw .... **SHAW**

SPELLED	PRONOUNCED
psittacosis	SIT uh KOH sis
psoriasis	suh RYE uh sis
psych	SYKE
psyche	SYE kee
psychedelic	SYE kuh DEL ik
psychiatric	SYE kee AT rik
psychiatrist	suh KYE uh trist ¶1
psychic	SYE kik
psycho	SYE koh
psychological	SYE kuh LAHJ i kul
psychology	sye KAHL uh jee
psychopath	SYE kuh path ¶18
psychosis	sye KOH sis
psychosomatic	
	SYE koh soh MAT ik ¶1
psychotic	sye KAHT ik
ptarmigan	TAHR muh gun
pterodactyl	TER uh DAK tul
Ptolemy	TAHL uh mee ¶20
ptomaine	TOH mayn ¶2
puberty	PYOOH bur tee
pubes	PYOOH beez
pubescent	pyooh BES unt
pubic	PYOOH bik
public	PUB lik
publication	PUB luh KAY shun
publicist	PUB luh sist
publicity	puh BLIS uh tee
publicize	PUB luh syze
publicly	PUB lik lee
publish	PUB lish
Puccini	pooh CHEE nee ¶1
puce	PYOOHS
pudding	POOD ing
pudendum	pyooh DEN dum ¶1, 21

SPELLED	PRONOUNCED
pueblo	PWEB loh
puerile	PYOOR ul or
	PYOOH ur ul ¶5, 22
puerility	PYOOH RIL uh tee ¶5
Puerto Rico	PWER tuh REE koh or
	PAWR tuh REE koh
Puget (Sound)	PYOOH jit
pugilism	PYOOH juh liz um
pugnacious	pug NAY shus
puisne	PYOOH nee
pulchritude	PUL kruh toohd ¶21
pule	PYOOHL
Pulitzer	POOL it sur ¶21
pullet	POOL it
pulley	POOL ee
pulmonary	PUL muh NER ee or
	POOL muh NER ee ¶23
pulpit	POOL pit or PUL pit
pulsar	PUL sahr or PUL sur
pulsate	PUL sayt
pulse	PULS ¶9
pulverize	PUL vuh ryze
puma	PYOOH muh ¶21
pumice	PUM is
pumpkin	PUM kin or PUNG kin or
	PUMP kin ¶9
puncheon	PUN chun ¶9
punctilious	pungk TIL ee us
punctual	PUNGK choo wul
punctuate	PUNGK choo wayt
puncture	PUNGK chur
pundit	PUN dit
pungent	PUN junt
Punic	PYOOH nik
punish	PUN ish

SPELLED	PRONOUNCED	SPELLED	PRONOUNCED

punitive .... PYOOH nuh tiv

Punjab .... PUN jahb *or* pun JAHB *or*
PUN jab

punster .... PUN stur ¶9

puny .... PYOOH nee

pupa .... PYOOH puh

pupil .... PYOOH pul

puppeteer .... pup i TIR

purblind .... PUR blynde

purchase .... PUR chus

purée .... pyoo RAY
sometimes pyoo REE ¶2

purgative .... PUR guh tiv

purgatory .... PUR guh TAWR ee

purify .... PYOOR uh fye ¶24

Purim .... POOR im *or* pooh REEM

Puritan .... PYOOR uh tun ¶24

puritanical ....
.... PYOOR uh TAN i kul ¶24

purity .... PYOOR uh tee ¶24

purlieu .... PUR looh *or* PURL yooh

purloin .... pur LOYN ¶2

purport *(verb)* .... pur PAWRT
also, and for the noun always,
PUR pawrt

purpose .... PUR pus

purse .... PURS

purslane .... PURS lin *or* PURS layn

pursue .... pur SOOH ¶21

purulent .... PYOOR uh lunt ¶21

purvey .... pur VAY

purview .... PUR vyooh

pusillanimous ....
.... PYOOH suh LAN uh mus

pussyfoot .... POOS ee foot

pustule .... PUS choohl ¶17

putative .... PYOOHT uh tiv

putrefaction .... PYOOH truh FAK shun

putrefy .... PYOOH truh fye

putrid .... PYOOH trid

Putsch .... POOCH

Pygmalion ... pig MAYL yun ¶5

pygmy .... PIG mee

pylon .... PYE lahn

pyorrhea .... PYE uh REE uh

pyramid .... PIR uh mid

Pyrenees .... PIR uh neez

pyrite .... PYE ryte

pyromania ....
.... PYE ruh MAY nee uh ¶1, 25

pyrotechnics ... PYE ruh TEK niks ¶1

Pyrrhic .... PIR ik

Pythagoras .... pi THAG ur us

Pythagorean .... pi THAG uh REE un

python .... PYE thahn
PYE thun *is now occasional* ¶8.

Q

quadrangle .... KWAHD rang gul

quadrant .... KWAHD runt

quadraphonic .... KWAHD ruh FAHN ik

quadratic .... kwahd RAT ik

quadriceps .... KWAHD ri seps

SPELLED	PRONOUNCED
quadrilateral	KWAHD ruh **LAT** ur ul
quadrille	kwuh **DRIL** ¶1
quadrillion	kwahd **RIL** yun
quadriplegia	
	KWAHD ruh **PLEE** jee uh ¶25
quadrivalent	KWAHD ruh **VAY** lunt *or* kwahd **RIV** uh lunt
quadruped	**KWAHD** ruh ped
quadruple	kwah **DROOH** pul *or* kwah **DRUP** ul
quadruplet	kwah **DRUP** lit *or* kwah **DROOH** plit
quadruplicate	kwah **DROOH** pluh kit
quaff	**KWAHF** ¶18
quagmire	**KWAG** myre ¶18
quahog	**KWAW** hawg *or* **KOH** hawg ¶19
qualification	
	KWAHL uh fi **KAY** shun ¶19
qualify	**KWAHL** uh fye ¶19
qualitative	**KWAHL** uh tayt iv ¶19
quality	**KWAHL** uh tee ¶19
qualm	**KWAHM** ¶19 *occasionally* **KWAHLM**
quandary	**KWAHN** dree ¶5, 19
quantify	**KWAHN** tuh fye ¶19
quantitative	
	KWAHN tuh tayt iv ¶19
quantity	**KWAHN** tuh tee ¶19
quantum	**KWAHN** tum *The plural* quanta *is* **KWAHN** tuh ¶19.
quarantine	**KWAWR** un teen ¶19
quark	**KWAWRK** ¶19
quarrel	**KWAWR** ul ¶7, 19

SPELLED	PRONOUNCED
quarry	**KWAWR** ee ¶19
quarter	**KWAWR** tur
quartet	kwawr **TET**
quarto	**KWAWR** toh
quartz	**KWAWRTS**
quasar	**KWAY** zahr *or* **KWAY** zur ¶14
quash	**KWAHSH** ¶19
quasi	**KWAY** zye *or* **KWAH** zee ¶14
quaternary	**KWAHT** ur **NER** ee *or* kwuh **TUR** nur ee ¶3, 23
quatrain	**KWAH** trayn
quaver	**KWAY** vur
quay	**KEE**
Quebec	kwi **BEK** *locally, usually* ki **BEK** *or* kay **BEK**
Québecois	kay be **KWAH**
quenelle	kuh **NEL**
querulous	**KWER** uh lus ¶21
query	**KWIR** ee *now occasionally* **KWER** ee
question	**KWES** chun ¶11
questionnaire	kwes chuh **NER** ¶11
quetzal	ket **SAHL**
queue	**KYOOH**
quiche	**KEESH**
quiddity	**KWID** uh tee
quidnunc	**KWID** nungk
quid pro quo	kwid proh **KWOH**
quiescent	kwye **ES** unt kwee **ES** unt *is now also often heard.*
quietude	**KWYE** uh toohd ¶21
quietus	kwye **EET** us
quince	**KWINS** ¶9

Quincy .... **KWIN** see ¶9
*Thus for the city in Illinois; the
city in Massachusetts is* **KWIN** zee.
quinella .... kwi **NEL** uh
kee **NEL** uh *is also heard.*
quinine .... **KWYE** nyne
quintessence .... kwin **TES** uns ¶9
quintet .... kwin **TET**
quintillion .... kwin **TIL** yun
quintuple .... kwin **TOOH** pul *or*
kwin **TUP** ul *or* **KWIN** too pul ¶21
quintuplet .... kwin **TUP** lit *or*
kwin **TOOH** plit
sometimes **KWIN** tooh plit ¶21
quire .... **KWYRE**
quirk .... **KWURK**
quisling .... **KWIZ** ling
Quito .... **KEE** toh
quittance .... **KWIT** uns
quiver .... **KWIV** ur
quixotic .... kwik **SAHT** ik
quizzical .... **KWIZ** i kul
Qumran .... koom **RAHN**
quoin .... **KOYN** *or* **KWOYN**
quoit .... **KWOYT** *or* **KOYT**
quondam .... **KWAHN** dum
Quonset (hut) *(trademark)* ....
.... **KWAHN** sit ¶9, 14
quorum .... **KWAWR** um
quota .... **KWOHT** uh
quotation .... kwoh **TAY** shun
quote .... **KWOHT**
quoth .... **KWOHTH**
quotidian .... kwoh **TID** ee un
quotient .... **KWOH** shunt

R

rabbi .... **RAB** eye
rabbinical .... ruh **BIN** i kul
Rabelais .... **RAB** uh lay
rabid .... **RAB** id
rabies .... **RAY** beez
raccoon .... ra **KOOHN** ¶1
raceme .... ray **SEEM** ¶1
racemose .... **RAS** uh mohs
Rachmaninoff ..... rahk **MAH** ni **NAWF**
racial .... **RAY** shul
Racine .... ruh **SEEN**
racism .... **RAY** siz um
racketeer .... rak uh **TIR**
raconteur .... rak ahn **TUR**
racquet .... **RAK** it
radar .... **RAY** dahr
radial .... **RAY** dee ul ¶25
radiant .... **RAY** dee unt ¶25
radiate .... **RAY** dee ayt
radical .... **RAD** i kul
radii .... **RAY** dee eye
radioactive .... **RAY** dee oh **AK** tiv
radiology .... **RAY** dee **AHL** uh jee
radioscopy ...... **RAY** dee **AHS** kuh pee
radiosonde .... **RAY** dee oh **SAHND**
radish .... **RAD** ish
radium .... **RAY** dee um
radius .... **RAY** dee us

SPELLED	PRONOUNCED
raga	**RAH** guh
ragged	**RAG** id
raglan	**RAG** lun
ragout	ra **GOOH**
raillery	**RAYL** ur ee
Rainier (Mount)	ray **NIR** ¶2
raison d'être	**RAY** zohn **DET** *or*
	RAY zohn **DET** ruh
rajah	**RAH** juh
rakish	**RAY** kish
Raleigh	**RAW** lee ¶19
rambunctious	ram **BUNGK** shus ¶9
ramekin	**RAM** uh kin
ramification	**RAM** uh fi **KAY** shun
rampage *(verb)*	ram **PAYJ**
also, and for the noun always,	
RAM payj ¶2	
rampant	**RAM** punt
rampart	**RAM** pahrt
RAM purt *has become infrequent*	
¶8.	
Ramses	**RAM** seez
ramshackle	**RAM** shak ul
ranchero	ran **CHER** oh ¶18
rancho	**RAN** choh ¶18
rancid	**RAN** sid ¶9
rancor	**RANG** kur
random	**RAN** dum
ransack	**RAN** sak
rapacious	ruh **PAY** shus ¶1
rapacity	ruh **PAS** uh tee
Raphael	**RAY** fee ul *or* **RAF** ee ul
The famous Italian painter is	
nearly always **RAF** ee ul.	
rapier	**RAY** pee ur ¶25

SPELLED	PRONOUNCED
rapine	**RAP** in
rapport	ra **PAWR**
An Englished pronunciation,	
ra **PAWRT**, *is occasionally heard.*	
rapprochement	ra **PROHSH** mah *or*
	ra prohsh **MAH**
Many non–French speakers	
attempt the nasalized vowel at	
the end.	
rapscallion	rap **SKAL** yun
rapture	**RAP** chur ¶12
rarebit	**RAR** bit ¶23
rarefy	**RAR** uh fye ¶23
rarity	**RAR** uh tee ¶23
rascal	**RAS** kul
raspberry	**RAZ** ber ee *or* **RAZ** bur ee
Rasputin	ras **PYOOHT** un
ratatouille	**RAT** uh **TOOH** ee *or*
	RAHT uh **TOOH** ee *or* raht uh **TWEE**
rather	**RADH** ur ¶18
for the interjection, ra **DHUR**	
rathskeller	**RAHT** skel ur *or*
	RATH skel ur
ratify	**RAT** uh fye
ratio	**RAY** shoh ¶25
ratiocinate	**RASH** ee **OH** suh nayt *or*
	RAT ee **OH** suh nayt
ration	**RASH** un *or* **RAY** shun
rational	**RASH** uh nul
rationale	rash uh **NAL**
The earlier pronunciation	
RASH uh **NAY** lee *is now rarely*	
heard.	
ratline	**RAT** lin
rattan	ra **TAN**

SPELLED	PRONOUNCED
rattler	**RAT** lur ¶5
raucous	**RAW** kus
raunchy	**RAWN** chee ¶19
ravage	**RAV** ij
Ravel	ra **VEL**
ravel	**RAV** ul
raven *(noun)*	**RAY** vun
ravening	**RAV** un ing
ravenous	**RAV** un us
ravine	ruh **VEEN**
ravioli	RAV ee **OH** lee
ravish	**RAV** ish
razor	**RAY** zur
re–	ree *or* ri *or* ruh

For following words formed with this prefix, in many instances, all three pronunciations may be heard ¶1.

reactionary	ree **AK** shuh **NER** ee
reactor	ree **AK** tur
readable	**REED** uh bul
readily	**RED** uh lee
reagent	ree **AY** junt
real	**REE** ul ¶7
realistic	REE uh **LIS** tik
reality	ree **AL** uh tee
realize	**REE** uh lyze ¶7
really	**REE** lee *or* **REE** uh lee

Increasingly **RIL** ee *is being heard, especially among younger speakers.* ¶8

realm	**RELM**
Realtor	**REE** ul tur *or* **REEL** tur ¶1, 5

REE luh tur *is not standard* ¶4.

SPELLED	PRONOUNCED
reason	**REE** zun
rebarbative	ri **BAHR** buh tiv
rebate *(noun and verb)*	**REE** bayt

For the verb, ri **BAYT** *is also heard* ¶2.

rebel *(verb)*	ri **BEL**
rebel *(noun)*	**REB** ul
rebellion	ri **BEL** yun
rebirth	ree **BURTH** ¶2
rebound *(verb)*	ri **BOWND** *or* **REE** bownd

in sports senses, usually **REE** bownd

rebound *(noun)*	**REE** bownd
rebuff	ri **BUF**
rebuke	ri **BYOOHK**
rebus	**REE** bus
rebut	ri **BUT**
recalcitrant	ri **KAL** si trunt
recall *(verb)*	ri **KAWL**

for the noun, especially for the calling in of faulty products, **REE** kawl

recant	ri **KANT**
recapitulate	REE kuh **PICH** uh layt
recede	ri **SEED**
receipt	ri **SEET**
receive	ri **SEEV**
recent	**REE** sunt
receptacle	ri **SEP** ti kul
reception	ri **SEP** shun
recess *(noun)*	**REE** ses

also, and for the verb usually, ri **SES**

recession	ri **SESH** un

SPELLED	PRONOUNCED
recherché	ruh **SHER** shay *or* ruh sher **SHAY**
recidivism	ri **SID** uh viz um
recipe	**RES** uh pee
recipient	ri **SIP** ee unt ¶25
reciprocal	ri **SIP** ruh kul
reciprocity	RES uh **PRAHS** uh tee
recitation	RES uh **TAY** shun
recitative	RES uh tuh **TEEV**
recite	ri **SYTE**
reclamation	REK luh **MAY** shun
recluse	**REK** loohs *or* ri **KLOOHS**
recognition	REK ug **NISH** un
recognizance	ri **KAHG** ni zuns *or* ri **KAHN** i zuns ¶9, 14
recognize	**REK** ug nyze
REK uh nyze *is generally disapproved.*	
recoil *(verb)*	ri **KOYL**
recoil *(noun)*	**REE** koyl *or* ri **KOYL**
recollect	rek uh **LEKT**
recommend	rek uh **MEND**
recompense	**REK** um pens ¶9
reconcile	**REK** un syle
reconciliation	REK un SIL ee **AY** shun
recondite	**REK** un dyte
occasionally ri **KAHN** dyte	
reconnaissance	ri **KAHN** uh suns ¶9, 14
reconnoiter	**REE** kuh **NOYT** ur *or* REK uh **NOYT** ur
record *(verb)*	ri **KAWRD**
record *(noun and adjective)*	**REK** urd
recoup	ri **KOOHP** ¶1

SPELLED	PRONOUNCED
recourse	**REE** kawrs *or* ri **KAWRS**
recreant	**REK** ree unt
recreation	REK ree **AY** shun
recrimination	ri **KRIM** uh **NAY** shun
recruit	ri **KROOHT**
rectangle	**REK** tang gul
rectify	**REK** tuh fye
rectitude	**REK** tuh toohd ¶21
rector	**REK** tur
rectory	**REK** tur ee ¶5
recumbent	ri **KUM** bunt
recuperate	ri **KOOH** puh rayt ¶21
redeem	ri **DEEM**
redemption	ri **DEMP** shun ¶10
redingote	**RED** ing goht
redolence	**RED** uh luns ¶9
redoubtable	ri **DOWT** uh bul
redraft *(verb)*	ree **DRAFT** ¶18
redraft *(noun)*	**REE** draft ¶18
redress *(verb)*	ri **DRES**
The noun is usually **REE** dres.	
reduce	ri **DOOHS** ¶21
reduction	ri **DUK** shun
redundancy	ri **DUN** dun see ¶9
redundant	ri **DUN** dunt
redux	**REE** duks
refectory	ri **FEK** tur ee ¶5
referee	ref uh **REE**
referendum	REF uh **REN** dum
referent	**REF** ur unt ¶5
referential	REF uh **REN** shul ¶9, 12
referral	ri **FUR** ul
refinery	ri **FYNE** ur ee
reflect	ri **FLEKT**
reflection	ri **FLEK** shun

reflex *(verb)* .... ri **FLEKS**

reflex *(noun)* .... **REE** fleks

reformation .... REF ur **MAY** shun

reformatory ... ri **FAWR** muh **TAWR** ee

refract .... ri **FRAKT**

refrigerate .... ri **FRIJ** uh rayt

refuge .... **REF** yoohj

refugee .... ref yoo **JEE** ¶2

refulgent .... ri **FUL** junt

refund *(verb)* .... ri **FUND**

>*Thus for the verb meaning to repay, but for the meaning to provide funds anew, it is* ree **FUND** ¶2.

refund *(noun)* .... **REE** fund

refurbish .... ri **FUR** bish

refusal .... ri **FYOOH** zul

refuse *(verb)* .... ri **FYOOHZ**

refuse *(noun)* .... **REF** yoohs

refutation .... REF yuh **TAY** shun

refute .... ri **FYOOHT**

regal .... **REE** gul

regale .... ri **GAYL**

regalia .... ri **GAYL** yuh ¶25

regatta .... ri **GAHT** uh ¶18

regency .... **REE** jun see ¶9

regent .... **REE** junt

reggae .... **REG** ay

regicide .... **REJ** uh syde

regime .... ray **ZHEEM** *or* ri **ZHEEM**

regimen .... **REJ** uh mun

regiment *(verb)* .... **REJ** uh ment

regiment *(noun)* .... **REJ** uh munt

region .... **REE** jun

register .... **REJ** is tur

registrar .... REJ i **strahr** ¶2

registration .... REJ i **STRAY** shun

regress *(verb)* .... ri **GRES**

regress *(noun)* .... **REE** gres

regression .... ri **GRESH** un

regular .... **REG** yuh lur

>**REG** lur *and* **REG** uh lur *are commonly heard but are not accepted as standard.* ¶5

regulate .... **REG** yuh layt

regurgitate .... ri **GUR** juh tayt

rehabilitate .... REE huh **BIL** uh tayt *or* REE uh **BIL** uh tayt

rehash *(verb)* .... ree **HASH**

rehash *(noun)* .... **REE** hash

rehearse .... ri **HURS**

Reich .... **RYKE**

reimburse .... ree im **BURS**

reincarnation .. REE in kahr **NAY** shun

reindeer .... **RAYN** dir

reinforce .... ree in **FAWRS**

reinstate .... ree in **STAYT**

reiterate .... ree **IT** uh rayt

reject *(verb)* .... ri **JEKT**

reject *(noun)* .... **REE** jekt

rejoinder .... ri **JOYN** dur

rejuvenate .... ri **JOOH** vuh nayt

relapse *(verb)* .... ri **LAPS**

>*The noun is also* **REE** laps.

relation .... ri **LAY** shun

relative .... **REL** uh tiv

relativity .... REL uh **TIV** uh tee

relaxation ...... REE lak **SAY** shun ¶1

relay *(noun)* .... **REE** lay

>*For the verb,* ri **LAY** *is also heard.*

SPELLED	PRONOUNCED
relegate	**REL** uh gayt
relevant	**REL** uh vunt
reliable	ri **LYE** uh bul
reliance	ri **LYE** uns
religion	ri **LIJ** un
religiosity	ri LIJ ee **AHS** uh tee
relinquish	ri **LING** kwish
reliquary	**REL** uh **KWER** ee ¶23
reluctance	ri **LUK** tuns ¶9
remake *(verb)*	ree **MAYK**
remake *(noun)*	**REE** mayk
Rembrandt	**REM** brant ¶18
remedial	ri **MEE** dee ul ¶25
remediation	ri MEE dee **AY** shun
remedy	**REM** uh dee
remember	ri **MEM** bur
remembrance	ri **MEM** bruns ¶9
reminisce	rem uh **NIS**
remiss	ri **MIS**
remission	ri **MISH** un
remnant	**REM** nunt
remonstrance	ri **MAHN** struns ¶9
remonstrate	ri **MAHN** strayt
remorse	ri **MAWRS**
remunerate	ri **MYOOH** nuh rayt
renaissance	
	REN uh sahns ¶2, 9, 14
renal	**REE** nul
renascent	ri **NAYS** unt *or* ri **NAS** unt
rendezvous	**RAHN** day vooh *or*
	RAHN dee vooh *or* **RAHN** duh vooh
rendition	ren **DISH** un
renegade	**REN** uh gayd
renege	ri **NIG** *or* ri **NEG** *or* ri **NEEG**
Renoir	ruh **NWAHR** *or* **REN** wahr ¶2

SPELLED	PRONOUNCED
renovate	**REN** uh vayt
renown	ri **NOWN**
renunciation	ri NUN see **AY** shun
reparable	**REP** ur uh bul
to be distinguished from repairable ri **PER** uh bul, *a less common word with the same meaning* ¶23	
reparation	REP uh **RAY** shun
repartee	rep ur **TEE** *or* rep ahr **TEE** *or* rep ahr **TAY**
repast	ri **PAST** ¶18
repatriate *(verb)*	ree **PAY** tree ayt
repatriate *(noun)*	ree **PAY** tree it
repellent	ri **PEL** unt
repentance	ri **PENT** uns ¶9
repercussion	REE pur **KUSH** un *or* REP ur **KUSH** un
repertoire	**REP** ur twahr ¶3
repertory	**REP** ur **TAWR** ee ¶3
repetition	REP uh **TISH** un
repetitive	ri **PET** uh tiv
replenish	ri **PLEN** ish
replete	ri **PLEET**
replica	**REP** li kuh
reportage	ri **PAWRT** ij
repose	ri **POHZ**
repository	ri **PAHZ** uh **TAWR** ee
reprehend	rep ri **HEND**
reprehensible	REP ri **HEN** si bul ¶9
represent	rep ri **ZENT**
reprimand	**REP** ruh mand ¶18
reprint *(verb)*	ree **PRINT**
The noun is usually **REE** print.	
reprisal	ri **PRYE** zul

SPELLED	PRONOUNCED	SPELLED	PRONOUNCED
reprobate	**REP** ruh bayt	resign	ri **ZYNE**
reproduce	ree pruh **DOOHS** ¶21	resignation	**REZ** ig **NAY** shun
reproduction	**REE** pruh **DUK** shun	resilient	ri **ZIL** yunt
reptile	**REP** tyle *or* **REP** tul ¶8	resin	**REZ** un
reptilian	rep **TIL** ee un ¶25	resist	ri **ZIST**
republic	ri **PUB** lik	resolute	**REZ** uh looht
repudiate	ri **PYOOH** dee ayt	resolution	**REZ** uh **LOOH** shun
repugnant	ri **PUG** nunt	resolve	ri **ZAHLV** ¶19
reputable	**REP** yuh tuh bul	resonance	**REZ** uh nuns ¶9
reputation	**REP** yuh **TAY** shun	resonate	**REZ** uh nayt
repute	ri **PYOOHT**	resort	ri **ZAWRT**
requiem	**REK** wee um *or*	resound	ri **ZOWND**
	RAYK wee um	resource	**REE** sawrs *or*
requisite	**REK** wuh zit		ri **SAWRS** ¶14
requisition	**REK** wuh **ZISH** un	respective	ri **SPEK** tiv
requite	ri **KWYTE**	respiration	**RES** puh **RAY** shun
rescind	ri **SIND**	respirator	**RES** puh rayt ur
rescue	**RES** kyooh	respiratory	**RES** pur uh **TAWR** ee *or*
research *(verb)*	ri **SURCH**		ri **SPYRE** uh **TAWR** ee
The noun is either ri **SURCH** *or*		respire	ri **SPYRE**
REE surch.		respite	**RES** pit
resect	ri **SEKT**	resplendent	ri **SPLEN** dunt
resection	ri **SEK** shun	responsible	ri **SPAHN** suh bul ¶9
resemblance	ri **ZEM** bluns ¶9	restaurant	**RES** tuh rahnt *or*
resent	ri **ZENT**		**RES** tuh runt ¶15, 8
reservation	**REZ** ur **VAY** shun	restaurateur	**RES** tur uh **TUR**
reservoir	**REZ** ur vwahr *or*	*In recent years an Englished*	
	REZ uh vwahr ¶3, 19	*spelling* restauranteur,	
reset	ree **SET**	*pronounced* **RES** tuh rahn **TUR**, *has*	
The noun is **REE** set.		*appeared.*	
reside	ri **ZYDE**	restitution	**RES** tuh **TOOH** shun
residence	**REZ** i duns ¶9	restive	**RES** tiv
residential	**REZ** uh **DEN** shul ¶9, 12	restless	**REST** lis ¶10
residual	ri **ZIJ** oo wul ¶17	restoration	**RES** tuh **RAY** shun
residue	**REZ** uh dooh ¶21	restore	ri **STAWR**

SPELLED	PRONOUNCED
restraint	ri **STRAYNT**
restrict	ri **STRIKT**
restriction	ri **STRIK** shun
result	ri **ZULT**
resume	ri **ZOOHM** ¶21
résumé	**REZ** oo may *or* **RAY** zoo may ¶2
resumption	ri **ZUMP** shun ¶9
resurgent	ri **SUR** junt
resurrect	rez uh **REKT**
resurrection	REZ uh **REK** shun
resuscitate	ri **SUS** uh tayt
retail *(noun)*	**REE** tayl
The verb is sometimes ri **TAYL.**	
retaliate	ri **TAL** ee ayt
retard	ri **TAHRD**
retardation	REE tahr **DAY** shun
retention	ri **TEN** shun ¶9, 12
reticent	**RET** uh sunt
reticulate *(verb)*	ri **TIK** yuh layt
The adjective is usually ri **TIK** yuh lit.	
retina	**RET** un uh
retinue	**RET** un ooh ¶21
retract	ri **TRAKT**
retractile	ri **TRAK** tul ¶22
retraction	ri **TRAK** shun
retribution	RET ruh **BYOOH** shun
retrieval	ri **TREE** vul
retrograde	**RET** ruh grayd
retrogress	**RET** ruh gres
retrospect	**RET** ruh spekt
Reuters	**ROYT** urz
reveille	**REV** uh lee
revel	**REV** ul

SPELLED	PRONOUNCED
revelation	REV uh **LAY** shun
revenge	ri **VENJ**
revenue	**REV** uh nooh ¶21
reverberate	ri **VUR** buh rayt
revere	ri **VIR**
reverence	**REV** ur uns ¶5, 9
reverend	**REV** ur und ¶5
reverential	REV uh **REN** shul ¶9, 12
reverie	**REV** ur ee
reverse	ri **VURS**
reversion	ri **VUR** zhun *or* ri **VUR** shun
revert	ri **VURT**
review	ri **VYOOH**
revile	ri **VYLE**
revise	ri **VYZE**
revision	ri **VIZH** un
revive	ri **VYVE**
revivify	ri **VIV** uh fye
revocable	**REV** uh kuh bul
ri **VOH** kuh bul *is now sometimes heard.*	
revoke	ri **VOHK**
revolt	ri **VOHLT**
revolution	REV uh **LOOH** shun
revolve	ri **VAHLV** ¶19
revulsion	ri **VUL** shun
reward	ri **WAWRD**
Reykjavík	**RAY** kyuh veek
rhapsodic	rap **SAHD** ik
rhapsody	**RAP** suh dee
rhea	**REE** uh
rheostat	**REE** uh stat
rhesus	**REE** sus
rhetoric	**RET** ur ik
rhetorical	ri **TAWR** i kul

rhetorician	RET uh RISH un	rigmarole	RIG muh rohl
rheum	ROOHM	*The variant form* rigamarole,	
rheumatic	roo MAT ik	RIG uh muh ROHL, *is not*	
rheumatism	ROOH muh tiz um	*uncommon.*	
rhinestone	RYNE stohn	rigor	RIG ur
rhinoceros	rye NAHS ur us	*in medical usage, also* RYE gur	
rhizome	RYE zohm	rigor mortis	RIG ur MAWR tus *or*
Rhodesia	roh DEE zhuh ¶25		RYE gur MAWR tus
rhodium	ROH dee um	Rilke	RIL kuh
rhododendron	ROH duh DEN drun	Rimbaud	ram BOH
rhomboid	RAHM boyd	Rimsky–Korsakov	
rhombus	RAHM bus		RIM skee KAWR suh kawf
rhubarb	ROOH barb	rind	RYNDE
rhyme	RYME	ringalievio	RING uh LEE vee OH
rhythm	RIDH um	rinse	RINS ¶9
ribald	RIB uld	Rio de Janeiro	
riboflavin	RYE buh FLAY vin ¶2		REE oh DAY zhuh NER oh
ribonucleic		*A number of variations are*	
	RYE boh nooh KLEE ik ¶21	*heard: for the third syllable, also*	
Richter (scale)	RIK tur	DEE *or* duh; *for the fourth, also*	
rickettsia	ri KET see uh	juh; *for the fifth, also* NIR.	
rickety	RIK it ee	Rio Grande	REE oh GRAND
ricochet	RIK uh shay ¶2	*Also quite common are*	
ricotta	ri KAHT uh	REE oh GRAN dee *and*	
ridable	RYDE uh bul	REE oh GRAHN day.	
riddance	RID uns ¶9	riotous	RYE ut us
ridicule	RID i kyool	riparian	ri PAR ee un ¶1, 23
ridiculous	ri DIK yuh lus	riposte	ri POHST
Riesling	REEZ ling	risible	RIZ uh bul
now also REES ling		risotto	ri SAWT oh *or* ree ZAWT toh
rifle	RYE ful	risqué	ris KAY
rifling	RYE fling	RIS kee *is sometimes heard as a*	
rigatoni	RIG uh TOH nee	*facetious variant.*	
righteous	RYE chus	rissole	ree SOHL *or* RIS ohl
rigid	RIJ id	ritual	RICH oo wul

rival .... **RYE** vul

rive .... **RYVE**

riven .... **RIV** un

riverine .... **RIV** uh ryne ¶22

rivet .... **RIV** it

Riviera .... RIV ee **ER** uh

rivulet .... **RIV** yoo lit

roan .... **ROHN**

Roanoke .... **ROH** uh nohk

robbery .... **RAHB** ur ee ¶5

Robespierre .... **ROHBS** pyer *or*
                      ROHBS pir

robin .... **RAHB** in

robot .... **ROH** baht
   ROH but *is now less common.* ¶8

robotics .... roh **BAHT** iks

robust .... roh **BUST** ¶2

rococo .... ruh **KOH** koh
   occasionally roh kuh **KOH**

rodent .... **ROHD** unt

rodeo .... **ROH** dee oh *or* roh **DAY** oh

Rodin .... roh **DAN**

roentgen .... **RENT** gun *or*
                      REN chun ¶9

rogue .... **ROHG**

roguish .... **ROH** gish

romaine .... roh **MAYN** ¶2

Roman .... **ROH** mun

romance *(noun)* .... roh **MANS** *or*
                ROH mans ¶2, 9
   The verb is usually roh **MANS**.

Romanesque .... roh muh **NESK**

romantic .... roh **MAN** tik

romanticism ...... roh **MAN** tuh siz um

romanticize .... roh **MAN** tuh syze

Romany .... **RAH** muh nee ¶20

Romulus .... **RAHM** yuh lus

rookery .... **ROOK** ur ee

room .... **ROOHM** *or* **ROOM**

Roosevelt .... **ROH** zuh velt *or*
                  ROOH zuh velt

ROH zuh vult *and* **ROHZ** velt *were
once common variants, but both
have now become rare.*

Roquefort (cheese) .... **ROHK** furt

Rorschach .... **RAWR** shahk

rosary .... **ROH** zur ee ¶5

rosé .... roh **ZAY**

roseate ...... **ROH** zee it *or* **ROH** zee ayt

rosemary .... **ROHZ** mer ee ¶23

roseola .... ROH zee **OH** luh
      The earlier standard
   roh **ZEE** uh luh *is becoming rare.*

Rosetta (stone) .... roh **ZET** uh

rosette .... roh **ZET**

Rosh Hashana ....
         RAWSH uh **SHAW** nuh ¶19
     The Hebrew is more like
   ROHSH hah shah **NAH**.

Rosicrucian .... ROH zuh **KROOH** shun

rosin .... **RAHZ** un

Rossini .... raw **SEE** nee

roster .... **RAHS** tur

rostrum .... **RAHS** trum

rotary .... **ROHT** ur ee

rotate .... **ROH** tayt

rotisserie .... roh **TIS** ur ee ¶5

rotogravure ....
         ROHT uh gruh **VYOOR** ¶24

rotund .... roh **TUND**

SPELLED	PRONOUNCED
rotunda	roh **TUN** duh ¶1
roué	rooh **AY**
rouge	**ROOHZH**
rough	**RUF**
roulade	rooh **LAHD**
roulette	rooh **LET**
roundel	**ROWN** dul
roundelay	**ROWN** duh lay
rouse	**ROWZ**
Rousseau	rooh **SOH**
route	**ROOHT** or **ROWT**
routine	rooh **TEEN**
royalty	**ROY** ul tee
rubella	rooh **BEL** uh
rubeola	ROOH bee **OH** luh
sometimes rooh **BEE** uh luh	
Rubicon	**ROOH** bi kahn
ruble	**ROOH** bul
rubric	**ROOH** brik
rudiment	**ROOH** duh munt
rudimentary	
	ROOH duh **MEN** tur ee ¶5
ruffian	**RUF** ee un ¶5
rugged	**RUG** id
ruin	**ROOH** in
rumba	**RUM** buh or **ROOM** buh
ruminant	**ROOH** muh nunt
ruminate	**ROOH** muh nayt
rummage	**RUM** ij
rumor	**ROOH** mur
runic	**ROOH** nik
rupee	**ROOH** pee
rupture	**RUP** chur ¶12
rural	**ROOR** ul ¶24
ruse	**ROOHZ**

SPELLED	PRONOUNCED
russet	**RUS** it
Russia	**RUSH** uh
rustle	**RUS** ul
rutabaga	ROOHT uh **BAY** guh ¶2
ruthless	**ROOHTH** lis
Rwanda	ur **WAHN** duh *or*
	ruh **WAHN** duh

S

SPELLED	PRONOUNCED
Saar	**SAHR** ¶14
sabbath	**SAB** uth
sabbatical	suh **BAT** i kul
sabot	**SAB** oh ¶2
sabotage	**SAB** uh tahzh ¶15
saboteur	sab uh **TUR** ¶24
saccharin	**SAK** ur in ¶5
sacerdotal	SAS ur **DOHT** ul
occasionally SAK ur **DOHT** ul	
sachet	sa **SHAY**
sacrament	**SAK** ruh munt
sacred	**SAY** krid
sacrifice	**SAK** ruh fyse
sacrificial	SAK ruh **FISH** ul
sacrilege	**SAK** ruh lij
sacrilegious	SAK ruh **LIJ** us
The earlier standard	
SAK ruh **LEE** jus *is much less*	
frequently heard.	

sacristy .... **SAK** ris tee

sacroiliac .... SAK roh **IL** ee AK
also, in the medical profession,
SAY kroh **IL** ee AK

sacrosanct .... **SAK** roh sangkt

sacrum .... **SAY** krum *or* **SAK** rum

Sadducee .... **SAJ** oo see ¶17

sadism .... **SAD** iz um *or* **SAY** diz um

safari .... suh **FAHR** ee

safflower .... **SAF** low ur

saffron .... **SAF** run

saga .... **SAH** guh
now sometimes **SAG** uh

sagacious .... suh **GAY** shus

sagacity .... suh **GAS** uh tee

sage .... **SAYJ**

Sagittarius .... SAJ uh **TAR** ee us ¶23

Sahara .... suh **HAR** uh *or*
suh **HAHR** uh ¶23

sahib .... **SAH** ib *or* **SAH** hib *or* **SAH** eeb
or **SAH** heeb

Saint Vitus' (dance) ....
.... SAYNT **VYTE** us

saith .... **SETH** *or* **SAY** ith

sake ("beverage") .... **SAH** kee

salaam .... suh **LAHM**

salacious .... suh **LAY** shus

salad .... **SAL** ud

salamander .... **SAL** uh **MAN** dur

salami .... suh **LAH** mee

salary .... **SAL** ur ee ¶5

salicylic (acid) .... SAL uh **SIL** ik

salient .... **SAYL** yunt ¶25

saline ..... **SAY** leen *or* **SAY** lyne ¶22

salinity .... suh **LIN** uh tee ¶1

Salisbury .... **SAHLZ** ber ee *or*
SAHLZ buh ree

saliva .... suh **LYE** vuh

salivary .... **SAL** uh **VER** ee ¶23

salivate .... **SAL** uh vayt

salmagundi .... SAL muh **GUN** dee

salmon .... **SAM** un

salmonella .... SAL muh **NEL** uh

Salome .... **SAL** oh may *or*
suh **LOH** mee ¶2

salon .... suh **LAHN** *or* **SAL** ahn

saloon .... suh **LOOHN**

salsify ...... **SAL** suh fee *or* **SAL** suh fye

salt .... **SAWLT** ¶19

salubrious .... suh **LOOH** bree us

salutary .... **SAL** yoo TER ee ¶23

salutation .... SAL yoo **TAY** shun

salutatorian ....
.... suh LOOHT uh **TAWR** ee un

salute .... suh **LOOHT**

salvage .... **SAL** vij

salvation .... sal **VAY** shun

salve .... **SAV** ¶18

salvo .... **SAL** voh

Samaria .... suh **MAR** ee uh ¶23

Samaritan ...... suh **MAR** uh tun ¶23

samba .... **SAM** buh ¶18

Samoa .... suh **MOH** uh

samovar .... **SAM** uh vahr

Samoyed .... **SAM** uh yed ¶1

sampler .... **SAM** plur ¶5

samurai .... **SAM** uh rye

sanctify .... **SANGK** tuh fye

sanctimonious ....
...... SANGK tuh **MOH** nee us ¶9, 25

sanction .... **SANGK** shun ¶9

sanctity .... **SANGK** tuh tee ¶9

sanctuary ....
.... **SANGK** choo **WER** ee ¶9, 12

sanctum sanctorum ....
..... **SANGK** tum sangk **TAWR** um ¶9

sandman .... **SAND** man ¶10

sandwich .... **SAND** wich ¶10

sangria .... sahn **GREE** uh ¶16, 18

sanguine .... **SANG** gwin

Sanhedrin .... san **HED** rin ¶18

sanitarium ... SAN uh **TAR** ee um ¶23

sanitary .... **SAN** uh TER ee ¶23

sanitation .... SAN uh **TAY** shun

sanitize .... **SAN** uh tyze

sanity .... **SAN** uh tee

sans .... **SANZ** ¶18

sansculotte .... sanz kooh **LAHT** ¶21

Sanskrit .... **SAN** skrit

Santa Claus .... **SAN** tuh klawz *or*
SAN ti klawz

Santiago .... SAN tee **AY** goh *or*
SAHN tee **AH** goh

São Paulo .... SOWN **POW** loo

sapient .... **SAY** pee unt ¶25

sapphire .... **SAF** eyre

Saracen .... **SAR** uh sun ¶23

Sarajevo .... SAR uh **YAY** voh ¶23

sarcasm .... **SAHR** kaz um

sarcastic .... sahr **KAS** tik

sarcoma .... sahr **KOH** muh

sarcophagus .... sahr **KAHF** uh gus

The plural is sarcophagi
sahr **KAHF** uh jye, *now also*
sahr **KAHF** uh gye.

sardine .... sahr **DEEN**

Sardinia .... sahr **DIN** ee uh ¶25

sardonic .... sahr **DAHN** ik

sari .... **SAH** ree

sarong .... suh **RAWNG** ¶19

sarsaparilla .... SAS puh **RIL** uh
also SAHRS puh **RIL** uh *or*
SAHR suh puh **RIL** uh ¶5

sartorial .... sahr **TAWR** ee ul

Sartre .... **SAHRT** *or* **SAHR** truh

sashay .... sa **SHAY** ¶2

Saskatchewan ..... sas **KACH** uh **WAHN**
or sas **KACH** uh wun

sasquatch .... **SAS** kwach ¶18

sassafras .... **SAS** uh fras

Satan .... **SAYT** un

satanic .... say **TAN** ik ¶1

sateen .... sa **TEEN** *or* suh **TEEN**

satellite .... **SAT** uh lyte

satiate .... **SAY** shee ayt

satiety .... suh **TYE** uh tee

satire .... **SA** tyre

satirical .... suh **TIR** i kul

satirize .... **SAT** uh ryze

satisfaction .... SAT is **FAK** shun

satisfy .... **SAT** is fye

satrap .... **SAY** trap *or* **SA** trap

saturate .... **SACH** uh rayt

Saturday .... **SAT** ur dee *or* **SAT** ur day

Saturn .... **SAT** urn

saturnalia .... SAT ur **NAY** lee uh ¶25

saturnine .... **SAT** ur nyne

satyr .... **SAYT** ur *or* **SAT** ur

satyriasis .... SAT uh **RYE** uh sis

saucy .... **SAW** see

Saudi .... sah OOH dee *or* SOW dee
   also SAW dee *which is relatively*
   recent but has been adopted by
   many people

sauerbraten .. SOWR braht un ¶7, 14

sauerkraut .... SOWR krowt

Sault Ste. Marie ....
   .... SOOH SAYNT muh REE

sauna .... SAW nuh
   Earlier SOW nuh *is still*
   occasionally heard.

saunter .... SAWN tur

sausage .... SAW sij

sauté .... saw TAY *or* soh TAY

sauterne .... soh TURN *or* saw TURN

savage .... SAV ij

savanna .... suh VAN uh

savant .... suh VAHNT *or* SAV unt

savoir–faire .... SAV wahr FER ¶3

savor .... SAY vur

savory .... SAY vur ee ¶5

saxophone .... SAK suh fohn

sayonara .... SAH yuh NAHR uh

scabbard .... SKAB urd

scabies .... SKAY beez
   also, especially formerly,
   SKAY bee eez

scabrous ...... SKAB rus *or* SKAY brus

scaffold .... SKAF uld *or* SKAF ohld

scalar .... SKAY lur

scald .... SKAWLD

scalene .... SKAY leen *or* skay LEEN

scallion .... SKAL yun

scallop .... SKAHL up ¶18

scaloppine ..... SKAL uh PEE nee ¶18

scalpel .... SKAL pul

scampi .... SKAM pee

scandal .... SKAN dul

Scandinavia ....
   .... SKAN duh NAY vee uh ¶25

scapula .... SKAP yoo luh

scarab .... SKAR ub ¶23

scarce .... SKERS ¶23

scathing .... SKAY dhing

scatological .... SKAT uh LAHJ i kul

scavenge .... SKAV inj

scenario .... si NAR ee OH
   occasionally si NAHR ee OH ¶23

scenery .... SEEN ur ee ¶5

scenic .... SEE nik
   occasionally SEN ik

scepter .... SEP tur

schedule .... SKEJ ool *or* SKEJ ul
   British, and often Canadian, is
   SHED yool.

Scheherazade .. shuh HER uh ZAHD *or*
          shuh HER uh ZAH duh

schema .... SKEE muh

schematic .... skee MAT ik ¶1

scheme .... SKEEM

scherzo .... SKERT soh

schism .... SIZ um *or* SKIZ um

schist .... SHIST

schizoid .... SKIT soyd

schizophrenia .. SKIT suh FREE nee uh
   or SKIT suh FREN ee uh ¶1, 25

schizophrenic .... SKIT suh FREN ik *or*
         SKIT suh FREE nik

schlemiel .... shluh MEEL

schlock .... SHLAHK

SPELLED	PRONOUNCED
schmaltz	**SHMAWLTS** ¶19
schmear	**SHMIR**
schnapps	**SHNAHPS** *or* **SHNAPS**
schnauzer	**SHNOW** zur
now also **SNOW** zur	
schnitzel	**SHNIT** sul
schnook	**SHNOOK**
scholar	**SKAH** lur
scholastic	skuh **LAS** tik
schooner	**SKOOH** nur
schottische	**SHAHT** ish
schuss	**SHOOS**
schwa	**SHWAH** *or* **SHVAH**
sciatica	sye **AT** i kuh
science	**SYE** uns ¶9
scientific	**SYE** un **TIF** ik
scientist	**SYE** un tist
scimitar	**SIM** uh tur
now also **SIM** uh tahr ¶8	
scintilla	sin **TIL** uh
scintillate	**SIN** tuh layt
scion	**SYE** un
scissors	**SIZ** urz
sclerosis	skluh **ROH** sis
sclerotic	skluh **RAHT** ik
scoff	**SKAWF** ¶19
sconce	**SKAHNS** ¶19
Scone (Stone of)	**SKOOHN**
also, but not among Scots, **SKOHN**	
scone	**SKOHN** *or* **SKAHN**
scorpion	**SKAWR** pee un ¶25
scoundrel	**SKOWN** drul
scour	**SKOWR** ¶7
scourge	**SKURJ**

SPELLED	PRONOUNCED
scribal	**SKRYE** bul
scribbler	**SKRIB** lur ¶5
scripture	**SKRIP** chur ¶12
scrofula	**SKRAHF** yuh luh
scrotum	**SKROHT** um
scrumptious	**SKRUMP** shus ¶9, 10
scruple	**SKROOH** pul
scrupulous	**SKROOH** pyuh lus
scrutinize	**SKROOHT** un yze
scrutiny	**SKROOHT** un ee
scuba	**SKOOH** buh
scullery	**SKUL** ur ee ¶5
sculptor	**SKULP** tur
scurrilous	**SKUR** uh lus
Scylla	**SIL** uh
scythe	**SYDHE**
séance	**SAY** ahns ¶9
search	**SURCH**
season	**SEE** zun
sebaceous	si **BAY** shus
seborrhea	**SEB** uh **REE** uh
secant	**SEE** kant *or* **SEE** kunt ¶8
secede	si **SEED**
secession	si **SESH** un
Seckel (pear)	**SEK** ul
seclude	si **KLOOHD**
seclusion	si **KLOOH** zhun
seclusive	si **KLOOH** siv
second	**SEK** und
SEK unt *is common and standard; before a word beginning with a consonant, the d may disappear, as in* second–class. ¶10.	
secondary	**SEK** un **DER** ee ¶23
secrecy	**SEE** kruh see

SPELLED	PRONOUNCED
secret	SEE krit
secretariat	SEK ruh TAR ee ut ¶23
secrete	si KREET
secretion	si KREE shun
secretive	SEE kruh tiv

also si KREE tiv, *which is the only pronunciation for the meaning of a secretion*

sectarian	sek TAR ee un ¶23
sector	SEK tur
secular	SEK yuh lur
security	si KYOOR uh tee ¶24
sedan	si DAN
sedate	si DAYT
sedation	si DAY shun
sedative	SED uh tiv
sedentary	SED un TER ee ¶23
Seder	SAY dur
sediment	SED uh munt
sedimentary	SED uh MEN tur ee
sedimentation	SED uh men TAY shun ¶1
sedition	si DISH un
seduce	si DOOHS ¶21
seduction	si DUK shun
sedulous	SEJ oo lus ¶17
seethe	SEEDH
segment *(noun)*	SEG munt
segment *(verb)*	SEG ment
segmental	seg MEN tul
segregate	SEG ruh gayt
segregation	SEG ruh GAY shun
Seidlitz *(powders)*	SED lits
seigneur	sen YUR *or* sayn YUR *or* seen YUR

SPELLED	PRONOUNCED
Seine	SAYN *or* SEN
seismic	SYZE mik ¶14
seismograph	SYZE muh graf ¶14, 18
seismology	syze MAHL uh jee ¶14
seize	SEEZ
seizure	SEE zhur
select	si LEKT
selection	si LEK shun
selectivity	si LEK TIV uh tee
selectman	si LEKT mun

also, in New England,
SEE lekt man ¶10

selenium	si LEE nee um ¶25
selvage	SEL vij
semanticist	suh MAN tuh sist
semantics	suh MAN tiks
semaphore	SEM uh fawr
semblance	SEM bluns ¶9
semen	SEE mun
semester	si MES tur
semi–	SEM i *or* SEM ee *or* SEM eye *or* SEM uh *variously*
seminal	SEM i nul
seminar	SEM uh nahr
seminary	SEM uh NER ee ¶23
Seminole	SEM i nohl
Semite	SEM eyte
Semitic	suh MIT ik
semolina	SEM uh LEE nuh
semper fidelis	SEM pur fi DAY lis
senate	SEN it
senator	SEN uh tur
senatorial	SEN uh TAWR ee ul
Seneca	SEN i kuh

SPELLED	PRONOUNCED
Senegal	**SEN** i gawl
senescent	suh **NES** unt
senile	**SEE** nyle *or* **SEN** eyle
senility	si **NIL** uh tee
senior	**SEEN** yur
seniority	seen **YAWR** uh tee ¶1, 19
señor	sen **YAWR**
señora	sen **YAWR** uh
señorita	**SEN** yuh **REET** uh
sensation	sen **SAY** shun
sense	**SENS** ¶9
sensitivity	**SEN** suh **TIV** uh tee
sensitize	**SEN** suh tyze
sensor	**SEN** sur *or* **SEN** sawr
sensory	**SEN** sur ee ¶5, 9
sensual	**SEN** shoo wul ¶9, 12
sensuality	
	SEN shoo **WAL** uh tee ¶9, 12
sentence	**SENT** uns ¶9
sententious	sen **TEN** shus ¶9, 12
sentience	**SEN** shuns ¶9, 12, 25
sentiment	**SEN** tuh munt
sentimental	**SEN** tuh **MEN** tul
sentinel	**SEN** ti nul ¶5
sepal	**SEE** pul
separable	**SEP** ur uh bul ¶5
separate *(verb)*	**SEP** uh rayt
separate *(noun and adjective)*	
	SEP rit ¶5, 9
sepia	**SEE** pee uh ¶25
September	sep **TEM** bur ¶1
septet	sep **TET** ¶2
septicemia	**SEP** tuh **SEE** mee uh
septuagenarian	
	SEP too wuh ji **NAR** ee un ¶13, 21

SPELLED	PRONOUNCED
Septuagint	**SEP** too wuh jint ¶21
septum	**SEP** tum
septuple	sep **TOOH** pul *or*
	sep **TUP** ul ¶21
sepulcher	**SEP** ul kur
sepulchral	suh **PUL** krul
sequel	**SEE** kwul
sequence	**SEE** kwuns *or*
	SEE kwens ¶8, 9
sequential	si **KWEN** shul ¶9, 12
sequester	si **KWES** tur
sequestration	**SEE** kwes **TRAY** shun
	or si **KWES TRAY** shun ¶1
sequin	**SEE** kwin
sequoia	si **KWOY** uh
seraglio	si **RAL** yoh ¶18
serape	si **RAH** pee *or* si **RAH** pay
seraph	**SER** uf
Serbia	**SUR** bee uh
Serbo–Croatian	
	SUR boh kroh **AY** shun
serenade	ser uh **NAYD**
serendipity	**SER** un **DIP** uh tee
serene	si **REEN**
serenity	si **REN** uh tee
serge	**SURJ**
sergeant	**SAHR** junt
serial	**SIR** ee ul ¶25
series	**SIR** eez
serif	**SER** if
serigraph	**SER** uh graf ¶18
seriocomic	**SIR** ee oh **KAHM** ik ¶1
serious	**SIR** ee us ¶25
sermon	**SUR** mun
serological	**SIR** uh **LAH** ji kul

serology .... si **RAHL** uh jee

serpent .... **SUR** punt

serpentine .... **SUR** pun teen ¶22

serrated .... si **RAYT** id

serum .... **SIR** um

serviette .... sur vee **ET** ¶1

servile .... **SUR** vyle *or* **SUR** vul ¶8

servitude .... **SUR** vuh toohd ¶21

sesame .... **SES** uh mee

sesquicentennial ....
.... **SES** kwi sen **TEN** ee ul

sestet .... ses **TET** ¶2

settee .... se **TEE** ¶1

settler .... **SET** lur ¶5

seventh .... **SEV** unth ¶9

sever .... **SEV** ur

several .... **SEV** rul ¶5

severance .... **SEV** ur uns ¶5

severe .... si **VIR**

severity .... si **VER** uh tee

Sèvres .... **SEV** ruh

sew .... **SOH**

sewage .... **SOOH** ij ¶21

sewer ("drain") .... **SOOH** ur ¶5

sewer ("one who sews") .... **SOH** ur

sexagenarian .... SEK suh ji **NAR** ee un

sextant .... **SEKS** tunt

sextet .... seks **TET**

sexton .... **SEKS** tun

sextuple .... seks **TUP** ul *or*
seks **TOOH** pul ¶21

sexual .... **SEK** shoo wul ¶5

sexuality .... SEK shoo **WAL** uh tee

shadow .... **SHAD** oh

shah .... **SHAH** ¶19

Shakespeare .... **SHAYK** spir

shallot .... shuh **LAHT**

In recent years SHAL *ut has
become common.*

shalom .... shah **LOHM**

shaman .... **SHAY** mun *or* **SHAH** mun

shampoo .... sham **POOH**

shamus .... **SHAY** mus *or* **SHAH** mus

shanghai .... **SHANG** hye ¶2

shantung .... shan **TUNG**

shashlik .... **SHAHSH** lik

Shawnee .... shaw **NEE** ¶2

shazam .... shuh **ZAM**

shears .... **SHIRZ**

sheath .... **SHEETH**

sheathe .... **SHEEDH**

shebang .... shuh **BANG**

sheik .... **SHEEK** *or* **SHAYK**

shekel .... **SHEK** ul

shellac .... shuh **LAK**

shelter .... **SHEL** tur

Shenandoah .... SHEN un **DOH** uh

shepherd .... **SHEP** urd

sherbet .... **SHUR** bit

*Either by mistaking the spelling
or by reduplication, some say*
SHUR *burt, but it is not standard.*

shibboleth .... **SHIB** uh luth

Shih Tzu .... **SHEED** zooh ¶2

shillelagh .... shuh **LAY** lee

formerly also shuh **LAY** luh

Shiloh .... **SHYE** loh

shirk .... **SHURK**

shirr .... **SHUR**

shish kebab .... **SHISH** kuh bahb

SPELLED	PRONOUNCED
shivaree	shiv uh **REE** ¶2:
see charivari	
shiver	**SHIV** ur
shofar	**SHOH** fur *or* shaw **FAHR**
shogun	**SHOH** gun *or* **SHOH** goohn
shortening	**SHAWRT** un ing ¶5
short–lived	**SHAWRT LYVDE** *or*
	SHAWRT LIVD: *see* –lived
Shoshone	shoh **SHOH** nee ¶1
Shostakovich	SHAHS tuh **KOH** vich
shout	**SHOWT**
shovel	**SHUV** ul
shrivel	**SHRIV** ul
Siam	sye **AM**
Siamese	sye uh **MEEZ**
also sye uh **MEES**	
Sibelius	si **BAYL** yus ¶25
Siberia	sye **BIR** ee uh ¶25
sibilant	**SIB** uh lunt
Sicilian	si **SIL** yun ¶25
Sicily	**SIS** uh lee
Siddhartha	si **DAHR** tuh
sidereal	sye **DIR** ee ul
sidle	**SYE** dul
siege	**SEEJ** ¶15
sienna	see **EN** uh
sierra	see **ER** uh
Sierra Leone	see **ER** uh lee **OHN**
Sierra Madre	see **ER** uh **MAH** dray
siesta	see **ES** tuh
sieve	**SIV**
signal	**SIG** nul
signatory	**SIG** nuh **TAWR** ee
signature	**SIG** nuh chur
signet	**SIG** nit

SPELLED	PRONOUNCED
significant	sig **NIF** uh kunt
signification	**SIG** nuh fi **KAY** shun
signify	**SIG** nuh fye
signor	seen **YAWR**
signora	seen **YAWR** uh
signore	seen **YAWR** ay
signorina	**SEEN** yuh **REE** nuh
signorino	**SEEN** yuh **REE** noh
Sikh	**SEEK**
silage	**SYE** lij
silent	**SYE** lunt
silhouette	sil oo **WET**
silica	**SIL** i kuh
silicate	**SIL** i kit *or* **SIL** i kayt
siliceous	suh **LISH** us
silicon	**SIL** i kun *or* **SIL** i kahn ¶8
silicone	**SIL** i kohn
silicosis	SIL uh **KOH** sis
silo	**SYE** loh
Silurian	si **LOOR** ee un
silva	**SIL** vuh
simian	**SIM** ee un
similar	**SIM** uh lur
similarity	SIM uh **LAR** uh tee ¶23
simile	**SIM** uh lee
similitude	suh **MIL** uh toohd ¶21
simon–pure	**SYE** mun **PYOOR**
simpatico	sim **PAHT** i **KOH** ¶18
simpleton	**SIM** pul tun
simplicity	sim **PLIS** uh tee
simplify	**SIM** pluh fye
simplistic	sim **PLIS** tik
simulacrum	SIM yoo **LAY** krum
simulate	**SIM** yoo layt
simulcast	**SYE** mul kast ¶18

simultaneous ..... SYE mul TAY nee us
also, but especially British,
SIM ul TAY nee us ¶5

Sinai .... SYE nye

since .... SINS ¶9

sincere .... sin SIR

sincerity .... sin SER uh tee

sinecure .... SYE nuh kyoor *or*
SIN uh kyoor ¶24

sine qua non ...... SIN ay KWAH NOHN
also, especially formerly,
SYE nee KWAY NAHN

sinew .... SIN yooh

sinewy .... SIN yoo wee ¶21

Singapore .... SING guh pawr *or*
SING uh pawr

singe .... SINJ ¶15

singular .... SING gyuh lur

singularity ....
.... SING gyuh LAR uh tee ¶23

Sinhalese .... sin huh LEEZ *or*
sin uh LEEZ
The final syllable may also be
LEES ¶14.

sinister .... SIN is tur

Sinn Fein .... SHIN FAYN

Sino— .... SYE noh *or* SIN oh

sinuous .... SIN yoo wus

sinus .... SYE nus

sinusitis .... SYE nuh SYTE is

Siouan .... SOOH un

Sioux .... SOOH
*The plural is spelled the same
way and is* SOOH *or* SOOHZ.

siphon .... SYE fun

siren .... SYE run

sirocco .... si RAHK oh

sisal .... SYE sul

Sistine .... SIS teen
occasionally SIS tin ¶2, 8

Sisyphus .... SIS uh fus

sitar .... si TAHR

situate .... SICH oo wayt

situation .... SICH oo WAY shun

sitz (bath) .... SITS *or* ZITS

Siva .... SHEE vuh *or* SEE vuh

skein .... SKAYN

skeleton .... SKEL uh tun

skeptic .... SKEP tik

skepticism .... SKEP ti siz um

skew .... SKYOOH

skirmish .... SKUR mish

skoal .... SKOHL

skua .... SKYOOH uh

slalom .... SLAH lum

slanderous .... SLAN dur us ¶5

slaughter .... SLAWT ur

Slav .... SLAHV ¶18

slaver ("drool") .... SLAV ur ¶18

slavish .... SLAY vish

sleazy .... SLEE zee

sleigh .... SLAY

sleight .... SLYTE

sleuth .... SLOOHTH

slimy .... SLYE mee

slippery .... SLIP ur ee ¶5

slither .... SLIDH ur

sliver .... SLIV ur

sloe .... SLOH

slogan .... SLOH gun

SPELLED	*PRONOUNCED*
sloth	**SLAWTH** *or* **SLOHTH** *or* **SLAHTH**
slough ("to shed")	**SLUF**
slough ("depression")	**SLOW**

When the word means swamp, *it is either* **SLOOH** *or* **SLOW**.

Slovak	**SLOH** vahk ¶18
Slovenia	sloh **VEE** nee uh ¶1, 25
slovenly	**SLUV** un lee
sluice	**SLOOHS**
slumber	**SLUM** bur
smidgen	**SMIJ** un
smithereens	smidh uh **REENZ**
smithy	**SMITH** ee

also, but chiefly British, **SMIDH** ee

smolder	**SMOHL** dur
smorgasbord	**SMAWR** gus bawrd
smother	**SMUDH** ur
snafu	sna **FOOH** ¶2
snivel	**SNIV** ul
snooty	**SNOOHT** ee
snorkel	**SNAWR** kul
sobriety	suh **BRYE** uh tee ¶1
sobriquet	**SOH** bruh kay ¶2
sociability	**SOH** shuh **BIL** uh tee ¶25
sociable	**SOH** shuh bul
social	**SOH** shul
socialism	**SOH** shul iz um
society	suh **SYE** uh tee
socio–	**SOH** see oh *or* **SOH** ~~shee~~ oh
sociology	**SOH** see **AHL** uh jee
sociopath	**SOH** see uh **PATH** ¶11, 18
Socrates	**SAHK** ruh teez
Socratic	suh **KRAT** ik ¶1

SPELLED	*PRONOUNCED*
sodium	**SOH** dee um ¶25
Sodom	**SAHD** um
sodomy	**SAHD** uh mee
soften	**SAWF** un
soiree	swah **RAY**
sojourn *(noun)*	**SOH** jurn

The verb is also soh **JURN**.

solace	**SAHL** is
solar	**SOH** lur
solarium	soh **LAR** ee um ¶1, 23
solder	**SAHD** ur
soldier	**SOHL** jur
solecism	**SAHL** uh siz um
solemn	**SAHL** um
solemnity	suh **LEM** nuh tee
solemnize	**SAHL** um nyze
solenoid	**SOH** luh noyd ¶20
solfeggio	sahl **FEJ** oh ¶25
solicit	suh **LIS** it
solicitude	suh **LIS** uh **TOOHD** ¶21
solidarity	**SAHL** uh **DAR** uh tee
soliloquize	suh **LIL** uh kwyze
soliloquy	suh **LIL** uh kwee
solipsism	**SAHL** ip siz um
solitaire	**SAHL** uh ter
solitary	**SAHL** uh **TER** ee ¶23
solitude	**SAHL** uh toohd ¶21
solo	**SOH** loh
solon	**SOH** lun *or* **SOH** lahn
solstice	**SAHL** stis ¶20
solubility	**SAHL** yoo **BIL** uh tee
soluble	**SAHL** yoo bul
solution	suh **LOOH** shun
solvent	**SAHL** vunt
Somalia	soh **MAHL** ee uh ¶1, 25

SPELLED	PRONOUNCED	SPELLED	PRONOUNCED
Somaliland ...	soh **MAHL** ee LAND ¶1	sorcery	**SAWR** sur ee
somatic	soh **MAT** ik	sordid	**SAWR** did
somber	**SAHM** bur	sorghum	**SAWR** gum
sombrero	sahm **BRER** oh ¶1, 20	sorority	suh **RAWR** uh tee
somebody	**SUM** bud ee *or*	sorrel	**SAWR** ul ¶19
	SUM bahd ee ¶8	sorrow	**SAHR** ow ¶19
somersault	**SUM** ur sawlt	sorry	**SAHR** ee ¶19
something	**SUM** thing ¶9	sortie	**SAWR** tee
somnambulate ...	sahm **NAM** byoo layt	sotto voce	SAHT oh **VOH** chee
somnolent	**SAHM** nuh lunt	soubrette	sooh **BRET**
sonar	**SOH** nahr	soufflé	sooh **FLAY** ¶2
sonata	suh **NAHT** uh	soul	**SOHL**
sonic	**SAHN** ik	soupçon	soohp **SOHN**
sonnet	**SAHN** it	*The n here indicates the*	
sonneteer	sahn uh **TIR**	*nasalized French vowel* ¶2.	
sonorous	suh **NAWR** us *or*	sour	**SOWR** ¶7
	SAHN ur us ¶1	source	**SAWRS**
soot	**SOOT**	sousaphone	**SOOH** zuh fohn *or*
SOOHT *and* **SUT** *are heard in some*			**SOOH** suh fohn
regions.		souse	**SOWS**
soothe	**SOOHDH**	south	**SOWTH**
soothsayer	**SOOHTH** say ur	*in terms like* southeast,	
sophism	**SAHF** iz um	southwest, south–southeast,	
sophist	**SAHF** ist	southwestern, *among sailors* **SOW**	
sophisticate *(verb)*	suh **FIS** ti kayt	souvenir	sooh vuh **NIR** ¶2
The noun is usually suh **FIS** ti kit.		sovereign	**SAHV** run
sophistication ...	suh **FIS** tuh **KAY** shun	*occasionally* **SUV** run ¶5	
sophistry	**SAHF** is tree	soviet	**SOH** vee it *or* **SOH** vee et *or*
Sophocles	**SAHF** uh kleez		soh vee **ET**
sophomore	**SAHF** mawr ¶5, 19	sow ("female hog")	**SOW**
sophomoric		sow ("to plant seed")	**SOH**
....	SAHF uh **MAWR** ik ¶5, 19	spacious	**SPAY** shus
soporific	SAHP uh **RIF** ik ¶20	spaghetti	spuh **GET** ee
soprano	suh **PRAN** oh ¶18	spangle	**SPANG** gul
sorcerer	**SAWR** sur ur	Spaniard	**SPAN** yurd

SPELLED	PRONOUNCED	SPELLED	PRONOUNCED
spaniel	**SPAN** yul	spelunker	spi **LUNG** kur
sparkler	**SPAHR** klur ¶5	Spencerian	spen **SIR** ee un
sparrow	**SPAR** oh	sperm	**SPURM**
sparse	**SPAHRS**	spermicide	**SPUR** muh syde
Spartan	**SPAHR** tun	spew	**SPYOOH**
spasm	**SPAZ** um	sphagnum	**SFAG** num
spasmodic	spaz **MAHD** ik	sphere	**SFIR**
spastic	**SPAS** tik	spherical	**SFER** i kul or **SFIR** i kul
spatial	**SPAY** shul	sphincter	**SFINGK** tur
spatula	**SPACH** uh luh	sphinx	**SFINGKS**
spavin	**SPAV** in	spicy	**SPYSE** ee
special	**SPESH** ul	spider	**SPYE** dur
speciality	SPESH ee **AL** uh tee	spiel	**SPEEL**
specialize	**SPESH** uh lyze	spigot	**SPIK** ut or **SPIG** ut
specie	**SPEE** shee or **SPEE** see	spina bifida	**SPYE** nuh **BIF** i duh
species	**SPEE** sheez or **SPEE** seez	*For the second word,* **BYE** fi duh *is*
specific	spi **SIF** ik	*also heard.*
specification	SPES uh fi **KAY** shun	spinach	**SPIN** ich or **SPIN** ij
specify	**SPES** uh fye	spinal	**SPYE** nul
specimen	**SPES** uh mun	spindle	**SPIN** dul
specious	**SPEE** shus	spinet	**SPIN** it
spectacle	**SPEK** tuh kul	spinnaker	**SPIN** uh kur
spectacular	spek **TAK** yuh lur	Spinoza	spi **NOH** zuh
spectator	**SPEK** tayt ur or	spinster	**SPIN** stur ¶9
	spek **TAYT** ur	spiny	**SPYE** nee
specter	**SPEK** tur	spiral	**SPYE** rul
spectral	**SPEK** trul	spirit	**SPIR** it
spectroscope	**SPEK** truh skohp	spiritual	**SPIR** i choo wul ¶5
spectroscopy	spek **TRAHS** kuh pee	spirituality	SPIR i choo **WAL** uh tee
speculate	**SPEK** yuh layt	spirochete	**SPYE** ruh keet
speculation	SPEK yuh **LAY** shun	spittoon	spi **TOOHN**
speculative	**SPEK** yuh luh tiv or	splendid	**SPLEN** did
	SPEK yuh layt iv	splendiferous	splen **DIF** ur us
speedometer	spi **DAHM** uh tur	splendor	**SPLEN** dur
speleology	SPEE lee **AHL** uh jee	splenetic	spli **NET** ik

spoilage	**SPOYL** ij	stable	**STAY** bul
Spokane	spoh **KAN**	staccato	stuh **KAHT** oh
spoliation	SPOH lee AY shun	stadium	**STAY** dee um
sponge	**SPUNJ** ¶15	Staël	**STAHL**
spontaneity	SPAHN tuh **NEE** uh tee	stagflation	stag **FLAY** shun
	or SPAHN tuh **NAY** uh tee	stagnant	**STAG** nunt
spontaneous	spahn **TAY** nee us ¶25	stagnate	**STAG** nayt
spoonerism	**SPOOH** nur iz um	staid	**STAYD**
spoor	**SPOOR** *or* **SPAWR**	stalactite	stuh **LAK** tyte
sporadic	spuh **RAD** ik ¶1	stalag	**STAL** ag *or* **SHTAH** lahk
sporangium	spuh **RAN** jee um ¶1	stalagmite	stuh **LAG** myte ¶2
spouse	**SPOWS**	Stalin	**STAH** lin
sprinkle	**SPRING** kul	stalk	**STAWK** ¶19
sprout	**SPROWT**	stallion	**STAL** yun
spumoni	spuh **MOH** nee	stalwart	**STAWL** wurt ¶19
spurious	**SPYOOR** ee us ¶24	stamen	**STAY** mun
sputnik	**SPOOT** nik *or* **SPUT** nik	stamina	**STAM** uh nuh
sputum	**SPYOOHT** um	stampede	stam **PEED**
squab	**SKWAHB** ¶19	stanchion	**STAN** chun ¶12
squabble	**SKWAH** bul ¶19	standardize	**STAN** dur dyze
squadron	**SKWAHD** run ¶19	Stanford–Binet (test)	
squalid	**SKWAHL** id ¶19		**STAN** furd bi **NAY**
squall	**SKWAWL**	stanza	**STAN** zuh
squalor	**SKWAHL** ur ¶19	staphylococcus	
squander	**SKWAHN** dur ¶19		STAF uh loh **KAHK** us ¶1, 5:
squash	**SKWAHSH** ¶19		*for plural see* coccus
squawk	**SKWAWK** ¶19	stapler	**STAY** plur ¶5
squeegee	**SKWEE** jee	starboard	**STAHR** burd
squelch	**SKWELCH** ¶9	**STAHR** bawrd *is occasionally heard*	
squirm	**SKWURM**	*but not from sailors or fliers.*	
squirrel	**SKWUR** ul ¶5		
squirt	**SKWURT**	startling	**STAHRT** ling ¶5
stabile *(adjective)*	**STAY** bil ¶22	starvation	stahr **VAY** shun
for the noun, usually **STAY** beel		Staten (Island)	**STAT** un
stability	stuh **BIL** uh tee	static	**STAT** ik
		station	**STAY** shun

SPELLED	PRONOUNCED
stationary	**STAY** shuh **NER** ee
stationery	**STAY** shuh **NER** ee
statistic	stuh **TIS** tik
statistician	**STAT** is **TISH** un
statuary	**STACH** oo **WER** ee ¶23
statue	**STACH** ooh
statuesque	stach oo **WESK**
statuette	stach oo **WET**
stature	**STACH** ur
status	**STAYT** us *or* **STAT** us
status quo	**STAYT** us, *or* **STAT** us, **KWOH**
statute	**STACH** ooht *or* **STACH** oot ¶21
statutory	**STACH** oo **TAWR** ee
staunch	**STAWNCH** ¶19
stead	**STED**
steadfast	**STED** fast ¶18 **STED** fust *is chiefly British.*
steady	**STED** ee
stealth	**STELTH**
stearic	stee **AR** ik ¶23 *occasionally* **STIR** ik
steelyard	**STEEL** yahrd *or* **STIL** yurd
steerage	**STIR** ij
stegosaurus	STEG uh **SAWR** us
stein	**STYNE**
stellar	**STEL** ur
stench	**STENCH**
stencil	**STEN** sul ¶19
stenographer	stuh **NAHG** ruh fur
stenotype	**STEN** uh type
stentorian	sten **TAWR** ee un
steppe	**STEP**
stereo	**STER** ee oh *or* **STIR** ee oh

SPELLED	PRONOUNCED
stereophonic	**STER** ee uh **FAHN** ik *or* **STIR** ee uh **FAHN** ik
stereotype	**STER** ee uh **TYPE** *or* **STIR** ee uh **TYPE**
stereotypic	STER ee uh **TIP** ik *or* STIR ee uh **TIP** ik
sterile	**STER** ul
sterilize	**STER** uh lyze
sterling	**STUR** ling
stern	**STURN**
sternum	**STUR** num
steroid	**STIR** oyd *or* **STER** oyd
stethoscope	**STETH** uh skohp
stevedore	**STEE** vuh dawr
stew	**STOOH** ¶21
steward	**STOOH** urd ¶21
stickler	**STIK** lur ¶5
stifle	**STYE** ful
stifling	**STYE** fling ¶5
stigma	**STIG** muh

The plural is stigmas **STIG** muhz, *but when the meaning is* a mark or scar on the skin, *it is stigmata* stig **MAHT** uh *or* **STIG** muh tuh.

stigmatic	stig **MAT** ik
stiletto	sti **LET** oh
stimulant	**STIM** yuh lunt
stimulate	**STIM** yuh layt
stimulus	**STIM** yuh lus

The plural is stimuli **STIM** yuh lye.

stinger	**STING** ur
stingy ("miserly")	**STIN** jee

not to be confused with stingy **STING** ee, *meaning* stinging

stipend	**STYE** pend *or* **STYE** pund

stipulate	**STIP** yuh layt
stipulation	STIP yuh **LAY** shun
stir	**STUR**
stirrup	**STUR** up *or* **STIR** up
St. Louis	saynt **LOOH** is
	saynt **LOOH** ee *is old--fashioned*
Stockholm	**STAHK** hohm *or*
	STAHK hohlm
stodgy	**STAHJ** ee
stogie	**STOH** gee
stoic	**STOH** ik
stoical	**STOH** i kul
stoicism	**STOH** i siz um
stolid	**STAHL** id
stollen	**STOH** lun *or* **SHTAW** lun
stomach	**STUM** uk
stomachache	**STUM** uk ayk ¶1
stooge	**STOOHJ**
stool	**STOOHL**
stoppage	**STAHP** ij
storage	**STAWR** ij
stout	**STOWT**
stow	**STOH**
Stradivarius	STRAD uh **VAR** ee us
strafe	**STRAYF**
straight	**STRAYT**
strait	**STRAYT**
strange	**STRAYNJ** ¶15
stranger	**STRAYN** jur ¶15
strangle	**STRANG** gul
strangulate	**STRANG** gyuh layt
strata	**STRAYT** uh *or* **STRAT** uh
stratagem	**STRAT** uh jum
strategic	struh **TEE** jik
strategist	**STRAT** uh jist

strategy	**STRAT** uh jee
stratification ....STRAT uh fi **KAY** shun
stratify	**STRAT** uh fye
stratosphere	**STRAT** uh sfir
stratum	**STRAYT** um *or* **STRAT** um
stratus	**STRAYT** us *or* **STRAT** us
Stravinsky	struh **VIN** skee
strawberry	**STRAW** ber ee *or*
	STRAW bur ee
strength ..	**STRENGTH** *or* **STRENGKTH**
STRENTH *has wide currency but is*
not heard in standard speech ¶9.
strenuous	**STREN** yoo wus
streptococcus	STREP tuh **KAHK** us
for plural see coccus
streptomycin	STREP tuh **MYE** sin
streusel ..	**STROOH** zul *or* **STROY** zul *or*
	SHTROY zul
striation	strye **AY** shun
stricture	**STRIK** chur ¶12
strident	**STRYDE** unt
stringed	**STRINGD**
stringent	**STRIN** junt
stroboscope	**STROH** buh skohp *or*
	STRAHB uh skohp
stroganoff	**STROH** guh nawf *or*
	STRAW guh nawf
stroll	**STROHL**
strontium	**STRAHN** shee um *or*
	STRAHN shum
occasionally STRAHN tee um ¶12
strophe	**STROH** fee
structural	**STRUK** chur ul ¶12
structure	**STRUK** chur ¶12
strudel ..	**STROOH** dul *or* **SHTROOH** dul

SPELLED	PRONOUNCED	SPELLED	PRONOUNCED
strychnine	**STRIK** nyne ¶22	subcutaneous	SUB kyoo **TAY** nee us
stubborn	**STUB** urn	subdue	sub **DOOH** ¶21
stucco	**STUK** oh	subgum	**SUB GUM**
student	**STOOHD** unt ¶21	subject *(noun)*	**SUB** jikt
studio	**STOOH** dee oh ¶21	subject *(verb)*	sub **JEKT**
studious	**STOOH** dee us ¶21	subjective	sub **JEK** tiv
study	**STUD** ee	subjugate	**SUB** juh gayt
stultify	**STUL** tuh fye	subjunctive	sub **JUNGK** tiv ¶9
stumble	**STUM** bul	sublease *(verb)*	sub **LEES**
stupefaction	STOOH puh **FAK** shun	sublease *(noun)*	**SUB** lees
stupefy	**STOOH** puh fye ¶21	sublet	sub **LET** ¶2
stupendous	stoo **PEN** dus ¶1, 21	sublimate *(verb)*	**SUB** luh mayt
stupid	**STOOH** pid ¶21	sublime	suh **BLYME**
stupidity	stoo **PID** uh tee ¶1, 21	subliminal	sub **LIM** i nul
stupor	**STOOH** pur ¶21	sublunary	sub **LOOH** nur ee *or*
sturdy	**STUR** dee		**SUB** loo **NER** ee
sturgeon	**STUR** jun	submarine	sub muh **REEN**
Stygian	**STIJ** ee un ¶25	submerge	sub **MURJ**
style	**STYLE** ¶7	submerse	sub **MURS**
stylish	**STYE** lish	submission	sub **MISH** un
stylistic	stye **LIS** tik	submissive	sub **MIS** iv
stylize	**STYE** lyze ¶5	submit	sub **MIT**
stylus	**STYE** lus	suborder	**SUB** AWR dur
stymie	**STYE** mee	subordinate *(verb)*	
styptic	**STIP** tik		suh **BAWR** duh nayt
styrene	**STYE** reen *or* **STIR** een	subordinate *(noun and adjective)*	
suable	**SOOH** uh bul		suh **BAWR** duh nit
suasion	**SWAY** zhun	suborn	suh **BAWRN**
suave	**SWAHV**	subornation	SUB awr **NAY** shun
		subpoena	suh **PEE** nuh

SWAYV *is facetious in the U.S. but was once standard in Britain.*

subaltern .... sub **AWL** turn

subconscious ....

.... sub **KAHN** shus ¶9, 12

subculture .... **SUB** kul chur

subpoena .... suh **PEE** nuh

Some people have opted for the euphonious suh **PEE** nee, *which is not generally considered standard.*

subrogate .... **SUB** ruh gayt

SPELLED	PRONOUNCED	SPELLED	PRONOUNCED
sub rosa	sub ROH zuh	succeed	suk SEED
subscribe	sub SKRYBE	success	suk SES
subscript	SUB skript	succession	suk SESH un
subscription	sub SKRIP shun	succinct	suk SINGKT
subsequent	SUB si kwunt	*now also* suh SINGKT	
subservient	sub SUR vee unt ¶25	succor	SUK ur
subset	SUB set	succotash	SUK uh tash
subside	sub SYDE	succubus	SUK yoo bus
subsidiary	sub SID ee ER ee ¶23	succulent	SUK yoo lunt
subsidize	SUB suh dyze	succumb	suh KUM
subsidy	SUB suh dee	sucrose	SOOH krohs
subsist	sub SIST	suction	SUK shun
subsistence	sub SIS tuns ¶9	Sudan	sooh DAN ¶1
substance	SUB stuns ¶9	sudden	SUD un
substantial	sub STAN shul ¶9, 12	sue	SOOH
substantiate	sub STAN shee ayt	suede	SWAYD
substantive	SUB stun tiv	suet	SOOH it ¶21
substitute	SUB stuh tooht ¶21	Suez	sooh EZ ¶2
substitution		sufferance	SUF runs ¶5, 9
.... SUB stuh TOOH shun ¶21		suffice	suh FYSE
subsume	sub SOOHM ¶21	*now less common* suh FYZE	
subterfuge	SUB tur fyoohj	sufficient	suh FISH unt
subterranean		suffix *(noun)*	SUF iks
.... SUB tuh RAY nee un ¶25		*The verb may also be* suh FIKS.	
subtle	SUT ul	suffocate	SUF uh kayt
subtlety	SUT ul tee	Suffolk	SUF uk
subtract	sub TRAKT	suffrage	SUF rij
subtraction	sub TRAK shun	suffragette	suf ruh JET
subtrahend	SUB truh hend	suffuse	suh FYOOHZ
suburb	SUB urb	sugar	SHOOG ur
suburban	suh BUR bun	suggest	sug JEST
suburbia	suh BUR bee uh	*British* suh JEST *is becoming*	
subversion	sub VUR zhun	*common in the U.S.*	
subversive	sub VUR siv	suggestion	sug JES chun ¶11:
subvert	sub VURT	*see preceding*	

suicidal .... SOOH uh **SYDE** ul ¶21

suicide .... **SOOH** uh syde ¶21

sui generis .... **SOOH** ee **JEN** ur is

suit .... **SOOHT** ¶21

suite .... **SWEET**

For the meaning a set of
matched furniture, *also*
SOOHT ¶21

suitor .... **SOOHT** ur ¶21

sukiyaki .... SOOH kee **YAH** kee

sulfa .... **SUL** fuh

sulfur .... **SUL** fur

sulfuric .... sul **FYOOR** ik ¶24

sulfurous .... **SUL** fur us ¶5

When the meaning is of or
containing sulfur, *it is usually*
sul **FYOOR** us ¶24.

sullen .... **SUL** un

sultan .... **SUL** tun

sultana .... sul **TAN** uh ¶18

sultanate ..... **SUL** tun it *or* **SUL** tun ayt

sultry .... **SUL** tree

Sulu .... **SOOH** looh

sumac ...... **SHOOH** mak *or* **SOOH** mak

Sumatra .... soo **MAH** truh ¶1

summa cum laude ....

.... **SOOM** uh koom **LOW** day *or*
SUM uh kum **LAW** dee

summarize .... **SUM** uh ryze

summary .... **SUM** ur ee ¶5

summation .... suh **MAY** shun

sumptuous ... **SUMP** choo wus ¶9, 10

sundae .... **SUN** dee

occasionally **SUN** day ¶8

Sunday ...... **SUN** dee *or* **SUN** day ¶8

sundry .... **SUN** dree

super– .... **SOOH** pur ¶21

superannuated ....

.... SOOH pur **AN** yoo **WAYT** id

superb .... soo **PURB** ¶1

supercilious .... SOOH pur **SIL** ee us

superego .... SOOH pur **EE** goh

supererogation ....‗‗.

.... SOOH pur **ER** uh **GAY** shun

supererogatory ....

.... SOOH pur i **RAHG** uh **TAWR** ee

superficial .... SOOH pur **FISH** ul

superfluity ... SOOH pur **FLOOH** uh tee

superfluous .... soo **PUR** floo wus

superintendent ....

.... SOOH pur in **TEN** dunt

superior .... suh **PIR** ee ur ¶1

superiority ....

.... suh **PIR** ee **AWR** uh tee ¶1

superlative .... suh **PUR** luh tiv ¶1

superman .... **SOOH** pur man

supernal .... soo **PUR** nul

supernumerary ....

SOOH pur **NOOH** muh **RER** ee ¶21,
23

superscript .... **SOOH** pur skript

supersede .... sooh pur **SEED**

supersonic .... SOOH pur **SAHN** ik

superstition .... SOOH pur **STISH** un

supervise .... **SOOH** pur vyze

supine .... soo **PYNE**

supplant .... suh **PLANT** ¶18

supple .... **SUP** ul

supplement *(noun)* ..... **SUP** luh munt

supplement *(verb)* ...... **SUP** luh ment

supplementary	SUP luh MEN tur ee	surrey	SUR ee
suppliant	SUP lee unt	surrogate	SUR uh git *or* SUR uh gayt
supplicant	SUP luh kunt	surround	suh ROWND ¶3
supplicate	SUP luh kayt	surtax	SUR taks
supposedly	suh POH zid lee	surveillance	sur VAY luns
supposition	SUP uh ZISH un		sur VAYL yuns *is infrequent, but*
suppository	suh PAHZ uh TAWR ee		sur VAY uns *is now sometimes*
suppurate	SUP yoo rayt		*heard.* ¶9
supra–	SOOH pruh ¶21	survey *(verb)*	sur VAY
supremacy	suh PREM uh see ¶1		*also, and for the noun usually,*
supreme	suh PREEM ¶1		SUR vay ¶2
surcharge	SUR chahrj ¶2	survive	sur VYVE
sure	SHOOR ¶24	susceptible	suh SEP tuh bul
surety	SHOOR uh tee ¶5, 24	sushi	SOOH shee
surface	SUR fis	suspect *(verb)*	suh SPEKT
surfeit	SUR fit		*for the adjective usually, and for*
surge	SURJ		*the noun always,* SUS pekt ¶2
surgeon	SUR jun	suspend	suh SPEND
surgery	SUR jur ee ¶5	suspense	suh SPENS ¶9
surgical	SUR ji kul	suspension	suh SPEN shun ¶9, 12
Suriname	SOOR i nahm *or*	suspicion	suh SPISH un
	SOOR i NAH muh ¶18, 24	Susquehanna	SUS kwi HAN uh
surly	SUR lee	sustain	suh STAYN
surmise *(verb)*	sur MYZE	sustenance	SUS ti nuns ¶9
	also, for the noun, SUR myze ¶2	suture	SOOH chur
surmount	sur MOWNT	suzerain	SOOHZ ur in
surname *(noun)*	SUR naym		SOOHZ ur ayn *is less common.*
	also, for the verb, sur NAYM ¶2	suzerainty	SOOHZ ur in tee
surpass	sur PAS ¶18	svelte	SFELT *or* SVELT
surplice	SUR plis	Swahili	swah HEE lee
surplus	SUR plus	swallow	SWAHL oh
surprise	sur PRYZE	swami	SWAH mee
surreal	suh REE ul ¶3, 7	swamp	SWAHMP ¶19
surrender	suh REN dur ¶3	swan	SWAHN ¶19
surreptitious	SUR up TISH us	swank	SWANGK

SPELLED	PRONOUNCED	SPELLED	PRONOUNCED

swap .... SWAHP ¶19

sward .... SWAWRD

swarm .... SWAWRM

swarthy .... SWAWR dhee ¶19

swash .... SWAHSH ¶19

swastika .... SWAHS ti kuh

   occasionally swah STEE kuh

swatch .... SWAHCH

swath .... SWAHTH ¶19

swathe .... SWAYDH

Swaziland .... SWAH zee land

sweat .... SWET

Swedenborgian ....

   .... SWEED un BAWR jee un *or*

   SWEED un BAWR gee un

swelter .... SWEL tur

swerve .... SWURV

swindler .... SWIN dlur ¶5

swinish .... SWYNE ish

swirl .... SWURL

swivel .... SWIV ul

swollen .... SWOH lun

swoosh .... SWOOSH *or* SWOOHSH

sword .... SAWRD

   The w was still sounded well

   into the 15th century.

sybarite .... SIB uh ryte

sybaritic .... SIB uh RIT ic

sycamore .... SIK uh mawr

sycophant .... SIK uh funt

sycophantic .... SIK uh FAN tik

syllabary .... SIL uh BER ee ¶23

syllabic .... si LAB ik

syllabify .... si LAB uh fye

syllable .... SIL uh bul

syllabus .... SIL uh bus

   The plurals are syllabuses *and*

   syllabi SIL uh bye.

syllogism .... SIL uh jiz um

sylph .... SILF

sylvan .... SIL vun

symbiosis .... SIM bye OH sis *or*

   SIM bee OH sis

symbiotic .... SIM bye AHT ik *or*

   SIM bee AHT ik

symbol .... SIM bul

symbolic .... sim BAHL ik

symbolism .... SIM bul iz um

symbolize .... SIM buh lyze

symmetrical .... si MET ri kul

symmetry .... SIM uh tree

sympathetic .... SIM puh THET ik

sympathy .... SIM puh thee

symphonic .... sim FAHN ik ¶6

symphony .... SIM fuh nee ¶6

symposium .... sim POH zee um

symptom .... SIMP tum ¶9

symptomatic .... SIMP tuh MAT ik ¶9

synagogue .... SIN uh gahg ¶19

synapse .... SIN aps ¶2

synaptic .... si NAP tik

synchromesh ....

   SING kruh mesh ¶1, 16

synchronize ..... SING kruh nyze ¶16

synchronous ..... SING kruh nus ¶16

syncline .... SING klyne ¶16

syncopate .... SING kuh payt ¶16

syncopation ....

   .... SING kuh PAY shun ¶16

syncope .... SING kuh pee ¶16

syndicate *(noun)* .... **SIN** duh kit
syndicate *(verb)* .... **SIN** duh kayt
syndrome .... **SIN** drohm
synecdoche .... si **NEK** duh kee
synergism .... **SIN** ur jiz um
synergy .... **SIN** ur jee
synod .... **SIN** ud ¶8
synonym .... **SIN** uh nim
synonymy .... si **NAHN** uh mee
synopsis .... si **NAHP** sis
   The plural is synopses
   si **NAHP** seez.
syntactic .... sin **TAK** tik
syntax .... **SIN** taks
synthesis .... **SIN** thuh sis
synthesize .... **SIN** thuh syze
synthetic .... sin **THET** ik
syphilis .... **SIF** uh lis ¶5
Syria .... **SIR** ee uh ¶25
syringe .... suh **RINJ** or **SIR** inj
syrinx .... **SIR** ingks
syrup .... **SIR** up or **SUR** up
   Both pronunciations seem to be
   heard with equal frequency.
systaltic .... sis **TAWL** tik ¶18, 19
system .... **SIS** tum
systematic .... **SIS** tuh **MAT** ik
systematize .... **SIS** tuh muh **TYZE**
systemic .... sis **TEM** ik
systole .... **SIS** tuh lee
systolic .... sis **TAHL** ik
syzygy .... **SIZ** uh jee
Szechwan .... **SECH** wahn
   SUH chwahn *approximates the*
   Chinese.

T

tabernacle .... **TAB** ur **NAK** ul
tablature .... **TAB** luh chur
tableau .... **TAB** loh
   The plural is tableaux *or*
   tableaus, *both* **TAB** lohz. ¶2
table d'hôte .... TAHB ul **DOHT** or
                        TAH bluh **DOHT**
tablet .... **TAB** lit
tabloid .... **TAB** loyd
taboo .... ta **BOOH** ¶1
tabor .... **TAY** bur
tabular .... **TAB** yuh lur
tabula rasa ... **TAB** yuh luh **RAH** suh or
           TAB yuh luh **RAY** suh ¶14
tabulate .... **TAB** yuh layt
tachistoscope .... tuh **KIS** tuh skohp
tachometer .... ta **KAHM** uh tur ¶1
tachycardia .... TAK i **KAHR** dee uh
tacit .... **TAS** it
taciturn .... **TAS** uh turn
taco .... **TAH** koh
   The plural tacos *is either*
   TAH kohz *or* **TAH** kohs.
tactician .... tak **TISH** un
tactics .... **TAK** tiks
tactile .... **TAK** tul ¶22
tactual .... **TAK** choo wul
taffeta .... **TAF** i tuh

Tagalog	tuh **GAH** lug or tuh **GAH** lawg ¶1, 19	tantra	**TUN** truh or **TAHN** truh
Tahiti	tuh **HEET** ee ¶1	tantrum	**TAN** trum
Tahitian	tuh **HEESH** un ¶1	Tanzania	TAN zuh **NEE** uh ¶18
tuh **HEET** ee un *is seldom heard, except in British usage where it prevails.*		*The nonstandard tan* **ZAYN** *ee uh is heard fairly frequently these days.*	
Tahoe	**TAH** hoh	Taoism	**DOW** iz um or **TOW** iz um
tai chi	**TYE JEE**	tapestry	**TAP** is tree
Taiwan	**TYE WAHN**	tapioca	TAP ee **OH** kuh
Taj Mahal	tahzh muh **HAHL** ¶15, 19	tapir	**TAY** pur
talcum	**TAL** kum	tarantella	TAR un **TEL** uh ¶23
tales ("jurors")	**TAY** leez	tarantula	tuh **RAN** choo luh ¶23
talisman	**TAL** is mun ¶14	tariff	**TAR** if ¶23
Talmud	**TAHL** mood or **TAL** mud ¶18	tarot	**TAR** oh or **TAR** ut or ta **ROH** ¶23
talon	**TAL** un	tarpaulin	tahr **PAW** lin or **TAHR** puh lin
tamale	tuh **MAH** lee	tarpon	**TAHR** pun
tambourine	tam buh **REEN**	tarragon	**TAR** uh gahn
tam-o'-shanter	**TAM** uh **SHAN** tur	tarsal	**TAHR** sul
tampon	**TAM** pahn	tarsier	**TAHR** see ur ¶25
tanager	**TAN** uh jur	tarsus	**TAHR** sus
tandem	**TAN** dum	tartan	**TAHRT** un
tangelo	**TAN** juh loh	tartar	**TAHR** tur
tangent	**TAN** junt	Tarzan	**TAHR** zan or **TAHR** zun ¶8
tangential	tan **JEN** shul ¶9, 12	Tass	**TAHS** ¶18
tangerine	tan juh **REEN** ¶2	tassel	**TAS** ul
tangible	**TAN** ji bul	tatami	tuh **TAH** mee
Tangier	tan **JIR**	Tatar	**TAHT** ur
tangle	**TANG** gul	tatterdemalion	TAT ur di **MAYL** yun ¶25
tango	**TANG** goh	tattoo	ta **TOOH**
tangy	**TANG** ee	taunt	**TAWNT** ¶19
tantalize	**TAN** tuh lyze	taupe	**TOHP**
tantamount	**TAN** tuh mownt	Taurus	**TAWR** us
		taut	**TAWT**

SPELLED	PRONOUNCED
tautological	TAWT uh **LAHJ** i kul
tautology	taw **TAHL** uh jee ¶1
tavern	**TAV** urn
tawdry	**TAW** dree
taxation	tak **SAY** shun
taxidermy	**TAK** si DUR mee
taximeter	**TAK** see MEET ur
taxonomic	**TAK** suh **NAHM** ik
taxonomy	tak **SAHN** uh mee
Tay–Sachs (disease)	**TAY SAKS**
Tchaikovsky	chye **KAWF** skee
tear ("rip")	**TER**
tear ("eye fluid")	**TIR**
teasel	**TEE** zul
teaser	**TEE** zur
teat	**TEET** or **TIT**
technical	**TEK** ni kul
technicality	TEK nuh **KAL** uh tee
technician	tek **NISH** un
technique	tek **NEEK**
technocracy	tek **NAHK** ruh see
technological	TEK nuh **LAHJ** i kul
technology	tek **NAHL** uh jee
tectonics	tek **TAHN** iks
Tecumseh	ti **KUM** suh
tedious	**TEE** dee us or **TEE** jus
tedium	**TEE** dee um
teethe	**TEEDH**
teetotaler	TEE **TOHT** ul ur ¶2, 5
Teheran	tay uh **RAHN** ¶18
Tel Aviv	tel uh **VEEV** ¶2
telecast	**TEL** uh kast ¶18
telegraph	**TEL** uh graph ¶18
telemeter	**TEL** uh **MEET** ur or tuh **LEM** uh tur

SPELLED	PRONOUNCED
telemetric	TEL uh **MET** rik
teleological	**TEE** lee uh **LAHJ** i kul or TEL ee uh **LAHJ** i kul
teleology	**TEE** lee **AHL** uh jee or TEL ee **AHL** uh jee
telepathic	TEL uh **PATH** ik ¶18
telepathy	tuh **LEP** uh thee
telephonic	TEL uh **FAHN** ik
telescope	**TEL** uh skohp
telescopic	TEL uh **SKAHP** ik
telescopy	tuh **LES** kuh pee
telethon	**TEL** uh thahn
televise	**TEL** uh vyze
television	TEL uh **VIZH** un
temerity	tuh **MER** uh tee
tempera	**TEM** pur uh
temperamental	TEM pruh **MENT** ul TEM pur **MENT** ul *is also heard in rapid speech.* ¶4, 5
temperance	**TEM** pur uns ¶5
temperate	**TEM** pur it ¶5
temperature	**TEM** pruh chur *Both* TEM pur chur *and* TEM puh chur *are heard in rapid speech.* ¶4, 5, 17
tempest	**TEM** pist
tempestuous	tem **PES** choo wus ¶1
template	**TEM** plit
temporal	**TEM** pur ul ¶5
temporary	**TEM** puh **RER** ee ¶5, 24
temporize	**TEM** puh ryze
tempura	tem **POOR** uh or TEM poo rah
tenable	**TEN** uh bul
tenacious	tuh **NAY** shus

SPELLED	PRONOUNCED	SPELLED	PRONOUNCED
tenacity	tuh **NAS** uh tee	tern	**TURN**
tenancy	**TEN** un see	Terpsichore	turp **SIK** ur ee
tenant	**TEN** unt	terrace	**TER** us
tendency	**TEN** dun see	terra cotta	TER uh **KAHT** uh
tendentious	ten **DEN** shus ¶9, 12	terrain	tuh **RAYN**
tenderize	**TEN** duh ryze	terrapin	**TER** uh pin
tenderloin	**TEN** dur loyn	terrarium	tuh **RAR** ee um ¶23
tendinitis	TEN duh **NYTE** is	terrazzo	tuh **RAZ** oh *or*
tendon	**TEN** dun		tuh **RAHT** soh ¶1
tendril	**TEN** drul	terrestrial	tuh **RES** tree ul
tenement	**TEN** uh munt	terrible	**TER** uh bul
tenet	**TEN** it	terrier	**TER** ee ur
Tennessee	ten uh **SEE**	terrific	tuh **RIF** ik
tenon	**TEN** un	terrify	**TER** uh fye
tenor	**TEN** ur	territorial	TER uh **TAWR** ee ul ¶25
tensile	**TEN** sul ¶9	territory	**TER** uh TAWR ee
tension	**TEN** shun ¶9, 12	terror	**TER** ur
tensor	**TEN** sur *or* **TEN** sawr ¶9	tertiary	**TUR** shee ER ee *or*
tentacle	**TEN** tuh kul		**TUR** shur ee
tentative	**TEN** tuh tiv	terza rima	**TERT** suh **REE** muh
tenuous	**TEN** yoo wus	tessitura	TES i **TOOR** uh
tenure	**TEN** yur	testament	**TES** tuh munt
tepid	**TEP** id	testate	**TES** tayt
tequila	tuh **KEE** luh	testator	**TES** tayt ur ¶2
tercet	**TUR** sit	testes	**TES** teez
tur **SET** *is sometimes heard.*		testicle	**TES** ti kul
tergiversate	**TUR** ji vur SAYT	testify	**TES** tuh fye
teriyaki	TER ee **YAH** kee	testimonial	
termagant	**TUR** muh gunt		TES tuh **MOH** nee ul ¶25
terminal	**TUR** muh nul	testimony	**TES** tuh MOH nee
terminate	**TUR** muh nayt	testosterone	tes **TAHS** tuh rohn
termination	TUR muh **NAY** shun	tetanus	**TET** un us
terminology	TUR muh **NAHL** uh jee	tête–à–tête	**TAYT** uh **TAYT** *or*
terminus	**TUR** muh nus		TET ah **TET**
termite	**TUR** myte	tether	**TEDH** ur

SPELLED	PRONOUNCED	SPELLED	PRONOUNCED

tetracycline .... TET ruh SYE kleen
*Doctors and patients alike have
settled on this pronunciation, but
formerly both* TET ruh SYE klin *and*
TET ruh SYE klyne *were common.*

tetrahedron .... TET ruh HEE drun

tetralogy .... te TRAL uh jee ¶1

tetrameter .... te TRAM uh tur ¶1

Teuton .... TOOHT un
also, more recently,
TOOH tahn ¶8, 21

Teutonic .... tooh TAHN ik ¶21

textile .... TEKS tyle ¶22

textual .... TEKS choo wul ¶5

texture .... TEKS chur

Thai .... TYE

thalamus .... THAL uh mus

Thames .... TEMZ
*The river in Connecticut is
usually* THAYMZ.

thanatopsis .... THAN uh TAHP sis

the .... dhuh
before vowels dhi *or* dhee; *also,
when emphasized,* DHEE

theater .... THEE uh tur
also thee AYT ur, *but this is
generally disapproved*

theatrical .... thee AT ri kul

theatrics .... thee AT riks

Thebes .... THEEBZ

thee .... DHEE

theism .... THEE iz um

thematic .... thee MAT ik ¶1

themselves .... dhem SELVZ ¶1

thence .... DHENS *or* THENS ¶9

theocracy .... thee AHK ruh see

theocratic .... THEE uh KRAT ik

theodicy .... thee AHD uh see

theologian ...... THEE uh LOH jun ¶2

theological .... THEE uh LAHJ i kul

theology .... thee AHL uh jee

theorem .... THEE uh rum *or*
THIR um ¶5

theoretical .... THEE uh RET i kul

theoretician ....
.... THEE uh ruh TISH un ¶5

theorize .... THEE uh ryze

theory ... THEE uh ree *or* THIR ee ¶5

theosophy .... thee AHS uh fee

therapeutic .... THER uh PYOOHT ik

therapy .... THER uh pee

thermal .... THUR mul

thermodynamics ....
.... THUR moh dye NAM iks

thermometer .... thur MAHM uh tur

thermos .... THUR mus

thermostat .... THUR muh stat

thesaurus .... thi SAWR us

Theseus .... THEE see us *or*
THEE soohs ¶21

thesis .... THEE sis

Thespian .... THES pee un

theta .... THAYT uh
occasionally THEET uh

thews .... THYOOHZ

thiamine .... THYE uh min ¶22

thievery .... THEE vur ee ¶5

thimble .... THIM bul

thine .... DHYNE

thingamajig .... THING uh muh JIG

third	THURD	thyme	TYME
thirst	THURST	*The spelling pronunciation*	
thistle	THIS ul	**THYME** *is not standard.*	
thither	THIDH ur *or* DHIDH ur	thymus	THYE mus
Thomism	TOH miz um	thyroid	THYE royd
thong	THAWNG ¶19	thyself	dhye SELF
thoracic	thaw RAS ik ¶1	tiara	tee AR uh *or* tee AHR uh ¶23
thorax	THAWR aks	Tibet	ti BET
thorough	THUR oh	tibia	TIB ee uh ¶25
THUR uh *is heard in some regions,*		tic douloureux	TIK dooh luh ROOH
especially the South.		ticklish	TIK lish
thoroughbred	THUR uh bred	Ticonderoga	TYE kahn duh ROH guh
thou	DHOW	tidal	TYDE ul
though	DHOH	tiddlywinks	TID lee wingks ¶5
thought	THAWT ¶19	tidy	TYE dee
thousand	THOW zund ¶10	tier	TIR
Thracian	THRAY shun	tiercel	TIR sul
thrall	THRAWL ¶19	Tierra del Fuego	
thread	THRED		tee ER uh del fooh AY goh
threat	THRET	tiffany	TIF uh nee ¶5
threepence	THREP uns *or* THRIP uns	tiger	TYE gur
	or THRUP uns ¶9	tightrope	TYTE rohp
threshold	THRESH ohld *or*	tigress	TYE gris
	THRESH hohld	Tigris	TYE gris
thrombosis	thrahm BOH sis	Tijuana	tee uh WAH nuh *or*
throng	THRAWNG ¶19		tee WAH nuh
throttle	THRAHT ul	tilde	TIL duh
through	THROOH	tillage	TIL ij
throw	THROH	timberland	TIM bur land
Thule	THOOH lee	timbre	TAM bur *or* TIM bur
in Greenland, TOOH lee		timely	TYME lee
thumb	THUM	timid	TIM id
Thursday	THURZ dee *or* THURZ day	timorous	TIM ur us ¶5
thus	DHUS	timpani	TIM puh nee
thwart	THWAWRT	tincture	TINGK chur ¶12

SPELLED	PRONOUNCED
tinder	**TIN** dur
tinge	**TINJ** ¶15
tingle	**TING** gul
tinnitus	ti **NYTE** us
tinsel	**TIN** sul ¶9, 14
tintinnabulation	TIN tuh **NAB** yuh **LAY** shun
Tipperary	TIP uh **RAR** ee ¶23
tirade	**TYE** rayd
Tirol	**TIR** ahl *or* **TYE** rohl
Tirolean	ti **ROH** lee un
tissue	**TISH** ooh
Titan	**TYTE** un
titanic	tye **TAN** ik
tithe	**TYDHE**
titian	**TISH** un
titillate	**TIT** uh layt
title	**TYTE** ul
titlist	**TYTE** list ¶5
titular	**TICH** uh lur *also, but especially British,* **TIT** yuh lur
Tivoli	**TIV** uh lee
toady	**TOH** dee
tobacco	tuh **BAK** oh
tobacconist	tuh **BAK** uh nist
Tobago	toh **BAY** goh ¶1
toboggan	tuh **BAH** gun ¶19
toccata	tuh **KAHT** uh ¶1
Tocqueville	**TOHK** vil *or* tohk **VEEL**
today	tuh **DAY**
toffee	**TAWF** ee ¶19
tofu	**TOH** fooh
toga	**TOH** guh
together	tuh **GEDH** ur

SPELLED	PRONOUNCED
toilet	**TOY** lit
toilette	twah **LET** *or* toy **LET**
Tokay	toh **KAY** ¶2
Tokyo	**TOH** kee oh
tolerable	**TAHL** ur uh bul ¶5
tolerate	**TAHL** uh rayt
toleration	TAHL uh **RAY** shun
Tolkien	**TAHL** keen
Tolstoy	**TOHL** stoy ¶2, 20
Toltec	**TAHL** tek ¶20
toluene	**TAHL** yoo ween ¶20
tomahawk	**TAHM** uh hawk
tomato	tuh **MAYT** oh tuh **MAHT** oh, *which is chiefly British, is no longer much heard in the U.S.*
tomb	**TOOHM**
tome	**TOHM**
tomfoolery	tahm **FOOHL** ur ee ¶5
tomorrow	tuh **MAHR** oh ¶1, 19
tonal	**TOH** nul
tonality	toh **NAL** uh tee ¶1
tongue	**TUNG**
tonic	**TAHN** ik
tonight	tuh **NYTE**
tonnage	**TUN** ij
tonsil	**TAHN** sul ¶9
tonsillectomy	TAHN suh **LEK** tuh mee ¶9
tonsillitis	TAHN suh **LYTE** is ¶9
tonsorial	tahn **SAWR** ee ul ¶25
tonsure	**TAHN** shur
tooth *(noun)*	**TOOHTH** *For the verb,* **TOOHDH** *is also heard.*

SPELLED	PRONOUNCED
toothed	TOOHTHT *or* TOOHDHD
toots	TOOTS
topaz	TOH paz
topiary	TOH pee ER ee
topic	TAHP ik
topographical	
....	TAHP uh GRAF i kul ¶18
topography ...	tuh PAHG ruh fee ¶19
topology	tuh PAHL uh jee
toque	TOHK
Torah, Tora	TOH ruh *or* toh RAH
popularly	TAWR uh
toreador	TAWR ee uh DAWR
torero	tuh RER oh
torment *(noun)*	TAWR ment
The verb is usually tawr MENT.	
tormentor	tawr MEN tur ¶2
tornado	tawr NAY doh
torpedo	tawr PEE doh
torpid	TAWR pid
torpor	TAWR pur
torque	TAWRK
torrent	TAWR unt ¶19
torrential ...	taw REN shul ¶1, 9, 12
torrid	TAWR id ¶19
torsion	TAWR shun
torso	TAWR soh
torte	TAWRT
tortellini	TAWR tuh LEE nee
tortilla	tawr TEE uh
tortoise	TAWR tus
tortuous	TAWR choo wus
torture	TAWR chur
Tory	TAWR ee
Toscanini	TAHS kuh NEE nee ¶19

SPELLED	PRONOUNCED
tostada	tohs TAH duh
total	TOHT ul
totalitarian ..	toh TAL uh TAR ee un *or*
	TOH tal uh TAR ee un ¶23
totality	toh TAL uh tee
totem	TOHT um
toucan	TOOH kan
touch	TUCH
touché	tooh SHAY
tough	TUF
Toulouse–Lautrec	
....	tooh LOOHZ loh TREK ¶14
toupee	tooh PAY
tour de force	toor duh FAWRS
tourism	TOOR iz um ¶24
tourist	TOOR ist ¶24
tournament	TOOR nuh munt ¶24
tourniquet	TOOR nuh kit ¶24
Tours	TOOR
tousle	TOW zul
tout	TOWT
tout de suite	tooht SWEET
toward *(preposition)*	TAWRD *or*
	tuh WAWRD
toward *(adjective)*	TOH urd
towel	TOW ul ¶7
tower	TOW ur ¶7
towhee	TOW hee *or* TOH hee
townsman	TOWNZ mun
toxemia	tahk SEE mee uh
toxic	TAHK sik
toxicity	tahk SIS uh tee
toxicology ...	TAHK si KAHL uh jee
toxin	TAHK sin
trachea	TRAY kee uh

SPELLED	PRONOUNCED
tracheotomy	... TRAY kee AHT uh mee
tract	.... TRAKT
not to be confused with track	
	TRAK
tractile	.... TRAK tul ¶22
traction	.... TRAK shun
tractor	.... TRAK tur
tradition	.... truh DISH un
traditionalist	.... truh DISH un ul ist
traduce	.... truh DOOHS ¶21
Trafalgar	.... truh FAL gur
tragedian	.... truh JEE dee un
tragedienne	.... truh JEE dee EN
tragedy	.... TRAJ uh dee
tragic	.... TRAJ ik
tragus	.... TRAY gus
traipse	.... TRAYPS
traitor	.... TRAYT ur
trajectory	.... truh JEK tur ee ¶5
trampoline	.... TRAM puh leen ¶2
occasionally TRAM puh lin	
trance	.... TRANS ¶9, 18
tranquil	.... TRANG kwul ¶16
tranquilize	.... TRANG kwuh lyze ¶16
tranquillity	.... tran KWIL uh tee ¶16
trans–	.... trans ¶9, 14
transaction	.... tran ZAK shun *or*
	tran SAK shun
transceiver	.... tran SEE vur
transcend	.... tran SEND
transcendental	....	
	.... TRAN sen DEN tul ¶1
transcribe	.... tran SKRYBE
transcript	.... TRAN skript
transcription	.... tran SKRIP shun

SPELLED	PRONOUNCED
transfer *(verb)*	.... trans FUR ¶2
The noun is always TRANS fur.	
transference	.... trans FUR uns *or*
	TRANS fur uns ¶9
transform	.... trans FAWRM ¶2
transformation	....	
	.... TRANS fur MAY shun
transfuse	.... trans FYOOHZ *or*
	tranz FYOOHZ
transgress	.. trans GRES *or* tranz GRES
transient	.... TRAN shunt ¶25
transistor	... tran ZIS tur *or* tran SIS tur
transit	.... TRAN sit ¶14
transition	.... tran ZISH un ¶14
transitive	.... TRAN suh tiv ¶9, 14
transitory	... TRAN suh TAWR ee ¶14
translate	.... TRANS layt ¶2, 14
translation	.... trans LAY shun ¶14
translator	...... TRANS layt ur ¶2, 14
transliterate	... trans LIT uh rayt ¶14
translucent	.... trans LOOH sunt *or*
	tranz LOOH sunt
transmission	..... trans MISH un ¶14
transmit	.... trans MIT ¶2, 14
transmitter	.... TRANS mit ur ¶2, 14
transmute	.... trans MYOOHT ¶14
transom	.... TRAN sum ¶9
transparent	.. trans PAR unt ¶14, 23
transpire	.... trans PYRE ¶14
transplant *(verb)*	....	
	.... trans PLANT ¶2, 14
transplant *(noun)*	....	
	.... TRANS plant ¶14
transport *(verb)*	....	
	.... trans PAWRT ¶2, 14

transport *(noun)*		treble .... **TREB** ul
.... **TRANS** pawrt ¶14		trefoil .... **TREE** foyl
transportation		tremble .... **TREM** bul
.... TRANS pur **TAY** shun ¶14		tremendous .... tri **MEN** dus
transpose .. trans **POHZ** *or* tranz **POHZ**		tremolo .... **TREM** uh loh
transposition .. TRANS puh **ZISH** un *or*		tremor .... **TREM** ur
TRANZ puh **ZISH** un		tremulous .... **TREM** yoo lus
Transvaal .... trans **VAHL** ¶14		trenchant .... **TREN** chunt
transverse .... trans **VURS** *or*		trepan .... tri **PAN**
tranz **VURS** ¶2		trepidation .... TREP uh **DAY** shun
transvestite .... trans **VES** tyte		trespass *(noun)* .... **TRES** pus
Transylvania		*also, and especially for the verb,*
.... TRAN sul **VAY** nee uh ¶14, 25		**TRES** pas ¶8, 18
trapeze .... tra **PEEZ** ¶1		trestle .... **TRES** ul
trapezium .... truh **PEE** zee um		trey .... **TRAY**
trapezoid .... **TRAP** uh zoyd		triad .... **TRYE** ad
trauma ...... **TROW** muh *or* **TRAW** muh		trial .... **TRYE** ul ¶7
traumatize .... **TROW** muh tyze *or*		triangle .... **TRYE** ang gul
TRAW muh tyze		triangulate .... trye **ANG** gyuh layt
travail .... truh **VAYL** *or* **TRAV** ayl		Triassic .... trye **AS** ik
travel .... **TRAV** ul		tribulation .... TRIB yuh **LAY** shun
travelogue .... **TRAV** uh lawg ¶19		tribunal .... trye **BYOOH** nul ¶1
traverse *(verb)* .... truh **VURS**		tribune .... **TRIB** yoohn
also, and for the noun and		*in names of newspapers, often*
adjective always, **TRAV** urs		tri **BYOOHN**
travesty .... **TRAV** is tee		tributary .... **TRIB** yoo **TER** ee ¶23
trawl .... **TRAWL**		tribute .... **TRIB** yooht ¶2
treachery .... **TRECH** ur ee ¶5		triceps .... **TRYE** seps
treacle .... **TREE** kul		triceratops .... trye **SER** uh tahps
tread .... **TRED**		trichinosis .... TRIK uh **NOH** sis
treason .... **TREE** zun		tricot .... **TREE** koh
treasure .... **TREZH** ur		trident .... **TRYDE** unt
treasury .... **TREZH** ur ee ¶5		trifecta .... trye **FEK** tuh
treatise .... **TREET** is		trifle .... **TRYE** ful
treaty .... **TREET** ee		trifocal .... trye **FOH** kul ¶2

SPELLED	PRONOUNCED
trifocals	**TRYE** foh kulz
trigeminal	trye **JEM** uh nul
trigonometry	TRIG uh **NAHM** uh tree
trillium	**TRIL** ee um
trilogy	**TRIL** uh jee
trimester	trye **MES** tur ¶2
trinitarian	TRIN uh **TER** ee un ¶23
trinity	**TRIN** uh tee
trinket	**TRING** kit
trinomial	trye **NOH** mee ul ¶25
tripartite	trye **PAHR** tyte
triple	**TRIP** ul
triplet	**TRIP** lit
triplicate	**TRIP** luh kit
tripod	**TRYE** pahd
triptych	**TRIP** tik
trisect	trye **SEKT** ¶2
triumph	**TRYE** umf ¶9
triumphant	trye **UM** funt ¶6, 9
triumvir	trye **UM** vur
triumvirate	trye **UM** vur it ¶5
trivet	**TRIV** it
trivia	**TRIV** ee uh ¶25
trivial	**TRIV** ee ul ¶25
triviality	TRIV ee **AL** uh tee
trochaic	troh **KAY** ik
trochee	**TROH** kee
troglodyte	**TRAHG** luh dyte
troika	**TROY** kuh
Troilus	**TROY** lus *or* **TROH** i lus
Trojan	**TROH** jun
troll	**TROHL**
trolley	**TRAHL** ee
trollop	**TRAHL** up
trombone	trahm **BOHN** ¶2

SPELLED	PRONOUNCED
trophy	**TROH** fee
tropic	**TRAHP** ik
tropism	**TROH** piz um
troposphere	**TROH** puh sfir ¶20
tropospheric	TROH puh **SFER** ik ¶20
troth	**TRAWTH** ¶19, 20
troubadour	**TROOH** buh dawr
trouble	**TRUB** ul
trough	**TRAWF** ¶19

In folk speech **TRAWTH** *or* **TROH** *is heard.*

SPELLED	PRONOUNCED
troupe	**TROOHP**
trousers	**TROW** zurz
trousseau	**TROOH** soh ¶2
trowel	**TROW** ul ¶7
truancy	**TROOH** un see ¶9
truant	**TROOH** unt
truce	**TROOHS**
truculent	**TRUK** yoo lunt
truffle	**TRUF** ul

rarely **TROOH** ful

SPELLED	PRONOUNCED
truly	**TROOH** lee
trumpery	**TRUM** pur ee
trumpet	**TRUM** pit
truncate	**TRUNG** kayt ¶16
truncheon	**TRUN** chun
trundle	**TRUN** dul
trustee	trus **TEE**
trusty	**TRUS** tee
truth	**TROOHTH**

The plural **truths** *is either* **TROOHDHZ** *or* **TROOHTHS**.

SPELLED	PRONOUNCED
tryst	**TRIST** *or* **TRYSTE**
tsar	**ZAHR** *or* **TSAHR**

tsetse .... **TSET** see *or* **TSEET** see *or* **SET** see *or* **SEET** see	
tuba .... **TOOH** buh ¶21	
tubal .... **TOOH** bul ¶21	
tube .... **TOOHB** ¶21	
tuber .... **TOOH** bur ¶21	
tubercular ..... too **BUR** kyuh lur ¶21	
tuberculosis .... too **BUR** kyuh **LOH** sis ¶21	
tubular .... **TOOH** byuh lur ¶21	
Tucson .... **TOOH** sahn	
Tudor .... **TOOH** dur ¶21	
Tuesday .... **TOOHZ** dee *or* **TOOHZ** day ¶8, 21	
tuffet .... **TUF** it	
Tuileries .. **TWEE** lur eez *or* tweel **REE**	
tuition .... too **WISH** un ¶21	
tularemia .... **TOOH** luh **REE** mee uh ¶25	
tulip .... **TOOH** lip ¶21	
tulle .... **TOOHL**	
tumble .... **TUM** bul	
tumbler .... **TUM** blur ¶7	
tumbrel .... **TUM** brul	
tumescence .... tooh **MES** uns ¶9, 21	
tumid .... **TOOH** mid ¶21	
tumor .... **TOOH** mur ¶21	
tumult .... **TOOH** mult ¶21	
tumultuous .... too **MUL** choo wus ¶1, 21	
tuna .... **TOOH** nuh ¶21	
tundra .... **TUN** druh *occasionally* **TOON** druh	
tune .... **TOOHN** ¶21	
tungsten .... **TUNG** stun	

tunic .... **TOOH** nik ¶21	
Tunisia .... tooh **NEE** zhuh ¶21 *also* tooh **NISH** uh	
tunnel .... **TUN** ul	
tupelo .... **TOOH** puh loh	
Tupi .... tooh **PEE** ¶2	
turban .... **TUR** bun	
turbine .... **TUR** bun ¶22	
turbocharger ...... **TUR** boh **CHAHR** jur	
turbot .... **TUR** but *sometimes altered, as if French, to* **TUR** boh, *which is not standard*	
turbulent .... **TUR** byuh lunt	
tureen .... too **REEN** ¶1	
turgid .... **TUR** jid	
turmeric .... **TUR** mur ik	
turmoil .... **TUR** moyl	
turpentine .... **TUR** pun tyne	
turpitude .... **TUR** puh toohd ¶21	
turquoise ...... **TUR** koyz *or* **TUR** kwoyz	
turret .... **TUR** it	
turtle .... **TURT** ul	
Tuscany .... **TUS** kuh nee	
tussock .... **TUS** uk	
Tutankhamen .... **TOOH** ahngk **AH** mun	
tutelage .... **TOOHT** ul ij ¶21	
tutelary .... **TOOHT** ul **ER** ee ¶21	
tutor .... **TOOHT** ur ¶21	
tutorial .... tooh **TAWR** ee ul ¶1, 21, 25	
tutti–frutti ..... **TOOHT** ee **FROOHT** ee	
tutu .... **TOOH** tooh	
tuxedo .... tuk **SEE** doh	
twaddle .... **TWAHD** ul	

SPELLED	PRONOUNCED
tweak	**TWEEK**
twelfth	**TWELFTH** ¶10
twelve	**TWELV**
twenty	**TWUN** tee or **TWEN** tee ¶10
twilight	**TWYE** lyte
twilit	**TWYE** lit
twine	**TWYNE**
twinge	**TWINJ** ¶15
twinkle	**TWING** kul
twirl	**TWURL**
twitch	**TWICH**
two	**TOOH**
twopence	**TUP** uns ¶9
twosome	**TOOH** sum
tycoon	tye **KOOHN**
tympanic	tim **PAN** ik
Tyndale	**TIN** dul
typhoid	**TYE** foyd
typhoon	tye **FOOHN**
typhus	**TYE** fus
typical	**TIP** i kul
typify	**TIP** uh fye
typist	**TYE** pist
typographical	**TYE** puh **GRAF** i kul ¶18
typography	tye **PAHG** ruh fee
typology	tye **PAHL** uh jee
tyrannical	ti **RAN** i kul
tyrannize	**TIR** uh nyze
tyrannosaur	ti **RAN** uh sawr or tye **RAN** uh sawr
tyranny	**TIR** uh nee
tyrant	**TYE** runt
tyro	**TYE** roh
tzar	**ZAHR** or **TSAHR**

U

SPELLED	PRONOUNCED
ubiquitous	yooh **BIK** wuh tus ¶1
UFO	**YOOH** foh or yooh ef **OH**
ufologist	yooh **FAHL** uh jist
Uganda	yooh **GAN** duh or ooh **GAHN** duh
ukase	**YOOH** kays ¶2, 14
Ukrainian	yooh **KRAY** nee un *occasionally* yooh **KRYE** nee un ¶25
ukulele	**YOOH** kuh **LAY** lee *The Hawaiian is* OOH koo **LAY** lay.
ulcer	**UL** sur
ulcerate	**UL** suh rayt
ulna	**UL** nuh
ulterior	ul **TIR** ee ur
ultimate	**UL** tuh mit
ultimatum	**UL** tuh **MAYT** um
ultra	**UL** truh
ultramontane	**UL** truh **MAHN** tayn or **UL** truh mahn **TAYN**
ululate	**YOOHL** yoo layt or **UL** yoo layt
Ulysses	yoo **LIS** eez
umbilical	um **BIL** i kul
umbra	**UM** bruh
umbrage	**UM** brij
umbrella	um **BREL** uh
umlaut	**OOM** lowt or **OOHM** lowt
unanimity	**YOOH** nuh **NIM** uh tee

SPELLED	PRONOUNCED
unanimous	yoo **NAN** uh mus ¶1
unawares	un uh **WERZ**
unbecoming	UN bi **KUM** ing ¶1
unblessed	un **BLEST**
unbridled	un **BRYE** duld
uncanny	un **KAN** ee
uncial	**UN** shee ul ¶25
unconscionable	
	un **KAHN** shun uh bul
unconscious	un **KAHN** shus ¶9, 12
uncouth	un **KOOTH**
unction	**UNGK** shun ¶9
unctuous	**UNGK** choo wus ¶9
undaunted	un **DAWN** tid ¶19
undecided	UN di **SYDE** id
undergraduate	UN dur **GRAJ** oo wit
undermine	un dur **MYNE** ¶2
underneath	un dur **NEETH**
underpass	**UN** dur pas ¶18
underprivileged	
	UN dur **PRIV** ul ijd ¶5
understand	un dur **STAND**
undulant	**UN** joo lunt ¶17
undulate	**UN** joo layt ¶17
undulation	UN joo **LAY** shun ¶17
undulatory	
	UN joo luh **TAWR** ee ¶17
unerring	un **UR** ing *or* un **ER** ing
UNESCO	yoo **NES** koh
unexceptionable	
	UN ik **SEP** shun uh bul
unfamiliar	UN fuh **MIL** yur
unflappable	un **FLAP** uh bul
ungainly	un **GAYN** lee
unguent	**UNG** gwunt

SPELLED	PRONOUNCED
unhallowed	un **HAL** ohd
unicameral	YOOH nuh **KAM** ur ul
unicorn	**YOOH** nuh kawrn
uniform	**YOOH** nuh fawrm
uniformity	YOOH nuh **FAWR** muh tee
unify	**YOOH** nuh fye
unilateral	YOOH nuh **LAT** ur ul
union	**YOOHN** yun
unique	yoo **NEEK** ¶1
unison	**YOOH** nuh sun ¶14
unit	**YOOH** nit
Unitarian	
	YOOH nuh **TAR** ee un ¶23
unitary	**YOOH** nuh **TER** ee ¶23
unite	yoo **NYTE**
unitize	**YOOH** nuh tyze
unity	**YOOH** nuh tee
univalent	YOOH nuh **VAY** lunt
occasionally yoo **NIV** uh lunt	
universal	YOOH nuh **VUR** sul
universality	
	YOOH nuh vur **SAL** uh tee
universe	**YOOH** nuh vurs
university	YOOH nuh **VUR** suh tee
unkempt	un **KEMPT** ¶9
unlearned	un **LUR** nid *or* un **LURND**:
	see learned
unmitigated	un **MIT** uh gayt id
unprecedented	un **PRES** uh **DEN** tid
unquestionable	
	un **KWES** chun uh bul ¶11
unrivaled	un **RYE** vuld
unruly	un **ROOH** lee
unscathed	un **SKAYDHD**
unseemly	un **SEEM** lee

unstrung	un **STRUNG**
untenable	un **TEN** uh bul
untoward	un **TOH** urd *or* un **TAWRD**
untutored	un **TOOHT** urd ¶21
unutterable	un **UT** ur uh bul
unwieldy	un **WEEL** dee
unwind	un **WYNDE**
unwonted	un **WUN** tid *or* un **WAWN** tid
upheaval	up **HEE** vul
upholster	up **HOHL** stur *or* uh **POHL** stur
upland	**UP** lund *or* **UP** land
uproarious	up **RAWR** ee us
upset *(verb)*	up **SET**

The noun is **UP** set, *and the adjective may be either, but usually the stress is nearly equal.*

upsilon	**YOOHP** suh lahn *or* **UP** suh lahn
upsy–daisy	**UP** suh **DAY** zee *or* **UP** see **DAY** zee
Ural	**YOOR** ul
uranium	yoo **RAY** nee um
Uranus	**YOOR** uh nus *or* yoo **RAY** nus
urban	**UR** bun
urbane	ur **BAYN**
urbanity	ur **BAN** uh tee
urbanize	**UR** buh nyze
urchin	**UR** chin
urea	yoo **REE** uh *or* **YOOR** ee uh
uremia	yoo **REE** mee uh ¶25
ureter	yoo **REET** ur
urethra	yoo **REE** thruh
urgency	**UR** jun see ¶9

urgent	**UR** junt
uric	**YOOR** ik ¶24
urinal	**YOOR** uh nul ¶24
urinalysis	YOOR uh **NAL** uh sis ¶24
urinary	**YOOR** uh **NER** ee ¶23, 24
urinate	**YOOR** uh nayt ¶24
urine	**YOOR** un ¶24
urology	yoo **RAHL** uh jee
Ursuline	**UR** suh lin ¶22
Uruguay	**YOOR** uh gway *or* **YOOR** uh gwye ¶24
usage	**YOOH** sij
use *(verb)*	**YOOHZ**

The past tense and past participle used *is* **YOOHZD** *in expressions like* "I used four quarts," *but* **YOOHS** *in* "I used to smoke" *or* "I'm used to it."

useful	**YOOHS** ful
useless	**YOOHS** lis
user	**YOOH** zur
usher	**USH** ur
usual	**YOOH** zhoo wul *or* **YOOH** zhul ¶5
usurp	yooh **SURP** ¶14
usury	**YOOH** zhur ee
utensil	yoo **TEN** sil ¶9
uterine	**YOOHT** ur in ¶22
uterus	**YOOHT** ur us
utilitarian	yoo TIL uh **TAR** ee un ¶23
utility	yoo **TIL** uh tee
utilize	**YOOHT** uh lyze
Utopia	yoo **TOH** pee uh ¶1
utterance	**UT** ur uns ¶5, 9

uvula	YOOH vyuh luh
uxorial	uk SAWR ee ul *or*
	ug ZAWR ee ul
Uzbek	OOZ bek
occasionally UZ bek	

V

vacancy	VAY kun see ¶9
vacant	VAY kunt
vacate	VAY kayt
vacation	vay KAY shun ¶1
vaccinate	VAK suh nayt
vaccination	VAK suh NAY shun
vaccine	vak SEEN ¶2
vacillate	VAS uh layt
vacuity	va KYOOH uh tee
vacuous	VAK yoo wus
vacuum *(noun)*	VAK yoo wum *or*
	VAK yoom

The adjective and verb are nearly always VAK yoom.

vagabond	VAG uh bahnd
vagary	vuh GAR ee ¶1, 23

Many people say VAY gur ee, *which is now also standard.*

vagina	vuh JYE nuh
vagrancy	VAY grun see ¶9
vagrant	VAY grunt

vague	VAYG
vagus	VAY gus
vainglorious	vayn GLAWR ee us
vainglory	VAYN glawr ee
valance	VAL uns *or* VAYL uns ¶9
valediction	VAL uh DIK shun
valedictorian	
	VAL uh dik TAWR ee un ¶25
valedictory	VAL uh DIK tur ee ¶5
valence	VAY luns ¶9
Valencia	vuh LEN see uh ¶11, 25
valentine	VAL un tyne
valet	VAL it *or* VAL ay *or* va LAY
valetudinarian	
	VAL uh TOOH duh NAR ee un ¶21, 23, 25
Valhalla	val HAL uh ¶18
valiant	VAL yunt ¶25
valid	VAL id
validate	VAL uh dayt
validity	vuh LID uh tee
valise	vuh LEES
Valkyrie	val KIR ee *or* VAL ki ree
valor	VAL ur
Valparaiso	VAL puh RAY zoh *or* VAL puh RYE soh
valuable	VAL yoo bul ¶5
valuation	VAL yoo WAY shun
value	VAL yooh ¶1
valve	VALV
vamoose	va MOOHS
vampire	VAM pyre
vampirism	VAM pyre iz um *or* VAM pi riz um
vanadium	vuh NAY dee um

vandal .... **VAN** dul

vandalize .... **VAN** duh lyze

vanguard .... **VAN** gahrd ¶16

vanilla .... vuh **NIL** uh

vanish .... **VAN** ish

vanity .... **VAN** uh tee

vanquish .... **VANG** kwish ¶16

vantage .... **VAN** tij

vapid .... **VAP** id

   occasionally **VAY** pid

vapor .... **VAY** pur

variable .... **VAR** ee uh bul ¶23

variant .... **VAR** ee unt ¶23

variation .... **VAR** ee **AY** shun

varicose .... **VAR** uh kohs

variegated .. **VAR** ee uh **GAYT** id ¶25

varietal .... vuh **RYE** uh tul

variety .... vuh **RYE** uh tee

various .... **VAR** ee us ¶23

varmint .... **VAHR** munt

varnish .... **VAHR** nish

varsity .... **VAHR** suh tee

vary .... **VAR** ee ¶23

vascular .... **VAS** kyuh lur

vas deferens .... VAS **DEF** uh renz

vase .... **VAYS** ¶14

   VAHZ *is chiefly British.*

vasectomy .... va **SEK** tuh mee ¶1

vasotomy .... va **SAHT** uh mee

vassal .... **VAS** ul

vassalage .... **VAS** ul ij ¶5

vaudeville .. **VOHD** vil *or* **VAWD** vil ¶5

vaunt .... **VAWNT** ¶19

vector .... **VEK** tur

vegetable .... **VEJ** tuh bul

vegetarian ....

   .... VEJ uh **TAR** ee un ¶23, 25

vegetate .... **VEJ** uh tayt

vegetation .... VEJ uh **TAY** shun

vehement .... **VEE** uh munt

   occasionally **VEE** hi munt

vehicle .... **VEE** uh kul

   occasionally **VEE** hik ul

vehicular .... vee **HIK** yuh lur ¶1

velar .... **VEE** lur

Velázquez .... vuh **LAS** kes *or*

   vuh **LAS** kwez ¶18

veld .... **VELT**

vellum .... **VEL** um

velocipede .... vuh **LAHS** uh peed

velocity .... vuh **LAHS** uh tee

velour .... vuh **LOOR**

velum .... **VEE** lum

velure .... vuh **LOOR**

velvet .... **VEL** vit

venal .... **VEE** nul

venality .... vee **NAL** uh tee ¶1

vendetta .... ven **DET** uh

vendor .... **VEN** dur

veneer .... vuh **NIR**

venerable .... **VEN** ur uh bul ¶5

venerate .... **VEN** uh rayt

venereal .... vuh **NIR** ee ul ¶25

Venetian .... vuh **NEE** shun

Venezuela .... VEN i **ZWAY** luh

   occasionally VEN i **ZWEE** luh

vengeance .... **VEN** juns ¶9

venial .... **VEE** nee ul ¶25

Venice .... **VEN** is

venire .... vuh **NYE** ree

venireman	vuh **NYE** ree mun	verify	**VER** uh fye
venison	**VEN** i sun ¶14	verisimilitude	
venom	**VEN** um		**VER** uh si **MIL** uh toohd ¶21
venous	**VEE** nus	veritable	**VER** i tuh bul
ventilate	**VEN** tuh layt	verity	**VER** uh tee

The first t is invariably sounded in standard speech; that is, not **VEN** *uh layt.*

		Vermeer	vur **MIR**
		vermicelli	VUR muh **CHEL** ee *or*
			VUR muh **SEL** ee
ventricle	**VEN** tri kul	vermifuge	**VUR** muh fyoohj
ventricular	ven **TRIK** yuh lur	vermilion	vur **MIL** yun
ventriloquism	ven **TRIL** uh KWIZ um	vermin	**VUR** mun
ventriloquist	ven **TRIL** uh kwist	vermouth	vur **MOOHTH**
venture	**VEN** chur	vernacular	vur **NAK** yuh lur ¶3
venue	**VEN** yooh	vernal	**VUR** nul
Venus	**VEE** nus	veronica	vuh **RAHN** i kuh
Venusian	vi **NOOH** shun	Versailles	vur **SYE** *or* ver **SYE**
veracious	vuh **RAY** shus		
veracity	vuh **RAS** uh tee		
veranda	vuh **RAN** duh		

vur **SAYLZ** *is the spelling pronunciation used for place names in the U.S.*

verbalize	**VUR** buh lyze	versatile	**VUR** suh tul ¶22
verbatim	vur **BAYT** um	verse	**VURS**
verbena	vur **BEE** nuh	versification	VUR suh fi **KAY** shun
verbiage	**VUR** bee ij ¶25	version	**VUR** zhun

VUR shun *is chiefly British.*

verbose	vur **BOHS**	versus	**VUR** sus *or* **VUR** suz
verbosity	vur **BAHS** uh tee	vertebra	**VUR** tuh bruh
verdant	**VURD** unt		
Verdi	**VER** dee		

The plural form vertebrae *is* **VUR** *tuh* bree *or* **VUR** *tuh* bray.

VUR dee *is also heard but is not applauded by those who play or listen to Verdi's music.*

		vertebrate	**VUR** tuh brit *or*
			VUR tuh brayt
verdict	**VUR** dikt	vertex	**VUR** teks
verdigris	**VUR** di grees *or* **VUR** di gris	vertical	**VUR** ti kul
verdure	**VUR** jur ¶17	vertiginous	vur **TIJ** uh nus
verge	**VURJ**	vertigo	**VURT** uh goh
verification	VER uh fi **KAY** shun	verve	**VURV**

SPELLED	PRONOUNCED
vesicle	**VES** i kul
vesper	**VES** pur
vessel	**VES** ul
vestal	**VES** tul
vestibule	**VES** tuh byoohl
vestige	**VES** tij
vestry	**VES** tree
vesture	**VES** chur
Vesuvius	vuh **SOOH** vee us
veteran	**VET** ur un ¶5
veterinarian	**VET** ur uh **NAR** ee un *or*
	VET ruh **NAR** ee un ¶5, 23
veto	**VEE** toh
vexation	vek **SAY** shun
via	**VYE** uh *or* **VEE** uh
viable	**VYE** uh bul
viaduct	**VYE** uh dukt
vial	**VYE** ul ¶7
viand	**VYE** und
vibrant	**VYE** brunt
vibraphone	**VYE** bruh fohn
vibrate	**VYE** brayt
vibration	vye **BRAY** shun
vibrato	vi **BRAHT** oh
vibrator	**VYE** brayt ur
viburnum	vye **BUR** num
vicar	**VIK** ur
vicarious	vye **KAR** ee us ¶1, 23
vice versa	**VYE** suh **VUR** suh

VYE see *and* **VYSE** *are also heard for the first word.*

SPELLED	PRONOUNCED
Vichy	**VISH** ee *or* **VEE** shee
vichyssoise	vee shee **SWAHZ** *or*
	vish ee **SWAHZ**
vicinity	vi **SIN** uh tee

SPELLED	PRONOUNCED
vicious	**VISH** us
vicissitude	vi **SIS** uh **TOOHD** ¶21
victim	**VIK** tum
victimize	**VIK** tuh myze
victor	**VIK** tur
Victorian	vik **TAWR** ee un ¶25
victorious	vik **TAWR** ee us ¶25
victory	**VIK** tur ee ¶5
victual	**VIT** ul
vicuña	vye **KOOHN** yuh

The variants vye **KOOH** nuh *and* vye **KYOOHN** uh *are common.* ¶21

SPELLED	PRONOUNCED
video	**VID** ee oh
vidicon	**VID** uh kahn
Vienna	vee **EN** uh
Vietnam	**VEE** ut **NAHM** *or*
	VYET NAHM *or* **VEE** ut **NAM**
vigil	**VIJ** ul
vigilance	**VIJ** uh luns ¶19
vigilant	**VIJ** uh lunt
vigilante	**VIJ** uh **LAN** tee ¶18
vignette	vin **YET**
vigor	**VIG** ur
vigorous	**VIG** ur us ¶5
viking	**VYE** king
vilify	**VIL** uh fye
villa	**VIL** uh
village	**VIL** ij
villain	**VIL** un
vinaigrette	vin i **GRET**
vindicate	**VIN** duh kayt
vindication	**VIN** duh **KAY** shun
vindictive	vin **DIK** tiv
vinegar	**VIN** i gur
vineyard	**VIN** yurd

vintage .... **VIN** tij

vinyl .... **VYE** nul

viol .... **VYE** ul

viola ("stringed instrument") ....
.... vee **OH** luh
occasionally vye **OH** luh, *but no*
viola player says it

viola ("plant") .... **VYE** uh luh *or*
vye **OH** luh

violable .... **VYE** uh luh bul

violate .... **VYE** uh layt

violation .... VYE uh **LAY** shun

violence .... **VYE** uh luns ¶5, 9

violent .... **VYE** uh lunt ¶5

violet .... **VYE** uh lut ¶5

violin .... vye uh **LIN**

violist .... vee **OH** list
Thus for a viola player, but for
a viol player, it is **VYE** uh list.

violoncello .... VEE uh lun **CHEL** oh
occasionally VYE uh lun **CHEL** oh

viper .... **VYE** pur

virago .... vi **RAH** goh *or* vi **RAY** goh

viral .... **VYE** rul

virelay .... **VIR** uh lay

vireo .... **VIR** ee oh

Virgil .... **VUR** jul

virgin .... **VUR** jin

virginity .... vur **JIN** uh tee

Virgo .... **VUR** goh
now sometimes **VIR** goh *as well*

virgule .... **VUR** gyoohl

virile .... **VIR** ul ¶22

virility .... vi **RIL** uh tee

virology .... vye **RAHL** uh jee ¶1

virtual .... **VUR** choo wul ¶5

virtue .... **VUR** chooh

virtuosity ...... VUR choo **WAHS** uh tee

virtuoso .... VUR choo **WOH** soh

virtuous .... **VUR** choo wus

virulent .... **VIR** yoo lunt ¶21

virus .... **VYE** rus

visa .... **VEE** zuh ¶14

visage .... **VIZ** ij

vis–à–vis .... VEE zuh **VEE** ¶1

viscera .... **VIS** ur uh

viscid .... **VIS** id

viscosity .... vis **KAHS** uh tee

viscount .... **VYE** kownt

viscous .... **VIS** kus

Vishnu .... **VISH** nooh

visibility .... VIZ uh **BIL** uh tee

visible .... **VIZ** uh bul

Visigoth .... VIZ uh gahth ¶19

vision .... **VIZH** un

visionary .... **VIZH** uh NER ee ¶23

visit .... **VIZ** it

visitation .... VIZ uh **TAY** shun

visor .... **VYE** zur

VISTA .... **VIS** tuh

visual .... **VIZH** oo wul

vita .... **VEE** tuh *or* **VYTE** uh
The plural vitae *is* **VEE** tye *or*
VYTE ee.

vital .... **VYTE** ul

vitality .... vye **TAL** uh tee

vitamin .... **VYTE** uh min

vitiate .... **VISH** ee ayt

viticulture .... **VIT** uh **KUL** chur

vitreous .... **VIT** ree us

vitriol	**VIT** ree ul *or* **VIT** ree ohl *or* **VIT** ree awl
vitriolic	VIT ree **AHL** ik
vituperate	vye **TOOH** puh rayt ¶1, 21
vituperative	vi **TOOH** pur uh tiv *or* vye **TOOH** puh rayt iv ¶21
vivacious	vi **VAY** shus ¶1
vivacity	vi **VAS** uh tee ¶1
viva voce	**VYE** vuh **VOH** see
vivify	**VIV** uh fye
viviparous	vye **VIP** ur us ¶1
vivisection	**VIV** uh **SEK** shun
vixen	**VIK** sun
vizier	vi **ZIR**
vocabulary	voh **KAB** yuh **LER** ee ¶1, 23
vocal	**VOH** kul
vocalic	voh **KAL** ik
vocalize	**VOH** kuh lyze
vocation	voh **KAY** shun
vocative	**VAHK** uh tiv
vociferous	voh **SIF** ur us ¶1, 5
vodka	**VAHD** kuh
vogue	**VOHG**
voilà	vwah **LAH**
voile	**VOYL**
volatile	**VAHL** uh tul ¶22
volcanic	vahl **KAN** ik ¶1, 19
volcano	vahl **KAY** noh ¶1, 19
volcanology	**VAHL** kuh **NAHL** uh jee ¶19
volition	voh **LISH** un ¶1
voltage	**VOHL** tij
Voltaire	vohl **TER** ¶20, 23

voluble	**VAHL** yoo bul
volume	**VAHL** yum *or* **VAHL** yoom ¶1, 8
voluminous ...	vuh **LOOH** muh nus ¶1
voluntary	**VAHL** un **TER** ee ¶23
volunteer	vahl un **TIR**
voluptuous ..	vuh **LUP** choo wus ¶12
voracious	vaw **RAY** shus ¶1
vortex	**VAWR** teks
votary	**VOHT** ur ee
votive	**VOHT** iv
vouch	**VOWCH**
vowel	**VOW** ul
voyage	**VOY** ij
voyeur	vwah **YUR** *or* voy **UR**
vulcanize	**VUL** kuh nyze
vulgar	**VUL** gur
vulgarity	vul **GAR** uh tee ¶23
Vulgate	**VUL** gayte *or* **VUL** git
vulnerable	**VUL** nur uh bul ¶5
vulpine	**VUL** pyne ¶22
vulture	**VUL** chur
vulva	**VUL** vuh

W

Waco	**WAY** koh
wad	**WAHD** ¶19
waddle	**WAHD** ul ¶19

SPELLED	PRONOUNCED
wadi	**WAH** dee
waffle	**WAWF** ul ¶19
waft	**WAHFT** ¶18
wager	**WAY** jur
Wagner	**VAHG** nur

Thus for the German composer, but the surname in America is commonly **WAG** *nur.*

Wagnerian	vahg **NIR** ee un
wahine	wah **HEE** nee *or* wah **HEE** nay
wahoo	**WAH** hooh ¶2
waif	**WAYF**
Waikiki	**WYE** kee kee *or* wye kee **KEE**
wainscot	**WAYN** skut *or* **WAYN** skaht
waistcoat	**WES** kut

The spelling pronunciation **WAYST** *koht is also heard* ¶10.

waitress	**WAY** tris
waive	**WAYV**
Walden	**WAWL** dun
Waldorf	**WAWL** dawrf
walk	**WAWK**
wallaby	**WAHL** uh bee ¶19
wallaroo	**WAHL** ur ooh ¶2, 19
wallet	**WAWL** it ¶19
Walloon	wah **LOOHN** ¶1
wallop	**WAHL** up ¶19
wallow	**WAHL** oh ¶19
walnut	**WAWL** nut
walrus	**WAWL** rus ¶19
waltz	**WAWLTS** *or* **WAWLS** ¶9
wampum	**WAHM** pum
wan	**WAHN** ¶19

SPELLED	PRONOUNCED
wand	**WAHND** ¶19
wander	**WAHN** dur ¶19
wanderlust	**WAHN** dur lust
wangle	**WANG** gul
Wankel (engine)	**VAHNG** kul *or* **WANG** kul
want	**WAHNT** ¶19
wanton	**WAHNT** un ¶19
wapiti	**WAHP** uh tee
warble	**WAWR** bul
warbler	**WAWR** blur ¶5
ward	**WAWRD**
warden	**WAWRD** un
wardrobe	**WAWRD** rohb
warehouse *(noun)*	**WER** hows

The verb is usually **WER** *howz* ¶14.

wariness	**WAR** ee nis ¶23
warlock	**WAWR** lahk
warm	**WAWRM**
warmonger	**WAWR** mung gur *or* **WAWR** mahn gur: *see* monger
warmth	**WAWRMTH** ¶9
warp	**WAWRP**
warrant	**WAWR** unt ¶19
warrantee	**WAWR** un tee ¶2, 19
warrantor	**WAWR** un tawr *or* **WAWR** un tur ¶19
warren	**WAWR** un ¶19
warrior	**WAWR** ee ur ¶19, 25
Warsaw	**WAWR** saw
wart	**WAWRT**
wary	**WAR** ee ¶23
wash	**WAWSH** ¶19
wasp	**WAHSP** ¶19

223

SPELLED	PRONOUNCED
wassail	**WAHS** ul *or* **WAHS** ayl
Wassermann (test)	**WAHS** ur mun *or* **VAHS** ur mahn
wastage	**WAYS** tij
wastrel	**WAYS** trul
watch	**WAHCH** ¶19
water	**WAWT** ur ¶19
watercraft	**WAWT** ur kraft ¶18, 19
Waterloo	**WAWT** ur looh ¶2, 19
WATS	**WAHTS** ¶19
watt	**WAHT** ¶19
wattage	**WAHT** ij ¶19
wattle	**WAHT** ul ¶19
waylay	**WAY** lay ¶2
weal	**WEEL**
weald	**WEELD**
wealth	**WELTH** ¶9
wealthy	**WEL** thee
wean	**WEEN**
weapon	**WEP** un
wear	**WER**
weary	**WIR** ee
weasel	**WEE** zul
weather	**WEDH** ur
weatherman	**WEDH** ur man
Wednesday	**WENZ** dee *or* **WENZ** day ¶8
weevil	**WEE** vul
weigh	**WAY**
weight	**WAYT**
Weimar	**VYE** mahr

occasionally Englished as **WYE** mahr

weir	**WIR**
weird	**WIRD**

SPELLED	PRONOUNCED
welcome	**WEL** kum
welfare	**WEL** fer
well–intentioned	**WEL** in **TEN** shund
well–spoken	wel **SPOH** kun
welsh	**WELSH** ¶12
Welsh corgi	**WELSH KAWR** gee
werewolf	**WIR** woolf *or* **WUR** woolf *or* **WER** woolf
Wesley	**WES** lee ¶14
Westminster	**WEST** min stur ¶9, 10
Westphalia	west **FAY** lee uh ¶25
wetland	**WET** land
wh–	hw *or* w

In America, this sound is made either with or without a slight puff of released breath. To show these variations, the words that follow represent wh– *as either* **(H)W** *or* **(h)w**.

SPELLED	PRONOUNCED
wharf	**(H)WAWRF**

The plural is wharves **(H)WAWRVZ** *or* wharfs.

SPELLED	PRONOUNCED
whatchamacallit	**(H)WUCH** uh muh **KAWL** it
wheal	**(H)WEEL**
wheat	**(H)WEET**
wheelbarrow	**(H)WEEL** bar oh ¶2
whence	**(H)WENS** ¶19
whenever	**(h)wen EV** ur ¶1
wherewithal	**(H)WER** widh awl *or* **(H)WER** with awl
whether	**(H)WEDH** ur
whey	**(H)WAY**
while	**(H)WYLE**

whimsy	(H)WIM zee
whinny	(H)WIN ee
whippet	(H)WIP it
whippoorwill	(H)WIP ur wil
whir	(H)WUR
whirl	(H)WURL
whirligig	(H)WUR li gig ¶1
whisper	(H)WIS pur
whistle	(H)WIS ul
whitewash	(H)WYTE wawsh ¶19
whither	(H)WIDH ur
Whitsunday	(H)WIT SUN dee *or* (H)WIT SUN day *or* (H)WIT sun day
who	HOOH
whole	HOHL ¶7
wholly	HOHL ee
whom	HOOHM
whoop	HOOHP *or* (H)WOOHP *or* WOOP
whoopee	(H)WOOH pee *or* (H)WOOP ee ¶2
whoops	(H)WOOPS *or* (H)WOOHPS
whore	HAWR
whorl	(H)WAWRL *or* (H)WURL
whortleberry	(H)WURT ul BER ee
whose	HOOHZ
why	(H)WYE
wicked	WIK id
wickiup	WIK ee up
widget	WIJ it
widow	WID oh
widower	WID uh wur ¶1
width	WIDTH ¶6
wield	WEELD
wiener	WEE nur

Wiener schnitzel	VEE nur SHNIT sul
Wiesbaden	VEES bahd un
wigan	WIG un
wigwam	WIG wahm
wild	WYLDE
wildebeest	WIL duh beest
wilderness	WIL dur nis
wildwood	WYLDE wood
williwaw	WIL i waw
wily	WYE lee
wimble	WIM bul
wince	WINS ¶9
Winchester (rifle)	WIN ches tur *or* WIN chis tur
wind ("to turn")	WYNDE
wind ("air movement")	WIND
in earlier poetry, occasionally WYNDE	
windage	WIN dij
winder	WYNE dur
windjammer	WIND jam ur ¶10
windlass	WIND lus
windmill	WIND mil ¶10
windrow	WIND roh
Windsor	WIN zur
windup	WYNE dup
windward	WIND wurd
among sailors WIN durd	
windy	WIN dee
wineglass	WYNE glas ¶18
winery	WYNE ur ee
winged	WINGD
in some lines of poetry WING id	
Winnebago	WIN uh BAY goh
winnow	WIN oh

SPELLED	PRONOUNCED
wino	**WYE** noh
winsome	**WIN** sum
wire	**WYRE** ¶7
wiry	**WYRE** ee ¶7
wisdom	**WIZ** dum
wise	**WYZE**
wiseacre	**WYZE** ay kur
wishful	**WISH** ful
wisteria	wis **TIR** ee uh
wistful	**WIST** ful
witchcraft	**WICH** kraft ¶18
with	**WIDH** or **WITH**

*depending usually on whether
the sound that follows is voiced
or voiceless (see the
Introduction)*

withal	widh **AWL** or with **AWL**
withdrawal	widh **DRAW** ul or with **DRAW** ul ¶7
withdrawn	widh **DRAWN** or with **DRAWN**
withe	**WITH** or **WIDH** or **WYDHE**
wither	**WIDH** ur
withers	**WIDH** urz
withhold	with **HOHLD** or widh **HOHLD**
within	widh **IN** or with **IN**
without	widh **OWT** or with **OWT**
withstand	with **STAND** or widh **STAND**
withy	**WIDH** ee or **WITH** ee
witless	**WIT** lis
witness	**WIT** nis
witticism	**WIT** uh siz um
wizard	**WIZ** urd

SPELLED	PRONOUNCED
wizened	**WIZ** und

occasionally **WYZE** und

woebegone	**WOH** bi gawn ¶1, 19
wok	**WAHK** ¶19
wolf	**WOOLF**

The plural wolves *is* **WOOLVZ.**

wolverine	wool vuh **REEN** ¶2
woman	**WOOM** un

The plural women *is* **WIM** in.

womb	**WOOHM**
wombat	**WAHM** bat
wonder	**WUN** dur
wonderful	**WUN** dur ful
wonderland	**WUN** dur land
wondrous	**WUN** drus
wont	**WAWNT** or **WOHNT**

occasionally **WUNT** ¶19, 20

won't	**WOHNT**
won ton	**WAHN** tahn
wood	**WOOD**
woodcraft	**WOOD** kraft ¶18
woodland *(noun)*	**WOOD** land or **WOOD** lund

The adjective is always
WOOD lund.

woodsman	**WOODZ** mun
woodsy	**WOOD** zee
woodwind	**WOOD** wind
woof ("fabric")	**WOOF** or **WOOHF**
woof ("dog's bark")	**WOOF**
woofer	**WOOF** ur
wool	**WOOL**
woops	**WOOPS** or **WOOHPS**
woozy	**WOOH** zee or **WOOZ** ee
Worcester	**WOOS** tur

Worcestershire (sauce) ....
...... **WOOS** tur shir *or* **WOOS** tur shur
word .... **WURD**
work .... **WURK**
workaholic .. WURK uh **HAWL** ik ¶19
workday .... **WURK** day
working .... **WUR** king
workman .... **WURK** mun
world .... **WURLD**
worm .... **WURM**
worrisome .... **WUR** ee sum
worry .... **WUR** ee
worrywart .... **WUR** ee wawrt
worse .... **WURS**
worship .... **WUR** ship
worst .... **WURST**
worsted .... **WOOS** tid *or* **WUR** stid
worth .... **WURTH**
worthy .... **WUR** dhee
would .... **WOOD**
wound ("injury") .... **WOOHND**
wound (*past tense of* wind) ....
.... **WOUND**
wraith .... **RAYTH**
wrastle .... **RAS** ul
wreak .... **REEK**
wreath (*noun*) .... **REETH**
wreathe (*verb*) .... **REEDH**
wreckage .... **REK** ij
wrestle .... **RES** ul
wretched .... **RECH** id
wristlet .... **RIST** lit ¶10
wristwatch ..... **RIST** wahch ¶10, 19
writhe .... **RYDHE**
wroth .... **RAWTH**

wrought .... **RAWT**
wry .... **RYE**
Wunderkind .... **VOON** dur kint
wurst .... **WURST** ¶24
Wyandotte .... **WYE** un daht

X

Xavier .... **ZAY** vee ur ¶25
now also ig **ZAY** vee ur
xenia .... **ZEE** nee uh ¶25
xenon .... **ZEE** nahn
xenophilia .... ZEN uh **FIL** ee uh *or*
ZEE nuh **FIL** ee uh ¶25
xenophobia ..... ZEN uh **FOH** bee uh *or*
ZEE nuh **FOH** bee uh ¶25
xerography .... zi **RAHG** ruh fee
Xerox (*trademark*) .... **ZIR** ahks
Xerxes .... **ZURK** seez
Xhosa .... **KOH** sah *or* **KOH** zah
In their African language, the
k–sound is actually a click.
Xmas .... **KRIS** mus
So pronounced because X is a
symbol for Christ; however, there
is also the popular **EKS** mus.
X–ray .... **EKS** ray
xylem .... **ZYE** lum *or* **ZYE** lem
xylophone .... **ZYE** luh fohn

SPELLED	PRONOUNCED	SPELLED	PRONOUNCED

Y

yacht .... **YAHT**

yachtsman .... **YAHTS** mun

Yahoo .... **YAH** hooh

Yahweh .... **YAH** we

yak ("idle talk") .... **YAK**
also, for a loud laugh, **YAHK**

yakety–yak .... YAK i tee **YAK**

yardman .... **YAHRD** mun *or*
YAHRD man ¶8

yarmulke .... **YAHR** mul kuh *or*
YAH mul kuh
YAH muh kuh *is now also heard.*

yaws .... **YAWZ**

yclept .... i **KLEPT**

ye *(article)* .... **DHUH** *or* **DHEE**
YEE *is a spelling pronunciation;
the word "the" was written with
an obsolete character that looked
like a* y, *which has been
substituted for it.*

ye *(old plural of* you*)* .... **YEE**

yea .... **YAY**

year .... **YIR**

yearn .... **YURN**

Yeats .... **YAYTS**

yellow .... **YEL** oh

Yemen .... **YEM** un

yeoman .... **YOH** mun

yeshiva .... yuh **SHEE** vuh

yesterday .... **YES** tur dee *or*
YES tur day

yeti .... **YET** ee *or* **YEET** ee

yew .... **YOOH**

Yiddish .... **YID** ish

yield .... **YEELD**

yock .... **YAHK**

yodel .... **YOH** dul

yoga .... **YOH** guh

yogi .... **YOH** gee

yogurt .... **YOH** gurt

yoke .... **YOHK**

yokel .... **YOH** kul

yolk .... **YOHK**

Yom Kippur .... YAHM **KIP** ur *or*
YOHM kee **POOHR** ¶19

yonder .... **YAHN** dur

yore .... **YAWR**

Yorkshire .... **YAWRK** shir

Yoruba .... **YOH** roo buh
also yoh roo **BAH**

Yosemite .... yoh **SEM** uh tee ¶1

youth .... **YOOHTH**
The plural youths *is* **YOOHTHS** *or*
YOOHDHZ.

yowl .... **YOWL**

Yucatán .... **YOOH** kuh tan *or*
yooh kah **TAHN**

yucca .... **YUK** uh

Yugoslavia ....
...... YOOH goh **SLAH** vee uh ¶1, 25

Yukon .... **YOOH** kahn

yule .... **YOOHL**

Yuma .... **YOOH** muh

Z

Zaire .... zah IR

Zambia .... ZAM bee uh

zany .... ZAY nee

Zanzibar .... ZAN zuh bahr

zeal .... ZEEL

zealot .... ZEL ut

zealous .... ZEL us

zebra .... ZEE bruh

in British, and often Canadian, usage ZEB ruh

zebu .... ZEE booh

Zechariah .... ZEK uh RYE uh

Zeitgeist .... TSYTE gyste

zenith .... ZEE nith

Zeno .... ZEE noh

Zephaniah .... ZEPH uh NYE uh

zephyr .... ZEF ur

zeppelin .... ZEP uh lin   ¶5

zero .... ZIR oh *or* ZEE roh

Zeus .... ZOOHS

Ziegfeld .... ZIG feld

Some people think "Ziegfield," and so ZIG feeld.

ziggurat .... ZIG oo rat

Zimbabwe .... zim BAHB way

zinc .... ZINGK

zinfandel .... ZIN fun del

Zinjanthropus ...... zin JAN thruh pus

zinnia .... ZIN ee uh   ¶25

Zion .... ZYE un

zircon .... ZUR kahn

zirconium .... zur KOH nee um

zither .... ZIDH ur *or* ZITH ur

zodiac .... ZOH dee ak

zodiacal .... zoh DYE uh kul

zombie .... ZAHM bee

zoological .... ZOH uh LAHJ i kul

zoologist .... zoh AHL uh jist

zoology .... zoh AHL uh jee

zooh AHL uh jee *is heard, but is not considered standard.*

Zoroaster .... ZAWR oh AS tur *or* ZOH roh AS tur

Zoroastrian ... ZAWR oh AS tree un *or* ZOH roh AS tree un

zowie .... ZOW ee

zoysia .... ZOY see uh   ¶25

zucchini .... zooh KEE nee   ¶1

Zulu .... ZOOH looh

Zurich .... ZOOR ik   ¶24

zwieback .... SWEE bak *or* SWYE bak   ¶14, 18

zygote .... ZYE goht

William S. Chisholm, Jr., Professor of English at Cleveland State University, served as Pronunciation Editor of *Webster's New World Dictionary*, Second College Edition, and is the author of three textbooks and numerous articles on the English language.